Other books by the author

SAMUEL HARRIS, AMERICAN THEOLOGIAN

LITTLE LESS THAN GOD

A Story of Down-East Religion and Politics

by

Frederick W. Whittaker, Ph.D., D.D.

President Emeritus
Bangor Theological Seminary
Bangor, Maine

Frederick W. Whittaker

Published by
Cay-Bel / New Markets Printing

LITTLE LESS THAN GOD

Library of Congress CC# 91-78187

ISBN 0-941216-53-5

Printed and published
in the
United States of America
by
Cay-Bel / New Markets Publications

E-92

Dedicated to

Shirley

My Wife for Fifty Years

Acknowledgements

I record my appreciation of three institutions which provided important assistance for the writing of this book. Gratitude is expressed to:

Bangor Theological Seminary, whose personnel past and present have contributed to the support of this project.

The Bangor Public Library, whose newspaper files and study space were made available to me.

The Bangor Daily News, for permission to reproduce some of the photographs used in the book.

"...what is man that thou art mindful of him...
thou hast made him little less than God...."

Psalm 8:4, 5 (RSV)

TABLE OF CONTENTS

INTRODUCTION

*By The Reverend Dr. Larry E. Kalp**

Believing wholeheartedly that there cannot be a separation of religion and politics in a person's life, Fred Whittaker provides a powerful personal document of his own struggle to be an effective Christian and citizen. His life reflects a splendid record of service in both arenas: as a local church pastor, seminary professor and president, city councillor and mayor, and state senator.

This very readable and lively account is more than a personal history. It takes the reader through a process of character growth and development as Fred's philosophy, faith, theology, and political ideas were nurtured. The integration of these areas of concern produced a citizen of integrity and sound convictions. An image of a committed and energetic churchman emerges from the book. Fred's concept of a "humanology" has grown from practical experiences in the settings of Church, education, and community. An underlying principle of humanology is a biblical understanding of men and women as contributors to the creative task of shaping God's world into a civilized and responsible sphere for life and work.

Little Less Than God is the sum of Fred's belief that humankind has been placed on this good earth by a caring and loving God who created us with the potential to be ourselves creative and effective citizens of the world we inherited. Fred sees in the biblical record a challenge for humankind to accept responsibility for shaping a world that is caring and productive. The tragic results of human neglect and immorality throughout history should drive us not to despair but to the renewed conviction that God calls every human to make a difference when and where he or she can. That is the truest meaning of faithful stewardship and citizenship. We are created with the power to reform our world.

* Senior Minister, The Community Church (U.C.C.) of Mountain Lakes, New Jersey; Former Publisher, The Pilgrim Press/United Church Press (United Church of Christ); Former Vice President, Bangor (Maine) Theological Seminary.

History need not be repeated since we have the God-given potential to make the world safe and secure for all creation. The historical record is replete with men and women who have caught this vision and have then committed themselves to making the world a better place in which to live and work. Fred would push us toward encouraging the development of our purest intentions to become creators of the world which a good God has intended. This calls us to be vigilant and responsible in our citizenship. Our human capacity to choose the good is a sign of our Creator's desire for us to develop fully our moral potential. It is this positive and hopeful understanding of human potential which becomes the key principle out of which Fred has established his own theology, which uses as cornerstones the development of faith and social justice.

This deeply personal and reflective study is more than an autobiography. In a real sense the book presses concerned readers into examining the issues which beg for responsible commitment and action in our day. As citizens of both Church and State, the issues of religion and politics become sharper and more focused as faith is brought to bear upon them. A life lived in the reality of these issues draws on the best of biblical, theological, historical, and political understandings in shaping decisions and actions. Fred Whittaker demonstrates, through his own case study, how his decisions and actions were shaped out of sound biblical and faith understandings. As a city councillor and mayor, a state senator, and a candidate for the Congress of the United States, Fred was able to translate theological, biblical, and historical perspectives into real-life dramas in the political setting. In a like manner his seminary classroom came alive with presentations of relevant issues which cried out for moral and religious values and perspectives. The real world became his place of work and ministry. On the seminary campus, often in the local churches of Maine, and in the wider community where Fred served so effectively, there were ample occasions for him to be a social critic on a diversity of issues involving both Church and State.

Fred's book is also an account of service as an innovative educator and effective seminary administrator. Bangor Theological Seminary grew in dramatic ways under his dedicated leadership.

His vision of a school "to serve the Churches" led him to establish a faculty and program with a high commitment to preparing men and women for ministry in local churches. Under his leadership a philosophy of seminary education emerged that was and remains truly unique in theological institutions. The "School of the Prophets" from its inception had developed a program of education for ministerial training that was non-traditional in approach and design.

Under Fred Whittaker's long tenure as a faculty member and president the concept of "The Bangor Plan" was firmly established. It was a unique approach to theological education which welcomed men and women into a program of both liberal arts and theological studies. Through the Plan students without a college degree were admitted to theological classes. Upon graduation they went into active and full-time ministry while at the same time finishing their college courses and degree work. Through the Plan many mature men and women were able to begin ministry early while they continued their degree studies. Fred nurtured "The Bangor Plan" because of his own experience and commitment to the need for a seminary that provided an "open door" to older men and women who had not been able to complete their liberal arts studies but who felt "called" to ministry in the Church. Bangor made it possible for them, and for Fred himself, to answer the late call and at the same time to acquire an outstanding education for the profession of ministry. Under Fred Whittaker's leadership the Seminary received national and international attention. The book provides an insightful historical record of his more than fifty years of continuing involvement with the Seminary.

Readers will see in this book a side of Fred Whittaker that may surprise and will surely please them. Here is an account of a devoted husband and father, told with sensitivity and a healthy sprinkling of humor. Fred shares the intimate details of life in the Whittaker household. Like the rest of the text, Fred's careful analysis, insight, and crisp writing style make it delightful and enjoyable reading. You will know more about Fred Whittaker, what motivated him, and the clearest outline of his theological thinking than is usually available on most public figures. The intimate details show how Fred worked out of assumptions and ideals that were formed early in his life and ministry. Especially interesting are the early sermons which trace the formative ideas that would later impel him to leadership in a number of important sectors of life and service. Here too are the lessons that he learned from mentors and teachers and colleagues through many years of religious and political life. What surfaces in the totality of the work is a churchman and world citizen of sound faith, and a politician with great acumen and sensitivity, who has lived out of principles and convictions that are at the core of his personality and character.

In his retirement years, Fred Whittaker continues as an active churchman, supporter of the Seminary and his local church, and a faithful social critic. He keeps abreast of the emerging issues in theological and historical studies. One is never surprised to turn to the newspaper in Maine or in Florida, where the Whittakers now reside, to see "A Letter to the Editor" which brings light to some public concern. He continues through writing and speaking to focus on some of his favorite topics: participation in the political process, paying equitable taxes as a civic responsibility, teaching about religion in the public schools, keeping the peace through the United Nations, and other issues of Church and State. His reading, research, and writing continue to benefit the Church and the wider community.

It is not easy to summarize the quality of the life of a person who has been so active and one who has impacted so many levels of life and faith. One gets a closer glimpse, however, in this account than is usual. It is the story of how one citizen and faithful Christian studied, worked, and served. It makes for good and helpful reading. I suspect that Fred's perspective on his early and latter days has been formed in the crucible of his theological and historical reflection. He models, in his writing, a style of reflection and analysis which might be borrowed by others who want to record their life and work. Fred's account never loses its way. It is clear and concise. He adds variety the way a composer or painter brings color and texture into a work of art. The result is a story that is at once informative and at the same time deeply personal and intimate.

It was my privilege to be Fred's colleague for more than nine years. In various capacities I came to know him as a very capable leader and helpful friend. He knew how to work with others, how to support them and how to give them valuable assignments to fulfill. He seemed never to tire of his work but came to his task as seminary president each year with a new openness and a willingness to move in some new directions. His own vision as well as confidence encouraged a team approach to many problems and projects. I learned some important administrative skills under his careful guidance. In those years, I found Fred to be a loving and caring person.

One could not know Fred Whittaker long without being struck by his thoroughness and care. It would be difficult to believe that he ever did anything carelessly or shoddily. I remember his many annual reports to the trustees of the Seminary that were detailed and helpful documents in terms of content and style. His ability to notice and master detail without ever losing sight of the whole has always been an awesome feat which I have admired in writers. It shows in the selection of words and phrases and in incidents and examples which have been selected for inclusion in his book.

But it would be unfair to see Fred Whittaker as a perfectionist. He never took himself with ultimate seriousness. I do, however, recall times when his tall stature and commanding voice could very nicely put a student, colleague, or political opponent in his or her place. He desired clarity and order in things but never let them stand in the way of good and open communication. He had a fine sense of humor and a comic sense which kept him close to others. He knew what to take seriously and what not to. Although Fred could at times be very task-orientated, he nevertheless exhibited a patience which made working with him a delightful exercise and experience. I remain grateful for his tutoring at a time in my life when I was shaping my own sense of worth and integrity.

My daughter and son speak fondly of "Dr. Whittaker" and the important role he played in their formative years as a family friend. The regular visits and family interchanges made Fred and Shirley Whittaker a part of our own family circle. A little over a year ago, when our daughter Karen was married she wanted the Whittakers to be a meaningful part of the family gathering. Fred served well as surrogate "grandfather" at the affair for Karen's two deceased grandfathers. Our whole family looks forward to an annual renewing of friendships each summer in Maine.

Fred's solid New England foundation and upbringing shows again and again in the values that shaped his life. His influence has been stamped on many others who have caught his vision of a world that is more just and a more humane social order for all people. This is the great lesson from the pages of this fine book. The person of integrity that Fred Whittaker was and is has been reflected in every page of this document which so carefully and completely details his life and work. Like a good teacher that he was and is, Fred concludes his book with the challenges for our future. As he began, so he concludes with the biblical conviction that because we are "little less than God" we have planted deep within us seeds of hope and promise, that once released can promote a better day and a more just society. This is the hope which faith and scripture promise. This book is an effort which deserves our careful reading and one that ought to be enjoyed for its deeply personal and human presentation.

LITTLE LESS THAN GOD

A Story of Down-East Religion and Politics

Foreword

For more than fifty years my life has been entwined with the history of Bangor Theological Seminary. This relationship began in 1939 when I matriculated at Maine's "School of the Prophets," as it is affectionately known. It continues today in my role as President Emeritus.

It is my desire and purpose to record the developing history of the Seminary during the past half-century, and my own growth from a young Christian layman to a theological administrator, a professor of Church History, and a political activist. The story is so complex that the narrative actually contains three or four books coalesced into one. "The Whittaker Years — Memoirs of a Seminary President" would have been an appropriate, all-inclusive title.

The book has strong theological foundations. And because I want to emphasize my basically liberal beliefs, I have chosen the title "Little Less Than God." It is one of my fundamental doctrines that the seminaries and the churches have over-emphasized the sinfulness of men and women while failing to proclaim the human moral potential of choosing the good over the evil, as revealed by the Psalmist and Jesus of Nazareth. I have incorporated this potential into a "humanology" for the decades immediately ahead.

The volume could have been called "Down-East Religion and Politics," which is its subtitle, thus reflecting a major theme of my writing: that the American theory of the "separation" of Church and State does not require the separation of religion and politics. I have demonstrated this thesis by avocational service as a Bangor city councillor and mayor, a Maine state senator, and a candidate for election to the Congress of the United States. Further, I have been a social critic on such issues as abortion, taxation, militarism, religion in the public schools, and international relations. My views on these and other issues are featured in the book.

Family history is another major emphasis in the manuscript. Frequent reference is made to events of my marriage to Shirley

Louise Johns, which culminated in a fiftieth wedding anniversary celebration in 1990. Life with our two children, Barbara and Mark, is a prominent part of the story. Thus the book might properly have been entitled "The 'Always Right' Reverend," which is a moniker given to me by my daughter and son, partially in frustration and partially in admiration.

The writing of this book began two days before my seventy-fifth birthday, and was finished about three years later. The task would not have been undertaken without the persistent and urgent request of my beloved wife that I leave a family record for our children and future generations. It is my hope that the alternation of chapters, not always in chronological order, will provide a change of pace and an anticipation which will maintain the interest of the reader.

This book has been written without the use of footnotes or the inclusion of a bibliography primarily because it is based in large measure upon the writings and the unpublished recollections of the author. The work is largely autobiographical in nature, and does not rely in any substantial way upon the published works of other writers. When third parties are quoted the sources are clearly indicated in the text itself.

The writings of the author included in this book are sermons, lectures, public addresses, newspaper guest columns, letters to editors, obituaries, legislative political statements, and reports to the board of trustees of Bangor Theological Seminary. In each case the source of the material is described within the text.

Most of the above writings are published in issues of The Alumni Bulletin of Bangor Theological Seminary, the files of the *Bangor Daily News* and the *Portland Press Herald / Sunday Telegram*, the Legislative Record of the 101st Maine Legislature (Augusta, Maine), and in *Theological Education* magazine of the Association of Theological Schools in the United States and Canada (Lancaster, Pennsylvania). In each case the identity of the particular writing is stated in the text.

The newspaper articles are identified by date, and copies may be found on microfilm in the Bangor Public Library. Other papers such as reports to Seminary trustees, also identified by date, are in the archives of the Moulton Library at Bangor Theological Seminary.

Also in the Moulton Library are the three major reference books used: histories of Bangor Seminary by Calvin M. Clark and Walter L. Cook; and the author's published work, a biography of *Samuel Harris, American Theologian.*

Frederick W. Whittaker, Ph.D., D.D.
January 1, 1992

PART I

*Years of
Preparation*

1.
The Beginnings
of a Seminary President

Early in the morning of January 26, 1913, a potential seminary president was born in a second-floor flat at 29 Judson Avenue in the city of New Haven, Connecticut. The mother was 24-year-old Annie May Penney Whittaker and the father was Frederick William Whittaker. Their first-born was given his father's name, plus the designation "Junior." No one at that time could have foreseen my future, and it was twenty-five years later before my life changed dramatically in a new direction. Years twenty-six to seventy-five had a significant quarter-century foundation which will be remembered in this first chapter.

My mother was a devoted housewife who spent all of her mature years taking meticulous care of her four children until they all received a high school education and eventually left the homestead. My father left his birthplace in Glendale, Rhode Island, at age 30 and moved to New Haven to marry his beloved. He earned his living at manual labor, first in a woolen mill, then in a dairy, and finally in an oven-manufacturing plant. It was not an easy life for him, but he did not complain.

The first crisis of my early years came with the influenza epidemic of 1918. My maternal grandmother, who lived with us, was one of its victims. I have only vague, but fond, memories of her.

3

She was a watchful grandmother on the few occasions when my parents took me on the trolley-car to the public beach at Lighthouse Point. My mother tells me that I, too, was seriously ill with the "flu;" however, she nursed me back to health.

The church and the school had its first impact upon me when I was five years old. My mother, who was raised a Methodist, took me to the neighborhood church, Plymouth Congregational, when I was very young. She attended Sunday worship on a regular basis, but I do not remember that my father ever was with her. He did attend my church wedding in 1940, however. Both my mother and father were conscientious persons with strong moral convictions, but "Dad" practiced his religion outside the institutional church. My sister, two brothers, and I were reared in a "Christian" home.

I have many fond memories of early school days in the Barnard grammar school, which I attended until I was ten years old. The educational experience was one which I enjoyed and appreciated from kindergarten through graduate school. I still recall with gratitude my first teachers: Miss Sullivan, Miss Beecher, Miss McGrail, and Miss Terrell. My principal physical activity at recess was playing "handball" in the schoolyard.

Ray Conniff and Dick Holabird were my inseparable pals until the family moved out of our Judson Avenue home in 1923. We three boys congregated in one another's homes every day. We played "piggie" on a regular basis, and I still have a scar in the middle of my forehead because I failed to duck the oncoming tapered wooden missile. Special treats for us boys were trips to the Holabird farms and orchards and to the Savin Rock amusement park, where we rode the rollercoaster and munched on popcorn and ice cream paid for by our neighborhood benefactor, Jules Wass.

Girls had little place in our lives during the early carefree days of youth. Ray had one sister, whom I remember as one who was vivacious and something of a tomboy. There were four girls in the Holabird family, all of them pretty, but their interests at the time did not include boys. I do recall that much later I had one date with the oldest Holabird girl on an occasion full of nostalgia.

A life-long interest in the church was nurtured for me by my mother. She was unswerving in her determination that my siblings

4

and I should be in Sunday school each week. Among my many religious teachers, Harry Hall Atwater is the one I remember most vividly. He was a successful lawyer who devoted each Sunday morning to explaining Christian truths to impressionable young boys like me. When I was seven, he gave me my first Bible as a gift from the church. He inscribed it to me with the scripture text I have never forgotten: "Be ye doers of the Word, and not hearers only."

Life among the new generation of Whittakers was mostly carefree and happy; although, looking back, it was somewhat circumscribed by the fact that there was no extra money available from my father's paycheck for frivolities. By the time I was nine years old, there were three other little ones in the household: Edward Richard, Dorothy Gertrude, and Stanley Earl. As the family increased, living quarters became smaller. I recall that after we moved from Judson Avenue to Winchester Avenue and later to Bassett Street, we had only two bedrooms in our five-room flat. One was for our parents and the other was fully occupied by my two younger brothers and me. It was not surprising that there was a certain closeness among us as we grew up. Our sister, we regretted, had little privacy since her bedroom was a corner of the dining area.

We did have some good times together as a family despite the fact that our only mode of transportation was the trolley-car or the train. There were occasional trips to a baseball game or the beach. Most memorable were the few times we took the train to Rhode Island so that we could become acquainted with a multitude of aunts, uncles and cousins — and one grandmother — who lived in the Woonsocket area. My father was the oldest of nine children born to my grandmother, Matilda. The others were Aunt Alice, Aunt Maria, Uncle Charlie, Uncle Jimmie, Aunt Tillie, Uncle Joe, Uncle Clarence and Aunt Elizabeth. They all treated us young Whittakers like royalty whenever we visited them.

After we moved to Winchester Avenue, my seventh and eighth grade training was received at Abraham Lincoln and Ivy Street schools. Since I was now ten years old, it was expected that I should begin to generate some income for the family budget in

5

view of the fact that my father worked for a minimum wage and my mother was engaged full-time as a wife and homemaker. So I went to work for Sam Most, my first but not last Jewish benefactor, in his neighborhood variety store. I delivered newspapers every morning and performed menial tasks in the store in the afternoon and on Saturday. My employer was not always satisfied with my diligence. If he thought I was loafing a bit he would bring me back to responsibility with the unforgettable Hebrew comment which sounded to me like: "Noo, noo, macher?"

As an eighth-grader, I earned my first and only dollars as an artistic performer. I played the fife in the school's fife and drum corps. We were all thrilled to be employed one week by the local Shubert Theatre, where dramatic professional productions were given a tryout before opening in New York City. The play was Channing Pollock's war drama, "The Enemy." We provided background fife and drum music from the basement of the theatre at an appropriate time in the stage production. This was the climax of my musical career!

When it was time for me to enroll in high school, there was very little question about which course I should pursue. No Whittaker had ever gone to college and there was no perceived purpose in enrolling in an academically-oriented high school like Hillhouse. So I enrolled as a freshman in Commercial High School in order to prepare for a vocation in the business world after graduation four years later. Whatever I might earn as wages would be a necessary supplement to my father's income. The long-range family plan was for me to become a second wage-earner until at least the time when my younger brothers and sister had received a high school education.

While in high school I continued my part-time employment, first by working several hours weekly in a neighborhood drugstore, where at the tender age of twelve I often had the responsibility of preparing chocolate and other syrups for use at the ice cream counter. Many times I was the "soda jerk" who concocted and dispensed sundaes, milkshakes, and other goodies to the waiting customers. Amazingly, I was also permitted to participate in the preparation of "citrate of magnesia" and other items sold at the drug counter.

When I was thirteen, I left my job as a "druggist" and spent all of my spare time working as a caddy at the Race Brook Country Club in nearby Orange. For three years I carried golf bags at this private course for men and women who were some of the leading citizens of the surrounding communities. Often I carried "double" — two bags — for which I received compensation at the rate of one dollar per bag. If I was lucky, a 50-cent tip might be added. Thus I was able to bring home about fifteen dollars per week to help augment the family income.

The years at Race Brook were important for another reason. As a caddy I learned to play the game of golf, and this recreational activity has been a major factor in my life since then for sixty-five years and more. It has undoubtedly been a significant contributor to my relatively good physical condition through the years, as well as an outlet for some of the frustrations which occur from time to time in one's personal and professional life. My first score on a regulation 18-hole course was 84. At age 78, I am still playing with a handicap of 12. Three times I have scored a hole-in-one, two of them after I was 70 years old. When I was 76 I "shot my age" for the first time.

High school was primarily an academic experience for me. I was only twelve years old when I entered as a freshman and just sixteen when I graduated. Skipping the fifth grade in grammar school brought an immature youth to high school. One result was a statistic in the class yearbook which indicated that I received the second-highest number of votes for "most bashful boy." However, in the graduation class I was ranked academically seventeenth in a class of more than three hundred, and third among the boys.

Athletically, I failed to make the first cut when I tried out for the varsity basketball team. Socially, my record was no better. When not studying, almost every spare moment was spent on the golf course as a caddy or a player. My interest in the opposite sex was keen enough, but largely unexpressed. I was well aware that there were some beautiful girls in my class: Edith, Marie, Alice, Evelyn, Helen, Dorothy, Rosemary. However, they were never more than good friends, except in my imagination. Actually, I was seventeen years old, and out of high school more than a year, before I had my first date.

My high school curriculum was designed to prepare me for a position in the business world. I became proficient at shorthand and typing, which led to my employment within a month of graduation as a clerk-stenographer in the Freight Traffic Department of the New York, New Haven and Hartford Railroad Company. For the next ten years I brought home a weekly paycheck, much of which was used to supplement the family income. My salary was especially important during the depression of the early 1930's when my father was without a job for several months.

In the early years of my railroad career I worked alongside a group of women in typing letters and statistics of various kinds. Since I was only a teenager, they looked kindly upon me as a "little boy." I remember with gratitude the helpful assistance given to me by Mary, Angie, and Grace. When I was nineteen, a most memorable social experience was a series of three or four dates with Grace, a 26-year-old, pretty brunette upon whom I had a "crush." She soon decided, unfortunately, that she was too mature for me. It was my only romantic involvement with an older woman.

After a year or two in the stenographic pool, I was promoted to the position of secretary to one of the department officers, Ray Gill. Later I spent some time as a diversion and reconsignment clerk in the office of Bill Foran, the Division Freight Agent in New Haven. In my later years with the railroad, I was secretary to the Assistant Freight Traffic Manager, Harry Sheffield. When I left in 1939 to begin preparation for another career, I was secretary to Frank Kinney, the Freight Traffic Manager. My decade of experience in the business world was to be a sound foundation for my new vocation. The men I worked for were a major influence in the shaping of my self-confidence and ability. Typing and shorthand are tools I have used ever since.

In evaluating the railroad years there are some outstanding memories. One was a privileged ride I took in the electrical engine of a passenger train from New Haven to New York City via Hell Gate Bridge to Pennsylvania Station. Sitting beside the engineer was a thrill in itself, as the train sped toward its destination at ninety miles an hour or more. Whenever the tracks entered a curve,

I wondered if we would meet head-on with another train moving in the opposite direction. Every time, however, the oncoming vehicle was on its own adjoining track. The climax of the ride was the passage through a tunnel under the East River and into the station. As a novice, it seemed to me that the tunnel walls were too small for the train and would squeeze us into oblivion. I was more than happy to see the light at the end of the tunnel and to arrive safety at the station platform.

Midway in my railroad vocation, a major change in policy moved the Freight Traffic Department from New Haven to South Station in Boston. Thus I spent two years away from home for the first time, living in a bachelor apartment with two other employees. It was a homesick time for me, and I returned to New Haven almost every weekend, especially to see my first serious girlfriend, Ellen Louise. There were to be only two other significant love affairs in my life, one with Mary Louise and the other with Shirley Louise, who has been my wife for half a century and more. It is easy to see my preference for middle names. As for the impact of my Boston experience, it was the opportunity to participate in the cultural advantages offered by one of the nation's great metropolitan centres.

One other event looms large in my recollection of railroad days. At twenty years of age, I was perhaps at the peak of my golf game. That year I played in the finals of the annual railroad golf tournament. My opponent was the company president, John J. Pelley, a friendly man but one who expected to win the championship. I had the temerity to defeat him, which created enough of a sensation to result in the publication of our picture in the roto-gravure section of the New York Herald-Tribune. From that day forward, I felt it was my destiny never to become the chief executive officer of the railroad.

Looking back on the 1930's, I recall that one of the pleasures of my secretarial job was the frequent travel with my boss on business trips he took to such metropolitan centres as Boston, New York, Philadelphia, Cleveland, and Chicago. I particularly enjoyed the overnight Pullman car travel to Chicago on the "20th Century Limited." It now seems anachronistic, but then it was considered socially inappropriate for a railroad official to travel overnight with a female secretary; hence only male secretaries were employed. I have never lost my love for rail transportation, and many years later I was a political leader in the unsuccessful attempt to maintain rail passenger service in the state of Maine. Today I still hold a firm conviction that the United States has neglected its railroads, to the detriment of its economy and its culture.

Golf was such a dominant part of my schedule during the ten years following high school graduation, that it deserves further mention. Every weekend four of us played thirty-six holes on Saturday, and again on Sunday very often. My associates were Al Davidson, Al Gesler, and John Robinson. Sixty years later, John is a member of the Race Brook Country Club, where once I was a caddy, and we still play together on occasions when I am visiting with family in the New Haven area. For many years I was a member of the New Haven Municipal golf team which played interstate matches with similar groups in Connecticut, Rhode Island, and Massachusetts. My first experience as "president" came as head of the Municipal Golf Club.

Plymouth Congregational Church was the place where I learned to be a Christian layman. Certainly it was the dominant influence upon me for twenty of my early years. In its Sunday school I learned to appreciate and understand the Bible, especially the teachings of Jesus. From its minister, Dr. Harold Gilbert Jones, came the ethical and moral training which has guided my behavior through the years. His sermons were in the liberal tradition and showed me how to apply religious principles to both personal and social problems. The Forum was a weekly gathering of young people where issues of the day were discussed in a worship context under the leadership of students from the Yale Divinity School who were employed on the part-time staff of the church. Two of these students, John McClelland and Dwight Large, were later to influence strongly my decision to study for the ministry.

The Forum also served as a social center for young church adults. After the meetings, some of us gathered at a nearby ice cream parlor for refreshments, good talk, and a general good time. Others preferred to pair off and travel homeward for private "dates."

The Forum was a place for meeting members of the opposite sex in a healthy church-oriented setting. It was here that I met all three of the girls who were most important in my life. It was here that as a one-time president of the Forum, I began to travel the road which led to the presidency of a seminary.

One other significant role of the church in my young life was the experience it gave me in amateur dramatics. In a well-directed program of theatrical productions, I was transformed from the bashful high school boy to one of "leading man" in such plays as "She Stoops to Conquer" and "Sun Up." It did wonders for my self-esteem and for my ability to express myself publicly.

There are at least two other aspects of the first quarter century of my life which stand out in my memory. One was the relationships which existed among my parents and my siblings. The other was the social realm in which I grew to maturity. As far back as I can recall, I have had kindly feelings toward members of the Jewish faith. The majority of the students in Commercial High School were Jews. I studied with them, played with them, and enjoyed with them a genuine mutual respect. At football games between the arch-rivals, Hillhouse and Commercial, one of the Hillhouse cheers was this: "Abie, Ikey, Jakie, Sam — all the boys that don't eat ham! Yea, Commercial!" But it was all taken in good fun. In the church, we had each year a joint worship service with the neighborhood synagogue. When I later became a church history professor, I always reminded my students of their great debt as Christians to the Old Testament and the Hebrew faith. It is no accident that today three of our closest family friends are Jewish. My wife and I have a similar attitude toward members of the black race. When I was in high school, I walked two miles each day through the black areas where "negroes" — as we called them — lived. There were no incidents of racial tension.

In terms of today's practice, I started late in my involvement with girls. My first date was with Leora, when I was almost eighteen years old. We went to the movies on the trolley-car. I was quite nervous about it all, and when I brought her home we soon parted, without a kiss, as I remember. It was our one and only date. When I first went out with Shirley, who is now my wife, some six years later, she commented that I had made up for lost time so far as boy-girl relations were concerned. Actually, in the interim I had dated a considerable number of girls, but only two are memorable now. They are part of my memoirs because they evoked in me for the first time romantic love.

Before marriage, the longest romantic involvement of my life was with Ellen. It lasted, with intermissions, for the better part of five years. One thing we had in common was our occupation: clerical and secretarial work. Another was our interest in the church. Our families were basically conservative. We were physically attracted to one another, but our ethical standards did not allow us to engage in anything beyond "petting," as it was called in the 1930's. We were very compatible about things like going to the movies, dancing, taking automobile rides, being at the beach, and participating in church activities. She was not very happy about my passion for golf on weekends. This probably was a factor in our eventual break-up. We did seriously consider marriage at one time, even to the point of buying some furniture for our future home. My two years in Boston and my tentative plans for going to seminary also cooled off the romance.

It is very likely that my relationship with Ellen was terminated by her because of a sudden interest I took in a pretty blonde named Mary Louise, who appeared one Sunday at the church Forum. Ellen and I had dated others occasionally, but I had never before been "smitten" by anyone else. Mary Louise was on a year's sabbatical from a music college and intended to return to her studies. She made an immediate impact upon several of the young men at the church. We dated over a period of several months and found one another mutually attractive and compatible. One Sunday I took her to my home for family dinner. On our walk to the church later that afternoon, we both confessed that we were in love. Our euphoria lasted only a few weeks. She returned to her college. We said goodbye one memorable evening in the Berkshire hills near her mother's home.

Following the episode with Mary Louise, Ellen and I did see each other on several occasions, but the relationship had changed. Eventually, she became interested in another man, whom she later married. Meanwhile, there was a new romance beginning in my life. Again it was the church young adult Forum which provided the opportunity for me to meet my future wife, Shirley Louise Johns. She was the eldest daughter of Blanche and Louis Johns and had recently moved to New Haven from Meriden, Connecticut, where she had been born on January 8, 1915. Her father was a top official of a major trucking company, and I had previously met him when he had business meetings with my boss at the railroad. Her mother quickly became active among the ladies of the church and was soon to become an important influence in my life.

Shirley was a graduate of Albertus Magnus College, a Roman Catholic school for women in New Haven. In September, 1937, she began teaching biology to college-preparatory students at Hillhouse High School, one of the premier institutions of its kind in Connecticut. During the summer months she was the director of a camp for girls at her parents' ocean-front home in Madison, Connecticut. I was impressed by the fact that she was a college graduate with a profession already in progress. But this was only one reason for my interest in her.

On our first date, it was apparent that Shirley and I were mutually attracted to one another. She was a pretty brunette with a fine figure and a winsome smile. She loved to dance, and I was quite willing to hold her in my arms. However, she has never found me very proficient in the dance department. She jokingly told me that I could fox-trot a waltz better than anyone she had ever known. Shirley has been an excellent swimmer all of her life, since college days when she swam competitively in the Yale University pool. I did not learn to swim until I was more than 70 years old.

Despite some of these incompatibilities, Shirley and I gradually grew fond of one another. We had a common interest in the church. I admired her teaching career. I once visited her at the high school, but did not go back again after she told me, with a laugh, that another teacher had asked if I was one of her students. Shirley's family, which included her younger sister, Barbara, were very kind to me and to my parents. My father did not have many social contacts, but he seemed to feel at ease when he was invited to the Johns' home. Blanche Johns was always a most gracious host. She had a large circle of friends, and everyone liked her. Actually, I fell in love with her before I had the same strong feeling about her daughter.

As Shirley and I began to spend more and more time together, we continued our interest in others. I had a few dates with Ellen, but our romance was definitely on the wane. Shirley went out with a handsome young baritone, and I was impressed by the the fact that an older man, a Jewish lawyer who was a family friend, also was enamored of Shirley. One humorous incident in my life occurred about this time. As an amateur thespian in the church drama society, the Plymouth Players, I was cast in a play's leading role which called for a love affair with the heroine. She was romantically involved with another man, but agreed that we might have one date during which we would practice our kissing technique. We could have become interested in one another except for the fact that her boyfriend, upon learning of our brief encounter, immediately asked her to marry him.

One of my last dates with Ellen also had a humorous side to it. One Saturday night she and I had plans to go to the movies. That same afternoon Shirley and I took a walk in West Rock Park, a favorite trysting spot, during which we expressed our growing fondness for one another. She had an engagement that night with one of her circle of admirers. However, we were both more interested in being with one another than we were in having dates that evening with someone else. So, we arranged a double-date, during which we tried not to show what were our romantic preferences. I never did know whether Ellen was aware of our subterfuge, but within a few short weeks she bid me a fond farewell which proved to be terminal.

The year was 1938, and I was now 25 years old. While marriage seemed to be a possibility, there was another desire growing within me which could not be ignored. My activity among the young people in Plymouth Church had brought me into contact with students from the Yale Divinity School who worked part-time on the church staff. One of these was John McClelland; the other was Dwight Large, who was also director of the amateur dramatics program. I visited several times with these theologues on the seminary campus and became increasingly determined to follow in their footsteps. I discussed the matter with my pastor, Harold Jones, who told me about Bangor Theological Seminary and its special program for non-college graduates who wanted to study for the ministry. After correspondence with President Harry Trust of the seminary, I was ready in the spring of 1939 to apply for admission to Bangor. My only doubts were centered about my future relationship with Shirley. She encouraged me to seek my chosen new vocation.

My mother and father were not as supportive. The idea of higher education for their son was foreign to their thinking. I was now in the tenth year of my employment with the railroad and my future in the business world looked bright. However, I did not want to be a railroad president; I wanted to be a Christian minister.

The Whittaker family was not a demonstrative one, but there was a deep affection for one another lying just below the surface of our relationships. I give full credit to my mother and father for establishing the kind of home, and exhibiting the kind of moral behavior, which taught me to have both sympathy and empathy for the needs of others and which enabled me to have innate knowledge of the difference between right and wrong whenever an ethical decision was to be made. Despite being relatively poor in material things, my parents were rich in moral and spiritual values.

I have no doubts that my father loved my mother, and that she reciprocated. However, I do not remember ever seeing them embrace or kiss one another. I determined to do better in showing affection in my own married life. Shirley will agree that I have succeeded. Dad was a hard-working man, probably to his own detriment and a resultant early death at age 60. He loved to eat ice cream and to listen to the radio. He was an ardent sports fan, especially with respect to baseball. When money was available he took me to watch the local minor league team. He was not a disciplinarian with his children. That was mother's department. He was secretly proud of me, I felt, when I decided to leave the railroad in favor of the seminary, despite his own judgment that I was making a mistake.

Mother was an excellent cook. She always provided tasty and nutritious meals for her family, in spite of her limited budget. She

15

welcomed the neighborhood children into our home as playmates for her own offspring. She expected my two brothers, my sister, and me to perform certain chores around the house. It was my job to empty the garbage, a job I detested because there were always bees swarming around the backyard waste receptacle. My own daughter has inherited my irrational fear of anything that stings.

The care of four children kept my mother busy most of the time. She showed no favoritism among us, and we were all anxious to please her. She did worry too much about us, we thought. She saw to it that we were faithful to the church and its programs. This religious training was a blessing upon all of us in later life. She and Dad planned that we would receive a good elementary and secondary education. I do not remember, however, that any of us received even rudimentary training in sexual matters. This seemed to be a taboo subject in the family. We learned what we had to know from our peers and from first-hand experience.

One incident from my teenage years left a lasting impression upon me. It was my practice, whenever possible, to hitch a ride from New Haven to the Race Brook Country Club, where I was a caddy. One day on the return trip I was riding in the cab of a truck when the driver, who had picked me up, asked me if I would like to go into the back of the truck with him. I was both frightened and embarrassed, but had sense enough to decline. It was my first experience with a homosexual. I did not confide in my parents, but from that day forward I stopped hitch-hiking.

After I began to date, my parents were always cordial to the few girls I brought home. Mother was often nervous about what might happen to her "innocent" first-born after he started to be interested in the opposite sex. She was always glad to see me come home safely, especially if I had been out in a car with a girl. Actually, I became the first driver in the family when I was more than twenty years old. Many times when I was going to see Shirley at her home, I walked the two miles which separated our residences. The pathway took me through an isolated area between two lagoons and mother worried about that, too. But I escaped all of the major hazards involved in growing to young manhood.

Mother was herself one of four children. Her brother Francis, my uncle, died at age 32 in the influenza epidemic of 1918 which also claimed the life of my grandmother. Her other brother, my Uncle Walter, was a veteran of World War I. My most vivid memory of him was of the day he took me fishing, the only time I have engaged in that sport. He loved the ocean waters and he gained the reputation of being our "swimming uncle" because of his habit of taking a dip in Long Island Sound on many a winter day. In much later life, after I had espoused some liberal social and political causes, Uncle Walter referred to me as "my nephew, the Communist." Mother's only sister was Aunt Bessie, and they adored one another. Bessie was married to Floyd Coddington, a candy manufacturer and retailer in Norfolk, Virginia. I well remember once visiting the candy store and enjoying some of the samples.

When sister Dorothy and brothers Edward and Stanley were born into the Whittaker family, life became more exciting and more crowded in our five-room flat. Ed was three years younger than I, and we had more interests in common during childhood days. We played together and slept in the same room. I remember some tennis games we had when I was not playing golf. Ed later married Beatrice Sterr and they established a home in Brockton, Massachusetts; there was born an only child, pretty daughter Laurel. By training, Ed was a "works simplification engineer." He was employed as what the layman would call an "efficiency expert" by the Winchester Repeating Arms Company in New Haven, the Gillette Safety Razor Company in Boston, and the Brockton Public Markets, successively. During World War II he served his nation as a non-military officer by directing the deployment and re-deployment of American personnel in the Italian theatre of operations. When he was only 53 he died prematurely because of a heart ailment, like his father.

My sister Dorothy and I have always had a close family relationship. I was happy when she arrived during my boyhood years, and she has always thought of me as her "big brother." I have regretted that lack of living space in our rented flats prevented her from having a room of her own during our growing years, but she did not complain about her lack of privacy in the dining room/bedroom she occupied. We three brothers did our best to take care of our only sister. "Dottie" followed me at Commercial High School and then went to work at the United Illuminating Company in New Haven. There was only one sweetheart in Dottie's life. She married Bradley Canada, and they had two sons, Jeffrey and Phillip. She now lives in Melrose, Massachusetts, and we still maintain a close relationship through writing and visitation, especially since the death of her husband.

My youngest brother, Stanley, was born in 1922 just before the family left my boyhood home on Judson Avenue. Stan and I resemble each other physically, and there has been a special bond between us since he reached the teenage years. I remember the many basketball skirmishes we had in our makeshift backyard court. Because of his proficiency at the game, we called him "Swish." For most of his adult life, Stan was an area salesman in western Connecticut and Massachusetts for a Boston-based hardware wholesaler. He served his country during World War II in the Pacific theatre of operations. He married Dorothy Thistle of New Haven and they were blessed with two lovely daughters, Cheryl and June. I shall always be grateful to Dot and Stan for their unselfish and loving care of my mother as a member of their household during her declining years. Shirley and I also cherish the many happy hours we spent with Dot and Stan in their Thomaston, Connecticut, home and in our Florida condominium during their frequent visits to Sarasota. Stan's early death at age 65 saddened us deeply.

When I was 25 years old, my youngest brother was a senior in high school. I knew that within a year all of my siblings would have completed their secondary education. The family financial situation was now stabilized with the help of my earnings and those of my brothers and sister. I was free to pursue a growing desire to change vocations and become a Christian minister. This yearning had been nourished by many years of watching and admiring the witness of my spiritual leader at Plymouth Congregational Church, the Reverend Harold Gilbert Jones. It was enhanced by my close friendship with John McClelland and Dwight Large, two of the many Yale Divinity School students who served on the Plymouth Church staff. Visits to the Yale campus only served to increase my determination to seek a college and theological education in preparation for ordination.

There were attractive alternatives for me: The possibility of an executive career with the railroad. The chance of a marriage to Shirley. There were also deterrents: The advice of my parents that I should keep my good job. My lack of funds to pay for a college and seminary education. The deciding factor was the encouragement of Harold Jones, my minister, and the information he gave me about Bangor Theological Seminary.

There was a school in Maine, he told me, which had a special program for non-college graduates who wished to change vocations. It offered pre-theological and theological studies on its own campus, in cooperation with the University of Maine at Orono. Miraculously, the school was so well endowed that it charged no tuition and offered board and room at affordable prices. I applied for admission in the spring of 1939 and was accepted. In September of that year I left behind me the railroad, my family and, most important, Shirley as I boarded a train for Bangor.

2.
A Double Life

The next nine years would be the busiest of my life. In the dual role of theologue and student-minister I would find my physical and intellectual capacities thoroughly tested. Four years of pre-theological and theological studies at Bangor would be followed by a summer and a year at Bowdoin College to complete work for a liberal arts degree. Then it was on to New Haven for four years of graduate study at Yale leading to a Ph.D. degree in religion. During all this time my double life involved serving as a youth assistant at Bangor's All Souls Congregational Church, as student-minister of the yoked Congregational Churches in Robbinston and Calais (Red Beach), Maine, and as minister and part-time student in Yarmouth, Maine, and Shelton, Connecticut, at the Huntington Congregational Church.

When I enrolled in Bangor Theological Seminary, my worldly goods consisted of 500 dollars I had saved during my working years with the railroad. This was enough to pay for room and board. Primarily because of a modest endowment and the general annual support of Maine churches, the Seminary had charged no tuition from the time of its opening in 1816; economic conditions forced a change in this policy in the mid-forties after I had graduated. During my tenure as president, when I was required to engage in vigorous fund-raising activities, I wondered about the wisdom of the no-tuition policy. However, I realized that without it many students like me could never have afforded to prepare for the ministry.

Bangor was, indeed, a unique theological school in 1939. Today other institutions have borrowed some features of its academic program, but then it was the only recognized protestant seminary which admitted students to its theological department who had not first completed a college education. I use the word "recognized" advisedly. Although it is a charter member of The Association of Theological Schools in the United States and Canada, the Seminary was given only "Associate" status by the ATS until 1974 because of its unorthodox admissions policy. Only after a 20-year struggle during the Whittaker administration did Bangor achieve full accreditation. The details of this story will be recorded in a later chapter.

My first impressions of the Seminary convinced me that it was a caring institution headed by a congenial and competent president, Dr. Harry Trust; that it was blessed with a scholarly friendly faculty; and that the student body was composed of young men like me, and a few women, who had left other vocations to follow a call into professional Christian service. New students were greeted by Elsie Olmstead, Secretary to the President. She served for 26 years in this capacity under three chief executive officers. She knew more about the school than anyone else on campus. She assigned me to Room 13 on the fourth and top floor of Maine Hall, the student dormitory, and I was ready to begin my life as a theologue.

My quarters consisted of a spacious living room, which also served as a study, and two small bedrooms. Howard Deming was my roommate. He had a beautiful tenor voice, and later sang at my wedding. Across the hall were Ed "Beau" Manning and Maldwyn "Mo" Parry. Mo and I have been life-long friends; he and his wife Alice visit with Shirley and me at least twice a year. Meals were served in an attractive dining room located in the "New Commons," where the Dorrs, "Ma" and "Pa," presided as stewards. The meals were hearty and usually tasty. They were served by students, who thus earned the cost of their board. The Dorrs were widely admired by the students, many of whom considered them to be foster parents when personal problems arose. The dining experience was "family living."

After a two-day period of orientation, my first class was scheduled. Because I had no previous post-high school education, except for a course in Public Speaking taken at a YMCA and a correspondence course in "Traffic Management," I was enrolled in the pre-theological department for two years of study in the liberal arts and sciences. These courses were taught both by resident faculty members and by visiting professors from the University of Maine at Orono who came to the Seminary campus twice a week. English Grammar and English Literature, Social Studies, Natural Science, and Psychology were offered by visiting University teachers. Introductory Old Testament and New Testament, Philosophy, Greek and Hebrew were taught by resident faculty who also offered the courses prescribed in the Theological Department.

The uniqueness of Bangor Seminary is seen in its dual program of studies. An increasing number of its students over the years have been college graduates who were thus qualified to begin a three-year theological course leading to a Bachelor of Divinity degree (now Master of Divinity). A majority of matriculants, however, have entered Bangor without a college degree. They, like me, have enrolled in pre-theological courses for two years, after which they engaged in three years of theological studies, upon the successful completion of which they received a diploma. The diploma graduates then transferred to some college or university of their choice, where they were given advanced standing toward an undergraduate degree. Upon achieving the Bachelor's degree in the Arts or Sciences, the student was required to write a theological thesis and thus became eligible for the Seminary's degree, a prerequisite for ordination. Another unusual feature of the "Bangor plan" is the employment of many students as part-time ministers of Maine churches, under faculty supervision. This enables them "to earn while they learn," an economic necessity.

During the first year of study at Bangor I met some of the men who were to influence greatly my own faith and practice. One of these was the instructor of the English grammar class, Professor

22

Cecil Reynolds of the University of Maine, a member of the visiting faculty. It was Professor Reynolds who made it possible for me to accelerate my academic program by his suggestion early in the course that I did not need instruction in the use of the English language. He realized that my ten years of experience as a private secretary was sufficient to qualify me for enrollment in English Literature, a sophomore course. Thus began a process which enabled me eventually to shorten my course at Bangor to four years instead of five. In the few weeks I spent in the classroom with Professor Reynolds, he and I developed a friendship which has remained through the years. He was a scholar of the first order and a social critic whom I still admire during the years of retirement for us both.

On the resident theological faculty at Bangor was Dr. Marion John Bradshaw. As professor of Philosophy of Religion he also taught a pre-theological course in the History of Philosophy. With his encouragement and permission I was allowed as a freshman to enroll in his sophomore class without benefit of introductory instruction in his subject. This illustrates another feature of "the Bangor plan": permitting mature students with intellectual capabilities to undertake advanced studies. This was another step, together with some extra academic work during the summer, toward my graduation with the Bangor diploma at the end of four years. Dr. Bradshaw was a profound philosopher, an impressive lecturer, and an instructor who challenged every student to use fully the mental capacities granted by the Creator. He was a dominant figure on the Bangor faculty for three decades, and was admired by his peers as well as those who sat in his classroom. He was my first academic "hero."

The Waldo Professor of Ecclesiastical History during my student days was Dr. Mervin M. Deems. He was inspiring both in the classroom and as a chapel speaker. I first came under his influence in a pre-theological course in medieval history. I knew then that I wanted eventually to be a history professor; this desire was reaffirmed during my theological studies with him in church history and missions. During all the rest of my days as a professor and churchman one of my dominant themes has been the significance of the missionary outreach of the church. I was so impressed by the personality and the professional competence of Dr. Deems that during my presidency I succeeded in bringing him back from Chicago Theological Seminary, where he had been teaching, to be the Dean of Bangor Seminary.

One of the strengths of the Bangor curriculum is the offering of studies in the Biblical languages. During my first year I was introduced to New Testament Greek by Dr. Alfred Morris Perry, the Hayes Professor of New Testament. Although I had taken three years of Spanish in high school, I was somewhat apprehensive, as are most freshmen at Bangor, about learning Greek. Dr. Perry soon made it evident that the task was achievable through reasonable academic effort. He was a superb teacher and a gentle man. I looked forward with keen anticipation to being a member of his theological class in New Testament during my junior year.

One of the "giants" on the faculty at Bangor during the twentieth century was Dr. Charles Gordon Cumming, the George A. Gordon Professor of Old Testament. He was a tall, handsome man with a shock of white hair that made him look like an ancient Hebrew prophet. I did not meet Dr. Cumming in the classroom until my junior year, but I was well aware of his reputation as a scholarly and dramatic lecturer; this was demonstrated in every one of his frequent chapel talks.

The shaping of my own theology began in my first year at Bangor when I met Dr. Andrew Banning in a pre-theological course called "Introduction to Reflective Thinking." His influence upon a generation of students (he taught at Bangor for 35 years) was enhanced by the reasonable and precise way in which he explained the many intricacies of theological doctrine. Trained at Harvard, he was the epitome of a true liberal. For many years he assumed the extra-curricular duty of Registrar, and during his final years at Bangor he was the Dean. Many students will remember fascinating evenings spent in Dr. Banning's home by invitation for informal discussion of theological themes by "The Fortnightly Club."

Banning, Bradshaw, Cumming, Deems, and Perry were "the big five" on the mid-century Bangor faculty. Three of them served under three presidents, and together they gave the Seminary an average of more than 25 years of academic leadership.

My "spiritual father" in the Christian ministry was Dr. Harry Trust, the president of the Seminary for 19 years (1933-1952). It was he who encouraged me to leave the business world and enter the "school of the prophets," as he loved to call the Seminary. He blessed the marriage bonds on my wedding day. He traveled half the width of the state of Maine and back again to preside at my first communion service as a student pastor. He prayed for me at the climactic time of ordination. It was his wish and plan that I return to the Seminary as a teacher, and eventually be his successor in the presidency. I shall pay further tribute to him when I recount my early days on the faculty. Suffice it to record here that during my student days, Dr. Trust, who was the Fogg Professor of Sacred Rhetoric and Oratory, taught me how to become an effective preacher and pastor.

Most important to a new student entering a seminary is the quality of its faculty. In this regard, Bangor was impressive. Another significant criterion is the physical environment in which study takes place. "The Seminary on the Hill," as it has been affectionately known, provided facilities which were adequate if not outstanding. There were twelve buildings on the ten-acre campus located on a hillside about a mile west of downtown Bangor, with an attractive view of the Penobscot River valley in the distance. Maine Hall, the student dormitory, was built in 1834 and contained twenty-four suites of rooms on three floors located above the first floor president's office, guest rooms, and a student recreational and social area. Each suite had a living room-study and bedroom area accommodating two students. There was a common bathroom on each student floor.

Classes were held in the Chapel Building, located on "Chapel Row" next to Maine Hall. It was constructed in 1859 and also contained the library in a somewhat antiquated and increasingly crowded setting. There was one classroom on the first floor, where traditionally the Greek language was taught. Up a long double stairway were two more classrooms, a lecture hall, and a chapel sanctuary. Towering over the library, class and chapel facilities was a belfry from which the peal of a bell could be heard throughout

25

the neighborhood. The bell is still rung by an attached hand-held rope. The historical tradition of Bangor is enhanced by the portraits of early faculty members and trustees hanging on classroom walls, by the imposing likeness of first president Enoch Pond which dominates the entrance hall, and by the impressive "Missionary Board" in one of the classrooms which lists the many graduates of Bangor who have served in the far corners of the world as Christian emissaries.

The newest building on campus at the time of my matriculation was the gymnasium, built in 1895 to house a small basketball court, a bowling alley, and a running track. The central heating plant was located in the basement. Many alumni will remember with nostalgia the intramural hoop contests which took place in the gym. It was also the scene of numerous seminary parties and dances. Sadly for some, the gym is now a memory for it has become the Wellman Commons, the school's dining facility and multi-purpose auditorium.

Until quite recently the seminary dining room was located on the first floor of the "New Commons," so designated because it was constructed in 1836, eight years after the "Old Commons." This building holds pleasant memories for me of good times and good food shared with my first-year classmates. Three years of different nostalgic reminiscences are associated with the New Commons. At one end of the building were two of the Seminary's student apartments, one of which became the Whittaker family home on campus for my wife and me. After my retirement as president, the building was renamed "Whittaker House" in my honor.

The "Old Commons," built in 1828, is the oldest building on campus. It is located next to the Chapel and has served through the years as housing for both faculty and students. In the early years all Seminary activity took place in this building, until Maine Hall became a reality in 1834. The old student living quarters can still be seen in their original condition on the fourth floor of the Old Commons. Several other buildings on the campus were faculty homes, including the historic Hannibal Hamlin House, where Dr. Warren J. Moulton was the first of Seminary presidents to take up residence after the home of Abraham Lincoln's first vice president was given to the school by the Hamlin heirs. It was the Whittaker family abode, thoroughly enjoyed for a period of 25 years.

Another major impression I recall from my early days at the Seminary was the attractive local community into which I had migrated from cosmopolitan New Haven. Bangor in 1939 was a city of about 30,000 inhabitants, primarily with equal numbers of Roman Catholics and Protestants, but with a goodly representation of people adhering to the Jewish and Greek Orthodox faiths. Only a few blacks lived in the area. An important cultural asset was the land-grant University of Maine, located at Orono eight miles away. There was considerable wealth among the inhabitants, much of it inherited from the lucrative timber business of the nineteenth century. Bangor's public library, one of the largest and best-endowed in a city of comparable size, was a valuable resource for the seminary student. Although most denominations had established substantial churches, I was most interested in the two Congregational parishes because of my background.

Although I was later to become affiliated for more than thirty years with the Hammond Street Congregational Church, located just two blocks away, my first Bangor religious connection outside the Seminary was with the All Souls Congregational Church in the eastern section of town. The minister was Dr. Frederick M. Meek, who later became pastor of the famous Old South Church in Boston. He was looking for a seminary student to work part time in the Church school. I was available, and I was chosen. It not only gave me a small but welcome income, it also gave me an opportunity for association with a man whom I consequently admired throughout my entire professional career. Our friendship continued in later years when we served together in national denomination work and when Dr. Meek became a member of the Seminary's board of trustees during my presidency.

The experience gained in the Church school at All Souls was a good beginning for a young theologue. It helped to put into perspective the studies I had begun, and working under Dr. Meek's supervision gave me a valuable measure of self confidence. The classroom work during the first semester did not prove to be difficult, although I had been out of school for ten years. Even the Greek

27

language was absorbed rather easily under Dr. Perry's skilled leadership. English Literature and Philosophy were two of my favorite subjects. However, not all of my attention was given to things academic and churchly. There was a certain young lady back in Connecticut who was often in my thoughts.

When Shirley and I parted in September of 1939, neither one of us would have believed that within a year we would be husband and wife. We had made no long-range commitment to one another. I would be busy with my studies, and I did not know what her future plans might be. We did correspond on a regular basis. She had presented me with a black cookie jar painted with bright flowers. It was twelve inches high, and she kept it filled with goodies, much to my delight as well as that of my roommate. Much as I enjoyed dormitory life, secretly I held the hope that one year without Shirley would be enough. Our affection for one another expanded through the courtesy of the U.S. mail service, and we keenly anticipated the long Christmas recess when we would be together again.

Eighteen consecutive days and evenings with Shirley over the holidays led to the mutual conviction that we could not survive a permanent separation. We resolved to find a way to bring her to Maine as my wife. There were obstacles. I did not have the kind of income needed by a married man. She was well established as a high school teacher. Our parents thought it was irresponsible, at best, for us to consider a wedding at any time in the near future. But love found a way!

Another of the features of "the Bangor plan" has been the opportunity given to mature students for service as part-time pastors of rural churches in Maine. In my day as many as twenty-five students would travel as far as 300 miles round-trip each weekend to distant parishes which otherwise would have no spiritual leadership. These were men, and an occasional woman, who had been lay leaders in churches before enrolling at Bangor. Most of them had also engaged in a trade or profession which they had abandoned in favor of the ministry. This maturity enabled them to be effective pastors, under supervision of the Seminary faculty, of churches to which they were assigned. It also enabled them to earn a modest income, thus helping them to pay some of their school expenses. The Bangor plan made it possible for me to bring Shirley to Maine as my wife.

Dr. Rodney W. Roundy, Superintendent of the Maine Conference of Congregational Christian Churches, will be gratefully remembered as the one who offered me an opportunity to become, in June of 1940, the student-minister of two small churches in Robbinston and Red Beach (Calais), located in Washington County on the St. Croix River, the boundary between the United States and the Canadian province of New Brunswick. The salary was twenty-five dollars per week, just about enough to give Shirley and me the courage to make our marriage plans.

Prior to the appointment by Dr. Roundy, Shirley and her parents made an automobile trip from New Haven to Bangor in February, 1940, during Shirley's one-week vacation from her teaching duties. It was a twelve-hour journey one way, but Blanche and Louis Johns were anxious to see first-hand what the future might hold for their daughter "way down East." Permission was given by President Trust for Shirley to visit my room on the fourth floor of Maine Hall. Without this approval, no women were allowed to venture beyond the first floor of the men's dormitory. How times have changed! When I first became president of the Seminary I did not even imagine that before the end of my incumbency Maine Hall would house both men and women students (although on separate floors). In any event, Shirley did come to my room, where she met several of my friends who lived on the fourth floor; I recall that they examined her with some curiosity, that they later gave me a hard time about being in love, but that they were more than a little envious of me.

Shirley's parents were favorably impressed by the Seminary campus, its program, and its personnel. They became particularly fond of President Trust because of his apparent sincere interest in the welfare of student Fred Whittaker as he made plans for his future personal and professional life. Shirley and her mother and father stayed at Bangor's premier hotel, The Bangor House, during their visit, and I well remember a cozy and friendly breakfast we had in their spacious room which overlooked Main Street. We did not talk much about wedding plans that February morning, but the

29

way was smoothly paved for the serious discussion at a later time which led to an engagement announcement in June.

It was shortly thereafter, as springtime came, that President Trust and Dr. Roundy spoke to me about a church appointment. Once my future part-time employment was determined, I pursued my studies during the second semester with renewed vigor and with keen anticipation of future events. Although Shirley's parents, and mine, remained most apprehensive about our meager economic resources, she and I went ahead with our plans for a September wedding two weeks before we would return to Maine as husband and wife. My bachelor life in the student dormitory was coming to an end.

When the Seminary year was over I went immediately to Washington County and began my work as student-minister of the Congregational Christian Churches in Robbinston and Red Beach (Calais). I did not even pause for a visit to New Haven when Shirley announced our engagement at a June party in her home. Later in the summer we had a reunion when she and her parents came to Maine and gained their first knowledge of the parishes where she and I were to spend two of the most exciting and rewarding years of our lives.

Robbinston in 1940 was a rural community of about 600 inhabitants. The only industry in town was a sardine canning factory. There was a local doctor and an officer of the U.S. Customs Service. Ernest Brown, the mail carrier, owned and operated Brook's Bluff, an attractive tourist facility for summer visitors with cabins overlooking the St. Croix River. The Brown family were to become close friends of the Whittakers. The children of Robbinston were educated in a local elementary school, but high school students were transported to Calais. Community social life centered in the Grange hall and in the Methodist Church on Robbinston "Ridge."

The Robbinston Congregational Church had been dormant for several years except for the summer months when there were enough visitors to support Sunday services. No new members had been added for twenty years, and the total membership had dwindled to six, all of them elderly. My instructions from Dr. Roundy of the Congregational State Conference were to seek additional members and to keep the church open throughout the year. I was inspired by the challenge and by the realization that the economic foundation of my forthcoming marriage depended upon the success of my mission. Two months of concentrated parish calling resulted in the enlisting of thirty-two new members, including several young people. Goal one was achieved!

It was a memorable Sunday in August of 1940 when the Robbinston Church received its class of new members at a Communion service conducted by President Harry Trust of Bangor Seminary. He had made the long trip to eastern Maine at my request since I was not permitted as a student minister to celebrate the eucharistic rite. It was one of the many ways in which Dr. Trust showed devotion to his office. Among those who joined the Church that day were six members of the Ernest Brown family, as well as a president emeritus of Colby College and a retired national officer of the Baptist churches, both of whom were summer residents. Nothing quite like it had ever happened before in this quiet little community. It was a red-letter day in my experience.

That summer without Shirley was a lonely one in many ways, but the days were brightened by the excitement of my new vocation and by the many friendships made, some of them to last a lifetime. Ernest and Princess Brown, and their four children, are those best remembered and most loved. When Shirley came to Robbinston in September as my wife, the Browns took us into their home as frequent guests. Princess, a lovely lady most aptly named, was in reality a surrogate mother to Shirley during the first months when my wife was adjusting to her new role in the parish. Tragedy struck in December of that year when Princess died of pneumonia at the age of forty-nine. Officiating at her memorial service was a traumatic experience for me. We laid her to rest in a beautiful hillside cemetery called "Picnic Hill," where her grieving husband joined her much later.

Betty was the eldest of the two Brown daughters. On my first visit to Robbinston it was she, then a pretty sixteen-year-old high school student, who escorted me around the town and introduced me to many of my potential parishioners. To this day Betty and her husband, Harold Blood, are among the Whittaker circle of friends.

31

They both became public school teachers, and he a superintendent of schools. The eldest Brown child, Harold, established a career in Philadelphia as an oral surgeon. The other son, Philip, found a vocation serving the state of Maine as a police trooper. Barbara Brown Barnes, the youngest daughter, was employed in the business world and still resides in the Robbinston homestead at Brooks Bluff. My wife and I have had two nostalgic reunions with the Brown family, one when I spoke at the dedication of a new organ in the Robbinston Church which Ernest gave in memory of Princess, and the other at the memorial service which I conducted following the death of Ernest. I noted then, with pride, that after his retirement as a rural mail carrier Ernest served as a representative in the Maine legislature, a role which I had earlier assumed as an avocation while president of the Seminary.

Other people and events of the Robbinston-Red Beach years are remembered with delight. Albion and Cora Goodwin, then seventy years old or more, lived frugally in a modest home two miles removed on a dirt road. Shirley and I often shared a meal with them during a pastoral visit; they were always in church on Sunday, weather permitting. Annie Lamb and her brother George, also in their seventies, provided shelter and food for me during my bachelor summer in the parish; she was the reliable and meticulous clerk of the church. Bob and Edith Seeley had little in the way of material goods, but they and their children were strong supporters of the church. Ivor Andrews, a farmer, and his invalid wife were people of sturdy faith; their children were in the developing Sunday school and young people's work. One tragic day, the Andrews' home and barn were destroyed by fire while the family watched helplessly from a nearby field. During an ensuing pastoral call I found them stoically accepting their fate and busily drawing plans for a new house.

Sadie Cox, the president of the Ladies Aide, was one of my severest critics, although I think she secretly approved my pastoral leadership. She taught me my first lesson about church politics. When I entered the Robbinston Church I was struck by the ugliness of the metal stove pipe which ran the length of the sanctuary from the wood-burning stove in the rear of the room. Moreover, if the

Church was to remain open during the winter, it would need a more adequate heating system. After due consideration by the members at a meeting which Sadie attended, it was voted unanimously to install a new furnace in the vestry, with appropriate hot air outlets in the sanctuary.

After it was installed the system worked perfectly, or so I thought. However, I noted that for several Sundays a group of members including Sadie gathered for conversation after the worship service on the spot where the old stove had been located. I could overhear some of the talk as I greeted members of the departing congregation. It became apparent that Sadie was mounting a campaign against the new heating system. Finally, in my brashness as a new minister, I decided to confront her. She complained that the Church was now drafty, that there was not enough money to buy wood, and, most important, that she and her cohorts "missed the old stove." I tried to be sympathetic, but eventually was moved to point out that the furnace had been approved by a unanimous vote of the congregation and the matter had been settled. Sadie was adamant. In my exasperation I blurted out: "But Sadie, you voted for the new furnace, didn't you?" Her reply was unforgettable: "Yes, I did, but you knew I didn't want it!"

A trial of a different kind also faced me during that first summer as a neophyte pastor. I had been in Robbinston only a month when Donny Goodwin, the 12-year-old son of his divorced mother, was killed in an automobile accident. I was called upon to conduct my first funeral service, a task made more difficult because of the tragic circumstances of the death. Donny was a Boy Scout and a beloved member of the community. His mother had raised him as a single parent and was herself living near the poverty level. I counselled with Dorothy, the mother, and did my best to comfort her in the memorial service. From the beginning of my ministry I have always planned the funeral rite as a memorial to the deceased, concentrating on the Christian faith in eternal life and on expressing thanksgiving for the positive aspects of the earthly life now ended. I was not certain that I had been helpful to the grieving mother until a week or two after the service when I stopped at Dorothy Goodwin's home and found her in the yard sitting on a wooden box before a large stone. In one hand she held a chisel and in the other a hammer. She was very much at peace when I talked with her and asked her what she was doing. She replied with some feeling: "Why, I am carving a tombstone for my son." That stone now rests in Picnic Hill Cemetery as a testimony to a mother's faith and love.

As the summer progressed, some basic work was done in reorganizing the program of the Robbinston Church. After the influx of new members, officers were elected and committees formed. A small Sunday school and a young people's group were organized. Pastoral calling resulted in increased attendance at weekly worship. Meanwhile there was work to be done in revitalizing the church at Red Beach.

For several years a small group of Christians had been meeting in the Congregational church located in an outlying ward of the city of Calais known as Red Beach. It was so named because of the color of a mineral once taken from a quarry on the banks of the St. Croix River. In 1940 the Red Beach Church was yoked with the larger Congregational Church in Calais. The resident minister at Calais went to Red Beach each Sunday afternoon to conduct worship. This assignment was now transferred to me, but with the understanding that the Reverend Thomas J. W. Cornish, the Calais minister, would be available for consultation and for emergency service in Red Beach. Tom Cornish, an alumnus of Bangor Seminary, became my very good friend over the years and was greatly helpful to me in my developing ministry.

Anna Chisholm was the clerk and matriarch of the Red Beach Church. With her assistance, and that of her daughter Carolyn, a systematic and largely successful effort was made to increase the membership of the church and to improve the attendance at weekly worship. My first wedding took place in this parish when two seventy-five-year-olds asked me to officiate at their marriage; this remains as a milestone in my ministry. The Chisholms and other new friends did more than their fair share of feeding and entertaining me during my bachelor summer in Washington County. Later they were most kind to Shirley and me. Living accommodations were provided in Red Beach for the newlyweds one summer and for a winter season.

When September came, it was time for a decision. Both of the churches voted to call me as their student minister under an arrangement which provided that I come to the parishes each weekend during the Seminary academic year and that I be in residence full-time during the summer. The combined salary was to be twenty-five dollars per week, fifteen from Robbinston and ten from Red Beach. Looking back, it seems like a very skimpy financial base for a man about to be married, but there were no apprehensions then. I left eastern Maine after Labor Day with a light heart for the long journey to Connecticut and my waiting bride.

3.
The Honeymoon Begins

The Whittaker-Johns wedding in New Haven on September 14, 1940, was an event of some social significance. Shirley's family had become well known in the community and church; she had completed three years of teaching at Hillhouse High School; she also had a circle of friends from her student days at Albertus Magnus College. I had lived in New Haven for twenty-seven years and had established many friendships at the railroad, in the church, and on the golf course. More than 400 people attended the marriage ceremony in Plymouth Congregational Church on a beautiful Saturday afternoon. The officiating clergymen were our pastor, the Rev. Harold G. Jones, and Dr. Harry Trust, president of Bangor Seminary. The attendants included Shirley's sister Barbara and cousin Virginia, my sister Dorothy and brothers Ed and Stan, one of Shirley's college classmates and one of her teaching associates, one of my golfing partners, and a close minister friend of both the bride and groom. A reception followed in the spacious and attractive garden behind the Johns' home at 460 Ellsworth Avenue. Blanche and Louis Johns were the proud and gracious hosts. Refreshments were served by pretty young ladies who had attended the summer camp conducted by Shirley.

The whole day was an exciting and satisfying experience still vividly remembered fifty years later. The beginning of the honeymoon also was memorable. We had planned to spend a few days at the World's Fair in New York City before heading for our new adventure in Maine. We left by automobile about seven in the evening with the idea of finding a motel enroute. We had hotel reservations in New York for the next few nights, but I had neglected to take care of accommodations for our wedding night. At ten-thirty we were still looking for a motel with a double bed; none was to be found, and we finally settled reluctantly for twin beds in a Greenwich motel.

The days at the World's Fair passed quickly, highlighted both by the wondrous things we had seen at the exhibition and by the glorious love found uniquely during a honeymoon. We were both anxious to start our married life in Maine. Waiting for us in Bangor was a cozy three-room apartment in the New Commons on the Seminary campus. It was one of the very few married student accommodations then available. The monthly rental was an amazingly low sixteen dollars, another feature of the "Bangor plan." Heat was included in the rental charge, but we paid our own utility bills. Located on the second floor, our apartment had a combination kitchen-dining room under a sloping roof with a dormer window, a living room, a bedroom, and a bathroom. It seemed to us ideal, and is remembered nostalgicly as the place where our first child was conceived two years later.

We furnished our living quarters largely with second-hand items and wedding gifts, augmented by the donation of a new refrigerator by Shirley's father after he discovered that some food had gone bad in the old one. Shirley had never learned to cook, but she became a fast learner with the help of some great recipes she had gleaned from her mother's file. To show how unaccustomed she was to kitchen duty at the beginning, I recall her early attempt at coffee-making via the "drip" method. She spooned in the proper amount of coffee and then poured in the hot water. Nothing happened. She took the contraption apart to see what was wrong, only to discover the compartment at the bottom where she should have put the grounds. This time there was coffee! Today, so far as I am concerned, my wife is the best cook in the world!

I was now a sophomore-junior under the Bangor academic program. Having completed some sophomore subjects in my freshman year, I was permitted to enroll in two courses normally reserved for those in the junior or first year of the theological department. For the first time I was privileged to study under the direction of Dr. Cumming and Dr. Deems, two of the professors I grew to admire so greatly. The instruction they gave me in Old Testament and Church History, respectively, was most helpful to me as I prepared weekly sermons for the churches I was serving.

In late September Shirley and I took our first weekend drive over U.S. Route 1, 135 miles to Robbinston and Red Beach. From the fall of 1940 until after Christmas in 1942, more than two years, this was our weekly routine during the academic year at the Seminary. Two automobiles were worn out during this period, but Shirley and I thought of the trip as exciting and romantic most of the time, even when we had to extricate the car from snowbanks. Usually we left Bangor on Friday afternoon or Saturday morning and returned on Sunday evening or early on Monday. Classes did not begin on Monday until the afternoon in deference to the many student pastors who were returning from their distant parishes that day. Again, the "Bangor plan" was considerate of the needs of new theologues.

The church people in our duel parish received the newlyweds with open arms. Shirley was warmly welcomed, and they were glad to see me back, too. The wedding trip became an extended honeymoon, at least for several weeks. I had spent the previous summer in Washington County, but for Shirley this was a transformation in lifestyle. She was used to the cosmopolitan atmosphere of New Haven with its Yale University influence. We were now about to begin a life together in Maine's "way down east." She made the adjustment admirably, thanks in good measure to the gracious and loving way in which Princess Brown and her family, in particular, received us into their home at Brooks Bluff. We often spent the weekends with the Browns during the first few months before Princess died. Several other parishioners also entertained us during that first year. While we were grateful for these courtesies, the experience of being in someone else's home

38

over a period of weeks did come to resemble extended pastoral calls. We felt constantly in need of being on our best behavior and did become a bit tired nervously. During the second and third seasons, we made arrangements whereby we lived in more private quarters most of the weekends.

As the weeks went by, Shirley became involved with me in the parish work. She helped in the church school and assisted in establishing a young people's group which met Sunday evening. One of the lasting results of our early years in the parish has been the continuing influence we had upon the lives of teenagers who are now engaged in adult careers far away from Washington County. One of these, Marjorie Vose Freeman, we hear from every year at Christmas. She is now well established as a teacher in California, and she never fails to comment in her annual greeting how she considers Shirley and me to be the principal inspiration for her useful Christian witness. We are rewarded.

One of the most helpful and best remembered academic experiences of Seminary days was the weekly "preaching exercise" under the direction of Dr. Trust. In addition to being president, he was also the Fogg Professor of Sacred Rhetoric and Oratory (a fancy title, indeed). Every Monday afternoon students in the theological department gathered in the Chapel to hear one of their number conduct worship and preach a sermon. The other students were expected to offer criticism after the benediction and then Dr. Trust would make his comments. As I remember it, much of the student reaction was negative, while the professor tried to say something positive. It was a most valuable and basic procedure for new theologues at the beginning of their ministry. I was greatly helped in the preparation of sermons for the weekly mission to Washington County.

The first year at Bangor passed quickly, happily, and successfully for Shirley and me. My wife was becoming adept in the kitchen and she was popular with my classmates, who felt free to come to our apartment and sample the always-full cookie jar. We looked forward to the weekends in the parishes, with its beautiful ride through the "Black Woods" to Cherryfield, Machias, and beyond. On several occasions we would stop halfway at picturesque

Jonesport, where classmate "Mo" Parry was the student pastor. He lived with his gracious mother, who always fed us well and was especially kind to my new young bride. Other good friends were Ruth and Preston Pennell of Dennysville; they served the Congregational Church in this small river town and in nearby Meddybemps. Preston was an earlier graduate of Bangor Seminary who brought honor to himself and to the school by his devoted and effective leadership, despite a slight speech impairment, to small rural parishes in Maine. Shirley and I learned much about ministry from him and from his wife Ruth, who made a distinct contribution to education in Maine.

There is an amusing and revealing incident associated with the Pennells. They were active in the local Grange, where Ruth played the piano at meetings. She was of German extraction and during World War II was the object of some ill-deserved local suspicion and criticism. One weekend I heard some idle talk in Robbinston, where the Pennells were known by reputation, about Ruth's alleged failure to stand up when the national anthem was sung at Grange meetings. Shortly thereafter Shirley and I spent a night in the Pennell home, as we did on more than one occasion. I told her about the rumor. She laughed, and slyly admitted that the rumor was true. When I expressed surprise, she explained: "Of course, I don't stand up for the 'Star Spangled Banner' in the Grange hall; I am the pianist!"

My wife and I continued to make new friends in Robbinston and Red Beach. One of these was Mildred Washburn, the daughter-in-law of Frank Washburn, a retired Commissioner of agriculture for the State of Maine who lived in the nearby town of Perry. Mildred played the organ in the Robbinston Church and her friendship has been meaningful through the years. One weekend we were invited to stay in the Frank Washburn home, where there was to be a Saturday afternoon tea. Shirley thought this would be an excellent time to display her set of matched silver fox furs, which she had not felt comfortable in wearing since leaving New Haven. The neckpiece was appropriately admired at the Washburn tea, but was given a different reception when she wore it to Sunday school the next morning. She was soon spotted by two of the young boys, one of whom exclaimed innocently enough: "Gee, she's gotta coupla skunks 'round her neck!" The furs were put back in storage for the duration.

One of the most challenging and time-consuming tasks of the student minister is the preparation of a weekly sermon. Usually I spent Friday afternoon and evening putting the finishing touches on the sermon and worship service for the coming Sunday. Since Dr. Trust had taught his students to prepare the sermon in manuscript form, it took several hours to complete the work. I include here, by way of example, excerpts from one of the sermons preached during my time at Robbinston and Red Beach. By necessity the same sermon was presented at each of the churches.

"Victory Is In The Heart" was the somewhat prosaic title. The text was Matthew 5:8 — "Blessed are the pure in heart, for they shall see God." As an opening illustration I recounted a report about a group of young men who were discussing religion in a college fraternity house. They protested: "Do you want to know what keeps us from being Christian? It's church people. They want us to be Christian, but they do not live right themselves."

The concept of right living is one which has permeated my theology since I learned it at my mother's knee. Thus I told my parishioners that "it is the sacred duty of each and every disciple of Jesus to 'live right' in the sight of God and other human beings; thus will we achieve the personal and social salvation of all who bear the name 'Christian.'"

In this sermon I also explained the importance of the weekly Sunday religious service. "The initial act in personal spiritual living is the worship of God; from that experience comes the guidance of the Holy Spirit and the revelation of Jesus Christ, which enables us to 'live right,' as fraternity members expressed it. It is important, I went on to say, that "in these hours of prayer and meditation we approach God with a pure heart." It does not matter, I suggested, whether our hands are clean or our clothes new; it does not matter where we were born or where we now live; God does not care whether the worshipper is rich or poor, educated or illiterate; all these things have nothing to do with religion.

What does matter, I concluded, "is that we come before God

humbly, acknowledging our sins — and we are all guilty before God because of the multiple sins of our evil world. What does matter is that we sincerely seek the forgiveness of God and resolve to serve Him to the best of our knowledge and ability. What does matter is that we banish from our hearts all thoughts of malice, of hatred, of greed and selfish desire. What does matter is that here in this holy place we cleanse our hearts so that we may see God and, having seen Him, there will come to us the faith which was in Christ Jesus. With this faith, victory is assured!"

My first Christmas Sunday in the yoked parishes was one to be remembered. It was the first time the Robbinston congregation had worshipped during this holy season in more than twenty years. I felt fulfilled as Shirley and I left the next day for what became an annual pilgrimage to the Johns family home in New Haven over a period of more than thirty years. So long as "Maga," the name given to Shirley's mother by her first grandchild, was alive it was a foregone conclusion that all the family would spend Christmas at grandmother's. It was a merry time for all, with great food, the exchange of presents, and carol-singing around the tree directed by Shirley's mother at the piano.

Soon after the New Year my wife and I returned to the Seminary where I became engaged in preparation for semester exams. They presented no problem so long as I took the time and effort to prepare. It was in January, too, that I attended my first Convocation Week at Bangor Seminary, an event unique in origin and in continuity.

Since 1905 Bangor Theological Seminary has offered a service to local and area lay people and ministers which was the first of its kind among theological schools and has the longest continuous history of similar events. Except for a few of the years during the two World Wars, the Seminary has brought to the Hammond Street Church for a series of lectures and worship services some of the most distinguished religious leaders of the twentieth century. The program was inaugurated by President David Nelson Beach, and the annual Quiet Hour is named in his honor. The major lectureships are the Enoch Pond Lectures on Applied Christianity, the Samuel Harris Lectures on Literature and Life, the Francis B. Denio Lectures on the Bible, the George Shepard Lectures on Preaching, and the Louis F. Stearns Lectures on Christian Theology.

Each year late in January, between the academic semesters, as many as 500 people from the Canadian maritime provinces and all of the New England states, plus a goodly number of alumni from other parts of the nation, spend three or four days at this religious festival. They are privileged to hear and to meet such distinguished speakers as Harry Emerson Fosdick, Washington Gladden, William Lyon Phelps, Walter Rauschenbush, Rufus Jones, Joshua Loth Liebman, Halford Luccock, Douglas Horton, Rabbi Abraham J. Heschel, Howard Thurman, Reinhold Niebuhr, and Paul Tillich. The Bangor Convocation has been a vital influence upon my own ministry, to say nothing of its profound effect upon thousands of other lives.

Inspired by my first Convocation experience, I faced with renewed vigor the remaining months of my first year in the dual role of theological student and parish minister. With Shirley at my side we cherished the long weekend trip to Robbinston and Red Beach, but were always happy to see the lights of Ellsworth on the nighttime return to Bangor.

It was not long before we began making plans for our first summer together in the parishes on the banks of the St. Croix River. Since the parsonage had been rented for many years to the family of the U.S. Customs officer, we needed to look elsewhere for housing. Fortunately, an offer came from a retired Episcopal priest who owned a summer home in Robbinston which he was not going to use that particular year. We were invited to use the premises for a modest fee, and we gladly accepted. It was a large rambling house close to the river and set back several hundred feet from U.S. Route 1. Actually, the house had quite a romantic aura about it, in addition to being a charming place in which to live. We occupied only the first floor, which had a bedroom corner in the spacious library area.

When June came we moved into the "Steenstra House," as it was known to the local residents, and began our initial concentrated effort as husband and wife to give full-time attention to our parish duties. I made pastoral calls in the two communities. Shirley shared leadership with me in the Sunday schools and in work with the young people; she also became active among the women. We even sang duets at morning worship, on occasion, when we felt the service needed something a little "different." It was a practice we did not repeat in later parish situations, although we did receive some favorable comments.

One of the big events of that summer of 1941 was the appearance in the Robbinston Town Hall of the Plymouth Girls Choir from New Haven, Connecticut. They were directed by William R. Mague and accompanied on the piano by Priscilla Mague. Both were talented musicians and graduates of the Westminster Choir School. Shirley and I had first met the Magues in our home church, where Bill was the choir director and Priscilla the organist. Both of them have impacted our lives at many points. I sang in Bill's choir at Plymouth Church. In the early 1940's Bill and Priscilla left Connecticut and moved permanently to a multi-acre farm owned by Priscilla's parents on the rock-bound coast of Maine seven miles off U.S. Route 1 in the Washington County town of Milbridge, where each summer for several years they conducted a music camp for some of the girls they had trained in New Haven. It was this group which gave a delightful concert in Robbinston to a most appreciative audience in what was undoubtedly the most auspicious cultural event ever to take place in this small rural community.

Bill and Priscilla Mague have a place in my memoirs quite distinct from all others. Educated and professionally active in metropolitan areas, they are indicative also of the sterling quality of Maine people. For more than forty years they gave their Christian witness in Milbridge and Bangor. They raised four children and educated them through grade 12 in their own isolated home. The eldest son went on to earn a Ph.D. degree and to become a university professor. They have been ardent supporters of the Milbridge Church and of the Boy Scout movement. Several years ago they made available a large acreage of their land holding as a wildlife refuge of the U.S. government.

After I became president of Bangor Seminary, I convinced the Magues to come out of their musical hibernation to create, direct, and accompany a choir at the school. This successful venture led to their employment as choir director and organist at All Souls Congregational Church in Bangor. Eventually, Bill became the chief executive officer of the Northern Conservatory of Music in Bangor. He served for many years as a valuable member of the Seminary board of trustees. Priscilla died a few years ago. As Bill and I continue our long friendship, we miss her very much.

Our personal lives during the first summer in the parishes were happy and productive. While the churches continued to grow in numbers and in activities, we were learning to live together as husband and wife in novel surroundings. We spent many quiet evenings in our rented home near the river. For the first and only time we had a pet in our household, a kitten named "Tippy" because of her propensity for going to sleep while sitting up and then tipping over on to her side. She was interesting to watch, and a comfort to Shirley when I was away. Our home was big enough so that we could do some entertaining, which is something Shirley has enjoyed and has done very well since the beginning of our marriage.

Well remembered is the visit of Shirley's parents, Louis and Blanche Johns, who drove up from Connecticut with ten of their long-time friends who had played pinochle together for many years. We had ample room for all of them on the second floor of our "mansion." They had a pleasant time exploring in Washington County in the daytime and playing cards at night. One evening a tremendous thunderstorm came down the St. Croix River valley and lingered all night just over our house, or so it seemed. As the lightning flashed and the thunder boomed around us, they quickly retreated from the second floor and spent most of the night with us in our library-bedroom. They never forgot that experience. Later in the summer we also had a good visit with two of Shirley's college classmates, Eileen O'Neill and Anita Flannigan, who came all the way by train from New Haven, including 135 miles on the Calais branch of the Maine Central Railroad, which at that time was still using potbellied stoves for heating purposes and oil lamps for lighting. It was a happy summer for us, but when September came we were ready and willing to go back to Bangor for the next academic year.

My third year at the Seminary, and my second in the theological department, was a busy one since I was taking an extra course in order to qualify the next year as a senior and thus shorten my time at Bangor by a full academic year. This was the time when I came under the influence of Dr. Alfred Morris Perry in New Testament studies and Dr. Andrew Banning in Theology. Both were thorough scholars in their respective fields and meticulous in their teaching process. Dr. Perry introduced me to Jesus of Nazareth as both an historic personality and as an object of faith, a liberal approach which I have always appreciated. He did his best to explain the letters of Paul, but I have never felt comfortable with some of the Pauline doctrine, especially the emphasis upon human sinfulness.

Dr. Banning was Harvard-educated and had a knack of simplifying even the most complex of theological doctrine so that it could be understood by the neophyte. He appealed to my own liberal tendencies by clearly delineating the relationship of faith and reason. He was not at all dogmatic, perhaps because of his leanings toward Unitarian thought processes. Dr. Banning gave me a sound theological base upon which I could later develop my own doctrinal positions. Another of the Bangor faculty members who had a lasting effect upon my ministry was Dr. Alex Dodd, under whom I studied "Abnormal Psychology," with clinical experience in the Bangor Mental Health Institute. Thanks to him, I have had a continuing appreciation of, and interest in, various types of mental health problems.

One of the helpful programs at Bangor Seminary was the daily chapel service, which gave students the opportunity to hear faculty members in a worship setting outside the classroom. We who were student pastors were grateful for any ideas we could glean from the chapel hours which would assist us in preparing our weekly sermons. Occasionally we would have an outside speaker as our chaplain for the week. It was the first week in December, 1941, when the Seminary brought to the campus as guest chapel speaker Dr. Hachiro Yuasa, president of Japan's Doshisha University. He was a Christian educator from another part of the world, and the students were deeply impressed by his personality and his message. We were sorry to see him leave on Friday for a weekend preaching engagement in Dover-Foxcroft. After the Sunday service Dr. Yuasa returned to Bangor and boarded a train for Boston.

While our newly-found Japanese friend was enroute, the military forces of his native land attacked the U.S. fleet at Pearl Harbor. Our country was involved in World War II as an active participant. We wondered what would happen to Dr. Yuasa. We discovered later that he was apprehended when his train arrived in Boston, was detained for questioning, and then released. On the Seminary campus there was much discussion about the relationship between the chapel messages we had heard the week before and the military actions against the United States. We concluded that the Christians of Japan had no more effect upon Emperor Hirohito than did the Christians of Germany upon Adolph Hitler. I have never forgotten that week with Dr. Yuasa; his name has been in my memory bank ever since.

The winter of 1941-42 was a traumatic one for Shirley and me so far as our living accommodations were concerned. We had determined not to spend another season with weekend visits in parish homes. In Red Beach the Nielsen family ran the local store and post office. In their living quarters they had a spare bedroom which was furnished but unheated. They graciously offered it to us for weekend occupancy. It was fine for the months of September and October, but when cold weather began it was difficult to stay warm in our second-floor single room. We did have a heated bathroom, but most of the night was spent huddled under voluminous covers in our double bed. In mid-winter, with the outside temperature sometimes hovering near zero, Shirley was still cold after wearing her clothes and a fur coat to bed. I was a little more warm-blooded, but still uncomfortable. We were young enough then, and sufficiently dedicated to our mission, to endure this rather simple hardship. As I recall it, Shirley complained less about the cold bedroom than she did about our drafty 1934 Ford with its faulty heater which was our transportation over 270 miles of snow-covered highway each weekend.

Speaking of transportation and of cold, the most frigid experience we ever had was a ride from Bangor to Providence in an old sedan with a classmate from Rhode Island. It was time to go to grandmother's for Christmas, but gasoline was rationed because of the wartime shortage. Five of us pooled what tickets we had and began the long trip shortly after midnight when all of us had returned from our student parishes. Also in the car was a small Christmas tree and a rather large dog. Despite the cramped quarters, all went well until the car heater stopped functioning and the windshield became covered with frost. So that the driver could see where he was going, he had to open both front windows of the car for de-icing purposes. Shirley and I were huddled in the back seat with another student and the tree. He and I tried to keep her warm, and she says she was never closer to another man than she was that wintry night. When nature called, we took turns relieving ourselves in the middle of U.S. Route 1, hoping that no other passing car would spot us. When we finally arrived in Providence the next morning, Shirley and I gratefully boarded a warm train for New Haven. It was a night to be remembered!

It was the same winter of the cold bedroom and the colder car that a much warmer event took place in Red Beach. The Church burned to the ground. We had worshipped in the sanctuary on Sunday afternoon and had returned to Bangor that evening. Sometime after midnight a defective furnace ignited the wooden structure and it was destroyed. I was notified the next morning by telephone. I went immediately to my faculty adviser, Dr. Mervin Deems, and asked him the question he has never forgotten: "What do you do when your church burns down?" I do not remember his reply, but for the final year of my ministry in Red Beach, we worshipped in the schoolhouse. Eventually the church was rebuilt.

Before the winter was over, death became poignant reality for me. On February 3, 1942, my father reached his sixtieth birthday. A month later he was fatally stricken by coronary thrombosis. Dad had not been in good health for some time, perhaps because of his reluctance to seek medical treatment. He suffered from shortness of breath and was no longer able to do the heavy lifting required by his manual work in a local dairy. He was also somewhat overweight. Since I was then a student at the Seminary I had not seen my father since the previous Christmas. When President Harry Trust called me out of a classroom on the morning of March 3rd, I was not prepared for the news of my father's passing. The sense of dismay and grief was quite overwhelming.

I have written earlier of my feelings about the one for whom I am named. Although we did not have a really close relationship, I had a genuine love and respect for my father. His moral influence upon me has been lifelong. By being a non-smoker and a non-drinker, he set an example for me which I have meticulously followed. I recall that when I was in my early teens he and mother learned of the Leopold Schepp Foundation in New York City, which offered awards of one hundred dollars to young boys who would promise not to smoke cigarettes until they reach maturity. I accepted an award and made the required promise, but it was really my father's example which had the greatest influence upon me. Dad is still frequently in my thoughts, and every year I visit his gravesite in New Haven's Evergreen Cemetery.

The spring of 1942 was relatively uneventful. Shirley and I were now beginning to make plans for the future. When the Seminary year ended we went back to our yoked parishes knowing that this would probably be our last summer there. The Steenstra House, which had been our home the previous year, was no longer available, so we made arrangements with a widowed member of the Red Beach Church to rent a spare room in her home. Meanwhile the financial strain of trying to live on twenty-five dollars per week was becoming oppressive. We briefly contemplated the possibility of establishing a summer camp back in Connecticut where Shirley had successfully earned extra dollars before we were married. This would have meant buying some new property with the help of her parents, since the old campsite had been washed away in the surprise hurricane of 1938. We soon abandoned that idea. Instead, we began to look for a new and more lucrative student parish somewhat nearer the Seminary, where I was about to begin my senior year. Our first attempt was unsuccessful. After another pleasant and satisfying three months in Robbinston and Red Beach, we returned to Bangor in September and began negotiations with Dr. Roundy of the Maine Conference for a change of parish.

In the fall of 1942 I was a candidate for the pastorate of the Dover-Foxcroft Congregational Church, located about thirty-five miles north of Bangor. It was my hope to serve this church during

49

my senior year at the Seminary and for at least two additional years while I attended the University of Maine at Orono for the completion of my liberal arts studies leading to the Bachelor of Arts degree. Under the "Bangor plan," I expected to receive the Seminary's diploma in June of 1943, but would then be required to secure the B.A. degree before becoming eligible for the Seminary's Bachelor of Divinity degree (now Master of Divinity) which was necessary for ordination.

Because I was to be a student-minister, the Dover-Foxcroft Church declined to call me. In retrospect, this disappointment turned out to be a blessing in disguise, for about a month later the First Parish Church of Yarmouth invited me to become its minister effective January 1, 1943. This meant that I would attend nearby Bowdoin College for the completion of my liberal arts studies. Bowdoin later offered me a graduate scholarship which started me on the road leading to an academic rather than a pastoral career. The Yarmouth Church offered me a parsonage and a cash salary of $1,800, which was a considerable economic improvement.

Shirley and I now faced the future with added confidence. We even began to talk about having a child. Meanwhile there was the senior year of study to think about. In addition, I had been elected president of the Seminary's student Christian Association, which involved some executive supervision of various campus activities. The fall semester was uneventful academically while we continued our ministry in Robbinston and Red Beach for its final months. Our living arrangements for this period were unique, indeed. We had no inclination to occupy again our heatless bedroom in Red Beach. Instead we established primitive accommodations in the vestry of the Robbinston Church. We had an out-house, a small stove, a wood-burning furnace, and two rather uncomfortable cots. We came to look upon this arrangement as one of pioneering and romance.

At the end of December I conducted with some sadness our final worship service. It was a particularly stormy day with much blowing snow. The afternoon congregation in Red Beach consisted of two hardy souls plus Shirley and me. We returned to Bangor the next day with mixed emotions. The Washington County experience was certainly a building block for my professional career. We have wonderful memories of many beautiful people. We recall with nostalgia long exciting rides over isolated roads, including a collision with a deer early one morning. We left the two churches in a much stronger condition than we had found them. They remained vital for several years until Robbinston's one industry, the sardine canning factory, closed its doors. Today the Robbinston Church is inactive again and the Red Beach congregation has been dissolved.

Before concluding the story of my first parishes, I recount three occasions when Shirley and I have returned for special events. When Ernest Brown died, his daughter Betty Blood asked me to conduct the memorial service; it was a memory-filled reunion with many dear friends when we laid Ernest to rest beside his beloved Princess. A few years earlier we had gone down east for the dedication of an organ given to the Robbinston Church by Ernest in honor of his deceased wife. Our last trip to the old parish was in 1978 when I was an independent candidate for election to the U.S. Congress from Maine's second district. I was greeted warmly at a political rally in the Robbinston Grange hall.

4.
A Wartime Ministry

We were now ready to move from the campus apartment in Bangor where Shirley and I had spent the first two years and more of our extended honeymoon. We will always cherish the memories of happy days there during family visits, and of good times with classmates. We remember when Shirley's sister, Barbara, stayed with us so that she could spend time with her boyfriend, Elmer Schlegel of New Haven, who was stationed at nearby Dow Air Force Base during the war years. She made the long trip by bus, but told her sister it was all worthwhile after she and Elmer were later married. Shirley and I were now prepared for a new adventure in the pastorate at Yarmouth.

For the next five months my wife and I had the longest separation of our married life. Because I still had to complete half of the senior year of studies at the Seminary, she stayed in the parsonage at Yarmouth while I was in Bangor Monday through Friday. It was a lonesome time for both of us, especially since Shirley soon discovered that she was pregnant with the child we had conceived shortly after the Yarmouth Church assignment was confirmed. We were eager for each weekend to come, but we had little time for personal concerns because of the demands of pastoral work and academic studies. The parsonage on Bridge Street was comfortable enough, but we were a bit apprehensive about her staying there alone at night. Mabel Ward, a widow and one of the saints of the Yarmouth Church, provided a refuge for Shirley overnight whenever I was out of town. We are forever grateful!

The First Parish Church of Yarmouth was a firmly established religious institution. I was its first minister who also had academic requirements to complete, which made my task as pastor an arduous one. However, I had strong help from the trustees and deacons, and Shirley was able to make her talents available in the parish on a more-or-less full-time basis. We lived in Yarmouth for only twenty months, but two events of great significance to us personally occurred during this short period. Our first child was born, and I was ordained to the Christian ministry. Certainly not unimportant were two other developments: I graduated from Bowdoin College and received a scholarship for graduate study at Yale University.

My pastorate at Yarmouth coincided with the middle years of World War II. One of my ministerial duties was to counsel with parishioners who had loved ones serving in the armed forces of the United States. It was also my sad responsibility to preside at memorial services for young men who gave their lives in the conflict. More than once I asked myself if I was being unpatriotic by taking advantage of my clerical exemption from military service. Perhaps it was a rationalization, but I concluded that my pastoral work on the homefront was also a contribution to national security. To illustrate, I recount here portions of a sermon preached at Yarmouth on Mothers' Day a few weeks after the death on the battlefront of Harvey Peterson, one of the town's bright young men. It reflects the influence of Bowdoin College upon me and shows the status of my own faith at the age of thirty. "Lullaby For The World" is the sermon title.

On the campus at Bowdoin College there is a beautiful chapel building known as Bannister Hall. Three times a week at eight o'clock in the morning a small group of students gathers in this building to hear the story of the history of music and to listen to the great masterpieces of the musical art. The inspiration for this message has come from the hours I have spent in that classroom.

There is something strangely comforting about a sonata by

53

Brahms heard at eight o'clock in the morning. In the early hours of the day the grandeur of a symphony by Mozart gives one a new sense of faith in God and faith in man. Within the spell woven by the majestic strains of a Beethoven concerto it is very easy to forget the confusion and turmoil of the world of reality in which we live. But one does not long dwell in ivory towers in our world today. Even the quiet campus of a small New England college is not immune from the noises of men at war. Just a mile from the college is the Brunswick Naval Air Station. All day long the planes are roaring over the campus, brushing the treetops and drowning out the voices of professors in their classrooms. Many times the glorious immortal music of the masters is silenced by the thunder of flying machines passing overhead. And yet when the terrifying sounds of war have gone, the music returns more beautiful than ever.

This brief picture of life in Maine is a parable for us today. Throughout the world, men, women and children are beset on all sides by the frightening noises of war. With fear in our hearts we listen for the latest radio reports from the battlefields of the world. With doubt in our minds we wonder whether God is still in control of his universe. Countless thousands of people are lying awake nights worrying about the safety of their loved ones who serve in the armed forces. We all need something to calm our fears, to ease our worries; we need something to renew our faith in God and man. I have found that faith in the enduring qualities of music, and my experiences in the music room at Bowdoin have suggested that the world needs a lullaby.

Who will sing this lullaby for the world? The answer comes quite naturally to mind: The frightened and bewildered child always runs to its mother for comfort. It is the mother who sings the lullaby. We have set aside this day in the church year to pay tribute to our mothers. In a time of peace we might very well spend this hour in speaking of the great love which we all feel toward our mothers. But the world is in great need this Mothers' Day, and I am sure that all mothers present will forgive us if we dispense with the usual expression of our loving sentiments toward them. Rather, I would call upon you mothers this morning to give a service which you are best qualified to perform. I ask you to soothe a troubled world with a lullaby of faith and love. And if I know anything at all about mothers — and I have had some experience with them — you will be much happier today if we come to you for help than you will be if we speak sweet words to you.

It is not an easy task to keep faith in a world engulfed by war. It is not an easy task to sing when loved ones are in danger. It is not an easy thing to keep faith when suffering and death stalk the earth. It is not an easy thing to sing when our families are broken by forces which we seem powerless to control. And yet someone, somehow, must help the world to rediscover a fundamental faith in the goodness and providence of God. I can think of no one better qualified to perform that task than the mother — the mother of whom the poet Wallace wrote: "The hand that rocks the cradle is the hand that rules the world."

If modern mothers are to be worthy of this high praise they must find some way to bind up the spiritual wounds of a world at war. They must learn to hold fast to a faith in God even when their hearts are broken; even when their throats are choked with sorrow, they must find the power to sing a lullaby before the cradle of their bewildered, frightened children. And so I call upon those of you who are mothers to revitalize your faith, through your own Christian experience, so that you may be able to comfort yourself and your family in these critical days.

I suggest, first of all, that a most vital stimulus to steadfast faith is a belief that wherever our loved ones are, they are in the presence of the same God whom we worship here in this hour. If we have learned anything from this war, we have discovered that we are living in one world. The sun rises and sets on Iwo Jima, on the Rhine River, in Burma, and in Italy. The boys who have gone from the Christian Church to serve in the armed forces have taken their faith with them. They can and do speak with God in the foxholes, in the bombers, in the submarines, or wherever they may be. If they take the wings of the morning and dwell in the uttermost parts of the sea, they will find the spirit of God traveling with them. You mothers whose sons have been trained in the Christian Church need have no fear for their welfare. They are well prepared to meet whatever may befall them anywhere in the world. If you can believe this, then your faith will enable you to sing the lullaby which will comfort those — in your own family and elsewhere — whose faith is weak.

I want to tell you the story of a young man and his mother whose faith has enabled them to overcome the greatest crisis that anyone is called upon to face. Harvey Peterson is one of thousands of young Christians who have given their lives in the war. Harvey was a regular attendant at church school and the morning worship service; he was active in young people's work and a leader in the Boy Scout program. He was just twenty years old when the bomber in which he was riding exploded. The telegram from the War Department was received by a neighbor, who asked me to deliver it to Mrs. Peterson. During my talks with Harvey's mother, I found her to be a woman of deep faith. The only thing she required of me was the assurance that her son had been given a Christian burial. I gave her that assurance.

I learned some other things about Harvey in talking with his mother. He had told her before he went into the army that he was not afraid to die. A few months before he left home he had attended the funeral service of one of his pals; he had learned that day to look upon death as a natural and normal procedure in the plans of God. Mrs. Peterson also told me that on the day before he was killed Harvey had written her a letter, telling how he had had a long talk with his chaplain that day. Harvey Peterson lived as one who was prepared to die, if necessary. I am sure that your sons have that faith, too. And Mrs. Peterson also still lives courageously in spite of the tragedy which has taken away her only son. More than that, this valiant mother, by her own example, is helping her husband and two daughters to retain their faith in God. I am sure of this because a few weeks after her brother's death, Harvey's sister joined the church. And on Easter Sunday the florist delivered a plant at the parsonage — from the Peterson family.

Harvey Peterson won no medals from his country, but in the eyes of those who know of his abiding faith he is a true hero. And this mother who hangs a gold star in her window is little known outside her hometown, but she is one of the dedicated Christian souls who is singing the lullaby of faith in a bewildered world.

Mothers, on this day when we think of all the joy and happiness which you have given to our lives, we call upon you to tell us that in spite of all its anxieties and trials, life is worth living. The poet has told us that it is you who rule the world. We want you to rule the world! We want you to show us a better way of life. This is the anguished cry of frightened humanity. Let me ask: What will your answer be, mothers? If you have succeeded in keeping faith alive within your own families in time of war you have accomplished much. But peace will come, and with it the far more difficult task of reviving the confidence, of soothing the fears, of that community of human beings which we Christians call the family of God. Speaking to you as Christian mothers on Mothers' Day, I am now going to suggest a way in which you may exert an influence which will extend far beyond the boundaries of your own immediate families.

St. Paul in his letter to the Ephesians speaks to his Gentile friends of "the Father of our Lord Jesus Christ, of whom the whole family on heaven and earth are named." That idea of one family in heaven and earth under the fatherhood of God is the goal toward which we should be striving — it is the strong foundation upon which our Christian faith is built. The goal has not been achieved, however, because our vision has not yet been broad enough to recognize the common bond which unites all human beings as the children of the Creator God. We have been too much concerned with the welfare of our own immediate families and too little concerned with the broader aspects of the Christian gospel which proclaims the universal Fatherhood of God and the brotherhood of man.

Consider for a moment the teachings of Jesus on this matter of family relationships. Matthew, Mark and Luke all tell the same story: One day Jesus was talking with his disciples and a large group of friends when word came to him that his mother and his brethren stood on the outside of the group and desired to speak with him. But he answered and said unto him who told him, "Who is my mother and who are my brethren?" And he stretched forth his hand toward his disciples and said, "Behold my mother and my brethren. For whosoever shall do the will of my Father which is in heaven, the same is my brother, and sister, and mother."

I do not intend to minimize the importance of the individual family life. Jesus teaches us to honor our fathers and our mothers. And as he hung in agony on the cross, one of his last earthly acts was to insure the welfare of his own mother by placing her in the care of his beloved disciple. What I do mean to suggest is that, for the Christian, concern for the well-being of his fellowmen must reach out beyond close family ties. And it seems to me that the mother, who is the very center and core of family life, is the one best qualified to teach her husband and her children that they have a mutual obligation to interest themselves in affairs outside their own home. The mother is uniquely equipped for this task because she is endowed with an instinct, an emotion, a passion — call it what you will — which we describe as mother love. I do truly believe that this love, if it is directed in the proper channels, can and must and will become the means whereby a more Christian world society is established.

You who are mothers, who are worried about the welfare of your own sons and daughters, must know that every mother, whether we call them friend or enemy, is also worried about the frightening events in a world at war. There are millions of mothers like you on every continent who are wishing, hoping, praying for the safety of their loved ones. Those mothers, too, many of them German and Japanese, love their sons and daughters just as much as you love yours. If you will but use your imagination you will know that there is a common bond of mother love which unites all mothers; knowing that, you will be compelled to so order your own lives in the future, and the lives of your husbands and your children, that never again will your present anxiety be brought upon you or any other mother. Thus may your song of love harmonize with your song of faith in a lullaby for the world.

Mothers, we do not love you less because this morning we have not spoken of our deep thankfulness for all your sacrifice on our behalf. We shall continue to honor and praise you in our daily lives. But today we are frightened. We dare not face the future without your hands to guide us. Help us, we beseech you, to keep our faith alive in a world at war. Teach us by the power of your *love to create a world of peace. We are fearful. We are tired. Sing us a lullaby!*

The response to this sermon by members of the congregation convinced me that the defense of the American way of life is enhanced by those who minister on the homefront as well as those who serve on the battlefield. In addition to my clerical duties in Yarmouth there was also work to be done in the classroom. The final months of my senior year at Bangor went by swiftly, probably because I was eager to leave my weekday room in the dormitory to be reunited with my pregnant wife in the parsonage on weekends. In June of 1943 I received the diploma of Bangor Theological Seminary. The next academic step under the "Bangor plan" was to complete the liberal arts study I had started at the Seminary with the help of visiting faculty from the University of Maine.

Thus in July I enrolled in Bowdoin College as a transfer student with advanced standing. Bowdoin was one of the Maine schools which cooperated with the Seminary under the Bangor plan. Because of my good academic record at Bangor, I was permitted to qualify for the Bowdoin A.B. degree by completing a summer term and one additional year. As an added bonus, Bowdoin kindly waived the required course in mathematics because I had studied the Greek language at the Seminary. A rather strange substitution, I thought at the time. During the summer session I took up language study again in preparation for the possibility that I might later engage in graduate work for a doctorate. I completed a year each in French and German, and then finished a second year as a senior at Bowdoin.

My double life as a student and minister continued during my stay at Yarmouth. Each class day I commuted the 32-mile round trip to and from Brunswick, which meant that I missed the experience of living on the college campus. It was during the summer of 1943 that I met a man who became a lifelong friend. John Whitney MacNeil graduated from Bangor Seminary in the spring of 1939, just before I entered the school in September. He lived in Auburn, Maine, with his wife Judith, and was the minister there of the Sixth Street Congregational Church. Like me, he was enrolled in a post-theological program at Bowdoin under the Bangor plan. We often spent the lunch hour together eating whatever goodies our wives had prepared for us. For more than forty-five years, until his death in 1979, John and I maintained a relationship of mutual admiration. His wife Judy and my wife Shirley are still the closest of friends. Over the years we have shared many memorable and some traumatic experiences.

One occasion which the MacNeils and the Whittakers have often recalled with nostalgia was a visit we had that summer in a camp which John and Judy had rented near Brunswick. We spent several days together, during which two remembered events occurred. One noontime while Judy was preparing lunch, she accidentally slashed a finger on the edge of a can; with the blood pouring out rather profusely she was about to faint when my pregnant wife came to the rescue and administered first aid. The other incident produced what have come to be known in the Whittaker family circle as "Shirley-isms." As the four of us relaxed one evening on the semi-darkened porch of the MacNeil cottage, there came an awkward pause in the conversation. After being together for two or three days, we had seemingly run out of subjects to talk about. Shirley rushed into the void with a question still remembered with amusement. Recalling our long unsuccessful attempt to find a double bed after our marriage a few years earlier, Shirley blurted out: "Did I ever tell you what my husband did to me on our wedding night?" After a few moments of embarrassed laughter by John and Judy, Shirley explained the import of the question. There were to be other "Shirley-isms" later.

As summer turned into autumn, all thoughts of church work and academic study faded into the background as Shirley and I prepared for the birth of our first child. Early in October a telephone call from the obstetrician in Portland gave us the somewhat disturbing news that natural childbirth would have to be replaced by a Caesarian section. An appointment was made for the operation. Shirley's parents came up from New Haven for the birth of their first grandchild, which was scheduled for October 8th. On the day before the appointed time, the four of us left Yarmouth for the hospital in Portland. Enroute the suggestion was made that a stop be made in a stationery story for the purchase of appropriate birth announcement cards. Shirley and her mother went into the store and asked a clerk for assistance. Showing friendly concern, the clerk asked: "When does your daughter expect her baby?" Came the casual reply: "Oh, she's on the way to the hospital now." The startled questioner could only exclaim: "Oh, my God!"

Right on schedule the next day there was born the most beautiful baby we had ever seen. We named our daughter Barbara Anne, first for Shirley's sister and second for my mother. The love we felt for our firstborn then has grown through the years, in times of joy and times of concern, and is now in full bloom. Her story has been an integral part of ours for forty-five years and more. Today Barbara Anne is in her second career as she serves as an ordained minister of the Unitarian-Universalist Churches. There will be much to tell about her in the intervening period as these memoirs unfold. Needless to say, life has never been the same for Shirley and me since the welcome birth of our only daughter.

My short career as a Bowdoin student was a happy and auspicious experience. Two of the professors made lasting contributions to my academic training: Herbert Ross Brown and Robert Peter Tristram Coffin. As an English major I am grateful to the first for making American literature come alive in the classroom; and to the second I am thankful for his disclosure of the intrinsic power of poetry. Especially memorable are the many evening seminars in Professor Coffin's home when we students sat around the fireplace and listened enthralled into the late hours as this master poet read and explained his lyrical productions.

Bowdoin has been very good to me. I was a James Bowdoin Scholar. Although it was an exception to the rule about transfer students, I was elected to Phi Beta Kappa. When I was awarded the Bachelor of Arts degree *magna cum laude* (the highest honor for a transfer student), the college also granted me a scholarship for graduate study. This opened the door to a career in teaching and, ultimately, to the presidency of a theological school. In 1964, twenty years after graduation, Bowdoin gave me its greatest accolade, the honorary degree of Doctor of Divinity; no other recognition has given me greater satisfaction.

Knowing that I would receive the B.A. degree from Bowdoin in June of 1944, I started early that year to qualify for the Bachelor of Divinity degree from the Seminary, which was a prerequisite for ordination. Under the Bangor plan I would be eligible for the B.D. upon award of the Bowdoin B.A. and the completion of a B.D. thesis for the Seminary. I had begun work on the thesis during my senior year at Bangor, but it still needed some finishing touches. The thesis illustrates my early, and still continuing, interest in promoting a vital and efficient relationship between Church and State so that these two institutions created by human beings may be mutually supportive in advancing the kingdom of God on earth. I have never been comfortable with the American doctrine of the absolute separation of Church and State.

My B.D. thesis was based upon a term paper written during my last year at the Seminary entitled "God and Caesar," a study of Church and State based on the thought of Thomas Aquinas, Dante Alighieri, and Marsilius of Padua. It is not important to recount the paper in detail, but its "Conclusion" will serve to illustrate my early thought on a recurrent theme in my later writings:

Now that we have studied the ideas of medieval scholarship with regard to the proper relationship between Church and State, it would seem profitable to draw some conclusion for our own age. St. Thomas, Dante, and Marsilius all attempted to create a situation wherein men could live in peace on earth and hope for eternal life with God; each suggested a different relationship between Church and State, but all three methods have failed to bring peace on earth. All three men were conscious of God as the supreme ruler of the universe.

St. Thomas maintained that God should rule through the Papacy, but his theory failed, perhaps because of corruption within the Church itself. Dante would separate the functions of Church and State and establish a supreme monarch to rule over all the world; his theory also failed, probably because of his naive belief that the temporal ruler of the world would receive and follow divine guidance directly from God. Marsilius saw the evil doings within the Church and turned to the State for salvation; he would have the Emperor rule on behalf of the sovereign people, but his plan failed, perhaps because he placed too little faith in the Church and things spiritual.

Marsilius would have the State correct the Church; today the State rules the temporal world, but we have no peace. Perhaps the Church needs to correct the State. Perhaps we have followed Dante too far in separating God and Caesar. The Caesar of Marsilius controls our peaceless world today. Perhaps we need the God of St. Thomas. Perhaps the Church should end its silence in the temporal world so that the State may know the Spirit of God. Perhaps?!

The diploma of Bangor Seminary which I received in June of 1943 was replaced a year later by the Bachelor of Divinity degree, giving me the academic credentials needed for ordination as a Christian minister. By pre-arrangement with the Committee on Ministerial Standing of the Congregational-Christian Conference of Maine, the Cumberland Association of CC Churches met in special session in the Yarmouth Church on June 6, 1944, to examine my "fitness for the Gospel ministry." After proper deliberation, the Association authorized my ordination at a service to be held on June 16th. That day proved to be one still remembered as one marking a transition in my life from theologue and student-minister to full-fledged Christian clergyman.

Most of those who participated in my ordination service were people who in one way or another had been important in shaping my career. President Harry Trust of the Seminary preached the sermon. The act of ordination was performed by my home church minister, Dr. Harold G. Jones of New Haven. The Maine Conference Superintendent, Dr. Rodney W. Roundy, gave the charge to the Church. Personal friends Maldwyn Parry and John MacNeil gave the invocation and read the scripture. The right hand of fellowship was offered by the Reverend Gladys D. York, minister of the North Yarmouth Church, who was particularly helpful to Shirley and me during our time in Yarmouth and has remained a valued friend until this day. George Hooten, a Seminary classmate, sang a solo. One of those who laid his hand upon my head was Dr. Nathanael Guptill, minister then of the South Portland Congregational Church, who later served on the Seminary's board of trustees and is today a bridge and golf partner.

It was during Yarmouth days that a lifetime relationship began with Ellison and Druscilla Beckwith. Both of them came from New Haven and were associated with us at Plymouth Church. El was an insurance company executive in Portland, Maine, when Shirley and I renewed our friendship with them. On occasion we would visit with them for a game of bridge. One memorable evening when our daughter Barbara was still a babe-in-arms, we returned from Portland to Yarmouth in a heavy snowstorm. Unable to negotiate the slippery hill from the highway into the town, we left the car and I carried our precious little girl for half a mile into the haven of the parsonage. A scary experience I have not forgotten! El Beckwith later became a most helpful trustee of the Seminary during my administration. When his wife died tragically, the victim of cancer, I participated in the memorial service, recalling all of the good times we had shared over many years in our respective homes. El and his second wife, Jane, are still today within the close circle of the Whittaker friends.

Throughout the final months of our time in Yarmouth, life took on a new and exciting dimension for Shirley and me. She devoted much of her talent and energy to being a mother. I had assumed a third role in addition to being a student and minister. Now I was a father for the first time — and a proud one at that. The members of the parish were pleased to have a baby in the parsonage. Their love for Barbara began before she was born with a generous shower of gifts. She was such a pretty child that admiration was widely shown whenever she appeared in public. Occasionally, when Shirley had an appointment out of the home, I assumed the task of babysitter. One Friday afternoon I was in charge of Barbara while Shirley was away. My sermon for the following Sunday was not finished and it was difficult to concentrate on theological matters while Barbara was in the room. I needed an hour without interruption. So I propped the baby up in her bassinet and put her before the full-length mirror in the bedroom. She seemed very happy with her new-found friend. When Shirley returned, she was at first furious that I had presumably let the baby have an unscheduled nap. She calmed down quickly when she discovered Barbara gurgling and cooing to her companion in the mirror.

Our pastorate in Yarmouth was all too short. I have had guilty feelings about its brevity from time to time, but I do believe we left the Church in a stronger condition than we had found it. In any event, when we left so that I could begin graduate study the congregation called another Bangor graduate, George Hooten, to be its minister; he also was a student at Bowdoin. Until Bowdoin offered me a graduate scholarship I had no real hope of engaging in further study, although I had secretly promised myself that I would try to become president of Bangor Seminary some day. The opportunity to work for a doctorate at Yale while serving as minister of the Huntington Church in nearby Shelton was irresistible.

The Charles Carroll Everett Scholarship for graduate study offered to me by Bowdoin College was a turning point in my career. Until then I had expected to continue my work as a parish minister. I had now been leading the double life of theologue and student-pastor for five years. Could Shirley and I endure another possible four years of this complicated lifestyle while I pursued studies for a doctorate? We decided that I could — and should. At about this time an offer came from the Chicago Theological Seminary to augment my Bowdoin award if I would enroll there for my graduate studies program. The offer came through the recommendation of Dr. Mervin Deems, my former teacher at Bangor who was now on the faculty at Chicago. It was with great reluctance that I finally decided not to accept this generous award, primarily because we had in hand a comparable offer from Yale University, but also because we had a family preference for remaining in New England.

In searching for an appropriate situation in which to continue my academic work, one of the crucial considerations was the availability of a church position which would be a residential and a financial base from which I could attend graduate school. Upon inquiry in the proper places, two possibilities presented themselves: one in the New York City area and one in Connecticut. I might have become an associate minister of a church in River Edge, New Jersey, and a graduate student at Union Theological Seminary in New York. However, I declined this opportunity when a more attractive one became available.

During this period of decision-making, I had been in

correspondence with Dr. James English, Superintendent of the Connecticut Conference of Congregational-Christian Churches, and with Dean Luther Weigle of the Yale Divinity School. After an interview with Dean Weigle, he set in motion a procedure which enabled me to enroll subsequently in the Department of Religion of the Yale Graduate School. He explained that the Yale Divinity School, where I actually pursued most of my course work, could not accept me as a graduate student on the basis of my Bachelor of Divinity degree from Bangor Theological Seminary because Bangor was an associate and not a fully-accredited member of the Association of Theological Schools. This was a technicality which could not be eliminated, but could be circumvented. Thus Dean Weigle arranged to have the Yale Graduate School accept my primary registration on the basis of my Bachelor of Arts degree from Bowdoin College, with secondary registration in the Yale Divinity School. The good Dean went a step further. Tuition in the Graduate School was more expensive than tuition in the Divinity School. He secured for me a scholarship which eliminated this cost differential. I shall be forever grateful to Dean Weigle for this and other later courtesies which enabled my career to progress.

With a choice of graduate schools settled, there remained the necessity of finding an employment opportunity as minister of a nearby church. Dr. English of the Connecticut Conference came to my rescue by recommending me to the Huntington Congregational Church in Shelton, which was about fifteen miles from New Haven. After the usual interviews and negotiations, the Church called me as its pastor, with the understanding that I would pursue part-time graduate study at Yale over a period of four years. My beginning salary was set at $2,400 per year, plus free use of the parsonage. Thus began a new and exciting chapter for the Whittaker family.

5.

The Turning Point

The next four years marked a turning point in my life. When I began my ministry in Huntington and my graduate study at Yale in September of 1944, it was still my plan to pursue a career as the pastor of a local church, at least for the immediate future. However, lurking in my innermost being were thoughts of a teaching vocation and the nebulous possibility of being a seminary president at Bangor. The turning point came in the spring of 1948 when President Harry Trust offered me a position on the Seminary faculty.

Meanwhile, momentous events occurred during this period in my personal life and in the world around me. Atomic bombs were dropped by the United States on Japanese cities, and World War II came to an end. President Franklin Delano Roosevelt died in office unexpectedly. The United Nations organization was created. I was asked by Plymouth Church in New Haven to play the role of Jesus in its annual Passion Play. Shirley delivered our one and only son, Frederick Mark. I completed my residence work for the Doctor of Philosophy degree from Yale University. It was, indeed, a unique quadrennium in my life.

The parish situation in Huntington proved to be a challenging one. The Congregational Church was a small one in a rural section of the city of Shelton which was just beginning to develop as a residential area for surrounding communities such as Bridgeport. For several years the church had been partially subsidized by the Connecticut Conference. It was my assignment to recruit and develop new personnel and financial resources. With the cooperation of old-time members of the church and several newcomers, we succeeded within the space of two years in changing the status of Huntington Congregational from a "mission-supported" church to one which was contributing to the Conference for the benefit of needy congregations elsewhere.

A valuable lesson was learned in the Huntington Church about the willingness of Christians to give generously to religious causes when they are properly motivated. Here was a parish which had routinely accepted financial help from other denominational churches in Connecticut when all the time it had been potentially capable of giving for missionary projects at home and in foreign countries. No one had heretofore challenged the church membership to widen their area of concern beyond the local community. At Bangor Seminary I had become aware through a course in "Missions" of the vast enterprise of the national Congregational-Christian Churches in support of educational institutions, medical facilities, agricultural projects, and developing churches in the United States and many areas of the world overseas. When this outreach of the Christian gospel was dramatized and explained to the Huntington Church, its members soon responded by giving rather than receiving. It became apparent to me then that a local church which supports the missionary program of its denomination will have no difficulty in raising the funds needed for its home expenses. This is a truth which I have preached throughout my ministry, and with eminent success.

Our four-year pastorate in Huntington was a happy time for Shirley and me. We were about thirty years old, and many of our parishioners were in our age group. We especially enjoyed "The Better-Half Club," which met regularly for social and semi-religious purposes. Several of its members have become our lifelong friends. While these younger people were on the growing edge of the church, many of its older members provided the stability which all local parishes need. 1945 was a pivotal year for a young minister trying to meet the spiritual needs of a growing congregation in a time of worldwide turmoil as World War II ended, and a time of national crisis as a long-term president died.

When I reached the legal voting age in 1934, Franklin Delano Roosevelt was already well into his first term as President to the United States. In my youth I had been vaguely aware of Warren Harding, Calvin Coolidge, and Herbert Hoover, but FDR was the only president who had really made an impact upon me. I had come to admire him for his executive skill in bringing the nation out of the economic depression which had left my father jobless, and for his diplomatic expertise in leading the nation to the brink of military victory in World War II.

When Roosevelt died unexpectedly on April 12, 1945, in Warm Springs, Georgia, the nation reacted in shock and disbelief. Its chief executive was gone in the first year of his unprecedented fourth term in office. Many Americans in their twenties and thirties had known no other president. The country was rudderless when it was still engaged in a world-wide military conflict. Religious professionals rushed into their pulpits the following Sunday in an attempt to assuage the national grief and to give some reassurance to millions of bewildered citizens. So did I. This is what I said to the Huntington congregation in a sermon entitled "A Time for Faith":

Just eighty years ago this morning a great wartime President of the United States lay dead. The nation was stunned, bewildered, fearful. But the nation survived. Today, within the hour, another great wartime President has been laid to eternal rest in a garden cemetery overlooking the beautiful Hudson River. The nation is stunned, the people of the world are fearful of what may happen in a future which seems suddenly darkened. But the nation will live on, and the world will survive. This is not a time for fear. This is a time for faith.

In the very hour of our distress we have for our inspiration the words of the man whose mortal presence has now been taken from us. Franklin Delano Roosevelt was a man of faith — faith in God, faith in his fellow-Americans, faith in the people of the world. Mrs. Roosevelt knew of that faith, and she has shown her own belief at this time of her greatest sorrow. For it was the loving wife of our departed President who requested the presiding clergyman at her husband's funeral service to read the words which now become a part of the American tradition. Thus Archbishop Angus Dun concluded his funeral prayers for the late President with these famous words: "The only thing we have to fear is fear itself."

Yes, this is a time, first of all, for faith in God. We have been prepared by the experiences of the Easter season to believe in eternal life. We see today in this seemingly untimely passing of a great man the orderly working of the natural laws of the universe. The sudden ending of a life upon which we had placed such a heavy burden has sobered this rather exuberant, self-confident nation, and turned the thoughts of the people toward the heavens. This nation and the nations of the world have been shocked into a realization that there is a God who enters into the affairs of men. In churches throughout the world, men and women are meeting today to call upon God in the hour of their common loss. Memorial services are attended by those who have never seen the President. Perhaps the most significant tribute of all is that presented by the major radio networks of America, who have cancelled all their regular programs in order to broadcast music and verse, thus to create a mood of meditation and prayer for those who seek divine guidance in this hour. The death of our President in this critical hour of history may in truth bring men to a new faith in God.

This is a time, too, for faith in our fellow-Americans. As the nation sorrows there has been created, almost overnight, a sense of unity among the people of the United States which even a worldwide war had failed to produce. We have suddenly realized that we are one people with a common bond of fellowship and purpose as symbolized by the man who has been President for more than twelve years, and by the man who now carries on in that high office. In the hour of crisis we realize — or we should realize — that the name "democrat" or "republican" is of little significance. The nation is the reality which we would preserve. To this end the members of all political parties are rallying around President Harry Truman, pledging their support to him in his efforts to carry on the policies in war and peace for which Franklin

70

Roosevelt gave his life. The success of this program will be the greatest monument we could erect in memory of our fallen leader.

At such a time as this we should set aside our petty differences of political affiliation. This is no time to criticize the domestic or foreign policies of the Roosevelt administration. Admittedly, mistakes have been made. But the fact remains that in spite of a worldwide economic depression and in the face of an international war, the internal and external integrity of our nation has been preserved. This is due in no small measure to the wisdom and strength of the man who has been our President for more than three terms. We should all be thankful in this hour for his consecrated leadership which has now come to an end. We should all be more willing to devote our best efforts to the tasks which lie before us. The nation suffered a relapse during the reconstruction period after the death of Abraham Lincoln. This must not happen again to a war-weary America. We must have faith in our new President and join with him in the unfinished work of building a peaceful world. This is no time for doubt, no time for quarreling, no time for fear, in our relationships with our fellow-Americans. It is a time for faith!

It is a time for faith in our fellow world-citizens. Even as Abraham Lincoln was the greatest domestic statesman of our nation, so Franklin Delano Roosevelt will go down in history as the greatest world statesman our nation has produced thus far. The name "Roosevelt" has become a symbol to the oppressed people of the world, a symbol of their hope for freedom and peace. The death of our President has affected the peoples of the world more than most of us realize. In England the British Parliament adjourned for the first time in its long history in honor of the memory of a foreign statesman. The Soviet Union, breaking all precedent, is in official mourning for a foreign citizen for the first time. All over the community of the United Nations there is grief today, deep personal grief, for a man known to many of the mourners only as a name and a symbol. It may very well be that the sense of loss is more deeply and sincerely felt in lands across the sea than it is in our own country, where partisan politics have created deep-seated prejudices.

In any event, we may be sure that the people of the world, especially the people of the smaller nations, are looking to us for leadership in the building of a better world. Franklin Roosevelt promised them that leadership. In what may prove to be his most significant contribution to world history, our late President led the United States out of a selfish isolationism to a place of power and influence in world affairs. He helped to create the Atlantic Charter. He invented the phrase "The United Nations." Franklin Roosevelt had faith in the other nations of the world. He led us to a union with many of them. They believed in him and in us. We must not fail now. We must keep faith with our fellow world-citizens. This is the Christian way of life: to be concerned with the welfare of our fellowmen throughout the world. Our beloved President has performed a Christian duty as well as an American responsibility in seeking to build a peaceful world for the mutual benefit of all humanity. We, as Christians and as Americans, are called upon to carry on the work so nobly begun.

It seems quite appropriate in this hour that we should remember another great American, whose words suggest a fitting climax for our meditation this morning. We shall always think of Abraham Lincoln when we hear the words, "that these dead shall not have died in vain —." And this reference to the honored dead of our Civil War reminds us that Franklin Roosevelt was truly a casualty in the present conflict. As Commander-in-Chief of the armed forces of the nation, he gave his life for his country in the performance of duty as a good soldier. What, then, shall we say about this soldier and the other thousands who have died on the battlefields of the world? We have been slow to consider the significance of the deaths of the common soldiers. May it be that the death of the Commander-in-Chief will awaken within each one of us a sense of the magnitude of the sacrifice which is being made on our behalf each day, each hour, as the war goes on. We need to ask ourselves, each one, whether we are worthy of this sacrifice. Are we willing, all of us, to redeem these spent and shortened lives given for us? Will we redeem these lives by creating that better world of peace for which our heroes have died? Again the words of Lincoln speak across the years: "It is for us, the living —." Yes, it is for us, the living, to have faith in God, faith in our fellow-Americans, faith in our

72

brothers across the seas. It is for us, the living, to put that faith into action. This we can do only as we interest ourselves in the affairs of government; this we can do by supporting our new President in the tremendous task he has inherited; this we can do by lending our moral strength to the United Nations' conference at San Francisco; this we can do by becoming good citizens and good Christians in search for enduring peace and goodwill among men.

Franklin Delano Roosevelt has done his work; he has accomplished the purposes for which God gave him the breath of life; his immortality is assured. It is for us, the living, to carry on, with steadfast faith, the work which he and our other honored dead have laid upon our hands and hearts. More than nineteen hundred years ago a man died. Those who knew this man, Jesus of Nazareth, could not believe that he had died. Their faith led them to build the Christian Church, which remains until this day as a godly force for good in our world. Now another man is dead. May it be that in his memory we shall build more securely the ever-increasing Kingdom of God as we live among our fellowmen and seek to bring them peace. God has spoken to His children in all generations. God has spoken to us in these past few days. He waits to lead us on. Let us march forward, with faith!

Just ten weeks after I preached the Roosevelt memorial, an event occurred in the city of San Francisco which had the potential of fulfilling all the dreams of universal peace held by religious people everywhere. The United Nations became a reality with the adoption of a charter by delegates of fifty nations who had been meeting for sixty-three days. The inherent "potential" for peace has failed to materialize, however, because of a fatal flaw in the charter which remains until this very day: the veto power given to each of the five major national powers on the Security Council — the United States, the Soviet Union, Great Britain, France and China. Until the charter is amended to remove this flaw, the peacekeeping functions of the United Nations will be ineffective.

When the United Nations charter was approved on June 26, 1945, it was reported in the press that President Harry Truman told a cheering throng: "Oh, what a great day this can be in history!" At the concluding session of the conference he told the assembled delegates that the world must now use the new "instrument of peace." By failing to use it, he said, "we shall betray all those who have died in order that we might meet here in freedom to create it. If we seek to use it selfishly — for the advantage of one nation or small group of nations — we shall be equally guilty of that betrayal."

This was the same President Truman who, less than two months later, authorized the dropping of atomic bombs on the Japanese cities of Hiroshima and Nagasaki. The resultant tragic devastation of human life and property did bring an end to World War II, but at what cost to the reputation of the United States as a civilized nation only the verdict of twentieth-century historians will determine. The official rationale for the decision to deploy the atomic bombs was that it saved the lives of hundreds of thousands of United States military personnel which would have been lost in the necessary invasion of Japan. Again, only future historians will be able to determine whether such an invasion was "necessary."

I well remember the vigorous discussions, pro and con, which took place in the Huntington community and at the Yale Divinity School after the atomic age was ushered in by the government of the United States. The concept of the United Nations as an instrument for worldwide peace was cast aside in the emotional atmosphere which marked the remaining months of the year 1945. Meanwhile, my divided attention was given to my duties as a Christian minister and as a graduate student.

To be a graduate student at Yale University is a natural goal for a young man born in New Haven. When it actually happened to me in September of 1944 I felt that my life had come full circle. I had admired the institution from afar through my friendship with theologues at the Divinity School. During the years of my early youth I had been an ardent fan of the Yale football team. Now I was ready to earn an academic degree which would open the door to a seminary teaching position. Because of my major duties as minister in Huntington, I planned to spend four years at Yale in order to complete my residence requirements for the Doctor of Philosophy degree in the Department of Religion. Most of my courses, however, were taken at Yale Divinity School.

Because I had established a friendly relationship with Dean

Luther A. Weigle during the admissions process, I decided to place major emphasis upon studies in his field of expertise, American Church History, with emphasis upon my favorite subject: Church and State. My curriculum also included two years of American History in the graduate Department of Religion. It was Dean Weigle who suggested that I write my doctoral dissertation on Samuel Harris, who was Dwight Professor of Theology at Yale during the last quarter of the nineteenth century. The subject appealed to me also because I had earlier discovered while a student at Bangor that Harris was born in Maine, graduated from Bowdoin College, taught theology at Bangor during the Civil War years, and was President of Bowdoin before going to Yale. As his biographer, my own theology has been deeply influenced by Harris.

It was my great good fortune to be a Yale Divinity School student during the mid-1940's. In addition to Dean Weigle, my professors included Roland Bainton, Kenneth Scott Latourette, Robert Calhoun, and Albert Outler. They made an indelible impact upon my eager intellect. When I knew I would soon be in one of their classes, the daily ride from Huntington of sixteen miles one-way seemed like a pleasure trip. Dr. Bainton, the noted Reformation scholar, was my mentor in Church History; I was excited to be in a seminar with him on Martin Luther during the time he was writing the definitive book on the reformer entitled, "Here I Stand"; he often brought parts of the manuscript into the classroom for discussion among the students. Dr. Latourette, author of the multi-volume "History of the Expansion of Christianity," filled me and my colleagues with awe as he demonstrated the tremendous influence of Christianity at home and throughout the world. I shall never forget Dr. Calhoun as he lectured day after day, without a note, on the history of Christian doctrine; although his vast knowledge of this intricate subject was never published in book form, the notes I took on his inspiring spoken words were the foundation blocks for my own teaching. And it was Dr. Outler who stimulated me to use all my rational powers in the development of a personal theology which led him to write this memorable comment on a term paper: "You are an unrepentant liberal." This paper will later serve as a transition piece between

Parts I and II of these memoirs.

The members of the Huntington Church were most generous and gracious to Shirley and me. Without their support and cooperation we could not have achieved the goals we had set for our professional careers and our personal lives. They were faithful in church attendance, singing in the choir, teaching in the Sunday school, and making financial pledges to the Church budget. They did not complain when their minister spent many hours each week in graduate study, knowing full well that he would probably leave the parish for a teaching position. They approved when he joined the Shelton Kiwanis Club in order to give himself an outreach into the larger community; this outreach has continued for more than forty-five years, in Bangor and in Sarasota. They responded when their pastor urged them to join him as members of the Village Improvement Society; one Saturday stands out in memory when more than fifty citizens turned out with rakes, shovels, and hoes to clean up the neglected local cemetery. They even applauded when their pastor became active in the Huntington Volunteer Fire Department.

The parsonage was a modern and commodious home for the Whittaker family. It was located in the center of town next to the schoolhouse and across from the fire department. Shirley was the exemplary homemaker; she prepared the meals, cleaned the rooms, cared for her husband, and reared our daughter Barbara Anne. When son Frederick Mark joined the family in 1946, she simply expanded her output of energy and love. For all the years of our marriage I have counted over and over again the multiple blessings of having a wife like Shirley. The parishioners appreciated Shirley, too. She was always the gracious hostess when visitors came to call or when social events took place in our home. When she needed help, for babysitting or other chores, someone was always available.

As a husband I suppose that my least helpful years were the ones in Huntington. I did do most of the grocery shopping on my way to and from my studies in New Haven. And throughout the years of our marriage I have always kept our financial accounts, for which Shirley is thankful. I have tried, too, to make possible every opportunity for my wife to visit with her mother and father. They often came to the parsonage and we were frequently in the Johns' homestead in New Haven. We spent every Christmas there, where we were often joined by my mother. I made every attempt to spend time with my children. Barbara Anne lived all of her preschool years in Huntington and was the "darling" of the parish. Babysitters were glad to have the assignment. She had a dislike only for the play-yard to which she was consigned when Shirley had some pressing other duties to perform. I remember one winter day when she was bundled up against the cold and put out in the yard for play. I was working on a sermon and Shirley was otherwise engaged. We did not immediately notice that a gentle snow had started to fall. An hour later we checked on our daughter and found her, snow-covered, asleep in the corner of the fenced-in yard. We were properly chagrined. After son Mark arrived, he and I soon became intimately acquainted. It was my task — and great personal pleasure — to hold him, give him his bottle, and change him at two a.m. each night.

A unique experience was mine in the spring of 1946. The significance of Plymouth Congregational Church in my life has already become evident. It reared me in the Christian faith, it inspired me to become a minister, and it was the scene of my wedding. While a theologue I had preached from its pulpit on more than one occasion. Now came an opportunity which was a mountain-top event for me. It is best described in a chapel talk I gave four years later at Bangor Seminary when I was a new young professor. The faculty and students were somewhat startled that morning when I announced that my topic would be "I was Jesus."

Four years ago, over a period of five short days just before Easter, I was Jesus. Or so I was in the eyes of more than three thousand residents of metropolitan New Haven. The occasion was the annual presentation in my home church of the Plymouth Passion Play, "From Manger to Throne," written and directed by Raymond L. Clarke, organist and choirmaster of the church. For nineteen consecutive years a cast of more than a hundred men, women, and children have lived out the greatest story ever told: the birth, the life, the death, and the resurrection of Jesus Christ, son of God.

On five consecutive nights during Lent the play is presented before a church full of worshippers; the action moves continuously from one to another of four specially-constructed stages, one of them the mountain built high up in the organ loft. The cast, in full costume, enacts the drama before a background of scenery skillfully painted to represent the the Palestinian countryside.

The manger is there; Mary sings a lullaby to her newborn son; the magi and the shepherds bring their gifts. The boy Jesus preaches in the temple, where he amazes the priests by his wisdom. Christ the man resists the temptations of satan in the wilderness; he walks by the sea of Galilee and calls the fishermen to be his disciples. The twelve gather with him on the mountainside and he gives them the gospel before sending them out to minister to the people. Christ heals the sick, gives sight to the blind, raises the dead, and feeds the hungry; he speaks his famous parables and gathers the children around him.

After the transfiguration, Christ prepares to visit Jerusalem; he makes his triumphal entry with the songs and cheers of the multitude sounding in his ears. He sweeps clean the temple and incurs the wrath of the scribes and Pharisees. He calls his disciples together in the upper room and breaks bread with them; then he goes to the garden of Gethesmane for prayer, and an angel ministers to him in song.

The soldiers arrive with Judas, who betrays his master with a kiss. Christ is taken before Caiphas, and Herod, and Pilate; the crowd demands his death. The march to Calvary begins, and Christ carries his cross — a realistically heavy cross — the full length of the church and on up the hill. He hangs there, high in the organ loft, accompanied by the two thieves on their crosses. The lightning flashes, the thunder rumbles from the organ, and one can feel the church building shake, as if in an earthquake. Then Christ suffers and dies.

The play draws to a close. Mary Magdalene finds the tomb empty; in her bewilderment and fear the risen Christ speaks to her. She runs and calls the other disciples; they gather at the foot of the mountain and listen to a final word from their Lord: "Lo, I am with you always." He stands before them high above all the people, dressed in a long white satin robe; then he turns and walks slowly upward until he joins a choir of angels, who sing in exultation.

As the final curtain closes and the church is dimly lighted, more than six hundred people file out quietly into the night. The members of the cast remove their costumes and their make-up in semi-silence, not wishing to break the spell of their communion with God. One figure lays aside the wig and the beard which for three hours have helped to make him look like Jesus, and he becomes a mortal man again. But none of those who have participated in or have watched this drama is ever quite the same again. This kind of personal and intimate experience with the living Christ revives one's soul and changes the whole perspective on life.

Consider first the people who come to see this Passion Play. I have been associated with the enterprise for more than fifteen years. Each season the church is filled every one of the five nights, and many are turned away for lack of room. A large number of people return year after year to see the drama; requests for tickets, which are free, come from all parts of the state of Connecticut. On any given night one can find in the congregation Roman Catholics, Jews, Negroes, people of many different national origins and from every walk of life. There are no distinctions of creed, color, nationality, or social standing in the presence of the living Christ. These people are hungry for faith, and under the spell of the Christian drama they find it. You would know this to be true if you could see these worshippers as I have seen them. If you could sit as Jesus — as I have sat — at the Last Supper and watch across the footlights a mass of upturned faces radiant with wonder and love, you would know the power of the sacrament of Holy Communion. If you could carry the cross of Christ, as I have carried it, through a congregation of hundreds of human beings, and hear their whispers of sympathy and their quiet sobbing, you would know the power of the Cross. If you could watch these multitudes leave the church at the close of the drama, as I have watched them many times, and see the marks of quiet confidence on many a countenance, you would know the reality of the resurrection. The lives of men are truly transformed when they know the Christ.

The wondrous effect of association with Jesus, though it be only in a sacred drama, is made manifest in the lives of those who play the supporting roles in the passion story. The one who sits year after year in the manger and sings a lullaby to the newborn Christ child has gained for herself something of the lovely spirit of Mary the mother. Another, a language teacher in a private school, has portrayed the role of Peter for ten years or more; I have walked with him on several occasions as his brother Andrew. I have seen the marks of Peter's character stamped upon this man in his personal life as a father, teacher, and church member. And most thrilling of all, perhaps, is the influence of Jesus upon the little children who make up an important part of the cast. One scene in particular I shall always remember: Jesus calls the children to him, holds one upon his knee, and tells them the parable of the lost sheep. If you could look into the faces of these babes who have seen Jesus, and see the light of divine love in their eyes, you would know what our Master meant when he said: "except ye become as little children ye shall not enter into the kingdom of heaven."

And what does it mean to the one who becomes Jesus for a few hours? Words cannot express what can only be experienced. I did not seek this opportunity. The part of the Christus is usually taken by a student at the Yale Divinity School, but when the chosen one fell ill a month before the scheduled presentation I was asked to take his place. By coincidence I was a Yale student myself at the time. When the church I was serving as minister granted me a week of time to devote entirely to the play, I accepted the invitation. On each of five nights, two hours were required for make-up and then three hours on stage. Each afternoon was spent in rest and relaxation. My diet for the week consisted primarily of scrambled eggs, milk and toast. This schedule was necessary because of the nervous tension which grips one who presumes to imitate the Master; the sense of responsibility is all but overwhelming. I learned then what all Christians should forever remember: To be like Jesus one must give all that he has of body, soul, mind and spirit.

I learned, too, what is equally important, that when mortal man gives all that he has in the service of God there is a Power from on high which will sustain him. When one seeks to be like Jesus he finds God. God was with me when I was Jesus! He taught me what to say, and when and how to say it. He put divine power in my voice, my eyes, my hands, so that through me He might reach the hearts of many hundreds of His children. As I prayed in the garden of Gethsemane, I knew the strength of God's authority, bending my will to His. As I hung upon the cross I knew the power of His love to save man in his suffering. As I stood on the steps to heaven among a choir of human angels singing the seven-fold amen, I knew the meaning of God's grace to grant eternal life to mortal beings.

All this was four years ago — when I was Jesus. Why do I tell you this story today? Because I know that when men and women see Jesus their lives are transformed, because I believe that this transformation is the one hope of saving our world today, and because I have faith that you and I can aid this transformation by: the use of the sacred drama, by the ministry of music, by speaking a prophetic word for God, but primarily by showing to spiritually hungry human beings the eternal Christ in our own lives.

A day or two after the final presentation, a letter came to me from the author and director, which I have cherished through the years. Raymond Clarke wrote:

"You have meant so much to the continuance and success of the Passion Play's sixteenth year that I cannot let it pass without writing you.

"You gave us an ideal interpretation and no one appreciates it more than the writer. The fact that you kept to the script unfailingly in spite of disruptions means everything. The ease with which you moved through the play, still keeping your mind on important things as well as non-important suggestions from all sources, is a real feat. Every word you spoke carried perfectly, so that nothing was lost. You looked and portrayed an ideal Christus. I thank you!"

Raymond Clarke's reference to "disruptions" during the Plymouth Passion Play warrants an explanation. An unexpected humorous incident occurred during the dramatic moment when Jesus and King Herod have a confrontation. On one occasion as Jesus approached Jerusalem he was warned that "Herod wants to kill you." His response was: "Go and tell that fox, 'Behold, I cast out demons and perform cures today and tomorrow, and the third day I finish my course.'" Later Jesus is brought before the King's court and hears Herod say, "So, thou thinkest me a fox. Perchance I am. Who knows?" The answer to the rhetorical question comes immediately — not from Jesus, but from the loud voice of a youngster sitting nearby in the congregation — "The Shadow knows!" This quotation from a well-known contemporary radio drama "stopped the show" momentarily as muffled laughter swept the church.

The Passion Play was not the only dramatic event of the spring of 1946. Shortly after Easter, on April 25th to be exact, Shirley was delivered of our second child, a son named Frederick Mark. The birth took place in Grace-New Haven Hospital, again by Caesarian section. Use of the surgical procedure for the second time meant, according to medical knowledge available in 1946, that our family would be limited to two children. Before the birth there was some concern about the health of the child since Shirley had been hospitalized during the third trimester of pregnancy for treatment of an acute ulcer. She had recovered nicely and, as the doctors had assured us, Mark came into the world in superb condition. We have called him Mark from the beginning to distinguish him from his father Frederick. He likes the name, but to this day honors his first name by signing himself "F. Mark Whittaker." Shirley and I were delighted to have a son who would be a brother to our beautiful daughter Barbara Anne.

In 1947 an announcement was made at Bangor Theological Seminary which set in motion a turning point in my career: the incumbent professor of Church History resigned in order to take another position. When I learned of this vacancy there was little doubt in my mind that I should seek to become a teacher at my alma mater. My residence graduate study at Yale would be finished in the spring of 1948, and the writing of my doctoral dissertation could be completed in conjunction with my faculty responsibilities at Bangor. President Harry Trust and I corresponded about this matter, and his enthusiasm was equal to mine. He was anxious to have another Bangor alumnus join him on the faculty. My candidacy was supported by Dean Luther Weigle of Yale and by Dr. Mervin Deems, who had been my professor of Church History at Bangor and was now on the faculty of the Chicago Theological Seminary. Eventually I was invited to join the Bangor faculty as an "Assistant Professor" effective September 1, 1948.

There was no hesitation on my part in deciding to leave the Huntington parish and to accept the invitation from the Seminary. This had been my dream since 1944 when Bowdoin College granted me a scholarship for graduate study. It was a stroke of good fortune that a vacancy occurred on the Bangor faculty at precisely the same time that I was ready to launch a teaching career. However, it was with a certain sense of guilt that I announced my resignation to the members of the Huntington Church. We had experienced four good years together as pastor and people. They had been most generous in giving me time for extra-curricular activities; it was as if they were willing to help me achieve the form of Christian service to which I had aspired. My conscience was clear that Shirley and I were leaving the Church in a spiritual and material condition stronger than that which prevailed when we first came to the parish. And I was gratified by the sentiment expressed in the following tribute read at the testimonial dinner honoring my wife and me:

"Fred Whittaker:
A man who walks with dignity and talks with grace.
Because he is a man of God he is a man of men,
Alike unfearful of the home, the market place,
The clash and conflict of the town and state.

Stand here upon the Church's steps,
Look westward to the school;
How many small, unknowing feet,
Ascending steps to school,
Will sound the rhythm of the praise
Of him they never knew.
How many teachers ardent in their work
Will find that work made easier.
How many better halves are better halves
Because of him. Unroof the homes that he has touched

83

And watch the mother laying down her book
and smiling at her husband say, How many times
Fred Whittaker has helped our Jane and Bill
And all their friends. So many of us know
That this is true, for Jane and Bill
And all their friends are his especial care.
For he has said, How little there is done
For our young people here. How much there is to do.
And others taking up this plea will some day build
A place for all this good community
Where young and old may work and play
And sing and dance. And should some one
Observe this house with visionary eye,
He then would see in every stone, each grain of sand,
The spirit of Fred Whittaker.

A change has come to Huntington. A light is lit,
A standard raised, a goal is set.
Nor will its people longer acquiesce
To stagnant civic carelessness.
Or watch with dull unseeing eye the country side
Neglected or misused.

Fred Whittaker:
Wherever you may go, how much success may come to you,
There will be days when dull distraction
Sits upon your desk, when mind will not
Respond to whip of will. When such days come,
Then think of us, your friends with you tonight,
Whose faith in you and loyalty are firm,
Though not so much to you, as to the things
You want for others.

Fred Whittaker:
We wish you well!"

Nine years in the parish ministry — at Robbinston, Red Beach, Yarmouth, and Huntington — were coming to an end. While my professional time during this period had been divided between formal study and church leadership, I had the satisfaction of knowing that my efforts as an ordained Christian minister had been widely appreciated. I still look back upon these years with nostalgia and have often wondered what might have happened if I had remained in parish work. One thing is certain: I have never wavered in my conviction that it is the witness of the lay people which determines the effectiveness of the local church program. Thus, since 1948 I have been an active layman — my ordination not withstanding — first in Bangor's Hammond Street Congregational Church and then, since retirement, in Sarasota's First Congregational United Church of Christ.

Now it was time to begin a new adventure, once again at Bangor Theological Seminary, where in 1939 I had enrolled as a student. The language and comprehensive examinations at Yale had been successfully completed. Shirley and I, Barbara and Mark, had said our goodbyes with some tears to our beloved friends in Huntington. In mid-summer 1948, after spending a few days with family in New Haven, we started our northward trek with Blue Hill, Maine, our interim destination. I had been invited to spend the month of August as guest minister of the Blue Hill Congregational Church. Four weeks in this delightful coastline summer resort community proved to be a happy interlude for the Whittaker family before we moved on to Bangor.

In Blue Hill that month we became intimately acquainted with the town's most famous personage, the Reverend Jonathan Fisher, who gave a lifetime of distinguished Christian service to the local church during the nineteenth century. The parsonage in which he lived with his family is now the headquarters of the Jonathan Fisher Memorial. It houses many of his artistic productions such as paintings and clocks. The Memorial is maintained by members of the Fisher family with the financial help of hundreds of friends and is open to the public during the summer months. Fisher is one of the founding fathers and original trustees of Bangor Theological Seminary. It is reported that he often walked the thirty miles or more to Bangor in order to attend meetings. The Jonathan Fisher Professorship of Christian Education was established at the Seminary during the Whittaker administration with the help of a generous donation from Miss Ethelwyn Hinckley, one of Jonathan's direct descendants. Shirley and I have continued our support of the Fisher Memorial through the years.

We lived in the spacious modern manse at Blue Hill, with its high ceilings and huge fireplaces. The home proved to be a fascinating place for our young daughter Barbara. She also enjoyed going to the beach with her mother and baby brother. Between Sunday sermons I relaxed by playing the picturesque nine-hole golf course. Shirley took pleasure in visiting Rowantrees, where the famous Blue Hill pottery is made and sold.

Blue Hill is fondly remembered as the stepping-stone for me from parish minister to theological professor. It was there, too, that I met for the first time a major benefactor of the Seminary. He was Walter Teagle, executive of a major oil company and a summer resident of Blue Hill. Shirley and I were entertained in his home that August, and in subsequent years I made annual visits to the Teagle Foundation offices in New York City. Since the administration of President Harry Trust the Foundation has made increasingly substantial annual scholarship grants to Bangor students until this very day.

From Blue Hill it was on to Bangor!

6.
The Unrepentant Liberal

Before telling the story of the years at Bangor in Part II of these memoirs, it will be revealing and pertinent, I believe, to disclose the theological basis upon which my life was predicated as a professor, a president, and a politician. In the spring of 1947 I was in my third year as a graduate student at Yale. I was thirty-four years old and probably at the height of my intellectual powers. In a term paper for Dr. Albert Outler entitled "The Prospects of Contemporary Theology," I set forth my candid opinion about major issues of Christian faith and practice; my life from that time forward has been an elaboration and an extension of the principles set forth in that paper. I have considered as a compliment Professor Outler's written comment: "You *are* an unrepentant and unreconstructed liberal!!" The remainder of this chapter is a verbatim reproduction of the document:

If theology is to be relevant to the contemporary scene, it must be a theology for laymen. If theology is to appeal to the twentieth century layman, it must be in accord with the WHOLE experience of modern man. Such a theology must lead man to a "saving" faith and therefore must proclaim a gospel for life in THIS world. I believe that contemporary theology has failed to meet successfully these three tests. This paper will attempt to validate this criticism and to suggest how future contemporary theology may avoid these faults.

The theology of the future must be a theology for laymen! Stanley High, journalist and ex-minister, maintains that Protestantism is beset by the evil of "clericalism"; this is made manifest, for example, in the proclaiming of "theological and ecclesiastical conceptions — the language of which is as unintelligible to the average layman as the meaning, if he could get it, would seem unimportant."

This judgment may be a bit extravagant, but there is more than a little truth in it. My own experience has been that while I was a layman in the church I was taught practically no theology. Now I understand why, for I have been a theological student for eight years: much of historical and contemporary theology is simply incomprehensible to most laymen.

Jesus was no theologian. His words, especially as recorded in the synoptic gospels, can be appreciated when their meaning is not obscured by theological speculation. The teachings of Jesus are primarily ethical in nature, and this is an aspect of his life which needs to be recaptured by contemporary theology. The ethics of Jesus have been subordinated to theological doctrines and dogmas concerning his person and his office. Paul began the process, which has continued to our day, of building a theological structure in which the person of Jesus as "Christ," "Saviour," "Master," God," etcetera, has been the foundation.

Augustine, Thomas Aquinas, Luther, Calvin, and countless others have all made significant contributions to historical theology. These four leaders were able by their own genius to formulate and explain a "contemporary" theology which captured the allegiance of their fellow Christians; this fact is self-evident in the records of church history. Theologians in our day have not had this genius, and the Christian faith is therefore weakened.

Neither the "dialectic" of Barth, nor the "Neo-Catholicism" of A.E. Taylor, nor the "paradoxes" of Reinhold Niebuhr, nor the "Unconditioned" of Tillich, are capable of saving modern man from his dilemma; and this, in part, because these theologians write for each other (or so it seems) and not for the great masses of the church who might hear them gladly if they could comprehend.

These theologies are insufficient also, I believe, because they are not truly contemporary but are re-statements of theologies of a historic past which have little or no vital significance for the twentieth century. I speak of Protestant theology. Thirteenth century Thomistic thought seems to have relevance for modern Catholicism, but this paper is addressed primarily to the Protestant situation. The only sure basis for a meaningful contemporary theology is not the doctrine of other Christians in earlier eras, but is the historic Jesus. This Jesus, through the simplicity, the rightness, and the challenge of his life and teachings (as recorded in the synoptic gospels), can be the inspiration of a gospel for today. But this gospel must be proclaimed in a theology for laymen.

I do not mean to suggest that theologians should omit the careful study of historical theology. This is essential background material for any contemporary theology. But the methods and content of historical theological controversies should not be emulated in our day. Modern theologians must abandon the "hair-splitting" tactics of Nicea and Chalcedon. Theological professors today should be prepared to restate for their students, in terms that can be used in the modern pulpit, those historical theological doctrines which have significance now; otherwise, such doctrines have only archaic value. The same thesis applies to theological writers. The only alternative, if we would keep Christian faith strong in the church, is to provide formal theological training for all our laymen. Even then, if my own experience is normal, there would be more theological questions asked than answers given. Perhaps God in His wisdom made us that way.

The lack of such a theology is the chief cause of the decline of the church in our day. This fact is implicitly validated by a report made in 1943 by Norman Pittenger after he had attended a conference of American educators, at which was represented "leaders of thought ... experts in the fields of science and philosophy, belles-lettres and art, history and political science. It would have been difficult to find a more distinguished company assembled at one place for one purpose." The conference discussed the subject of religion, and, before suggesting a list of essentials for modern religion, they agreed in the judgment that "the churches simply do not count in the American scene."

Mr. Pittenger's report suggests the second essential factor for the theology of the future: it must be in accord with the WHOLE experience of modern man. Theology should welcome with gratitude the assistance rendered by the physical sciences in unveiling more and more of the mysteries of the universe. Theology may legitimately move beyond science by faith into the realm of the unknown, but should not dogmatically proclaim as religious truth any hypotheses which are patently contrary to the findings of the physical sciences. In the field of physical science there seems to be an ever-widening horizon of knowledge available to modern man; theology must be willing to make use of such knowledge, by revising its own findings if necessary, if it would remain relevant. In this connection, theology would do well to consider what part the psychological behavior patterns known as "projection" and "identification" play in the formulation of its doctrines.

Anthropology and sociology, too, in their disclosure of hereditary and environmental factors which affect the life of man have valuable contributions to lay at the footstool of the "Queen" of the sciences. In this country the "separation" of church and state has obscured the kinship of political science and theology; this is a vast area where contemporary theology should and must offer guidance and moral persuasion if it is not to succumb to the pseudo-religion of nationalism. In addition to its own religious history, contemporary theology should be keenly aware of the facts of secular history, including the history of other faiths, and should be ready to temper its own dogmatic utterances when this is suggested by the facts of "profane" history. D.C. MacIntosh in his "Pilgrimage of Faith" finely demonstrates this moderating attitude without undermining his own particular faith.

Another technique of the twentieth century which theology could use to its advantage is that employed by the writers of so-called "cultural" history. No longer is it legitimate to write history in terms of wars and revolutions, kings and presidents, without reference to the thoughts and deeds of the great masses of humanity, often inarticulate, who really are the essence of history. The theology of the future, if it would be a living thing, must not be written on the mountaintops by a Barth or Tillich but must spring up out of the valleys where the world of men is engaged in toiling, suffering, and hoping.

The whole experience of modern man includes, of course, both rational and aesthetic factors which may be classified under the general terms philosophy and art. I have never been certain where to draw the line between philosophy and theology; perhaps there is no real distinction. I doubt that either can exist independently of the other. In any event, the future of theology will depend upon how wisely it makes use of the suggestive rational patterns developed by philosophy and science. At the same time theology may and must move beyond the point where philosophy and science stop to rest. Theology must set the pace, so to speak, and this it can do not by being dogmatic and static but by a dynamic changing of the speed and direction of its own course as it is challenged by other forces in the "game" of life. To continue the metaphor, theology will find a great source of strength and inspiration for its pace-setting task in the nourishment it receives from the aesthetic realities which pervade the life of man.

Theology should be grateful for, and willing to accept help from, the poet, the musician, and the artist. A rational theology alone will not survive in modern culture; it must also take into account the emotional and the spiritual factors which are a vital part of the whole experience of man. Contemporary theology has vast resources of human experience from which to draw its content. The chief task of theology may be to make real the relationship between God and man; however, this relationship must be stated in terms which take into account all the factors I have named, and some which I may have overlooked. If contemporary theology can develop a system of doctrine which represents in equilibrium the whole experience of man, and can proclaim this doctrine in language comprehensible to laymen, then — and only then — will it no longer be true to say that "the churches simply do not count in the American (or world) scene."

There are theologians who do not seem to care whether or not the church does "count" in the world scene; their chief emphasis and only hope is centered in some "other" future existence. Modern

91

man, I believe, needs and wants a faith which will "save" him from the physical trials and spiritual turmoils of life in THIS world. This third essential of a contemporary theology is closely allied with the second, outlined above, but deserves emphasis on its own validity. One of the most widely quoted secular speeches of our day is that of General Douglas MacArthur, made in Tokyo Bay in August, 1945, in which he stated that the problems facing the world are "basically theological." I agree with the General and hasten to add that unless theology accepts the responsibility of suggesting valid answers to the questions men are asking about this present life and its meaningfulness, it will be relegated to comparative oblivion as a purely academic exercise indulged in by theologians who are in the world but not of it. I cannot believe that the theology of Reinhold Niebuhr, for example, with its low estimate of the value of life in this world, is capable of capturing the allegiance of modern man. Such a theology and all others which despair of this life but make rosy promises of something better beyond are rightly criticized by Marxist sympathizers as an "opiate of the people."

It is true, of course, that Christianity received its impetus and much of its sustaining force from the faith of its adherents in the promise of eternal life. This is one aspect of Christian theology which must always be emphasized. But it is only ONE aspect! Christianity, if it is to be the religion of those who follow the teachings of the historic Jesus, has also an ethical aspect. Jesus preached rules for living to human beings who existed in the same world of which we are a part. Contemporary theology should rediscover the power of ethical transformation which lies dormant in the teachings of Jesus; therein is a gospel for today.

To be sure, Jesus had a firm belief in the reality of eternal life, but he ALSO appreciated the wonder and beauty of the natural world in which he lived as we live, and he saw real worth in the developing lives of his fellowmen. Both man, even the sinful man, and his world were for Jesus the creatures of God and were therefore good in His sight. It is this aspect of the teachings of Jesus — that this life and those who live it are essentially good — which offers to contemporary theology perhaps its greatest opportunity to validate itself in the world of men. The prospects of *contemporary theology are bright, challenging, seemingly unlimited — IF it is a theology, simply and succinctly stated, in accord with the whole experience of man in this world.*

There are certain specific aspects of Christian doctrine which, it seems to me, stand under indictment by modern man because they do not meet successfully the three tests herein outlined. The Christian doctrine of God is, of course, the basic factor in all Christian theologizing, and yet much of modern thought in this area is unintelligible to the layman; so much so that skepticism and atheism are quite in evidence even among professed Christians. How can I, a parish minister, explain the nature of God to my parishioners in terms of the "Wholly Other," or "The Given," or "The Unconditioned"? It is much easier for me and for them to understand and appreciate what John Dewey means by his naturalistic "God," which at least has the virtue of being related to the world in which we live. And yet this all-imminent "God" is not sufficient to satisfy the aesthetic and spiritual "feeling" of man which demands a God who is also transcendent.

I have written that Jesus was not a theologian. By this I mean primarily that, according to the Bible record, he rather assumed than explained the existence of God. This fact has significant implications for contemporary theology. The doctrine of God is the most difficult, I believe, and the one least likely to be finally agreed upon of all Christian doctrines. This is as it should be, for a God who was fully known to man would no longer be God. Edgar Brightman, in his book "The Finding of God," writes that "There is more to learn about God's nature and his purpose than stands written in any book or has been thought by any human mind." The testimony of Jesus and of his modern disciple should warn contemporary theologians against the tendency either to deny the existence of an ontologically real God or to proclaim as final the revelation of God in Jesus Christ. Theology should admit its inability to define precisely the nature and will of God. No doctrine of God should be dogmatic, but should be presented tentatively for testing by the whole experience of man. The whole experience of man suggests that God IS a reality which defies definition, but a God nevertheless who does create, sustain, and guide human life. God is not to be defined but to be experienced. Jesus knew God in this way, and the God whom he discovered can also be known to us, perhaps even in fuller measure since we have in our scientific world means of discovery (or revelation) of the secrets of the universe not available to Jesus.

I have implied in the above sentence that "discovery" and "revelation" are practically synonymous. Some contemporary theologians would not agree, and here is another instance where a rather simple relationship between man and God has been confused unnecessarily by men eager to establish the authority of their own viewpoint. The Bible is at the center of this confused situation. Many a good Christian has become indifferent or antagonistic toward the Protestant church because he could not reconcile the facts of human experience with the doctrine that the Bible contains the final and only authoritative revelation of God's nature and will. To be sure, the Bible contains a revelation of God, but man is involved in the process and without his recognition or discovery of the fact that God was speaking to him there could have been no revelation.

"But the initiative is always with God!," cry the critics. Of course the initiative is with God, since it was God who created man in the first place with the ability to communicate with God; but because man is free to use or not use this ability, revelation by God always requires discovery by man. The Bible would not have been written without cooperative effort on the part of both God and man; God revealed, man discovered and wrote. Contemporary theology can perform a valuable service by cleaning up this misunderstanding as to what constitutes revelation. More important, contemporary theology could and should reassure modern man that revelation continues in our day. It is conceivable that a new Bible could be written in the twentieth century. God speaks to us just as surely as he spoke to the original writers of the Bible; it behooves us to listen to Him now while at the same time we seek new light from His revelation of old.

I believe that the most important developments in contemporary theology for the immediate future will be concerned with the doctrines of man, Jesus Christ, and the church. In this connection I do not concede that nineteenth century "liberalism" is dead; on the contrary, it is and will be an important factor in twentieth century theology — the popularity of John Dewey's thought in educational circles is one piece of supporting evidence. Other factors will be: probably a good measure of Reinhold Niebuhr, although I cannot imagine that his pessimistic analysis of the human predicament will ever supplant the idea of progress in the development of human character. It seems to me that the Christian doctrine of man is at the moment suffering from a distorted historical perspective; two worldwide wars with their concomitant evils have undermined man's faith in himself and in his God. Perhaps the social scientist can help the theologian at this point.

Trite as it may sound, there is a "cultural lag" in our fast-moving industrial age which has had much to do with the chaotic historical events of the twentieth century. The human race is in the midst of severe "growing pains" as it develops slowly but surely from a group of isolated communities toward the ideal of "one world," one family under God, which has been the goal of the Christian kingdom. It is unfortunate, I think, that contemporary theologians are kicking man when he is down. There is no doubt that man has committed sins, but theology does not help the situation by assuring man that this is his natural state, from which he can never hope to escape in this world. And theology is certainly unnecessarily grotesque in its doctrine that even the man "redeemed by grace" must remain a sinner. Neither the judgment nor the wrath of God will suffice to convert modern man; forgiveness and love at least have a better chance to lead man to his salvation.

I have heard more than one testimony to the effect that the Christian pulpit today is not providing a gospel for admittedly sinful man. At the moment I am myself preaching a series of Lenten sermons on the theme, "Our Sins," but I never fail to end the sermon on the hopeful note that these sins are not an inseparable part of human nature, but can be overcome. It is perhaps a judgment upon contemporary theology, and a validation of my thesis that theology must be in accord with the whole experience of man in this world, that a biologist has recently been widely publicized as "God's Newest Witness." Dr. Lecomte du Nuoy, in his book entitled

"Human Destiny," sets forth the thesis based upon scientific investigation, that man does not represent the end of evolution but only a middle stage between the past, with all the memories of the beast, and a future rich in the promise of the soul. So from now on, he says, our progress will not be physical but spiritual. The man of the future will be completely liberated from destructive human passions. Though he will enjoy the pleasures of the body, he will not be ruled by them. A book reviewer comments that the author wrote this book to doubters and skeptics — "to increasing millions whose despair makes them wonder whether life is worth living." Contemporary theology, if it is to fulfill its mission, should find a challenge here to convince despairing man that this life is worth living. And this can be done on no less an authority than the founder of the Christian faith, who thought highly enough of the nature of man so that he could charge his disciples: "Be ye therefore perfect."

The salvation of man, it seems to me, depends upon the realization of the simple concept set forth by Jesus in the prayer he taught his disciples: "Thy kingdom come on earth as it is in heaven." Contemporary theology should center its thinking about Jesus Christ and human redemption in this area. Man wants to know two things: First, that there is a "life" beyond what man calls "death." Second, that there is a God-given purpose in this life which is progressively revealed to men who earnestly strive to overcome their sins and to build a human community worthy of the title, "City of God." Jesus Christ has given men assurance that these things are so. It is the task of theology to state these facts convincingly.

Men before Christ believed in a life after death. Christ believed in a life after death. Christ's contemporaries believed in a life after death. Christians throughout the centuries have believed in a life after death. It is a basic tenet of the Christian faith that the professed followers of Christ are reunited with him and with God after death. This proposition can be neither proved nor disproved by mortal man; there is no evidence available to us. It is entirely a matter of faith, but it is a faith so common to men, the creatures of God, that to deny its validity without evidence is to deny that man is a creature of God. Let theology state these propositions simply but firmly, without attempting to describe the nature of the future life (which attempt must necessarily go beyond faith into the realm of fantasy) and it will find eager believers among the masses of men. Jesus will thus become a savior of men from death, not because he was God incarnate but because, in spite of his essential humanity, he was and is able to lead his fellowmen to a vital faith. Then, with this issue settled insofar as it is possible for mortal man to comprehend the purposes of God, let Christology concentrate on the task of presenting a way of salvation for sinful men in this world.

Jesus Christ came not to be ministered unto but to minister. One of the weaknesses of orthodox Christianity has been its proneness to so exalt the person of Jesus Christ, even to the point of identifying him with God, as to lead men to worship him but not to follow him. The ethical teachings of Jesus have been obscured by doctrines of his supernatural person and office. He has been pictured as a person different in kind from other mortal beings, as one "without sin," as essentially "divine." I do not believe that modern man will any longer be captured by this concept. The theology of tomorrow should proclaim a Jesus who is kin to all mankind, one who is divine in the sense that all men are divine because they partake of a portion of the spirit of God who created them, one who developed to the fullest extent possible the divine resources which were given to him by the Creator, one who calls men to follow him not because he was by an act of God "without sin" but because he faced the same temptations which confront other men and did not sin. Christology should emphasize Christ's complete faith in a God whom he called Heavenly Father; his willingness to give his very life for the task which he believed God had given him; his kindness and unselfishness in helping those who needed physical or spiritual healing; his ability to make real to others his own ideas about God; his understanding of human nature and his wisdom as a teacher; these are factors which the common man can comprehend and can aspire to accomplish on his own behalf.

Modern man does not want to be saved; he wants to cooperate in his own salvation. For orthodox Christianity, the cross of Christ has been looked upon as the means of salvation for sinful man, but man can no longer believe in the atonement theory which pictures Christ as the "lamb of God" who takes away the sins of the world. And this because of the quite obvious fact that the sins are very much still in the world. It is too easy a way to salvation, and not a convincing one, which claims that Christ died for our sins and that, therefore, we are saved. If we would have salvation through Christ we must incorporate in our own way of living those characteristics of his life which we admire. We, too, must learn faith, humility, submission, mercy, love, forgiveness, and a desire to serve our fellowmen. We must learn from Christ of the beauty, dignity, and worthwhileness of life and then seek, like him, to enrich our own lives and those of our "neighbors" by developing to its utmost the divine side of our nature. The gospel of tomorrow must be an ethical gospel which inspires men, through the guidance of Christ's still largely untried but still pertinent teachings and his ever-present spirit, to seek the completion of a kingdom of God on earth.

I feel certain that contemporary theology faces a vital opportunity to proclaim a more meaningful doctrine of the church. The ecumenical movement demands it, secular society needs it, and the man in the pew wants it. It is a doctrine of the "church militant" of which I speak. Many of my lay friends tell me that they have had enough of pious platitudes, of brilliant analyses, and of abstract ideals, from the pulpit. Now they want to know what to do about making effective in secular society the program of living for which the church stands. This will involve a revision in orthodox theology so that the church may become the conscience of the world. Neither identification of the church with individual national secular states nor the separation of church and state will any longer suffice. In the first case the church loses its distinctive universal character; in the latter case it loses touch with the reality of life. In the first case the church cannot be the conscience of the world; in the second case it does not wish to be the conscience of the world.

Contemporary theology should point out, to Americans in particular, that there can be no actual separation of church and state, any more than there can be a separation of the various parts of the human body without endangering the whole structure of society or of the individual. Both the state and the church have no objective existence in themselves; they are composed of human beings. These human beings created the state and created the church in order to meet certain fundamental needs of human nature. These needs may be classified as material and spiritual; however, they cannot be separated from each other either in the individual or in society; they are interdependent and they are best satisfied when the state and the church cooperate as a unit. The state does not properly fulfill its function if it ignores spiritual values. The church does not properly fulfill its function if it does not interest itself in secular matters. A church member does not meet his obligation to society unless he puts his religion into action and becomes a good citizen of the state. A citizen of the state is able to perform his duty to society best when he is guided by the spiritual values of religion. In the truly integrated personality or society, there can be no separation of those functions which are delegated to the state or to the church.

John Bennett in "Christianity and Our World" suggests that "if the Christian is not to be an ineffectual spectator concerned more about the purity of his own soul than about results in society, he must cooperate with those political and social movements which at a given time seem most promising in the light of Christian ideals." Contemporary theology should point out that the church must stop being a spectator, that it must discard the theory of being in the world but not of it. The church should be called upon to take an active part in the establishment of the kingdom of God on earth, and this through the corporate efforts of its members who are conscious of the guidance of God and who then follow that guidance in effective action.

The church has the potential power — political and educational power through its worldwide supra-national organization; spiritual power in the faith and ethical teachings of its Christ — to become the conscience and thus the salvation of the bewildered world of men. For too long that power has lain comparatively dormant; now theology must release it for God's sake and for man's sake. I well realize that such a course of theological action may threaten the greater unity of the Christian church envisioned in the ecumenical movement. It may also alienate from the church those who insist that religious faith should be concerned only with individual salvation. Should these developments arise they may well be a blessing in disguise. The church may have to become smaller before it can become stronger. An ecumenical church without a social gospel allied to an individual gospel will not suffice. God reveals, Jesus Christ exemplifies, and the church should proclaim, a message of good news for the common man in this world. The prospectus of contemporary theology centers in this task.

PART II

Bangor Years

7.
Professor and Dean

My return to Bangor Seminary in September of 1948 began an exciting adventure which was to last for thirty years until retirement. Less than ten years earlier, I had been a private secretary for a railroad official, with no post-high school education except a Y.M.C.A. course in public speaking and an extension course in traffic management from LaSalle University in Chicago. Now I was to teach church history to prospective Christian ministers, some of whom were older than my thirty-five years. It was the beginning of a dream coming true which would reach fruition four years later with my election as president of the school.

One of the most satisfying aspects of the experience was the reunion with my former teachers. It did not matter that for three probationary years I would have the title of "assistant" professor. I would be the only teacher of church history and I would be on the same faculty with the men I idolized: Harry Trust, Charles Cumming, Alfred Perry, Marion Bradshaw, and Andrew Banning. I shall always be grateful that they welcomed me with affection and enthusiasm as a new colleague.

My annual salary of $3,500 plus housing was a major improvement over the $2,400 I had received as minister of the Huntington Church. Our assigned residence was located on the campus at 199

Cedar Street. It was a large house with eight rooms, an attached barn which served as a garage, and a spacious fenced-in yard which became a playground for our two children. The barn was especially fascinating to five-year-old Barbara, who soon discovered that it contained two stalls which had long ago been occupied by horses; she insisted that she could still smell the animals. As our two-year-old son grew older, he was happy to find that a family of eight boys named Hansen lived next door; he became one of them and once identified himself as "Mark Hansen."

Almost as soon as the Whittaker family was settled in its new home, Shirley and I joined the Hammond Street Congregational Church and thus began an active affiliation which continued for three decades. It has been one of my deliberate purposes through the years to play a vital role in the life of the local church, not so much as an ordained minister but as a concerned layman. I have filled most of the offices of the church: moderator, deacon, trustee, member and chairman of various committees, and delegate to county association and state conference. Daughter Barbara was enrolled in the church school, as was son Mark when he reached the proper age; both children later became members of Hammond Street Church and active in its youth program. Shirley has given many years of service as church school teacher and as a leader in women's work.

When the Seminary formally opened its 133rd year on September 20, 1948, and even before I had made my initial appearance in the classroom, I was thrust center-stage, and introduced to the school and local community by the invitation extended to me by the faculty to give the opening address. I well remember the emotional impact of this occasion, which at that time called for the wearing of a tuxedo under the traditional academic robe and hood. The title of the address was "The Government of God," and it reflected my keen interest in the theology of Martin Luther which had been developing since my days in the classroom of Roland Bainton, Yale's Reformation scholar. Because it illustrates some major convictions about the relationship of Church and State, which have been a hallmark of my professional career, and because it was my first public pronouncement as a member of the Seminary faculty, I include here some extended excerpts. These were later

104

published in the October, 1948, issue of the B.T.S. "Alumni Bulletin."

One of the most lively subjects of discussion among modern churchmen is the relationship of Church and State as institutions designed to secure the welfare of mankind. Since Martin Luther's time there has been a rather sharp difference of opinion on this matter between Roman Catholic and Protestant leaders. I should like to share with you tonight the results of a study I have made of the theology of Luther as it pertains to this important subject of the proper place of the Church and the State in our society.

According to Luther, there are two regimes or kingdoms — the spiritual and the worldly or secular — which comprise God's government of human life. God has ordained both of these regimes and the Christian is subject to both. Luther writes: "Christians are subjects of two kingdoms — they have experience of two kinds of life. Here on earth where the world has its home and its heavenly kingdom we surely are not citizens. But being obliged to continue in this wretched state so long as God wills, we should mingle with other mortals, eat and drink, make homes, till the soil, fill civil offices and show good will toward our fellows, even praying for them, until the hour arrives for us to depart unto our home."

Luther supported his conception of the worldly kingdom as a part of God's governmental plan by quoting the familiar words of Paul in Romans 13 and Peter in the second chapter of his first epistle. He points out that the "children of Adam" must all be divided into two classes, one group belonging to the kingdom of God and the other to the kingdom of the world. The first group is comprised of all true believers in Christ and they need no secular law or sword. The second group, much larger than the first, is the worldly or the non-Christian. In order to control this group and to provide some sanctuary for the true believers, God has established a worldly government with its law and its sword, which is not a terror to good works, but to evil, as St. Paul has declared.

Luther explains further: "These two kingdoms must be sharply distinguished and both be permitted to remain, the one to produce piety, the other to bring about external peace and prevent evil deeds; neither is sufficient in the world without the other. For no one can become pious before God by means of the secular government. Where, on the other hand, the spiritual government reigns alone over land and people, there evil is given free rein and the door is opened for every kind of knavery." The distinction between the two kingdoms is not as sharp as would seem to be indicated here, for the members of the Kingdom of God are expected not only to subject themselves to the authority of the kingdom of the world, but also to serve actively the purposes of this secular power. This may even involve bearing the sword, not for one's own protection but for the benefit of others. "As concerns yourself," adds Luther, "You would abide by the Gospel and govern yourself according to Christ's word, gladly turning the other cheek and letting the mantle go with the cloak. In this way, then, things are well balanced, and you satisfy at the same time God's kingdom inwardly and the kingdom of the world outwardly."

In this connection, Luther makes a significant statement which has implications for twentieth century concepts of the proper relationship between Church and State: "It would indeed be good and profitable if all princes were real and good Christians, for the sword and the government, as a special service of God, belong of right to Christians more than to all other men on earth."

I am reluctant to accept the concept of Paul and Luther that the secular rulers receive their power and authority directly from God by ordination. History, ancient and modern, is replete with evidence that this theory results in tyranny, and when two or more temporal rulers are convinced that they are God's agents they come into conflict and the result is a "holy" war. Luther's doctrine that the powers that be are ordained of God becomes positively dangerous to the welfare of the people in this era of the modern secularized state. In this connection it seems to me quite naive for Luther to hold that the temporal authorities will be controlled by God's threat of eternal damnation for their souls. There is little historical evidence that many civil rulers, or even all popes, have been deterred from tyranny because of their fear of God. Certainly in the twentieth century such a doctrine has little relevance to the facts concerning temporal government. I think it in order at this point to suggest that Christians of Protestant lineage have been much too prone to *ignore their responsibilities as citizens of this world, leaving it to God and to the Roman Catholic Church to guide the civil state.*

However, Luther speaks to all ages when he assigns a divine significance to the temporal sphere of government. Without accepting the extreme teaching that the powers that be are ordained of God, we modern Protestants, particularly in the United States where the "tradition" of the separation of Church and State needs new interpretation for our time, should more fully acknowledge the importance of civil government as a means toward establishing the Kingdom of God on earth. It is the duty of the Christian, as Luther points out, to fill civil offices; in fact, Christians are the best qualified to hold positions of temporal authority. There should be more deacons in the State House at Augusta and in the Capitol at Washington!

I am convinced that many modern Protestants, in their irrational zeal to avoid following the example of their Roman Catholic brethren in all things and in their misunderstanding of Protestant doctrines of Church-State relationships, have failed to exercise their proper influence in and upon secular government. Luther has something to say to these people: Fill civil offices! Make all your princes Christian! Pray for the temporal powers! Preach God's Word to them!

My final word to you tonight is this: The government of God cannot prevail without our Christian participation in the affairs of state. We Protestants, in good Lutheran tradition, must assume our responsibility for guiding the policies of the temporal powers of our world. Thus will we demonstrate that Luther is not a museum-piece, but that he speaks a vital word for twentieth-century Christianity.

This treatise on the government of God would within ten years have an important influence upon my life as I began a five-year span as an elected official in city and state politics. However, my immediate attention was directed to the church history classroom where I was scheduled to give my first lecture the next day. For the initial teaching year I was expected to offer two courses each semester so that I might devote some time to the completion of my doctoral thesis; I have remained ever grateful to the faculty and trustees of the Seminary for this concession.

One course was in "Early and Medieval Church History." It was offered to juniors, or first-year theological department students. The catalog carried this description: "A lecture course surveying the internal development and the external environment of the Eastern and Western Churches from the New Testament period through the Middle Ages." This required first-semester course was followed in the second with one entitled "Reformation and Modern Church History"; the catalog gave this outline: "A survey of the Church in western Europe, the British Isles, and the Near East from the Reformation to the present time." Each of these two courses was offered for three semester hours, and were prerequisites for further study in the Church History department.

There were two other courses in the Church History department which were required for graduation. One was a three semester-hour study in American Church History, which was a survey of the development of Christianity in America from the colonial period to the present time. The other was Christian Missions, which met three times each week to study the missionary activities of the Christian Church from the early to the modern periods, but with emphasis upon developments since 1800. These two courses were offered to Middlers (second-year students in the Theological Department).

After I completed the writing of my doctoral dissertation in 1949, two electives were added to my teaching schedule. One of these was a seminar, with supervised study in selected fields of student interest. The most popular offering was an in-depth examination of the history of Church-State relationships, popular perhaps because it my own favorite subject. The other elective was entitled "Studies in Christian Doctrine." In a two-year cycle this course considered the theology of leading Christian thinkers and of the Church from the early days to the modern period. The first year dealt with the Church Fathers, Augustine, the Ecumenical Councils, and the Scholastic theologians. During the second year consideration was given to the doctrines of the Renaissance and Reformation periods, and the development of Christian thought from the rise of modern Rationalism in the seventeenth century to the Ecumenical movement.

The general description of the courses offered in the Church History department, as I announced it in the first catalogue after joining the faculty, is of particular interest because it has withstood the test of time and has remained unaltered to this day during the incumbencies of my two successors in the Church History chair; it declares:

"The primary purpose of the work in this department is to enable the student to see contemporary Christianity in the light of a proper historical perspective. Major emphases will include the place of doctrine as an impetus to social action, the relationship of Church and State, the importance of Christian missions, and an estimate of the Ecumenical movement. Constructive attitudes toward the Roman Catholic and other non-Protestant groups will be inculcated. While a study of the Church in western Europe will necessarily occupy a large part of the curriculum, the courses will be directed toward a preparation of the student for service in the Christian Church at home or in the mission field."

After the normal three-year probationary period, I was inaugurated on September 18, 1951, as the Waldo Professor of Ecclesiastical History, a position I held until my retirement in 1978 after thirty years on the faculty. The Waldo chair was established in 1856, the result of a gift from Miss Sarah Waldo of Worcester, Massachusetts. President Enoch Pond was the first incumbent and in the ensuing years the chair has been occupied by the following professors: Levi L. Paine, Henry W. Hulbert, Calvin M. Clark, Mervin M. Deems (twice), C. Howard Hopkins, myself, and Roland H. Wessels.

On the occasion of my installation as Waldo Professor I was again invited to give the address at the opening of the Seminary year, the second time this honor and privilege was bestowed upon me in my three years on the faculty. My topic was "The New Christendom," and the following excerpts will illustrate another facet of my developing thought on the proper relationship between Church and State:

My studies have convinced me that history suggests a tenable plan for the redemption of contemporary civilization. I have used the term, "The New Christendom," to describe what I have in mind; this is my thesis: Classical Christendom, now defunct, contained certain ideas and ideals which can and should be revived and given new form in the twentieth century. The basic principle of "The New Christendom" is that human life in this world is a part of eternal life, and is therefore sacred. This concept presupposes a spiritual unity between the sacred and the secular, between the Church and the State — a unity which is an integral part of the order of things as created by God. In this order of things man is essentially good and only relatively evil; man is capable of cooperating with God for the building of a worldwide society which is worthy to be called the "kingdom of God" or the "New Christendom." The chief instruments for the building of this new order are the Church and the State, both of which are of equal significance in the economy of God. Both the Church and the State have coordinate responsibilities in a vast program designed to permeate all of society with Christian beliefs and practices.

If the new Christendom is to emerge, its citizens must find a method of overcoming the two social forces which led to the downfall of classical Christendom, namely, nationalism and sectarianism. Nationalism must be transformed into world-loyalty, and sectarianism must give way to ecumenicity. I believe that the United Nations and the World Council of Churches, imperfect and often impotent as they are, can effect that transformation if they are given the wholehearted support and guidance of the Christian peoples of the world. Specifically, then, what shall we do?

First, if Christendom is to be the order of the new day we must see to it that the story of Jesus Christ and his way of life is told in every corner of the earth. This will mean that we shall give of our money and our prayers for the support of the missionary enterprise of the Church. The International Missionary Council has been the guiding light in the formation of the World Council of Churches, and the missionary emphasis continues as the pulse of the World Council's program. There can be no new Christendom until Christ's name and Christ's way is universally acclaimed by the nations of the world. My greatest joy in teaching is to tell the story of Christian missions. It is one of the chief sources of my optimism. What shall

110

you do? Say, "I believe in missions!" And let your deeds support your words! You will soon find your national provincialism and your sectarian bias being given new horizons.

Second, if you want the United Nations to succeed in establishing permanent international peace, do your part toward establishing lasting denominational peace within the Church. It is a platitude — but an inescapable truth — that a divided Church cannot minister to a divided world. In the new Christendom the United Nations and the World Council of Churches will exchange delegates for mutual advice and counsel, but this will not come to pass until the political leaders know that the World Council speaks for a Christian Church which is united in spirit and purpose. Within the Council itself, the consolidation of the Faith and Order and the Life and Work movements has resulted in the proclamation of prophetic words of wisdom by the Council on practically all the major problems facing modern society. But the world will not listen to a Council which represents a sharply divided Church.

What can you do? Become familiar with the program of the World Council through reading and study. Learn about the work of its counterparts, the National Council of Churches, and state and local councils. All of these groups are seeking to build the new Christendom through devotional, educational and legislative projects. Then make your local church and yourself a living part of this ecumenical movement by avoiding undue emphasis upon denominational traditions and practices, by cooperating with plans for organic and federative unions which promise to strengthen the total witness of the Church in the world, and by effecting at the local level the various programs for individual and social improvement suggested by the state, national, and world councils of churches.

Thus far I have been dealing with methods designed to strengthen the Christian Church for its part in the building of the new Christendom. What can be done to bring the State into partnership with the Church for the cooperative task assigned to them by God? The timid may answer that the State now looms so large in human affairs that it will never condescend to a partnership with the Church. But I maintain that if the Church acknowledges its inter-dependence upon the State in the divine order, if the Church calls upon the State for assistance in bringing its Gospel to the people of the world, and if the Church will provide new and consecrated leadership for the State, there will emerge a new era of Church-State relationships leading toward human social salvation. The "separation" of Church and State will not suffice at this point.

The Church and the state are associations of human beings like you and me. Under God's guidance we can make of them what we will! Here are a few quick suggestions: Let church members take more seriously their responsibility to participate in the political arena. This will involve the establishing and maintaining of social action organizations throughout the whole ecclesiastical structure, from the local church to the World Council. The Church must, in effect, become a "pressure group" against war and all other corporate evils which threaten human civilization. Again, church members must offer themselves as public servants in high and low places. The most effective way to Christianize the State is to elect and appoint more and more Christian men and women to positions of political leadership. Moreover, Christians should become active members of some political party so that the influence of the Church may be felt at the grassroots, where candidates and policies are chosen. I am confident that the widespread adoption of these procedures would immeasurably aid the progress of the new Christendom from town government to United Nations.

One other important suggestion is in order: As a Christian minister I know the primary significance of spiritual forces in shaping the destinies of men and nations. Men and women must have an experience of faith which cleanses their hearts before they can properly and fully use their minds and bodies in effective social action. However, as a Christian teacher, I also know that the process of education is an invaluable ally in developing the spiritual life and in leading faith into good works. Thus I am convinced that the new Christendom demands the cooperation of Church and State in the realm of education.

The Church should call upon the State for help in providing a public education for young people which places religion in its proper perspective as the most powerful single force in all of human history. An education which fails to acquaint the student with the dramatic story of human relationship with God — and particularly the Jewish-Christian aspects of that story — is an education which leaves the student ignorant of facts which give life its true meaning. Furthermore, it performs a distinct disservice to religion and to civilization itself by separating religion from the rest of life. There is a rapidly growing movement in the United States to re-introduce religion as a fourth "R" in the curricula of our public schools. With this basic training in non-sectarian religion provided in cooperation with the State, the churches would then have some hope of completing the religious education of their members through weekend instruction. This whole area of religion in education is one which deserves careful but immediate consideration of the leaders of both Church and State, lest the realization of the new Christendom go by default through human ignorance of God's place and promise in history. (It is pertinent to note that the suggestion set forth in this paragraph was adopted twelve years later by the Supreme Court of the United States in its 1963 decision banning prayer and Bible reading in the public schools but *allowing* students to be taught *about* religion.)

This, then, has been a presentation of my faith and my hope. If it has been idealistic it is because I believe that idealism is the true realism in a civilization where pseudo-realism has led humanity to the brink of physical, moral, and spiritual chaos. If it has been optimistic, it is because I believe in the omnipotence of God and in the ability of His human creatures to cooperate with Him for the temporal and eternal redemption of men and women. If it has been utopian, it is because I believe that most children of God would rather spend their earthly lives seeking the new Christendom than accept the verdict of the pessimists that the earthly plight of humanity is hopeless.

Within a year after I gave the 1951 opening address as Waldo Professor, a major change occurred in my professional career when I was chosen to be the fifth president of Bangor Seminary effective August 1, 1952. This meant that I carried a full teaching assignment in the Church History department for a relatively short time.

However, my love of the classroom experience did not diminish, and I continued to teach a limited number of courses each semester throughout the twenty-six years of my presidency. During my early years on the faculty I was keenly aware of my neophyte status as a teacher. I felt like a pygmy among giants when I realized that my colleagues were the very men I had so admired during my student days at Bangor. Furthermore, I had received no teacher training in graduate school (a glaring curriculum omission, in my opinion). And so I was forced to rely upon my own judgment in selecting teaching techniques I had observed during student days.

The senior members of the Bangor faculty were very kind to me. They accepted me as an equal and almost immediately gave me committee assignments to carry out. One which I remember vividly was on a special committee chaired by Dr. Marion Bradshaw, which was charged with the responsibility of examining the need for student discipline, with particular reference to the drinking of alcoholic beverages. Our committee submitted its report on December 3, 1948, less than three months after I had joined the faculty, and I record the content here as illustrative of social conditions on the Bangor campus near the middle of the twentieth century. The faculty minutes of the above date contain the following item:

Recognizing the grave social problems connected with the use of alcoholic drinks, the real physical, moral and professional dangers involved, and the damage done to the Seminary's reputation through reports of Seminary members indulging in intoxicants, the faculty has by unanimous vote made the following provisions effective as of December 8, 1948:

a. Aware of the great dangers in drinking, dangers long recognized but now intensified in our age, we join in admonishing students of this seminary against indulging in any drinking of alcoholic beverages. Any students found guilty, in the judgment of the faculty, of being under the influence of alcohol will be instantly dismissed.

b. Any student thinking that this announcement of new regulations constitutes an invasion of student rights may withdraw at the close of the present semester with full credit, and in good and regular standing.

That students be requested not to seek entertainment at public places of amusement which are of questionable reputation and character.

The student response to this new ruling was less than enthusiastic. There was widespread criticism of the administration for not providing the means of more adequate social life on the campus. After due deliberation the faculty finally adopted the following addendum at its meeting on February 9, 1949:

The faculty recognizes that the question of student attendance in places of public entertainment is related to the larger question of providing a more adequate program for the development of a healthy social life on the campus.

The faculty realizes that dancing is now an accepted custom in the social program of a large number of churches, and we feel that the Seminary would do well to help prepare prospective ministers for participation in such a program.

Therefore, the faculty will recommend to the Trustees that the Christian Association, under proper faculty supervision, be granted permission to sponsor occasional social evenings with dancing in the gymnasium as one means of improving the social life of the Seminary.

My service on this special faculty committee during the first year was a forerunner of events to come. President Trust realized that the students needed someone on the faculty who would represent their legitimate interests in academic and social affairs; he also felt the need for staff assistance in the recruiting of new students. He requested the Board of Trustees to appoint me to the office of Dean of Students effective September 1, 1949. In his letter making the appointment, Dr. Trust commissioned me to "act as personal

115

counselor in matters pertaining to life of the students on campus and in relation to their church work. Where students need help in personal affairs you will officially represent the Seminary." I was paid an addition $250 per year for this task. A year later my portfolio was expanded to include service as "recruiting agent" for the school.

My appointment as recruiting agent may have been inspired by my report as Dean of Students at the conclusion of my first year in that office. In May of 1950 I wrote to President Trust as follows:

The general morale of the students this year has been good. A revised edition of the Students' Guide has been prepared, which should result next year in still further improvement in the tenor of student life. My office and my home have been open at all times to students who wished to confer with me; there has been a good deal of personal counseling during the year, especially when you have been absent from the city. Under your supervision I have assisted in placing and advising student pastors; in your absence I have interviewed prospective students who have called at your office.

A statistical study of the enrollment in the school reveals some interesting facts: At the beginning of the academic year there were sixty-two students on the campus; the present number is fifty-five. Of the seven students who left during the year, three did so for reasons of personal or family health, two because of unsatisfactory academic work, and two by personal choice. Of the fifty-five students now in school, twenty-four are in the pre-theological courses and thirty-one in the Seminary proper; nine will leave through graduation and two others have indicated that they plan to study elsewhere next year. Twenty-eight students are receiving aid from the Veterans' Administration. Twenty-six students are married. The age factor is worthy of note: eighteen of the present students, or roughly one-third of the total, entered the school before they were twenty-one years old; at the present time the same number, eighteen, are twenty-two years old or less, eight of them being under twenty.

I draw certain conclusions from these figures, as follows: First, the Seminary is enrolling a large proportion (almost fifty percent) of students who are married or who marry while here. As a result the school is facing a serious family housing problem; some prospective students, as you know, cannot enroll until they have

116

promise of a house in which to live. Second, the catalog of the Seminary states in its opening narrative paragraph that the school "occupies a unique place among the seminaries of the Congregational tradition and of the northeastern United States by reason of the special opportunity it offers to mature men who have felt the call to Christian service after experience in other fields and who have not previously had the benefits of college education." In view of this "unique" function of our Seminary I feel that we may be accepting a disproportionate number of young men just out of high school who might well spend four years in college before seeking seminary training. Third, with fifty-five students enrolled the Seminary is operating at less than capacity, and, further, there are not enough applicants to allow for careful screening and selection of students. There are now eleven vacancies in the dormitory, and the number will probably increase as the large number of veterans now receiving government aid (twenty-eight) gradually diminishes. These conclusions lead me to make the following recommendations:

(1) In view of the apparent need for recruiting new students, and since much of your time and energy is now taken up with the campaign for funds, I propose that as Dean of Students I be authorized to devise a plan whereby a considerable part of my weekend time would be spent in recruiting new students, especially the more mature men to whom this school offers a "unique" opportunity. The principal part of this plan, as I envision it, would involve my speaking in the larger — and later the smaller — churches of New England on appointed Sundays, and on Mondays at service clubs, junior colleges and other preparatory schools. Since I am myself a product of the unusual academic plan offered by our Seminary, I am confident that my effort to recruit new students, especially among mature men who do not now know of the possibilities at Bangor, would bring substantial results. And, incidentally, this recruiting program would be good advertising for the school and would probably bring it additional money as well as men.

The adoption of this recommendation would involve some extra expense, principally in the form of traveling costs and an increase in my salary sufficient to compensate for the net amount I am now earning through supply preaching on Sundays. In this connection, during the past academic year I have served two long interim pastorates and have preached every Sunday but two since last September. Since I must have this additional income in order to meet current family expenses and to pay off debts incurred during the long period of scholastic preparation for my teaching work, I feel that my time and energy may best be spent in the service of the Seminary in recruiting students rather than in supply preaching.

(2) The large number of married students now enrolled, and the prospect that many future students will be married, clearly indicates the need for additional student apartments if the Seminary is to attract mature men.

I realize that the adoption of these recommendations will involve new expenditures at a time when the financial condition of the Seminary is somewhat unstable. However, I believe that an accelerated program for recruiting students is essential to the future welfare of the Seminary, and that money invested now in such a program will bring substantial dividends to the school.

My report to President Trust was presented to the Board of Trustees at its meeting on June 5, 1950, with the result that I was re-appointed as Dean of Students and also commissioned to serve as recruiting agent for the Seminary. I continued in this dual role for two additional years until my election in 1952 as president to succeed Dr. Trust upon his retirement. During this period the student enrollment increased to seventy the first year and to eighty the second year. The dormitory was again being used to its normal capacity of two students in each suite of rooms. The pattern for the recruiting program was roughly the same each year. I made something over twenty trips annually to various places in New England, preaching sermons, speaking to college and young people's groups, and addressing denominational meetings; in each case the story of Bangor Theological Seminary and its unusual mission was told. In my final report as Dean of Students I recommended that a way should be found to continue direct recruitment. After I became president one of my early accomplishments was the establishment of a staff position for this purpose. Meanwhile, the need for

118

additional student apartments was left unmet for lack of funds until the early years of my administration.

While the Seminary has always remained solvent and free of debt, due largely to heroic efforts at fund-raising by its presidents and other officers adept at public relations, the struggle for financial stability has been continuous and arduous. Bangor has consistently been blessed by a Board of Trustees which was generous in making personal gifts to the school and wise in the investment and spending of the limited funds made available to the Seminary. One such trustee was the Reverend Clarence W. Fuller, who served for twenty-five years as chairman of the Board beginning in 1956. When I joined the faculty in 1948, Fuller was on the staff in his second year as Assistant to the President. Thus began a friendship which grew in intensity throughout his lifetime.

"Chuck" Fuller was an alumnus of Bangor Seminary who graduated in 1937. After ten years in the parish ministry he was called by President Trust in 1947 to assist in raising new funds for the school. The announcement of his appointment was made in the leading article of the January, 1947, issue of The Alumni Bulletin. With confident boldness the article proclaimed:

"The die has been cast. The Trustees of Bangor Theological Seminary have authorized the inauguration of a program which it is believed will keep B.T.S. abreast of the times and fit into the needs of the churches for the next fifty years. The goal has been set financially for at least ONE MILLION DOLLARS. In terms of service that means an ever increasing list of men well-trained for the Christian ministry. It means maintaining the same high standards of scholarship as in the past. It means a larger faculty to broaden the base of education. It means buildings now in use and suitable for a long-range program to be put into proper condition, and buildings now outdated to be replaced by modern structures."

The Seminary acknowledged that this was an ambitious program which would take several years to achieve. Clarence Fuller was appointed Assistant to the President to begin the process. Fuller was then the minister of the East Congregational Church in Springfield, Massachusetts, and had been a leader in denominational and ecumenical activities in the local area. He was a graduate of

Amherst College. He and his wife Anora moved to the Bangor campus in the spring of 1947 to begin his new assignment.

The April, 1947 issue of The Alumni Bulletin contained an admonition in large letters, "Remember our Million Dollar Campaign in Your Prayers." It also published a letter which Fuller had sent to all Bangor alumni telling them that "we are going to keep reminding you of the Seminary's drive for a million dollars through every available medium. We must keep you thinking about it because you are the most significant factor in the success of the campaign." He announced the formation of an alumni committee to promote the campaign and closed the letter with a personal word which expressed both negative and positive impressions. He wrote:

"I have been on campus now about a month. I have found some problems. The Seminary obviously has certain needs which viewed superficially may create an unfortunate impression. But underneath I have found a large and profound faith in the mission which Bangor has traditionally undertaken, and a universal desire to make the Seminary a more effective instrument for the fulfilling of that mission. And it is not ballyhoo to say that I am encouraged. A great many of the difficulties we of the alumni have been hearing about can be surmounted if adequate funds are available. One seminary president after another, and many denominational leaders, have written us that Bangor Seminary, continuing in its traditional role, is essential in the training of ministers. There must be a school, they agree, continuing the job we are doing. And I am convinced that the staff and the faith are here to do this job if you and I can see that it is adequately undergirded financially."

Fuller was undoubtedly encouraged further by the action of the Executive Committee of the General Council, Congregational Christian Churches, on May 1, 1947, endorsing Bangor's unique academic program and its so-called "Forward Movement." Optimism about "The Million Dollar Campaign" reached its height later that year and was reflected in The Alumni Bulletin for October, which contained enthusiastic articles written by President Trust and Clarence Fuller. A General Alumni Committee had been named, and its members were exhorted to make their own sacrificial gifts to the campaign; more importantly, they were requested to submit to the Seminary the names of prospective donors among alumni-served churches who might make substantial gifts to the school. Dr. Trust declared that "the success of the campaign is largely dependent upon the cooperation of you, our alumni."

Three months later, however, it was apparent that the solicitation of funds was not gaining momentum. Fuller's report of campaign news in The Alumni Bulletin of January, 1948, indicated that eight unsolicited pledges from alumni had been received, averaging $132. Only 170 names of possible donors among church members had been submitted; the reluctance of ministers to supply names of prospective givers was acknowledged. Before the end of 1948 approximately fifty percent of the alumni had made gifts or pledges, but the total amount was below expectations. A campaign for seed money from friends of the Seminary in the Bangor area failed to materialize a year after it had been announced; no reason for this failure was ever publicized, but it was known privately on the campus that one or more of the local trustees of the Seminary were hesitant about the community appeal. There was a growing consensus among Seminary personnel that the campaign goal of one million dollars was unrealistic.

President Trust announced in The Alumni Bulletin of July, 1949, that in the spring of the year Clarence Fuller had, by mutual consent, been released from his contract as Assistant to the President. With the help of Dr. Trust, Fuller was soon called to be the minister of the First Congregational Church of Melrose, Massachusetts, a position which he filled with great distinction for thirty years until his retirement in 1979. In the year we had spent together on the Bangor campus Chuck and Anora Fuller, Fred and Shirley Whittaker established a friendship which has endured and grown through the years. The two years of heroic but sometimes frustrating effort as a fund-raiser was soon supplemented by the more than three decades of dedicated service which Clarence Fuller gave to the Seminary as a member of the school's Board of Trustees and as its chairman from 1956 throughout my administration and beyond.

In his announcement of the termination of Clarence Fuller's contract, President Trust paid tribute to the work of his colleague; here are some excerpts:

"Without a background of experience in the difficult field of fund raising, Clarence faced his task with courage and optimism ... As the campaign progressed it became evident we were not securing the larger gifts which were essential to our ultimate success. No one saw this more clearly than Clarence Fuller, and in one of his reports to the trustees he urged securing the services of a man experienced in institutional finance ... It is with very sincere appreciation and affection that I write this tribute to a faithful friend and servant of B.T.S. who has sown much seed which will be productive to the advancement of our beloved Seminary. Clarence W. Fuller has done a noteworthy piece of work, and now goes on to a still greater task of serving in the parish ministry."

The seeds sown by Clarence Fuller have indeed been nurtured by those who have succeeded him in office. The campaign for new funds continued for the remaining years of the Trust administration under the leadership of David Q. Hammond, a professional public relations expert living in Augusta, Maine. He promoted the concept of "Partnership" between church people and the Seminary, later to be known as "The Fellowship" and, eventually, as "The Annual Fund." However, the first real advance in the continuing campaign occurred during the Whittaker administration with the installation on September 22, 1953, of the Reverend Daniel W. Fenner, an alumnus, as the first Vice President of the Seminary. His story will be told in later pages. Meanwhile I shall record some of the memorable personal and professional events which were a prelude to my election as the fifth president of the Seminary in 1952.

8.
Doctor of Philosophy

The culmination of my formal academic preparation came on a cold February morning of 1950 when the postman delivered to me at my Bangor campus home the inscribed degree of Doctor of Philosophy from Yale University. It was a far cry from my dream of receiving this document in person at a ceremony in Yale's Woolsey Hall at New Haven, where I had been presented with my high school diploma in 1929. But I had completed all the requirements for the doctorate in the fall of 1949, and the University would not allow me to wait for the degree to be awarded at the next public ceremony scheduled for June. My gratitude to Yale was only slightly diminished by the timing. I could now use the title "Doctor" and was fully prepared scholastically for my faculty position at Bangor Seminary.

My colleagues at Bangor rejoiced with me. In the spring of 1950, President Trust expressed his pleasure by inviting faculty and trustees, together with their wives, to a testimonial dinner at the Bangor House, with Shirley and me as the guests of honor. I shall always remember that night in May for two special reasons. One of my very favorite Bangor professors, Dr. Charles Gordon Cumming, the senior member of the faculty, spoke for his colleagues and described me as "a spiritual son." Only one thing pleased me more. When Dr. Trust spoke of our close personal relationship he concluded his remarks by presenting to me a Yale University Ph.D. academic hood. It was the same hood which his first son, Harry Knowlton Trust, had earned just a year or two earlier. The son's life had come to a tragic early end on August 26, 1949, after a fatal attack of poliomyelitis.

The writing of the doctoral dissertation was a milestone in my life for more than one reason. It was my final qualification for the Ph.D. degree, but more than that, it brought me into vital contact with a man, Samuel Harris, who was to have a tremendous influence upon my thought and practice for the rest of my life. Harris had come into my consciousness as early as January, 1940, when at my first Seminary Convocation I heard a "Samuel Harris Lecture on Literature and Life." I learned then that Harris had been Bangor's Professor of Christian Theology for twelve years (1855-1867), including the Civil War period. I met Harris again when I was a student at Bowdoin College in 1944 and discovered that he had been president of the school from 1867 to 1871. Soon after I started my graduate study at Yale I found that Harris had again preceded me when I saw a memorial plaque on the campus honoring him for twenty-five years of service (1871-1896) as Dwight Professor of Systematic Theology. Needless to say, when Yale's Dean Luther A. Weigle, my professor of American Church History, suggested that I write my doctoral thesis on Samuel Harris, I was more than ready and willing.

Dean Weigle was anxious to have the story of Harris publicized since no one had yet written the biography of this distinguished Yale theologian. Moreover, at his death Harris had left an unpublished manuscript of several hundred pages which contained his mature thought not revealed in three previous books on theology. These pages were in the Sterling Memorial Library at Yale, waiting for someone to study and edit them. During the summer of 1949, after my first year of teaching at Bangor, Shirley and I took our two children to New Haven and established our residence in the spacious home of her parents, Louis and Blanche Johns. I was permitted to use a recreation room in the basement as a private study and spent the better part of three months working on the manuscript of my thesis. I came out into daylight primarily to work in the Yale library or to visit locales in Massachusetts and Connecticut where Harris had served pastorates and had later lived in retirement.

Writing the biography of Samuel Harris was one of the most arduous tasks of my lifetime. It required complete concentration throughout the summer. Only when the walls of my study area seemed to close in around me after two or three weeks of writing, did I engage in a few hours of much-needed recreation. My principal hobby of golf then came to the rescue. Hitting the little white ball through eighteen holes of the New Haven Municipal Golf Course, where I had spent countless hours of my younger years, did wonders for my mental health and sent me back to the typewriter with renewed vigor. When the manuscript was completed early in the fall I sought to redeem the written promise I had made to Yale, as a condition to receiving the Ph.D. degree, that I would arrange for the publication of the dissertation. That this effort failed was a source of keen disappointment to me. A dozen or more book publishers indicated that the story of Harris did not have sufficient public appeal to justify the printing and marketing costs involved.

The manuscript entitled "Samuel Harris, American Theologian" had a niche in my private library for more than thirty years as I devoted full time to my professional career. When I retired, my first priority was to arrange for the publication of my book. I prepared a revised and updated manuscript and submitted it once again to several book publishers, but with the same negative response. I have never understood why The Yale Press, in particular, was not interested in this story of one of the University's most illustrious faculty members. I felt so strongly that Samuel Harris deserved a more notable place in the history of American theology that in 1981 I arranged to have the book published by Vantage Press in New York City, with a financial subsidy provided by the author. While the book has had a fairly wide distribution in libraries and educational institutions, the Harris story is still largely unknown. For this reason, and because Samuel Harris has had such a profound effect upon my own theology and upon my participation in the political process, I devote most of this chapter to a synopsis of his biography and writings.

Samuel Harris was born on June 14, 1814, in that section of Maine's Washington County now known as East Machias. He was the ninth and last child born to Lucy Talbot and Josiah Harris. Thus he became a member of the Harris family which for five generations maintained a high degree of respectability and character — according to the family historian — and participated in many activities which were for the welfare of the town. Young Samuel's interest in the Christian Church undoubtedly stemmed from his father's concern for the religious welfare of the community. When in 1802 there was formed an association of subscribers for the purpose of erecting a "House for the Public Worship of the Supreme Being," Josiah Harris was named clerk of the group and a member of the building committee.

Josiah's greatest service to the community was probably his work on behalf of Washington Academy, the local elementary school which gave his most famous son an early training and an opportunity to begin his career as an educator. Josiah was a trustee of the Academy for five years and secretary for another fifteen. Samuel continued his father's interest in the school by serving as its principal from 1838 to 1840. In 1892 he made what was probably his last trip to the scene of his childhood in order to speak at the centennial celebration commemorating the founding of Washington Academy.

All the records and testimony at hand indicate that Samuel Harris was a gentleman and a scholar from youth to old age. An early manifestation of this fact marked his years as a student at Bowdoin College. He entered the school at the age of fifteen and in spite of his youth was a leading scholar. Henry Wadsworth Longfellow came to Bowdoin at the same time (1829) as professor of modern languages and literature, and his influence upon Harris was significant. Harris learned from Longfellow the German, French, Spanish and Italian languages and their literature, an important asset in his later career as a theologian. The interest of Harris in the physical sciences gained impetus at Bowdoin under the tutelage of Parker Cleaveland, one of the pioneers in American science. Certainly his basic training in the scientific methods of his day was a primary factor in his later ability to reconcile the findings of science and religion.

Young Harris was very much aware of religion during his Bowdoin days. This was the period of revivals which marked the "second Great Awakening," so-called, of early nineteenth century America. In the fall of 1830 a vigorous outpouring of spiritual power swept the Bowdoin campus; Harris, then a sophomore, was among the twenty-five or more students "cordially receiving the Redeemer." After graduating from Bowdoin, Harris received his theological training at Andover Seminary in Massachusetts. In contrast to the more liberal atmosphere at Bowdoin, where Longfellow, for example, was favorably inclined toward Unitarian doctrine, Andover was a school which, according to its historian, was "built sturdily to breast the gales that beat against Puritan orthodoxy."

Under the leadership of Leonard Woods and Moses Stuart, Samuel Harris was well trained in the conservative New England theology during his years at Andover. The evidence is not conclusive as to just how much he was influenced by the experiences of his formal education. His nephew, George Harris, characterized him as a young man who did his own thinking and as not very much directed by others. This judgment is borne out by the testimony of Professor Charles Dinsmore of Yale, who writes in the Dictionary of American Biography that Harris as a theologian belonged to no school, but occupied a transitional position between the old dialectical theology of New England and the more modern methods of thinking.

Soon after his graduation from Andover in 1838 Harris married Deborah Robbins Dickinson, a Machias girl. No children were born to them; but they adopted one daughter, Lucy Marsh, who later became the wife of Edwin Pond Parker, a graduate of Bangor Seminary famous for his 60-year pastorate in the Second Church of Christ at Hartford, Connecticut.

Samuel Harris was ordained to the Christian ministry in the Congregational Church at Conway, Massachusetts, on December 22, 1841, a church which he served as pastor for fourteen years. During the early years of his ministry he was threatened with blindness by an eye ailment which prevented him from reading during a period of three years. An admiring classmate wrote concerning this affliction: "A misfortune which might have crushed a less heroic spirit was the occasion of a self-discipline that was of great advantage to him through life. Doomed to a dark room and with the peradventure that he might ultimately lose his sight, he calmly gathered in his mind and memory's clear intelligence all the facts and principles and truths he had ever known, classifying and arranging everything so it could be seen under its proper head." Despite his physical affliction, Harris was a living example of the application of Christian principles to various phases of community life. He maintained a keen interest in the local school system at Conway, and served on the school board for many years.

Mrs. Harris was a blessing upon her husband during the early trying years of his blindness, and throughout her life. When she died, Samuel had engraved on her tombstone these words of gratitude: "Faithful and Beloved." Harris looked upon his affliction as an act of grace, for it forced him to think out his sermons and to preach them extemporaneously. One who knew him well reports that he cultivated a kind of preaching "that for clearness of thought, finish of style and felicity of illustration, was almost matchless... If you had closed your eyes you could not have told he was not reading a most carefully prepared manuscript."

In a dissertation on Christian truth Harris demonstrates his homiletical skill, while at the same time disclosing a portion of his early theology. In one of the most picturesque passages in all his writings, he says that "truth cannot be given; it must be bought. We must use the wells which our fathers opened, but we must draw the living waters ourselves; if necessary, removing the stones with which the Philistines have stopped them. The formulas and systems of the past are bequeathed to us; the living truths of these formulas every man must find for himself. The pot that held yesterday's manna is spoiled; with the new morning each man must gather for himself the heavenly food. Hence truth, though old, is always new. Christianity itself, though eighteen centuries old, is as new to us as to the first generation that received it. Each man must receive it for himself as really as if he were the first to whom it was preached. Through forgetfulness of this comes the phenomenon of ancient creeds, old and sublime declarations of human rights, time-honored formulas of political truths, custom-worn words of high significance, which everybody utters and few obey — the tombstones of departed thought."

I dwell for a moment on the subject of Samuel Harris as a preacher, for here is a man who was an eloquent and prophetic pulpit orator and, at the same time, a sound philosopher and theologian. He believed with firm conviction that the pulpit was the proper place to discuss any matter which affected the public welfare, and so he spoke out fearlessly on such subjects as war, slavery, and abstinence. In his earliest sermon extant, entitled "The Mexican War," delivered at Conway in 1846, he voices his opposition to the war and then makes this clarion call:

"The pastor is appointed as a watchman over the interests of morality and religion. According to the perfect ideal of his office it is his business — rising above the bias of party or sect, above partiality or fear, or any selfish consideration — to plead for humanity against all wrongs, to proclaim the truth in its severe and simple majesty, and to vindicate all God's claims on men. In the discharge of this duty he is called to speak upon all the relations and spheres of action belonging to human life; for man cannot act except as a moral and accountable being. If the minister sees men acting on principles contrary to the gospel, if he sees measures adopted which are undermining morality and religion — whether in politics, in trade, or in whatever department of action — he is not only justified in speaking, but forbidden under awful penalties to be silent. The preacher can have no respect for himself, and deserves none from his hearers, who models his preaching only by the desire to please. If his office has any claim to be an embassy from God, the preacher must be guided in what he says simply by the will of Him who sent him."

Samuel Harris came to Bangor after eight years at Conway and four years as pastor of the Congregational Church in Pittsfield, Massachusetts. He served the Seminary for twelve years, 1855 to 1867, as Professor of Systematic Theology. One who knew him well says that "his career at Bangor as a citizen was perhaps even more notable than that of the theologian and the preacher." Certainly he brought fame to himself in all three capacities. He was much in demand as a preacher both locally and throughout the state. Yale University earnestly sought his transfer to New Haven as a teacher of theology; and his influence on civic life was so pronounced that political leaders urged him to seek election to the Congress of the United States.

Harris reached the climax of his Bangor career during the Civil War when he was a favorite speaker at mass meetings of the citizenry. In 1860 he presided over a session of the Central Congregational Church which passed the following resolutions on slavery: "Resolved, that the holding of human beings in bondage as slaves, and treating them as property, is contrary to the law of God and the spirit of Christianity. Resolved, that every person claiming to belong to the Christian Church who intentionally gives his influence to sustain the system of American slavery, furnishes mournful evidence of professing a spirit not in accordance with the mind of Christ."

On election eve, 1864, Harris reached a high point in his role as a political speaker. On the same program with Vice President Hannibal Hamlin, Harris addressed a rally in Bangor's Norumbega Hall. Here is the citizen-patriot speaking: "Look at Maryland! Just voted herself free! (Applause) Look at the District of Columbia — no more slavery there! Look at Missouri, and other states coming in as free states, forever to remain free! (Applause) Would you put the black robe on them again? ... The great events of this war are going to settle this question by destroying the slave-holding aristocracy. The principles of the Union and the Constitution are to be sustained ... The Union, once sustained, is the hope of all mankind and permanent peace is guaranteed to future generations. We will transmit to our children through this great glorious country, for all time to come, the noblest birthright of an American citizen."

If Samuel Harris was a man with a social gospel, if he was a man heard gladly in the classroom, the pulpit, and the auditorium, it was because his faith was so comprehensive as to see the divine significance of every aspect of life. He could speak with authority on such social issues as slavery, abstinence, and politics because his thinking on these subjects was grounded in a sound theology.

In 1863 he preached a sermon before the Maine Missionary Society which sets forth important aspects of the theology he was teaching and preaching during his Bangor period. The sermon was entitled "The Son of Man," and its theme was "the human nature of Christ."

Harris wrote that the Son of Man "presents human nature in its completeness...in Jesus is a humanity perfect in its relationship with both God and man." Thus Christ saves men by taking on their human nature, showing them thereby their own worth in God's sight as brothers to one another and as the children of God. "Because the Savior took human nature in its completeness, he consecrated all that is human ... all that belongs to humanity is hallowed ... In any human life, however ordinary, a man may be godlike ... in every affection and condition. This thought should inspire and ennoble us every day ... Christ is God in humanity coming down to us to lift us to his likeness ... Here is courage for every Christian enterprise and hope for every Christian endeavor."

As these memoirs continue, it will become evident that the author was guided theologically by the Harris doctrine of the human potential. The point will be elaborated in a later chapter, "Theological Analyst," which features my last commencement address at Bangor Seminary in 1978, entitled "Little Less Than God." Another major influence upon my life and practice was an essay published by Harris in 1854 on the subject of "Politics and The Pulpit." It was the inspiration for my own political career as councilman and mayor of the city of Bangor, as a Maine state senator, and as a candidate for election as a representative in the Congress of the United States. This story will be told in later chapters.

Ministers of the Gospel, declared Harris, have the same rights as other citizens to vote, to participate in political caucuses and conventions, to deliver political addresses, and otherwise to exert an influence in political affairs. Preaching is one medium which is at the disposal of the minister in the exercise of his influence, and Harris exhorts the clergy to abide by Christ's instruction — "Preach the Gospel" — in the use of the pulpit to discuss political issues:

"No minister has a right to preach politics. Every minister is bound to preach the gospel in its application to politics. Hence in preaching on a proposed act of government the preacher is not to discuss its constitutionality, for he is not commissioned to draw his instructions from the constitution. He is not to discuss its financial bearings, for he is not commissioned to draw his instructions from the science of political economy. He is not to discuss it as a question of jurisprudence, for except as the principles of jurisprudence are identical with the principles of God's law, he is not appointed to expound that science. But he is to draw his instructions from the word of God. He is to bring out from the Bible the eternal principles of God's law and apply them to the political action alike of individuals, of parties, or of the government itself."

Harris deals with some objections put forth against clerical participation in politics. With regard to the alleged ignorance of ministers in this realm, he suggests that if our government is such a mystery that a plain man cannot judge of the right or wrong of its acts, then we may well abandon our democracy and commit the government to a nobility born and trained for statesmanship. Ministers are sometimes criticized for a lack of common sense, and this because their ideas seem visionary and impractical. Harris replies that many principles propounded by ministers, which have been ridiculed by their contemporaries, have in later times been incorporated into the institutions of society because they have been found true. Further, although the minister is liable to error, he performs a significant civil duty by compelling men to bring their political opinions into the light of the Christian gospel, to test them before the court of heaven, and to make political decisions under the vivid consciousness of a responsibility to God.

Harris justifies by several positive arguments his contention that the pulpit and politics cannot rightly be separated. In the first place, the Bible itself is much concerned with political subjects; it contains the history of the entire growth, the decline, and final overthrow of a nation; it declares the principles upon which its prosperity depended and the reasons for its decline. The number of sermons relating to politics would be greatly increased if they were proportionate to the attention given in the Bible to political subjects. Second, the Bible is designed to purify human character, both individually and socially, in the present life; the Gospel fits men for the future world by requiring them to be holy now. Preaching should not be a lullaby for those who would be at ease in sin, or a plaything for an hour of vacancy, but it should be a power to quicken the careless and to rebuke the sinful. In our country, Harris maintained, "all men are politicians," and a large portion of daily conversation and action is political; therefore, to exempt the preaching of the Gospel in its application to politics is to exempt it from one of the large and significant areas of human life. Rather, let every faithful minister aim to apply the Gospel in such a way that every political act, from the casting of a vote to the filling of high civil office, shall be subjected to the will and to the judgment of God.

Third, the results of political action are inseparable from the advancement of Christ's kingdom. The church and the state are "instruments by which God evolves His purpose of grace." Christianity is the only philosophy of history; neither the history of secular society nor the history of Christianity can be comprehended in isolation and, therefore, the acts of government can never be matters of indifference to the preacher of the Gospel. On the contrary: "He must study the age in which he lives, keeping his hand upon its pulse, that he may know the dangers which threaten the Church and the hopes which dawn before her ... He keeps alive in the community the awe-inspiring knowledge of God's providence and sovereignty among the nations, and of the subserviency of all national acts and revolutions to that higher and more glorious end, the advancement of Christ's kingdom on the earth."

In the fourth place — and here Harris certainly has something to say to the American people today — he points out that while in the United States "we have separated the Church and the State, we have not separated — and we cannot with impunity separate — religion and politics. These are the two themes which surpass all others in intrinsic dignity and practical importance." The separation of Church and State, Harris goes on to say, does but render it the more necessary to healthy political action that, throughout the entire population, the true principles of religion and their proper application to all human affairs should be clearly explained and diligently inculcated. This is essential to preserve to politics their true dignity, and to make the political agitations incident to a democracy purifying and ennobling rather than corrupting and belittling. Harris then adds a concluding comment, as prophetic now as it was then: "When the politics of a nation are made contemptible in the eyes of the people, and statesmen begin to be despised as political hacks, then the nation is far advanced in degeneracy, and every political agitation hastens its decay."

In 1867, Samuel Harris resigned his professorship at Bangor Seminary, wherein he had served for twelve years, and became for the next four years the president of Bowdoin College. While he proved to be an innovative and productive administrator, his first love was teaching. In 1871 he accepted an invitation from Yale University to become the Dwight Professor of Systematic Theology. He remained there for twenty-five years, during which time he produced his major writings. In 1874, at the age of 60, he sent to the press a series of twelve lectures entitled "The Kingdom of Christ on Earth," and its theme has been called the central principle of the Harris theology. Not until 1883, when he was 69 years old, did he publish the first of his major works. This was "The Philosophical Basis of Theism," and it is probably better known than his later publications. In it he postulates God as "Absolute Reason" and thus lays a foundation upon which to build his theological faith. The book was widely read, was translated into Japanese and other foreign languages, and was generally hailed as one of the century's outstanding publications in the field of the philosophy of religion.

Four years later Harris produced another volume, called "The Self-Revelation of God," which carried the philosophical argument over into the realm of Christian doctrinal theology. The basic premise of this work is that "the three factors in the knowledge of God are divine revelation, religious experience and rational thought." Harris then began to prepare for publication his complete system of theology, but he was not permitted to finish this work. In 1896, at the age of 82, he finished and gave to the world two volumes entitled "God The Creator and Lord of All," which comprise about half of his projected plan. The other half of his system is in large measure complete in manuscript form. When Harris died in 1899 he had written almost 700 pages under the title "God Our Saviour," most of which is devoted to his concept of the Christian plan of redemption. The work is preserved in the Sterling Memorial Library of Yale University, and much of it is summarized in my book on "Samuel Harris, American Theologian."

I have included this introduction to Samuel Harris not only because of the profound effect he has had upon my life, but because I believe that his rightful place in American church history has not yet been established, more than ninety years after his death. It is my hope that other scholars will be inspired to read one or more of the published works of this Christian son of Maine. For it is my firm conviction that when the final history of nineteenth century Christianity in American is written, the name of Samuel Harris will be placed alongside those of Horace Bushnell, Washington Gladden, and other heroes of the faith. And it is conceivable that Harris will someday be known, along with Jonathan Edwards, as a "great" American theologian.

Samuel Harris preaches no superficial Gospel. He believes in man's ability, with the ever-present help of the Creator, to make real on earth the kingdom of God. At the same time he insists upon the need of sinful man to be redeemed by a God who in Christ was reconciling the world unto Himself. And he grounds his whole theological system in a realistic philosophy which identifies God with "Absolute Reason." Thus Harris presents what I believe the twentieth century Christian so desperately needs: A realistic theology based upon a sound philosophy and vitalized by an evangelistic fervor growing out of experience with the living God. We may yet praise him for revealing God to us, even as he has been highly praised by others in the epitaph on his tombstone: "The Pure In Heart Shall See God."

When I was writing my doctoral thesis on Samuel Harris during the summer of 1949 in the New Haven home of my wife's parents, I could not foretell that in less than a year one of my principal benefactors would die unexpectedly, thus breaking the close ties which united the Johns family. Louis August Johns had treated me like the son he never had, especially since the passing of my own father in 1942. He was intensely proud of his two daughters and of the four grandchildren they had brought into the world. And his devotion to Blanche, his beloved wife, was a joy to behold. When I was asked to give the memorial address at his funeral on June 12, 1950, I was honored to do so but challenged to utter words which would bring comfort to those who loved him. Portions of the address are reproduced here as a record of family history for the benefit of future generations, but also as an expression of my own Christian faith just a few weeks after I became a Doctor of Philosophy. This is what I said, in part:

We are assembled on this sacred occasion for what I like to think of as a memorial service, not a funeral. For the Christian believer this is a time when two purposes should be uppermost in our minds and hearts: This is a time for revitalizing our faith in a God of love, and it is a time for giving thanks to God for the beauty and inspiration of the life now taken from us into the nearer presence of its Creator. I want to share with you my own thoughts at these two points.

Last summer I sat in the garden of Louis and Blanche Johns on Ellsworth Avenue. As I wondered at the color and fragrance of the flowers, suddenly I realized that there before me, in full bloom, was an Easter lily. Easter in June! This was a new idea to me, and yet as a Christian minister I should have known that the experience of Easter, with its promise of eternal life, is not restricted to one Sunday in the spring of each year. Easter comes to us, in June or October, in March or December, as a gift from God whenever we are ready to trust Him and to believe that He loves each one of us as a father loves his child.

The Easter lily, blooming in June, is a sign of God's central revelation in Christ that this earthly life of ours is but an episode in the larger and fuller life to come when we shall all be with our heavenly Father and know Him more perfectly. Christian men and women from the first disciples down through the centuries have believed that this was what God was saying to them through Jesus Christ: "God so loved the world that He gave His only begotten Son, that whosoever believeth in Him should not perish, but have everlasting life." This faith has given us confidence that our God is with us in this life and that death is but a part of the plan of the

Creator by which He brings all believers into closer harmony with Himself. This faith has enabled men and women to enjoy this good life on earth with thankful hearts, to quietly meet its problems and its sorrows, and to face the dimly lighted future with peace of mind.

We are mortal humans and we cannot know all of the reasons why God has created us and placed us in this world; we cannot know why He calls each one of us, at an appointed time, to leave our friends and to join those who have been called before us. We cannot draw a blueprint of the future life, but we can — we must — believe that a glorious new experience awaits each one of us beyond this earthly life. The promise of God is summed up in the words of our Lord Jesus Christ himself when he said: "I am the resurrection and the life; he that believeth in me, through he were dead, yet shall he live; and whoever liveth and believeth in me shall never die."

Yes, this is a time for revitalizing our faith in a God of love, but it is also a time when we honor the memory of our loved one, now taken from our sight for a while. There are many manifestations of the love of God in this good world of ours — the beauty of nature, the loyalty and friendship of our neighbors, the glory of a newborn child, and the devotion which binds us together as families. We find God, too, in the lives of individuals who have mirrored in their own words and deeds the divine spark placed in them by their Creator. Not the least of these was Louis Johns, and this memorial service would be incomplete if we did not give thanks for the joy he has brought to us and for the influence of his spirit which shall be ever with us.

We have known Louis Johns in many different capacities. Some of you have known him as a businessman, some as a Mason and a Shriner, some as a churchman, others as a loyal friend. You know what kind of gentleman he was, and you will utter your private prayers of gratitude.

I stand in the enviable position of having known Louis Johns as a family man, and his gracious influence in this capacity is difficult to put into words. I have seen him as a faithful and devoted husband, one whose chief interest in life was to please his mate. One simple

137

illustration of this fact is that for thirty-five years, until her recent death, he provided in his own home a haven for his wife's mother. The married life of Louis and Blanche Johns has been a joy and inspiration to all who have witnessed it. I for one am convinced that such a marriage was conceived in heaven and will continue there when God so wills it.

I have seen Louis Johns as a father, intensely proud of his two daughters and always anxiously watchful of their best interests. I have known him as a father-in-law; in fact, for eight years he has been my only earthly father. I count this relationship as one of the richest blessings of my life and I rejoice in the opportunity to give this testimony. Louis Johns has welcomed both of his sons-in-law into his family and has always been keenly concerned for their welfare. No four children ever had a finer father.

And, finally, I have seen him as a grandfather, a role in which he excelled beyond measure. He gloried in all that the little ones were and did. During the days of his recent illness his thoughts were constantly on the children and nothing brought him greater comfort than to hear and talk about them. The four grandchildren called him "Pompie," a name given to him by the eldest granddaughter in her early attempts to say "Grandpa." The flowers in the vase on the mantel were placed there in the name of the grandchildren to show their love for "Pompie." I close with a story out of the mouth of a babe, which should make this occasion a time of faith and thanksgiving, with rich promises for the future. On Saturday morning, the four-year-old grandson listened to his mother explain that God had taken his grandfather to live in heaven. He thought for a moment, then announced to his mother: "I'm going outdoors and look up in the sky to see if I can find Pompie." Jesus has taught us: "except ye become as little children, ye shall not enter the kingdom of heaven." May we all find an entrance there!

During the summer of 1950 Shirley and I spent a considerable amount of time with her mother as she prepared to begin what proved to be more than thirty years of widowhood. We returned to Bangor in September for the 1950-1951 academic year, during which I continued my work as professor and dean of students.

138

Armed with my Yale doctoral degree, I contemplated a long and fruitful career at the Seminary. As indicated in an earlier chapter, I was installed as a full professor in 1951, but the most significant event of the year for me was the announcement of President Harry Trust that he would resign at the end of the academic year in 1952.

My own appreciation of Dr. Trust will be made known at an appropriate later time. One factor I note here: He was delighted when I was called to fill the faculty vacancy in 1948, and he now revealed to me that he would be pleased to have me succeed him in the presidency. This emboldened me to pursue a goal which I had held since student days: I advised the chairman of the board of trustees, Willard S. Bass, that I should like to be considered as a candidate for the office of president of the Seminary.

Before reaching a decision in the naming of a successor to President Trust, a trustee committee engaged in two major procedures. First, a letter was sent to all installed faculty members inviting them to comment "freely and frankly" on a series of questions concerning the future of the Seminary and the qualifications to be desired in a new president. I replied in a twelve-page, single-spaced letter, the principal points of which I shall summarize below.

On July 12, 1951, I wrote of my firm belief that the Seminary has its central mission in the "unique plan of providing a theological education for students whose academic preparation has been irregular." Thus I agreed with a comprehensive report of 1946 made by Professors Bradshaw, Cumming and Hopkins. This report contained a key recommendation that there should be "a courageous, intensive, prolonged effort ... to strengthen the finances of the Seminary, to increase the number and improve the quality of the students, and to enhance the Seminary's relations with the churches. I concurred, but added the suggestion that the Seminary should also seek to establish more effective relationships with colleges and universities, with denominational officials and representatives of other theological schools, and with the citizens of Bangor and vicinity.

The faculty report of 1946 recommended that the "Junior College," or pre-theological course, be discontinued. I strongly disagreed, and made several suggestions for improving the program, many of which were subsequently implemented. For example, the minimum age for admission of non-college students to the pre-theological department should be raised to 21 years. Further, more of the college-level courses should be taught by adjunct professors from the University of Maine, thus reducing by fifty percent the teaching responsibilities of resident theological faculty. Also, arrangements should be made with other Maine schools such as the University, Bowdoin, Bates, and Colby whereby students with superior academic records at Bangor in the combined pre-theological and theological five-year program would be given senior or advanced-junior standing. This would reduce the time for pre-ordination study from seven to six or six-and-one-half years, thus providing an added incentive for mature students to enroll in the "Bangor plan" and to strive for academic excellence.

My letter contained the following pertinent comment: "Ministry to the rural churches is another important aspect of Bangor's unique mission. During the year just ended, thirty-one of our students served as pastors of churches, some as far away as Washington and Androscoggin Counties. Many of these churches would be closed for lack of leadership if the Seminary were not here ... The Seminary should offer adequate training in rural sociology, a course in pastoral theology which takes account of attitudes and situations peculiar to rural peoples, and supervision of student pastors by a member of the faculty called for this specific purpose ..." (During my administration and beyond, these ideals were effectively fulfilled by Dr. Walter L. Cook as Harry Trust Professor of Preaching and Pastoral Relations and as Field Education Director.)

Another continuing purpose of the Seminary should be to enroll in the theological department an increasing number of students who have completed two years of college work. Such students, I predicted, will undoubtedly constitute the major portion of the student body in the foreseeable future. Bangor would have no unique mission if this were no so. On the other hand, I concurred with the suggestion in the 1946 faculty report that the Seminary should recruit a larger number of college graduates. In this endeavor, however, we are in competition with the better-known standard theological schools. Nevertheless, I maintained that "Bangor offers certain distinct advantages which should appeal to prospective ministers, viz., it has a comparatively small seminary family wherein students receive more individual attention from faculty members and wherein they enjoy intimate personal fellowship. The cost of living and studying at the Seminary is considerably lower than that afforded by other schools. And the opportunities for actual pastoral experience are more numerous and extensive than elsewhere."

In concluding my response to the trustees with respect to the mission and purpose of the Seminary, I emphasized the importance of providing a first-class theological education at a minimum cost to the students. This would involve the establishing of more financial aid and the providing of additional housing for the ever-increasing number of married students coming to the Bangor campus.

Turning to the matter of "Curriculum Needs," I repeated my first priority of adding to the faculty a field education supervisor, and suggested that such an appointee might also serve in my stead as dean of students. I then wrote about another pressing need in the field of Religious Education: "It was my own experience as a Bangor graduate that I was very poorly equipped in this important aspect of modern church leadership; I know that others have had the same problem. Correspondents have told me that there is a serious shortage of directors of religious education and of associate ministers trained in this field. The Seminary has had many requests in recent years for the names of candidates for such positions, but all too often this school has been unable to supply such names. Instruction in religious education would also include the use of audio-visual aids as indispensable to the teaching program of the modern church. (Early in my administration, the first full-time professor of Religious Education was added to the faculty.)

In the area of curriculum needs, I made three other suggestions to the trustees: (1) While the 1946 faculty report had talked about combining the position of Librarian and professor of Religious Education, I believed that two full-time faculty members were required. (2) With the retirement of President Trust, there would be need to add to the faculty a full-time professor to train students in Homiletics and Pastoral Theology. (3) A program of clinical training

141

should become a permanent part of the curriculum through the cooperative efforts of a resident faculty member working with the Eastern Maine General Hospital and the Bangor State Mental Hospital.

My letter to the trustees next turned to another of the principal concerns of the governing board: "The Needs of the Faculty." Historically, the basic cash salary of faculty members had increased over a 20-year period from $3,200 per year to $4,200. I expressed the opinion that the Seminary would not be able to retain its present younger faculty members and secure adequate replacements for those due to retire soon unless a substantial increase in salary was forthcoming. I also questioned the desirability of the common practice among faculty members of supplementing their income by major extra-curricular activity such as interim pastoral work. Other faculty needs delineated were: a formal system of sabbatical leaves, which might encourage an increase in scholarly publication; an addition to the office staff in order to provide secretarial assistance to the Registrar, the Librarian, the Dean of Students, and other faculty members; and continued improvement in retirement provisions through participation in Social Security and the Annuity Fund for Congregational Christian Ministers.

Another major area of concern among the trustees was the matter of physical equipment needs. In my response I underlined the importance of using all available space for the provision of additional apartments for married students, since the number of families had reached fifty percent and was increasing. The student dormitory, Maine Hall, needed greater protection against fire, an ever-present danger because of faulty wiring, lack of electrical outlets, unrestricted smoking, antiquated ladders instead of modern fire escapes, and no sprinkler system. I suggested a long-term plan for a major building program, with special emphasis upon the construction of a new fireproof library. (The Moulton Library was opened in 1957, five years after I became president of the Seminary.)

The most crucial problem facing the Seminary, as I saw it, was the need for additional financial resources. The current operating budget was approximately $80,000. This must be raised to at least $100,000 during the next fiscal year "if the most pressing of the short-term needs of the Seminary are to be met." In this connection I recommended the continuation and the expansion of the "Fellowship" for the purpose of securing additional annual donations from a wide constituency. Long-range, I envisioned a major fund-raising campaign under professional leadership in order to increased the endowment of the Seminary and to provide for necessary capital improvements.

In the immediate future I called for "the adoption of an aggressive and vigorous program of public relations and advertising." I suggested the appointment of a "Field Representative" to the Seminary staff, whose full-time job would be to travel throughout New England and the eastern states telling the "Bangor story," recruiting students, and soliciting financial support. This idea was based upon my railroad experience, which taught me that the placement of field representatives at strategic centers throughout the nation is essential to economic success. I predicted that within the first year such a program would bring returns to the Seminary far in excess of the cost of the project.

Before closing my letter to the trustees with a section on "Qualifications of the President," I included three other suggestions: (1) The number of trustees should be increased to thirty in order to provide for additional alumni members, representatives of denominations other than the Congregational Christian, and more business executives from outside the state of Maine. (2) Since the three groups most concerned with the welfare of the Seminary are the Trustees, the Faculty, and the Alumni, every effort should be made to "keep open and active the various channels of communication among these three groups, to the end that through consultation and concerted action all may make the greatest possible contribution toward the upbuilding of the Seminary." (3) The practice of asking the President of the Seminary to serve as chairman of the Board of Trustees should be discontinued; the Board will function more effectively in the future if the President is associated with it only in an *ex officio* and advisory capacity.

The Board of Trustees asked other faculty members and me to put into writing a list of qualifications for the new President. I listed first, scholastic ability and effectiveness as a teacher. The

President should be of equal stature with other faculty members, and should be enough of a scholar to command the respect of his colleagues. He should be a teaching member of the faculty; close contact with students will be helpful to him when he is called upon to deal with them in an executive capacity.

Second, the President should have enough business and executive ability to visualize and effect a progressive, as distinguished from a conservative or liberal, program for the institution. He should be able to gather a competent and loyal support staff, and then delegate to each member the authority and responsibility which his or her position deserves. He should be qualified to make valid suggestions to the Trustees concerning expenditure of Seminary funds. He should be sympathetic to the personal and professional needs of the Faculty. He should show a genuine interest in the problems of the Alumni. In dealing with students, the President should combine empathy and firmness with regard to such matters as academic standing and financial obligations to the Seminary.

Third, the ability to establish and maintain good public relations is an important attribute of general executive capacity. On the local level the President should maintain active participation in the community through a church and service club, for example. On the wider level, he will promptly answer all correspondence, make personal appearances at significant Church functions, and show a keen interest in denominational affairs. Good public relations will surely include proclaiming the unusual opportunities offered by Bangor Seminary in training a mature Christian ministry for the churches. It will involve asking, without apology, for financial support of the school.

My long letter to the chairman of the Board concluded: "The views expressed in this letter purposely reflect the fact that I am a candidate for the position of President of the Seminary ... Whatever may be the decision of your committee, I trust that the man you choose will be one who knows and appreciates the special place under the sun reserved for Bangor Theological Seminary, and who by his own faith in the divine purpose of the school will evoke the enthusiastic loyalty of its Trustees, its Faculty, and its Alumni."

Apparently my letter to the Board of Trustees struck a responsive chord. The committee to select a new President continued its deliberations throughout the remainder of 1951, but early in the new year I was invited to spend an afternoon in the office of George Eaton, senior member of Bangor's prestigious law firm, Eaton and Peabody. George was a long-time trustee of the Seminary and a member of the selection committee. It was a memorable two hours. George and I also knew each other as fellow members of the Hammond Street Congregational Church. The meeting was friendly enough, but I was somewhat apprehensive because I sensed that my appointment as President of the Seminary hung in the balance. To the best of my ability I answered all of the many questions directed to me. George inquired about my personal and family life, my theology, my political outlook, my relationship with other faculty members, and my attitude toward the Bangor community. When he ended the conversation, we shook hands with a smile and I departed, not really knowing what kind of an impression I had made.

The answer to my dreams and my ambition came three months later at a special meeting of the Seminary Trustees held in Portland, Maine, on May 14, 1952. The official record, communicated to me by Dr. Cornelius E. Clark, Secretary of the Board, tells the story:

"You were unanimously elected the new president of Bangor Theological Seminary, and were authorized to assume the duties of the office on July 1, 1952. The salary is $6,000, plus living accommodations and an annuity. You will be entitled to a vacation of four weeks annually."

9.
President: The Early Years

As I begin the story of my 26-year presidency, it is most appropriate that I start with an expression of gratitude to Dr. Harry Trust, my predecessor. Here was a man who served the Seminary unselfishly and devotedly for nineteen years at an annual cash salary which never exceeded $5,000. My beginning compensation was $1,000 more than he ever received. In remembering Dr. Trust, I recall also the distinctive contributions made to the Seminary by the other presidents who came before me. Without their devoted leadership the Seminary would not now be celebrating the 175th anniversary of its opening in 1816.

Bangor Seminary is more — much more — than the life of its presidents, but occasionally we do well to recollect the heritage they have left to those who carry on the noble tradition of this "school of the prophets," a phrase which was often on the lips of Harry Trust. It is pertinent to note that the first five presidents of Bangor served for a total span of exactly 100 years, with an average tenure of precisely two decades. The historian in me calls attention to the fact that the Seminary managed to survive two long periods — from 1816 to 1857 and from 1882 to 1903 — without presidential leadership. This twice-used practice of leaving the administrative tasks to the senior faculty member has happily been abandoned

146

since the early twentieth century.

Enoch Pond was officially the president of the Seminary — or rather "The Maine Charity School," as it was then known — for twenty-five years. His service to the school spanned half a century, however, beginning in 1832 when he became Professor of Christian Theology. He is widely acknowledged to be the one who established the Seminary on a firm foundation. The western boundary of the campus, Pond Street, is named in his honor, as is the old schoolhouse in which student families now live. The Enoch Pond Lectures on Applied Christianity remind us at Convocation time of our debt to the first president. His portrait hangs in the entrance to the Seminary chapel.

The influence of David Nelson Beach upon the Seminary has continued far beyond his eighteen-year term as President, which ended in 1921. His spirit has lived on the campus in recent years through his son who bore the same name and was a trustee emeritus until his death in 1990. President Beach will be perpetually memorialized for establishing the unique and widely-famous Convocation program, which has been an annual feature of the Seminary year since 1905. Equally important to the school and its constituents is the Bachelor of Divinity (now Master of Divinity) academic degree, which was formalized during the Beach administration. It is entirely fitting that the Seminary's second president should be honored each year during the David Nelson Beach Quiet Hour at Convocation, and that his portrait should hang in the beautiful and worshipful chapel sanctuary which bears his name.

When Warren Joseph Moulton became Bangor's third president in 1921, he had already served the school with distinction for sixteen years as its Professor of New Testament Language and Literature. His twelve years as chief executive, although comparatively short in duration, were filled with major achievements. He was widely acclaimed as a New Testament scholar, served as director of the American School of Oriental Research in Jerusalem, and was president for two years of the forerunner of the Association of Theological Schools in the United States and Canada. Some of his administrative accomplishments included the improvement of buildings and grounds, a doubling of the endowment, a substantial increase in the number of students, and the addition of two new academic departments. He also inaugurated "The Alumni Bulletin" as the Seminary's scholarly journal. When he died he left the school a bequest of $200,000, part of which was inherited from his wife Helen. (He could not have saved such a sum from his meagre salary.) When the new library was built in 1958 there was unanimous agreement that it should be named for Warren and Helen Moulton.

Dr. Moulton made one other vital contribution to the Seminary: he nominated as his successor the Reverend Harry Trust, an alumnus who had been one of his students twenty years earlier. It was the friendship, the guidance, the encouragement, and the example of Harry Trust which enabled me to become a theological student, a Christian minister, a professor of history, and a seminary president. My earliest recollection of Dr. Trust is related to the correspondence we exchanged which led to my acceptance as a student at Bangor after ten years of work with a railroad company. He assured me that there was a place for me under "the Bangor plan." It was the fourth president who perfected this unusual program in 1938 by adding a second year of liberal arts study and establishing the "pre-theological department" for non-college graduates.

From my student days through my early presidential years until his death, Harry Trust was my "pastor." This was a witness which came naturally for him, for he had served for twenty years as minister to churches in Maine and Ohio before coming to the Bangor presidency. When Shirley and I were married in 1940, Harry Trust was there. When I needed him to celebrate communion and receive church members when I was a student pastor in remote eastern Washington County, Harry Trust was there. When my father died prematurely during my student days at Bangor, Harry Trust was there. When I was ordained as a Christian minister, Harry Trust was there. And when I aspired to be a professor of church history, and later the president, at Bangor Seminary, Harry Trust was there.

My illustrious predecessor was a man of piety and of faith. He transformed a storage room on the second floor of the chapel building into a beautiful sanctuary, complete with stained glass windows and organ, which was the worship center for a generation

148

of Bangor students and faculty. Services were held five days a week and the president was always in attendance unless he was away from the city. Moreover, he expected the students to join him in worship — and he told them so! My own absence was a rarity, as it was throughout the years. Unfortunately, one of the failures of my administration was the inability to inspire, despite precept and example, the kind of piety through corporate worship which permeated the old chapel in the "upper room."

The faith of Harry Trust, nurtured by nineteen years of daily worship on the Seminary hill and in a local church, was manifested in numerous ways. He presided over the school during the years of the "great depression" and World War II in the decades of the thirties and forties. Through diligent work and in confidence that his God would sustain him, he brought the Seminary through the most difficult administrative years any Bangor president has known. By personal testimony, he exemplified belief in the gospel of eternal life proclaimed by Jesus Christ when death twice came to the Trust household; Harry and his wife Lillian were both seriously injured in an automobile accident which eventually was a contributing cause of her early demise; an even greater tragedy was transcended when the first son of the Trust family, Knowlton, was a victim of polio at the age of twenty-six, just a few months after he had earned the Ph.D. degree and had begun a teaching career.

Harry Trust was a churchman from the day he began his Christian service in his native England as an agent of the British Colonial Missionary Society. While he was Bangor's president emeritus and until shortly before he died, he was pastor of a church in Lenox, Massachusetts. His belief in the institutional "body of Christ" never wavered as he gave himself freely as both a minister and a layman to churches in Maine and in many places beyond. He often remarked that Seminary professors would be most effective if they maintained an active relationship with a local congregation. This is a bit of advice which I have taken seriously throughout my career — still another reason why I am deeply grateful to my predecessor.

Before ending this tribute, I call attention to one other lesson learned from Harry Trust. His first address as president of Bangor

Seminary was entitled, "A Creative Ministry." Here are a few excerpts: "The modern minister must live among men. He cannot live apart or expect to be placed on a pedestal as an idol. He must show that the Christian life can be lived on the ground floor of everyday human experience ... In order to exercise a creative ministry a pastor must have a real understanding of modern problems ... He will know the story of outstanding political movements. He will familiarize himself with the social and welfare life of his community ..."

Harry Trust was a distinguished citizen of Bangor. He was a principal organizer and then president of the Bangor Executives' Club. Following the example of his predecessor, Warren Moulton, he was president of the Bangor club and later district governor of Rotary International. He was a pioneer in efforts to unite in cooperative endeavors the local Jewish and Christian communities; before the ecumenical movement reached its fruition, he was a leader in creating friendly relationships between Roman Catholic and Protestant groups in Bangor. Needless to say, I am one among many who are indebted to Harry Trust for his social and cultural vision.

It has been almost thirty years since Harry Trust finished his earthly pilgrimage. His mark is indelible upon the history of Bangor Seminary. His Christian witness will not be forgotten, especially if his admirers proclaim their debt to him from time to time. Thus I deem it an honor and a privilege, as I recount my own presidency of the Seminary, to recall the life and ministry of one of our "saints who from their labors rest."

In announcing the transition from the Trust to the Whittaker administrations, The Alumni Bulletin of July, 1952, carried the headline, "The Mantle of Elijah ... Upon Elisha Falls." One of my first duties as the new president was to submit to the Board of Trustees a budget report for the coming fiscal year beginning July 1, 1952. In that report I set forth principles which became hallmarks of my long administration: "It is the president's place to ask for sufficient funds to support an adequate faculty, to employ a competent staff, to keep the buildings and grounds in good repair, and to make possible a program of ever-expanding influence and

150

service by the Seminary. It is also the president's place to cooperate with the trustees in devising ways and means of securing the necessary funds." There was no major deviation from these principles at Bangor for the next twenty-six years.

My first request was for the addition of two members to the resident faculty. One of these was to be a professor of rural sociology and pastoral theology, who would also serve as director of field work with the thirty-five students then serving as pastors of churches. When the new academic year opened in September the Reverend Leonard M. Sizer began his work in this new position. He was a native of Iowa and came to the Seminary from a position as an associate pastor of the First Baptist Church in Iowa City. He was a graduate of Andover Newton Theological School and a Ph.D. candidate at the State University of Iowa. As a Baptist, Sizer added a welcome ecumenical dimension to the Bangor faculty.

My second budget request was for funds to permit the appointment of a full-time professional librarian, who might also be qualified to assume some teaching responsibilities in the pre-theological department. The trustees fulfilled this request by calling the Reverend David J. Siegenthaler of Baltimore, Maryland, to be Seminary librarian effective September 1, 1952. Mr. Siegenthaler was a graduate of Franklin and Marshall College and Yale University. He was an ordained minister of the Evangelical and Reformed Church and had been employed as a serial cataloguer in the Yale Divinity School library. He represented a denomination which later merged with the Congregational Christian Churches to form the United Church of Christ.

My first budget also proposed to raise the salaries of the four installed members of the faculty by $500 to $4,500. I was careful to point out that the new figure was no higher than the salary received by at least four of the ministers serving local Bangor churches. The increase was granted, perhaps because I also reminded the trustees that the four professors involved — Charles Cumming, Alfred Perry, Marion Bradshaw, and Andrew Banning — had given a total of one hundred years of devoted service to the Seminary. Modest salary increases were also requested, and granted, for members of the visiting faculty from the University of Maine, for

151

the secretary to the president, and for the maintenance staff.

From the first days of my tenure as president I was keenly aware of the vital importance of the faculty to the Seminary. I shall always remember with deep gratitude the kindness of the four senior professors — Cumming, Perry, Bradshaw, and Banning — in accepting and supporting the new young president who had only a decade earlier been one of their students. I record also my longstanding appreciation of the University of Maine and its officers for permitting its faculty members to teach in the pre-theological liberal arts and sciences program at the Seminary. Without their dedicated and effective service the famous "Bangor plan" for non-college graduates would never have been possible. The name of David W. Trafford deserves special mention. He taught history courses at Bangor throughout my administrative years and beyond. While I was president, he was given faculty status at the Seminary and for many years filled with distinction the office of Director of Liberal Studies, all the while carrying out his responsibilities as a full-time professor at the state university. When he retired during the administration of my successor, Dr. Wayne Glick, Dr. Trafford was appropriately named Professor Emeritus of the Seminary.

In 1952 the secretary to the president was Elsie M. Olmstead. She had held this position since the time of President Warren J. Moulton and throughout the incumbency of Dr. Harry Trust. For more than twenty years she had been the only office staff member at the Seminary and, except for the president, she was the chief executive officer of the school in practice if not in title. She was much beloved by a generation of students and alumni, who came to depend upon her for many services. She was of invaluable help to me in the first years of my presidency, but grew restive and unhappy as the Seminary policies changed and the office staff expanded. Her service with me ended after six years.

The maintenance staff of the Seminary has always been underpaid and too few in number. During my early years as president there were only three men employed to care for fifteen old buildings (1895 was the construction date of the newest one), to keep up the appearance of a 10-acre campus, and to operate an antiquated central heating plant. That I inherited some deferred maintenance is illustrated by the list of improvements in the physical property contained in my first budget report to the trustees: new roof shingles on a wing of the New Commons (built in 1836), on the ell of a student apartment building, and on the home of one of the professors; a new kitchen and bathroom in another faculty home; replacement of stair treads in the student dormitory; new floor covering and wallpaper for the Seminary dining room; and improvements in the boiler room. A cost-of-living salary increase of five dollars per week for the maintenance staff was really not adequate compensation for Elwood Cookson, the superintendent of buildings and grounds, and his assistants, John and Donald Knowles; these three and those who followed after them were unsung heroes of life on the Bangor campus.

One of the distinguishing features of Seminary social life through the years has been the continuous operation of a campus dining room. Not many theological schools as small as Bangor have successfully maintained such a facility. In my student days we could always count on Albert Dorr and his wife to provide three good meals a day for hungry young men and women. Mrs. Gladys Covel was the steward in the 1950's, and she faithfully carried on the tradition of being a "mother" to many students by feeding them and counselling them when homesickness or other personal problems arose. The dining room was also the perennial setting for hospitality during Convocation Week, meetings of the board of trustees, and special events for students and faculty. This facility, so vital to campus living, was located in the New Commons for generations until it was relocated during the Glick administration in the "Wellman Commons," formerly the gymnasium. Subsidizing the dining room operation was a continual drain on the Seminary budget, but has been a feature of gracious significance well worth every dollar spent.

During my first year as president, steps were taken to enhance the financial condition of the Seminary. A modest increase was made in student charges. Since its establishment Bangor has been a low-cost school. No tuition was charged until the mid-1940s; it was indeed, as the early name implied, "The Maine Charity School." In 1952 the annual academic charge was only $150; it was raised then to $200. Similar modest increases were made in dormitory fees and dining room costs. It was obvious, however, that only a major campaign for additional annual gifts and capital funds would meet the needs of the school, not the least of which was a new library. The financial fortune of the Seminary took a significant upward turn with the appointment by the trustees of a vice president, effective September 1, 1953.

Daniel W. Fenner was a graduate of the Seminary in 1951. He had entered the school in 1948 as a student, the same year I began my Bangor career as a professor. I was favorably impressed by his academic ability and by his speaking talent. In order to provide for his wife Robin and their three children, he had successfully candidated, before enrolling at the Seminary, for the pastorate of the Federated Church in Solon, Maine. In 1949 he moved to Skowhegan and became minister of its Federated Church. He had studied at Hamilton College in Clinton, New York, and was a recent graduate of Colby College. After he had been on the Seminary staff for a few years he was awarded the Doctor of Divinity degree by New England College. I was also aware of Dr. Fenner's success in the business world before he came to the Seminary. In this respect he was typical of the many hundreds of non-college graduates who enrolled in the unique "Bangor plan" in order to prepare for a second career in the Christian ministry after being an active layman. For ten years he had been a salesman for the American Rolling Mill Company of Middletown, Ohio. Later he was the founder and owner of an insulating and waterproofing concern in Glens Falls and Utica, New York.

I knew that Dan Fenner was the man I wanted to be vice president of the Seminary in charge of its fund-raising activities when I discovered during his Bangor student days he was earning more money as a minister in Skowhegan than the professors who were teaching him at the Seminary. At least, that was one of the selling points I used in convincing the trustees to employ him. During his tenure as vice president the financial status of the school improved and a capital gift campaign succeeded in raising $300,000 for a new library. This story will unfold as these memoirs continue.

Early in my presidency, attention was also given to strengthening

154

the governing board of the Seminary by adding trustees with experience in the business world. At the semi-annual meeting of the board in December of 1952 there was acceptance of my nomination of Ellison F. Beckwith of Lexington, Massachusetts. He and his wife Druscilla had been my friends since early church days in New Haven. Beckwith had long been associated with the Phoenix Mutual Life Insurance Company of Hartford, Connecticut, and had served as field supervisor in their offices from Portland, Maine, to Washington, D.C.; he was then an executive field underwriter with offices in Boston and Lexington. Throughout my administration and beyond, "El" Beckwith has been my personal friend and strong supporter in Seminary affairs. Within a year he had succeeded in bringing to the Board James U. Crockett of Concord, Massachusetts, a horticulturalist with strong church affiliation who served the school effectively and loyally during all the years of my tenure. Jim later became famous as author of the Time-Life series of books on gardening and as host of the popular television show "Crockett's Victory Garden." Jim and Margaret Crockett became life-long friends of the Whittakers.

During the 1950's the Board of Trustees performed yeoman service in guiding and supporting the new young president. For four years, until his death in 1956, Willard S. Bass of Wilton, Maine, senior officer of the Bass Shoe Company, led his colleagues in a cooperative venture with the president which greatly strengthened the academic and financial condition of the Seminary. He and I had a kind of father-son relationship, and I still wear with pride his academic robe, which he gave to me before he died. His successor as Board chairman was alumnus Clarence W. Fuller, who filled the office with wisdom and integrity for more than two decades while also serving as minister of the First Congregational Church of Melrose, Massachusetts.

Among the first trustees with whom I worked were men I have long remembered with admiration and gratitude. They included: Dr. Rodney W. Roundy, who as Maine Conference Minister, gave me my career start as student-minister in Washington County; his successor, Dr. Cornelius E. Clark, long-time secretary of the Board; Dr. Frederick M. Meek, for whom I worked as student assistant

155

during my first year at Bangor and with whom I was associated in ecumenical endeavors later on; Charles F. Bragg 2nd, leading Bangor business executive and Seminary treasurer for many years; two justices of the Maine Supreme Court, Robert B. Williamson and Donald W. Webber; John Lowell of Boston and Fred Goodrich of New York, both of them bank executives; James A. Gannett, registrar of the University of Maine at Orono, and Dr. Athern P. Daggett, professor at Bowdoin College; Dr. Fred Thompson, minister of Woodfords Church in Portland; Dr. David Nelson Beach, pastor of Center Church in New Haven and same-name son of the Seminary's second president; Bangor insurance executives Donald S. Higgins and Arthur G. Eaton; the Reverend Frederick D. Hayes of High Street Church in Auburn; L. Felix Ranlett, librarian of the Bangor Public Library; and alumni Richard Beyer, Ned McKenney, and Alfred Hempstead.

The dedicated Bursar of the Seminary was Franklin W. Eaton of Bangor, an investment specialist who later became a trustee of the school. He, Charles Bragg, and I managed to keep the financial affairs of the Seminary on an even keel through the years, although the two of them were more conservative than I in fiscal matters. I was always certain that more unrestricted funds would be forthcoming when needed to balance the annual budget, while they argued that we should not spend in any given year more dollars than we received in annual gifts. In any event, for twenty-six years the Seminary remained free of debt and balanced its annual operating budget with the help of a few thousand dollars taken from unrestricted funds functioning as endowment; the saving factor, I confess, was the continuing donation to these endowment funds by Seminary benefactors. Despite our frequent skirmishes in meetings of the Board, Charles, Franklin, and I are still good friends.

The first momentous event of my presidency was my inauguration as the Seminary's fifth chief executive at a formal ceremony on June 1, 1953, in the Hammond Street Congregational Church. I was escorted to the church by a procession which included the inaugural officers, the board of trustees, the faculty, the senior class, and the delegates representing educational institutions throughout the United States. The induction of the president was performed by Willard S. Bass, chairman of the trustees, and the charge to the president was given by Dean Vaughan Dabney of Andover Newton Theological School. Dr. Harry Trust, president emeritus of the Seminary, offered the inaugural prayer, and the benediction was given by Dr. Charles Gordon Cumming, senior member of the Seminary faculty. A dinner honoring the new president was attended by 200 guests at the Bangor House. Among the speakers were Dr. Roswell P. Bates, speaker of the Maine House of Representatives, who brought greetings from Governor Burton M. Cross; Dr. Tertius VanDyke of the Hartford Theological Seminary, who spoke on behalf of the Association of Theological Schools; and President James Stacy Coles, president of Bowdoin College.

The inaugural address was entitled "Toward a More Mature Ministry." It is included in these memoirs in its entirety because of its significance as an historical document and because it sets forth the philosophy and the program which became the platform of the Seminary for many years to come. The address was published in the July, 1953, issue of the Seminary's "Alumni Bulletin," as follows:

In the Gospel according to St. Matthew it is recorded that, "Jesus, walking by the Sea of Galilee, saw two brethren, Simon called Peter, and Andrew his brother, casting a net into the sea; for they were fishers. And he saith unto them, follow me, and I will make you fishers of men. And they straightway left their nets and followed him." From this humble beginning on the shores of an ancient sea there has grown the worldwide Christian enterprise of which we are a part today. The churches in which we worship, the schools in which we teach, the professions in which we work, the homes in which we live, have all been influenced — directly or indirectly — by what one of our great historians, Kenneth Scott Latourette, has called "the impulse from Jesus." For more than nineteen hundred years men and women have continued to hear the call of the Master and have become his disciples. It is this fact which makes possible the sacred occasion we celebrate today. We have not gathered here to honor an individual human being. At the very least we are met together to bring tribute to an institution

157

which for 139 years has been educating leaders for the ongoing Christian movement.

All of us who have been associated in any way with Bangor Theological Seminary are immensely proud of its long record of service to the Kingdom of God. But it is my earnest desire that what is said here now shall rise above praise for person or institution into the realm of what Jesus called "good works" for the glory of our "Father which is in heaven." To that end I speak to you concerning my conception of the role to be played by the Seminary as one instrument of the divine purpose. The theme of this address, "Toward a More Mature Ministry," requires development in three different phases, although all of them are interrelated. The three phases may be symbolized by the simple interrogations: "Why?," "Who?," and "How?"

The first question to be asked is, "Why is there need for a more mature ministry?" The answer to this inquiry calls for a definition of the term "mature," and this will be given in due time. Meanwhile, my concern is to show the apparent failure of the leadership of the modern church to inspire a faith in the laity sufficient for their salvation. It is true, as Dr. Latourette has pointed out, that Christianity is more widely spread, more deeply rooted, among more diverse peoples, than ever before in its history. **It is also true that church membership and church attendance in the United States** is at a record height. And still the civilized world totters on the brink of chaos, in spite of all that Christianity can do. On the international scene, where the Christian doctrine of the brotherhood of all men has the potential power to insure peace, the nations stand poised for a third world war in half a century. In our national life, this land which was founded by men of strong faith now is encompassed by fear and distrust, by lust for wealth and power. As a people we spend many times more money for gambling and alcoholic beverages than we do for education and philanthropy. In our personal lives the signs of spiritual and moral decay are all too manifest. The family is the basic unit of the Christian life, but the percentage of divorce is at an all-time high and continues to advance. And what of individual souls, who by the grace of communion with God in Christ should find contentment in their *daily work and comfort in their times of trouble? Statistics tell us that our mental hospitals cannot possibly admit all their prospective patients, and there is abundant evidence that as a whole we are a highly nervous people.*

Some of you will say that I paint too dark a picture, and others will suggest that the Christian ministry is not wholly to blame for the plight of modern man. These are valid criticisms, but I do insist that the human situation is not nearly as hopeful as it might be under more effective leadership by those in high clerical office. It has been a part of my philosophy to retain as much as possible of the layman's point of view toward the role of Christianity in our contemporary society. Before beginning theological studies it was my privilege to serve in various lay capacities in a large city church. This is an experience indispensable to what I have called "a more mature ministry." Throughout the ensuing years many of the most valuable contributions to my own thinking — to my own theology, if you will — have been made by my intimate friends among the laity. Much of what is to follow will reflect this fact. Only recently two of these friends have urged upon me the importance of evaluating the effectiveness of seminary training in terms of service rendered by the ministers it produces. These two friends represent a widely-held opinion that the Christian Church has not yet activated its potential power for good in the world, and in view of the actual condition of our civilization in the so-called Christian era there seems to be ample evidence to answer the question, "Why is there need for a more mature ministry?"

The next consideration involves a definition of the term "mature." In this connection permit me to quote from a "Prospectus for Bangor Theological Seminary" which I presented earlier today to the Board of Trustees. In this document the following is set forth as the "General Objective" of the Seminary: "To train ministers for Christian churches who will be prepared to meet the changed and changing religious needs of individuals, and who will so lead the local and worldwide Christian movement that the corporate witness of the Church will be a redemptive factor in the continuing society of man." In explanation of this objective the Prospectus lists three "Specific Aims" of the Seminary, and reference to these will further illustrate the meaning of maturity in the ministry.

The first specific aim is "to produce ministers adequately trained in all fields of knowledge related to their total task, including practical as well as academic disciplines." For example, the minister should be acquainted with modern sociology, psychology, and business practice. The second aim is "to train ministers who will preserve whatever values there are in denominational doctrine and polity, but who will be leaders in the ecumenical movement toward a united Christian fellowship." And the third specific aim of the Seminary, as I envision it, is "to train ministers who will be active in the life of the community as a whole while not neglecting the appointed work of the Church. For example, the minister should participate in educational, civic, and public service activities."

This definition of a "mature" ministry involves certain theological presuppositions which deserve expression. It is my conviction that the religious needs of individuals and of social institutions can only be met in our day by a theology which is essentially optimistic about the relationship existing between God and man, and which gives man a role to play in the divine drama of personal and corporate salvation. The mature minister is one who believes in a God who is both transcendental and imminent, a God who is both the Creator and the Sustainer of the universe. This God partially reveals Himself in THIS world through the natural order of physical being, through the spiritual and moral factors which distinguish men from other creatures, and reveals Himself especially through the life and teachings of Jesus Christ. However, for the full revelation of God, men must await the eternal life yet to come for all who accept the Gospel proclaimed by Christ.

The mature minister is one who believes that Jesus Christ is the Son of God, but who believes that men are the sons of God and that they differ from Christ in degree but not in kind. He believes that the apparent sinfulness of man is a relative phenomenon; that man, the creature of a good God, is himself basically good; and that man has the power, through the free will granted by the Creator, to diminish progressively the control of evil over his individual and corporate life as he responds more and more to the gracious influence of God's continuing and manifold revelation. There is need for a more mature ministry so that this kind of a Gospel may be preached to a waiting world.

The second major question to be discussed is this: "Who will provide this more mature ministry?" It will be most adequately offered, I believe, by men who can explain from personal experience the meaning of birth and death, of suffering and sorrow. It will be given in fullest measure by men who, from first-hand knowledge, can teach the significance of the moral law with regard to marriage, labor-management problems, political issues, and the social evils of drinking, gambling, and war. It will be provided by men who have lived for a while among the people to whom they must preach the Word of God. Candidates for the ministry who move from home to college to seminary to parish are less likely to be adequately prepared for their chosen profession than those who have dwelt for a time in the world where laymen live.

Today's Church needs ministers who have mingled with the crowds of the marketplace; who have felt the give-and-take of the business world; who have lived long enough to marry, to become fathers, to know disappointment, and to experience the pangs of suffering and sorrow. The man who has sold life insurance will know how to sell the Christian Gospel. The man who has managed his own business will be more efficient at managing God's business in the Church. The man who has served in political office will recognize the proper relationship between Church and State as two co-relative instruments of the divine purpose. The man who has studied human laws will know how to apply more wisely the laws of God. The man who has taught the facts of human history will be better able to explain the controlling and guiding power of the Creator in this dramatic narrative. The man who has seen his loved ones suffer and die will speak with authority about the Christian faith and hope.

There is today a serious shortage of workers in practically every phase of professional Christian service. I believe that the Church has a comparatively untapped source of supply in this hour of its need. Sitting in the pews of our sanctuaries each Sunday morning are thousands of mature men and women who would gladly leave their present occupations and prepare for full-time service as leaders of the Church if they were encouraged by their ministers and shown how they could become "fishers of men." The first ministers of Christ were men called by Jesus to leave their nets by the Sea of Galilee and follow him. There are many such dissatisfied "fishermen" among the laity of our churches who are unhappy about the way they are spending their lives and who are waiting only for a "call" challenging them to change vocations.

I know whereof I speak, for I spent ten years in the employment of a railroad company before deciding to study for the Christian ministry. Moreover, during the past three years I have been presenting that challenge from the pulpits of many New England churches, with encouraging results. But the most convincing proof of my proposition is to be found in the history and the present status of Bangor Theological Seminary. Since the granting of its charter in 1814 this school has specialized in offering a thorough and scholarly training to mature men who have felt the call to Christian service after years of work in other fields. Half of the present student body consists of married men, many of whom have left other occupations in order to become leaders of the Church. One of our students is a man over fifty years of age, three others are in their forties, several are in their thirties, and a large number of others are more than twenty-five years old.

Among our recent graduates there are some outstanding illustrations of the unique mission of Bangor in making it possible for older men to prepare for the ministry. One such alumnus was thirty-five years old when he enrolled as a student. He had come to this country from his native Holland in search of a theological education, and because his academic training had been somewhat irregular he found that our program best fitted his needs. For several years he had been a book publisher and salesman in his native land and in the Dutch East Indies. During World War II he had been captured by the Japanese in Java and interned for three years in a prison camp. He served as a lay chaplain to his fellow prisoners, and out of that experience grew a conviction that he wanted to become a minister of the Christian Gospel. Today he is the pastor of one of our New England churches, and he is a living example of my conviction that the modern Christian movement will prosper under a more mature ministry.

The pastor of one of our larger churches in Maine came to this Seminary for training at the age of thirty-nine after a successful career as the principal of a private school in Massachusetts. One who now serves in a metropolitan church in New Hampshire was educated here after several years of experience in a retail clothing business in Florida. And still another left the advertising business in order to prepare for a ministry which has called him to Connecticut, then to Rhode Island, and now to Massachusetts. These are but a chosen few of the long line of men who have changed vocations in order to answer the ancient call of the Master. The following is a partial list of the professions and trades which have provided a background of experience for the mature ministry being given by Bangor graduates: teaching, accounting, insurance, advertising, baking, banking, farming, printing, salesmanship, lumbering, tool-making, textiles, shoe-making, mining, clerical work, Y.M.C.A. work, and, of course, the original Christian trade of carpentry.

Thus I present to you my answer to the question, "Who will provide this more mature ministry?" The position presented here is subject to criticism by those who believe that the principal supply of candidates for the ministry must continue to be young men just out of high school and college. There is no doubt that this source should be thoroughly cultivated. Bangor Seminary will always welcome qualified candidates among the younger men, especially those who have met their military obligations to the nation. It is my thesis, however, that there is a huge reservoir of potential ministers among mature men, and it is my intent that Bangor shall continue to provide an "open door" for them. This has been the Seminary's unique mission, and we are encouraged to maintain it by testimony such as this from the spiritual leader of one of our larger denominations: "There is increasing demand everywhere for men in the ministry who have had first-hand experience in the areas in which the people of the pews live their lives ... If institutions like Bangor did not exist, they would have to be invented."

There remains to be answered this third major question: "How shall a more mature ministry be trained?" My reply is colored by the fact that I believe the so-called "Bangor plan" to be an adequate and proper instrument for the educating of such a ministry. My conviction at this point was an important factor in the decision of the Board of Trustees to elect me to this cherished position. It is my purpose to carry out the wishes of the Trustees so long as it is their considered judgment, concurred in by the faculty, that our training program is valid and necessary. We are strengthened in our aim by the testimony, for example, of the president of a most prominent theological school, who has written: "Bangor is performing a unique function and one which is indispensable in the total program of theological education in the country."

Reference to the charter of the Seminary will disclose the clue to its unusual academic policy. The school was established for the avowed purpose of "promoting religion and morality, and the education of youth in such languages, and in such of the liberal arts and sciences, as the Trustees thereof shall from time to time judge the most useful and expedient for the purposes of said Seminary." Under the provisions of this charter, the Seminary has continued to educate prospective Christian ministers in both general and theological subjects. The major exception to this policy is that students holding the A.B. degree or its equivalent from some accredited college or university are required to study only theological subjects. At this point Bangor follows the standard practice of other seminaries and grants the Bachelor of Divinity degree upon the successful completion of the three-year curriculum.

However, the great majority of students who matriculate at Bangor come to the school with little or no formal training in general subjects beyond the high school level. To these students the Seminary offers on its own campus, in cooperation with the University of Maine, a two-year course in the liberal arts and sciences. Most of the subjects are taught by visiting professors from the University, although in two or three instances instruction is given by resident members of the Seminary faculty. All of the subjects are carefully prescribed in accordance with the recommendations of the American Association of Theological Schools in its "Statement on Pre-theological Studies." The two-year course includes sixty-eight semester hours of study divided among the following subjects: English composition and literature, philosophy, Bible, history, psychology, Greek language, the natural sciences and the social sciences.

Upon the successful completion of the pre-theological course, students are admitted to the Seminary's three-year course in theological subjects; this latter course is similar to that offered in other seminaries. The Bangor plan deviates from the norm by admitting students to the theological curriculum on the basis of two years rather than four years of pre-seminary college work. It does so for reasons which will be explained in a moment. When students have met all the requirements of this combination five-year course, the Seminary awards them a diploma but no degree. In order to qualify for the Bachelor of Divinity degree the graduates of the Seminary diploma course must then complete their arts and sciences studies by enrolling as transfer students in some accredited college or university of their choice. Only when students have achieved the Bachelor of Arts degree or its equivalent do they become eligible for the Seminary's degree. This usually requires one and a half to two years in addition to the five years spent in the Seminary, the length of time depending upon the academic ability of the individual student.

To state the case more simply, under the "Bangor plan" qualified candidates for the Christian ministry may earn the A.B. and B.D. degrees in seven years, the normal time required under the standard plan of theological education. The standard plan calls for four years of college studies plus three years of theological work. The Bangor plan divides the four years of college studies by interposing the three-year theological curriculum between the sophomore and junior years. We at Bangor recognize the value of the standard four-plus-three program of theological education, but we believe that our unusual two-plus three-plus two program is providing a valid and necessary medium for the training of the mature men and women we have traditionally served. There are at least three reasons why this is so.

First, there is a psychological reason for the appeal which our program has for older men. Many of them are willing to begin their college studies in a seminary where other older men are enrolled, whereas they would hesitate to enter a regular college as freshmen. They feel, too, that they are closer to their chosen profession as members of a seminary family. As a matter of fact, many of these older men begin actual work as student pastors in neighboring churches within a short time after entering the school. This suggests a second, and very practical, reason for the appeal of our program: Tuition and other costs are unusually low, and apartments for married students are available at a nominal rental. Moreover, the strategic location of the Seminary in the heart of rural Maine affords ample opportunity for competent men to serve as student pastors. This service, which is carefully supervised by our Director of Student Field Work, is welcomed by the fifty churches now receiving their ministry, and, in turn, the students are grateful not only for the experience itself but for the chance to earn a portion of their expenses. Thus many men begin their actual ministry long before such an opportunity would be available to them if they were enrolled in a four-year college course, and this means that through the Bangor plan the way is opened to large numbers who could not otherwise afford to enter the clerical profession.

In the third place, I dare to suggest in this learned company that there are pedagogical reasons why our program is desirable. It is quite possible that our students receive more benefit from their liberal arts and theological studies under our two-plus three-plus two schedule than do other students under the standard four-plus three plan commonly in use. Graduates of our five-year combination course certainly have the advantage in their last two years of college of knowing exactly which studies to pursue, and their three years of training in theology is a distinct asset to them. Moreover, students trained in our two-year pre-theological course, which is planned for a specific vocation and in accordance with the recommendation of the American Association of Theological Schools, are at least as well prepared for theological studies as many graduates of four-year college courses who have not concentrated their attention and interest upon the recommended pre-theological liberal arts subjects. Bangor Theological Seminary offers an integrated course of college and theological studies to men and women who are committed throughout a seven-year period of preparation to the high calling of ministering in the name of Christ. It has proven through the years, by the witness of its alumni in large and small parishes throughout New England and beyond, that it is capable of training both older and younger students for a mature Christian ministry.

Permit me to make a few comments concerning the future. The "Prospectus" to which I referred earlier, and which was approved by the Board of Trustees at its annual meeting today, calls for a program of expansion between now and 1964, when the Seminary will celebrate the 150th anniversary of the granting of its charter. It is our purpose to conduct a research project designated to determine the strengths and weaknesses in the present ministry of Seminary graduates; to discover the actual religious needs of individuals; to re-examine the place and promise of the Church in society; and to suggest remedial action to be taken through the faculty and the curriculum of the Seminary. The curriculum will be established in accordance with the findings of the research project, and a resident and visiting faculty will be engaged to fulfill the curriculum needs.

It is our plan to enroll eventually a student body of two hundred, comprised approximately as follows: fifty percent mature students with incomplete academic preparation, but with some experience in another vocation; twenty-five percent college graduates; and twenty-five percent young students of unusual promise with good high school academic records. The realization of this goal will require an enlarged faculty and a new-building program. In the way of buildings we shall need at least the following: adequate dormitory space, apartments for married students, a fire-proof library, a chapel, auditorium, infirmary, administration offices, and classrooms. It will be necessary, of course, to conduct a campaign for new funds adequate to meet the needs of the Seminary's expanded program; these funds should include permanent endowments, annual gifts for operating expenses, and special gifts.

A most important step has already been taken toward the goal we seek. The Board of Trustees created last December the new office of Vice President of the Seminary, and this office will be occupied, effective September 1st of this year, by the Reverend

167

Daniel W. Fenner, now minister of the Federated Church in Skowhegan, Maine. Mr. Fenner is himself a product of the "Bangor plan," having come to the Seminary for theological training after thirteen years as a business executive. Out of this background of training and experience he will travel extensively in order to recruit students and solicit funds; with the assistance of the President he will carry on the Seminary's program of promotion and public relations. I would urge upon you, however, that the administrative staff will need in this whole expansion project the consecrated support of the faculty, the trustees, the alumni, the churches, and that ever-increasing host of Christian friends who comprise the "Fellowship" of Bangor Theological Seminary.

This, then, is my answer to the question, "How shall a more mature ministry be trained?" But some will surely ask, "Can it be done?" In reply I tell you a short story: Under the glass top of my office desk, where I see it every day, is a clipping from Time magazine dated September 8, 1952, which reports the completion of the new building program of Colby College and the establishment of the beautiful campus on Mayflower Hill in Waterville. Credit for this seven million dollar achievement is given primarily to Dr. Franklin W. Johnson, former president of the College, for it was his faith and hard work that gave impetus to the project. Dr. Johnson's philosophy is summed up in one sentence — which I have taken as my own, and offer now to you — "ANYTHING that OUGHT to be done CAN be done!"

Throughout the preparation of this address — and during its delivery — I have been conscious of a Presence telling me that what we have done and what we plan to do at Bangor Theological Seminary is something that ought to be done. It is the Presence of the One who spoke to the Galilean fishermen long ago and called them to a divine task. This same Jesus the Christ, who inspired the early disciples to build the Church, is today summoning us to strengthen that Church as we train in this Seminary a mature Christian ministry. This is a ministry, as Jesus has taught us, of healing the sick, of comforting those who mourn, of peace-making, of mercy, of righteousness, and of the preaching of the gospel of the kingdom even in the face of persecution. This is something that *ought to be done — and can be done — not for the glory of this institution or any human individual, but for the sake of Him who is our Master and who has said to us, "Ye are the light of the world ... Let your light so shine before men that they may see your good works and glorify your Father which is in heaven." Amen.*

Implementation of the goals set forth in my inaugural address began in earnest with the installation on September 22, 1953, of the Reverend Daniel W. Fenner as Vice President of the Seminary. Operating as a team in a vigorous development program, aided by an expanding and dedicated Board of Trustees, we saw the culmination of our efforts during the decade of the 1950's with the dedication of the new and beautiful Moulton Library in the fall of 1959. Other note-worthy achievements of the year were a record-high enrollment of 106 students and the reception of the largest amount ever given in one year to defray Seminary operating expenses. One contribution alone was for $2,500, a donation from the 50-year class of 1909, four of whose six living members were on campus with their wives for a reunion celebration. I record their names here for posterity: Milton V. McAlister, John H. Moseley, William H. Curtis, and Stephen C. Lang.

Construction of the new library was begun in 1957, and its dedication two years later was the first major improvement in the physical facilities of the Seminary envisioned in the 150th Anniversary Development Program scheduled for completion in 1964. The building was constructed at the amazingly low cost of $300,000. It was named in honor of Dr. Warren J. Moulton, Bangor's third president, and his wife Helen Winifred Moulton; the Moultons left a $200,000 trust fund for the perpetual support of the Seminary. The following is a description of the library published in the November, 1959, edition of the "Bangor Seminary Herald": "It is primarily of brick, aluminum and glass. Interior woodwork is of red birch in driftwood finish. The building contains a reading room which will accommodate seventy students and has bookstack area comprising three floors capable of housing 70,000 volumes. The stacks also contain study carrels for twenty-four students. Seminary offices are located on the second floor and include accommodations for faculty and administration. There is also a spacious meeting room for trustees and faculty, and a large business office."

The Moulton Library is one of two accomplishments of the Whittaker years in which I take the greatest satisfaction; the other is the accreditation of the Seminary, a story which will be told later. At the dedication of the new library, recognition of its significance was given both locally and nationally. John T. Barry, Jr., mayor of Bangor, brought greetings and congratulations from the city. Dr. Wesley A. Hotchkiss of New York City represented the Congregational Christian Churches as an officer of its Board for Homeland Ministers. The dedication address was given by the Reverend Clarence W. Fuller, chairman of the Seminary trustees; he said in part: " Now in a time of increasing standardization in educational procedures, a seminary which deliberately and purposefully contravenes the generally-accepted pattern of theological education — though it accepts no less from the candidates for its degrees — and which is located off the beaten path and away from the largest sources of wealth, goes ahead and optimistically builds a fine new library and administration building to prepare itself for the next century. This is a fact, I think, of which we can be justifiably proud."

Before the Moulton Library became a realty the Seminary's rich treasure of books was stored and used in antiquated quarters on the first floor of the Chapel building. Since 1924 the library had been under the supervision of Dr. Alfred Morris Perry, who also served the Seminary as Hayes Professor of New Testament Language and Literature. Unfortunately, Dr. Perry did not live to see the Moulton Library, which was the fulfillment of a dream he and his president envisioned as early as the mid-1920s. His sudden death on January 14, 1954, following a heart attack, created the first vacancy in the faculty I had come to know and love. Dr. Perry was a graduate of Marietta College, Harvard University, and Hartford Theological Seminary; he received a Ph.D. degree from the University of Chicago in 1918. He was married to the former Florence May Hodges and was the father of three daughters and two sons.

Morris Perry and I were close friends, both during my student days and as faculty colleagues. We were members of the Bangor

Kiwanis Club, and sat together at a noon luncheon meeting the day before his death. He was a master teacher of the Greek language, and three decades of Seminary students admired his scholarly interpretation of the New Testament. In 1949, he gave the school's opening address entitled "Modern Criticism and the Preaching of the Gospels," in which he said: "We live by faith, not by fact. It is not the historical Jesus who is the object of our faith ... Our faith is in the ever-living Christ, not in the Galilean carpenter, however good and kind his life, however beautiful and wise his words. Our faith is not in history, but in the spirit which shone in the life of that Galilean teacher, shone so clearly that men felt they had a new vision of God — in the spirit which somehow was communicated to those who were closest to him, and from them passed on to others until the movement which claimed his name became a world religion."

In a memorial service I spoke these words about my beloved professor: "We of the Seminary family, both past and present, are deeply grateful to God for the witness of His servant among us — and in the further reaches of Christendom — during these past thirty years. By using to the utmost the intellectual powers bestowed upon him by the Creator, this Christian teacher, preacher, and author has spread abroad the vast riches of God's Word as contained in the Holy Bible. More than that, by freely sharing his spiritual endowments he has been, in truth, a disciple of the Master. Those of us who have known him intimately will recognize the validity of these words written by a prominent businessman: 'Your people at the Seminary will miss his kindness and his understanding as much as his brilliance as a teacher.' To this holy moment of faith and thanksgiving, there is one brief thought to be added: Not long ago the one we love was asked by a friend: 'What do you plan to do after you retire?' The answer came back quickly: 'Why, I'll stay right here and teach!' Alfred Morris Perry has retired to his God, but his spirit lives with us and, in the name of Christ, he will continue to teach."

The year 1954 was a momentous one for the Seminary and for my administration in that two appointments of major significance were made to the faculty. In September Dr. Mervin M. Deems, who had been my professor of Church History during student days, returned to Bangor as the first Dean of the Seminary. At the same time Dr. Burton H. Throckmorton, Jr., began his thirty-five years of service as professor of New Testament Language and Literature as successor to Dr. Perry. For the next fourteen years, Dr. Deems and I shared both the administration of the Seminary and the teaching of courses in Church History. The appointment was a source of deep personal satisfaction to me.

From 1943 to 1954 Dr. Deems had been Michigan and Sweetser Professor of the History of Early Christianity and Missions at the Chicago Theological Seminary. In earlier years he was a member of the faculty of William Jewell College in Missouri and Carleton College in Minnesota. He was an ordained minister of the Congregational Christian Churches (now the United Church of Christ). From 1932 to 1936 he was pastor of the Congregational Church in Norway, Maine, before coming to Bangor Seminary for seven years as Waldo Professor of Ecclesiastical History. While in Chicago, Dr. Deems was in wide demand as a preacher and lecturer. He has served as interim pastor of several churches in Illinois, and in 1952 he gave the Samuel Harris Lectures on Literature and Life at the Bangor Seminary Convocation.

Born in Baltimore, Maryland, in 1899, Dr. Deems holds the A.B. degree from Johns Hopkins University, the Th.M. of Southern Baptist Theological Seminary, and the Ph.D. degree of the University of Chicago. He is a member of Phi Beta Kappa and of the American Society of Church History. While at Chicago he was editor of The Chicago Theological Seminary "Register." He and his late wife, Cleta, are the parents of two daughters, Margaret and Mary. In his second term at Bangor, Dr. Deems was not only a professor of Church History, but also Fogg Professor of Sacred Rhetoric. In addition, he served as editor of "The Alumni Bulletin," a scholarly quarterly published by the Seminary. As the first Dean of the school the contribution of Mervin Deems proved to be invaluable.

The premature death of Alfred Morris Perry challenged the new administration to find a qualified faculty replacement for one who had made the New Testament and the Greek language come alive for a generation of Bangor students. It was the very good fortune of the Seminary to discover the availability of a young 33-year-old scholar, the Reverend Burton H. Throckmorton, Jr., who was then a member of the faculty of Wellesley College. Earlier he had been an instructor in New Testament at Union Theological Seminary in New York City; he also had taught Bible courses at New York University, Princeton University, and Drew Theological Seminary. He is an ordained minister of the Presbyterian Church, U.S.A.

Born in Elizabeth, New Jersey, Dr. Throckmorton holds the A.B. degree of the University of Virginia and the B.D. degree of Union Theological Seminary. He did his graduate work at Union and at Columbia University, which awarded him the Ph.D. degree. He is a member of the Society of Biblical Literature and Exegesis, and is a Kent Fellow of the National Council on Religion in Higher Education. He is well known in the theological world as the editor of "Gospel Parallels," a standard text for New Testament students, and as the author of "The New Testament and Mythology."

Almost immediately after he began his career at Bangor in September, 1954, Dr. Throckmorton was recognized as an exceptionally talented teacher. It was predicted by many that he would eventually leave Maine to become a professor at some larger theological school. He remained for thirty-five years, until his recent retirement, and thus became one of the several faculty members who have been inspired to remain at unique Bangor Seminary for three decades and more. Burton is married to the former Ansley Coe and is the father of two sons, Hamilton and Timothy. Both Hamilton and his mother are graduates of Bangor. I have happy memories of Ansley as one of my students. She was for several years my pastor during her service as minister of Bangor's Hammond Street Church. I am proud of her current top-executive leadership of the national United Church of Christ.

One other change in Seminary personnel took place in 1954. The Reverend David J. Siegenthaler, librarian and instructor in Church History since 1952, resigned his position in order to continue graduate study. He was replaced by Miss Charlotte M. Torrey of Bangor, who for eleven years had been employed by the Bangor Public Library. Miss Torrey graduated from Bangor High School and received her A.B. degree from the University of Maine in 1943. Since 1948 she had been head of the Extension Department at the Public Library, in which capacity one of her responsibilities was to provide service to the Seminary library.

1955 was another significant year in the development of the Seminary faculty. Walter L. Cook and Stephen Szikszai joined the teaching staff, and each thus began a service of more than thirty years to the school. Cook was an ordained minister of the American Baptist Convention and for seven years had been minister of the First Baptist Church in Bangor, during which time he had for the past three years taught a course in preaching as a member of the Seminary's visiting faculty. His appointment completed the plan of the Whittaker administration to strengthen the school's department of homiletics and practical theology, which had not had a full-time faculty member in residence since the retirement of President Trust in 1952.

Walter Cook's appointment coincided with the completion of three years of service to the Seminary by Dr. John Burford Parry as a visiting professor of Homiletics and Pastoral Theology. Dr. Parry was a graduate of Bangor and of Yale University. For twenty years he was the minister of the Wellesley Congregational Church after an earlier pastorate in the Hope Congregational Church in Springfield. Before Walter Cook joined the full-time faculty, instruction in preaching was also given by Dr. Milton M. McGorrill, minister of the Bangor Universalist Church, and lectures on pastoral theology were given by the Reverend Edward G. Ernst, minister of the Hammond Street Congregational Church. Walter Cook occupied the chair named in honor of Bangor's fifth president, the Harry Trust Professorship of Preaching and Pastoral Relations. In addition he was Director of Student Field Work, in which capacity he was responsible for supervision of the relationship between the Seminary and the more than sixty churches served by student pastors in central and eastern Maine.

Walter Cook was especially well-qualified for his new position. From sixteen years of pastoral experience in Maine he knew the churches of the state and the needs of the people. Before his seven years at First Baptist he had served pastorates in Hebron, Calais and Farmington. He was born in Somerville, Massachusetts, and was a graduate of Greenville College in Illinois (B.A.) and of Andover Newton Theological School (B.D.). Later he was granted the honorary degree of Doctor of Divinity by Ricker College in Houlton, Maine. Dr. Cook proved to be the most prolific writer on the Seminary faculty. He published several volumes of meditations for young people which were widely used and acclaimed. He wrote "The Story of Maine Baptists, 1904-1954" and "The History of Bangor Theological Seminary." His volume with the humorous title "Send Us a Minister — Any Minister Will Do," is a popular account of his long and effective career as student field work director at the Seminary. Walter and his wife Merle were the parents of two sons, Richard and Bradford. Mrs. Cook was also an ordained Baptist minister, and served Maine pastorates in West Minot, East Hebron, Farmington Falls, and Bangor.

When Charles Gordon Cumming retired in 1955 as the Seminary's George A. Gordon Professor of Old Testament Language and Literature he had completed thirty-six years of unparalleled service to the school. He was to continue for another three years on the part-time faculty as lecturer on the History of Religions. The Board of Trustees praised him with a resolution which read in part: "We convey to Dr. Cumming our profound gratitude for these long years of noble Christian service; for his faithfulness in scholarship, his brilliance of interpretation and appreciation, his dramatic and imaginative insights, and the love and humor that have always characterized his teaching and leadership; for his profound and eloquent preaching at our Seminary and in the pulpits of Maine, wherein he did honor God and this institution and all who were associated with it — for all these graces, gifts, and accomplishments, and for the abundant friendliness of heart and soul that gave of himself at all times and hours other than and more than was required of him, so that he has been a father and adviser to class after class of students who were enriched and blessed by his great heart and prophetic wisdom."

The faculty joined in the universal acclaim of Dr. Cumming with a statement of its own, from which the following excerpts are taken: "He has brought to our understanding the interpretation of the Old Testament linguistic competence, taste for literature, knowledge of other religions, acquaintance with philosophy, sound and shrewd judgment, glowing personal faith, and unfailing discernment of the difference between the trivial and the weightier matters of vital religion ... It has long been said that the Prophets live again in Dr. Cumming's classroom. It may be more accurate to say that instead of impersonating men of ancient times, renowned as spokesmen for God, he had himself been a prophet in our midst, mediating wisdom or laying down the law in classroom and in chapel, enabling others to perceive things invisible..."

Dr. Cumming was a native of Nova Scotia and an ordained minister of the Presbyterian Church of Canada. He held the A.B. degree of Dalhousie College, the B.D. of New York's Union Theological Seminary, and the Ph.D. degree of Columbia University. He was an instructor in Old Testament at Union for three years before coming to Bangor in 1919. During a sabbatical year in 1932-1933 he taught in the American Schools of Oriental Research in Jerusalem. In 1954 he gave the Samuel Harris Lectures on Literature and Life at Bangor's annual Convocation, one of the very few Seminary faculty members to be so honored. Upon his retirement "The Alumni Bulletin" commented editorially: "It is impossible to express adequately the esteem with which hundreds of alumni regard Dr. Cumming and the love which he has engendered in the hearts of us all." My wife Shirley and I looked upon Charles Cumming as a "father" figure and we were delighted to have him reside in an apartment of our Hannibal Hamlin home during his retirement years. With other faculty family members, we recall also with affection Lenore Cumming, who was described in a faculty resolution as "a wife gratefully remembered among us for her highly-endowed and alert mind, for the extent and vitality of her interests, and for her scintillating speech."

The vacancy left by Charles Cumming was not easy to fill. By good fortune, however, the Seminary was able to secure the services of the Reverend Stephen Szikszai, Th.D., to become the new professor of Old Testament Language and Literature effective September 1, 1955. Dr. Szikszai was born of Hungarian parents in Pola, Austria-Hungary, in 1914. He studied for four years at the

Reformed Theological Seminary at Sarospatak, and later continued his studies in the fields of philosophy and Old Testament at Debrecen University in Hungary. In 1945 he fled before the Russian army from Hungary to Germany, where he lived in the American Zone and served until 1951 in the Hungarian Reformed Pastoral Service among Hungarian displaced persons. In 1951 he married Hildegard Schaffelhofer, and in the same year the Szikszais entered the United States as immigrants. They were granted full American citizenship in 1957.

Dr. Szikszai graduated from Union Theological Seminary, New York City, in 1954 with the degree of Doctor of Theology in Old Testament studies. He was an ordained minister of the Evangelical and Reformed Church. His ethnic and theological background added a new and welcome dimension to the ecumenicity of the faculty. Fluent in many languages, he established the popularity of Hebrew among Bangor students. Like many others, Dr. Szikszai helped to train a generation or more of ministers at Bangor during his tenure of thirty-two years. He also served for many years as Registrar, Director of Admissions, and Director of Liberal Studies.

One of the most unusual careers as a Bangor Seminary faculty member ended in June, 1957, when Dr. Marion John Bradshaw retired after thirty-two years as Professor of Philosophy of Religion. Thus, during the first five years of my administration as President, four of the teachers during my student days at Bangor — Harry Trust, Alfred Morris Perry, Charles Cumming, and Marion Bradshaw — had completed their distinguished careers. These four men gave the Seminary one hundred seventeen years of devoted service, a record that may never be equalled.

Dr. Bradshaw was born in Salem, Ohio, in 1886. He graduated from Hiram College with the degrees of A.B. and M.A. He received the B.D. degree from Union Theological Seminary in New York City and was honored by the University of Maine as a Doctor of Divinity. He was an ordained minister of the Congregational-Christian Churches. Before coming to Bangor he served on the faculty of Hiram College, Grinnell College, Union Theological Seminary, and in pastorates in Ohio, New Jersey, and Massachusetts. Dr. Bradshaw was the author of several published books: "Third

Class World," "Philosophical Foundations of Faith," "Free Churches and Christian Unity," "Baleful Legacy," and three beautiful volumes on the state of Maine illustrated with superb photographs.

On the occasion of his retirement I spoke these words in appreciation of Dr. Bradshaw for the inspiration he gave me as a student, as an alumnus, and as a faculty colleague: "I choose first words which he published some years ago in which he proclaimed that one of the things most needed in the life of the church and of the seminary is a profounder love of God with our minds. I can say as a former student that he taught me what I know about the use of reason in its relationship to faith ... I have reason to be grateful to him personally for his willingness during my administration to serve in several capacities, notably as the genial manager of the Seminary bookstore, and as Dean of the Chapel ... There are two phrases spoken often by him whom we honor which will live with me forever, and will have a meaning perhaps deeper than even he intended. You have heard these words many times from one who was both a theologian and a philosopher. First, 'O thou whom no man has seen at any time,' the assurance that through the ministry of this Christian scholar we have come as close as mortal man can to seeing God. And second, the benediction which we have heard over and over again, a benediction which has assured us of the reality of eternity: 'Till time shall be no more.'"

A year after Dr. Bradshaw retired, the Reverend Arnold W. Hearn joined the faculty as his successor. Hearn became Visiting Lecturer in Philosophy and Christian Ethics at the beginning of the 1958-59 academic year. He was an ordained Methodist minister and had served a four-year pastorate in New York City. He had been an instructor at Princeton University and at New York's Union Theological Seminary. He held the B.A. degree of the University of Missouri and the B.D. of Union. He was a candidate for the Ph.D. degree from Columbia University. Upon receiving the doctorate he later became an associate and then a full professor at Bangor.

Meanwhile, the year of 1957 had seen the realization of another goal of the Whittaker administration: the establishment of a department of Christian education at the Seminary. On July 1st the

Reverend David W. Jewell was appointed Associate Professor of Christian Education, thus raising to equal status with other academic disciples an essential field of study which had heretofore been taught by visiting instructors. Since 1955 David Jewell had been an instructor in the department of Religious Education and Psychology at Union Theological Seminary in New York City. He was an ordained minister of the Congregational-Christian Churches and had served as minister of education in the Union Church of Tarrytown, New York. He held the the B.A. degree of Carleton College in Minnesota, the B.D. of Union, and the Doctor of Education degree from Teachers College, Columbia University.

Many changes took place in Seminary personnel during the early years of the Whittaker presidency. Not the least of these was caused by the death of Willard Streeter Bass, a distinguished Christian churchman and Maine business leader, the chief executive officer of the famous Bass Shoe Company in Wilton, Maine. He had been a member of the Seminary's Board of Trustees for thirty-six years and its chairman from 1952 until his death in 1956. The faculty joined the trustees in adopting resolutions praising Mr. Bass for his devotion to the Seminary. "The Alumni Bulletin" of April, 1956, published my own tribute to him, and I quote it in part below:

"The earthly life of Willard Bass spanned seventy-nine years. He was a man of strong faith, a faith which grew in power during his sixty years of membership in the Christian Church. This faith sustained him during the several months of his last illness, and he left instructions that the memorial service should be one of 'confidence and triumph.' For thirty-two years he was a deacon of the Wilton Congregational Church and, most remarkably, was superintendent of its Sunday School for forty-seven years. His interest in the church extended to the Congregational-Christian Conference of Maine, which he served in several official capacities — director, president, trustee — over a period of thirty-five years.

"Willard Bass was led by his Christian faith into Christian action. He put his Christianity to work in many places: in Wilton Academy, the Chicago Institute, and as a teacher during his early career; in the shoe-manufacturing business organized by his father,

G.H. Bass and Company, where he worked for forty-eight years, serving as president since 1925; in his 'alma mater,' Bowdoin College, as a member of the Board of Overseers for twenty-six years; in the Boy Scout movement, the state Y.M.C.A., the Franklin County Memorial Hospital, the Wilton Water Board, the Wilton School Board, and the Wilton Lions Club ... He held the A.B. degree, Phi Beta Kapa, from Bowdoin College, and the A.B. and A.M. degrees from Harvard University. In 1954 Bowdoin awarded him the honorary degree of Doctor of Humane Letters for his 'humanitarism and support of all things worthwhile in his greater community' ..."

The history of Bangor Theological Seminary from 1956 to 1978 should be known as "The Fuller-Whittaker Years." Following the death of Willard Bass, the Reverend Clarence W. Fuller was elected as chairman of the school's Board of Trustees, a position which he held throughout my administration and beyond. As an alumnus and former assistant to President Harry Trust, Clarence was fully cognizant of, and devoted to, the unique mission of the Seminary. As my "boss" and close personal friend, he was to labor in tandem with me for more than two decades on behalf of the school we both loved. As the decade of the 1950's drew to a close — a decade which saw the completion of the work of such "giants" as Harry Trust, Alfred Morris Perry, Charles Gordon Cumming, and Marion John Bradshaw — the Seminary was now ready to face with confidence — with a new and augmented faculty and the recently-completed Moulton Library — the challenges of the 1960s and 1970s. At this moment my own personal career was about to take on a new dimension as I entered the world of politics in fulfillment of an avocational goal.

10.
Mayor and State Senator

In the fall of 1959, with the permission of the Seminary trustees, I announced my candidacy for election to the Bangor City Council. This was the beginning of my involvement in practical politics as an avocation over a period of thirty years. During this time I have been a city councillor and mayor, a Maine state senator, a delegate to a national Republic convention, an independent candidate for governor, an independent candidate for the U.S. Congress, and a member of the Democratic Executive Committee of Sarasota County in Florida.

My political activity should come as no surprise to readers of these memoirs who have noted the influence upon my life of such historical figures as Martin Luther, John Calvin, and Samuel Harris. From my opening address as a seminary professor and my doctoral thesis I have emphasized the importance of "cooperation" rather than " separation" of Church and State, together with the admonition that the Christian citizen has a moral obligation to put faith into action by serving as an elected civil servant.

At the October municipal election I was second among three candidates chosen to serve for three years on the Bangor City Council. A popular medical doctor finished first by a margin of seven votes. I thus became part of a nine-person policy-making board of directors. Under the city council-manager form of government, a full-time City Manager bears the responsibility of administering municipal affairs and effecting policies determined by the Council. The incumbent manager during my tenure was Joseph R. Coupal, Jr., a most competent official with whom it was a pleasure to work. Coupal was ably assisted by the long-term City Clerk, Jay Alley. I came to admire both men, both as friends and as co-workers for the benefit of the city. Outstanding colleagues were Dr. Carl Blaisdell and attorney Edward Gross.

The Bangor City Council met in regular session twice a month. There were always routine matters of business to consider. The preparation and adoption of budgets took a good measure of thought and time. With some regularity there were committee meetings to attend. Serving on the Council was a fulfilling experience, especially when major issues were debated and resolved. I take pride in knowing that my name is etched on three plaques in different parts of the city commemorating civic improvements in which I played a leading role. One is in downtown Bangor on the Kenduskeag Stream just south of the State Street bridge. Another is in the "new" Bangor High School, which opened in 1964 at its campus site east of outer Broadway. A third is adjacent to the clubhouse of the Bangor Municipal Golf Course, a unique recreational facility which was my brainchild while mayor of Bangor in 1962 during my third year on the City Council.

In 1956 the Kenduskeag Stream was an open sewer flowing through the heart of downtown Bangor to the nearby Penobscot River. The City Council of which I was a member initiated a process which several years later saw the completion of an interceptor sewer along the Stream which restored the flowing water to its pristine beauty and at the same time established the Kenduskeag Parking Plaza on both sides of the Stream between State and Washington Streets, thus solving both a serious sanitation problem and the city's desperate need for more downtown parking space. Today the Kenduskeag upstream has a beautiful park and walkway along its banks, and it flows by a modern residential condominium in the center of the city on Franklin Street which takes pride in calling itself a waterfront facility.

Being a professional educator, I quite naturally was keenly interested during my term on the City Council in a proposal to build a new municipal high school to replace the building on Harlow Street. As a member of the Council I was asked to serve as vice chairman of the High School Building Committee. In that capacity I supported the point of view that a new and modern facility should be built at an available site east of outer Broadway at the growing edge of the city. The estimated cost was $3,264,820. Another city councillor, John Barry, was the leader of a group of citizens who favored a plan to renovate and enlarge the old high school. In an address to the Bangor Kiwanis Club and at a public hearing in the City Hall I argued that a new campus-type structure at the Broadway location would accomplish at least three purposes: It would provide a physical plant large enough for the necessary classrooms, gymnasium, and auditorium; it would enhance land and property values in a developing outlying area, and it would assure the school of accreditation.

After much debate, and considerable delay, the new high school was opened on a beautiful campus on outer Broadway. Time has proven the wisdom of the decision. The building is a showcase for the city, its facilities have met all the educational and social needs of succeeding generations of students, and the area surrounding the school has seen continuing residential and commercial growth for more than two decades.

During my year as Council Chairman and Mayor in 1962, my fellow councillor, attorney Edward Gross, and I began a campaign to convince the Council that it should propose the building of an eighteen-hole municipal golf course on the intown location known as the old city farm. The land was directly on the approach to Dow Air Force Base (now Bangor International Airport) and could not be used for residential or commercial development. The idea was cooly received at first, but by 1963 the Council authorized the project and appointed a Golf Course Advisory Committee, of which I was a member. In July of 1964 the Bangor Municipal Golf Course became a reality, and it has been a recreational asset of the first magnitude ever since. Austin Kelley has been its professional for more than twenty-five years. Under his guidance the facility has become one of the outstanding public courses in the United States. In 1978 it hosted the National Public Links championship, the first time a New England municipal golf course had received this honor. In 1989 nine additional holes were opened, and I had the privilege of playing in the first threesome on inaugural day. It is doubtful that any other American city of its size has such a splendid public golf course located near the geographical center of the community.

While I was a member of the Bangor Council I was involved in discussions about compulsory ROTC programs in the Bangor High School (which I opposed), and the denying of liquor licenses to local hotels which featured "strip tease" entertainment (I approved the denial). Much more significantly, I was an ardent opponent of the Maine Central Railroad and its plan to end all railroad passenger service in Maine. The *Bangor Daily News* on February 25, 1960, published a front-page account of my address the previous day before the Bangor Kiwanis Club under the headline: "Whittaker Raps PUC, Railroad — Hits Passenger Service." Here are some excerpts:

"Within a year Bangor may become a second-class city and Maine a second-class state through the abandonment of all passenger train service ... The so-called 'passenger trains' on the Maine Central are really mail, express and merchandise trains with the passenger coach attached at the end. The needs of the passengers are all but forgotten as they ride in the tail-end coach, yet they are admonished by the Public Utilities Commission to patronize these trains or face the loss of all railroad transportation ... The PUC should require the Maine Central and Boston and Maine railroads to provide five-hour service between Bangor and Boston in both directions with convenient arrival and departure times ... There should be two round-trips daily on trains reserved for passengers, without mail and other 'head end' traffic; mail and merchandise should be handled in separate trains."

Later in 1960 I made the following remarks to my colleagues at a regular meeting of the Bangor City Council on August 8th: "On September 6th the city of Bangor will be left without passenger service as a result of action taken by the Maine Central Railroad and a decision rendered by the Maine Supreme Court. It is my opinion that this situation can only result in a deterioration of Bangor's status as a modern city ... It seems to me inevitable that a city isolated from the rest of the United States so far as railroad passenger service is concerned will find it more difficult to attract new business and industry, teachers and students for its own and nearby educational institutions, patrons for its area-wide recreational facilities, and permanent residents for its homes ... I suggest that the Bangor City Council should acknowledge the seriousness of this situation and seek whatever remedial measures may be available."

I further pointed out that in the present case the Maine Central Railroad, a public utility, had denied any responsibility to provide passenger service on its lines in spite of a decree by the Maine Public Utilities Commission requiring it to provide such service. While the Maine Supreme Court had sustained the position of the railroad, nevertheless the need for railroad passenger service from and to Bangor remained. Ample evidence of this fact was given at a public hearing before the Maine Public Utilities Commission in Bangor on November 4, 1959. Additional testimony concerning need is given in letters written to the editor of the *Bangor Daily News*, in communications addressed to the Maine Public Utilities Commission, and in requests made of me personally as one who is vitally interested in this problem.

I then suggested three possible courses of action:

1. An interested party — such as the Bangor City Council, Bangor Chamber of Commerce, or some other group of citizens — should petition the Maine Supreme Court for a review of its decision.
2. The Boston and Maine Railroad or the Bangor and Aroostook Railroad should be requested to provide, voluntarily, passenger service between Portland and Bangor by leasing the Maine Central Railroad facilities for the purpose of operating one or two round-trips daily.
3. Since the continuation of railroad passenger service in Maine is of vital importance to the welfare of the whole State, the Governor and the State Legislature should be asked to take whatever executive or legislative action may be necessary

and legally possible to protect the public interest.

I then made the following enabling motion: "that the Bangor City Council authorize its Public Relations committee to study the potential impact of the railroad passenger situation upon the welfare of the city; to solicit and receive comments and suggestions from interested citizens; and to recommend to the Council what action, if any, should be taken to protect the public and civic welfare."

The Public Relations committee of the Council did take this matter under advisement. I was chairman of the committee at the time, having been the councilman responsible for initiating the establishment of this new standing committee. However, neither the committee nor the Council itself was able to prevent the Maine Central Railroad from abandoning all passenger train service from and to Bangor in 1961. Two years later, while serving as a Maine State senator, I did introduce legislation proposing to have the State of Maine subsidize a two-year trial period of rail passenger service between Bangor and Portland, but that is a story to be recounted later.

My first two years on the Bangor City Council had been productive and satisfying. I had proven the validity of my long-held opinion that church-oriented persons had both the responsibility and the ability to serve in elected public office. My colleagues on the Council showed their agreement with my opinion by choosing me to be chairman of the Council, and thus Mayor of the city, for the year 1962. A front-page headline of the *Bangor Daily News* described the uniqueness of this choice: "Dr. Whittaker First Cleric Named to Head City Council." I may have been the only president of a theological seminary to be elected as head of a municipal government.

The year as Mayor passed quickly, with principal attention being given to the three major projects previously described: the Kenduskeag interceptor sewer, the new Bangor High School, and the proposed municipal golf course. In this endeavor I was blessed by the support of such distinguished colleagues as attorney Edward Gross, mentioned earlier, and by new members of the Council: Carl Delano, churchman and railroad official, and well-known respected member of the legal profession, Nicholas Brountas.

My experience on the Bangor City Council so fulfilled my long-held desire to put my Christian principles into political action that I was not satisfied to withdraw from public service at the end of the three-year term. In 1962 I had been a member of the Seminary faculty for fourteen years and had not yet taken a sabbatical. In 1955 I had been entitled to a six-month leave of absence with full salary or a sabbatical of one year with half pay. Since I was then in the early years of my presidency, I decided to forego this academic privilege. In 1962 my second seven-year period of service to the school was completed, and I had in mind a definite program for a sabbatical. I asked the Board of Trustees for permission to be a candidate for election as a State Senator in the Maine legislature. Thankfully, the Board gave a positive response to my request.

My name was entered in the June, 1962, primary as one of several Republican candidates from Penobscot County for the office of State Senator. This was my first endeavor in partisan politics, since the Bangor City Council election was non-partisan. The primary election gave me one of the four seats available, and in the November general election my position as a State Senator in the 101st Maine legislature was confirmed automatically because the Democratic party did not field a slate of candidates. Thus in January, 1963, I took my assigned seat in the Senate chamber at the State capitol in Augusta. It is probable that I thus became one of the very few, if not the only, theological school president to serve concurrently as an elected official in state government.

The remainder of this chapter will describe my activities as a State Senator. Before beginning this story, however, I interject here excerpts from an address on "The Legislative Function in Community Improvement," which I presented before the annual meeting of the New England Managers' Institute at the University of Maine in Orono on August 20, 1963. The purpose of the Institute is to improve municipal management throughout New England by continuing in-service training of responsible municipal officials. My appearance was arranged and sponsored by Joseph R. Coupal, Jr., the City Manager of Bangor with whom I had recently served as City Council Chairman and Mayor. My assigned topic was "Interpreting the Popular Will," and my remarks will illustrate some of the philosophy and practice which permeated my public service in local and state government. This is an abridged version of my address:

The peace and prosperity of a city or state depends in large measure upon the quality of the legislative function. No public activity by the individual citizen is more important than the process of law-making. Improvement of community life will be realized in direct proportion to the wisdom, courage, and integrity displayed by the elected representatives of the people.

"Interpreting the Popular Will" is my assigned topic. However, experience has taught me that the "popular will," so called, is a nebulous thing not easily to be defined or understood ... Thus I am convinced that the responsible legislator, in his efforts to achieve community improvements, should be concerned not so much with the "popular will" as with the "public welfare." These two concepts are not always compatible, and I believe that priority for the public welfare is essential to good government ... With apologies, then, to the institute chairman, and without seeking your popular will through a test vote, I propose to continue this representation with major emphasis upon interpreting the "public welfare."

When a legislator gives primary allegiance to the public welfare he or she does not cast votes for the sole purpose of assuring re-election, does not seek acclaim by irresponsibly supporting all so-called popular civic programs, and does not succumb to the political pressure of special interest groups. On the contrary, the lawmaker who is a good servant of the people acts as protector of the community health and culture, and as leader in the development of new programs and services which promise to enhance the standard of living for all constituents. The elected civic official is in fact a trustee, a member of the board of directors, of a corporation which expends many thousands, and often millions, of tax dollars. Through governmental actions the lawmaker literally exercises vast control over the lives of fellow citizens. Consciously or unconsciously, these citizens depend upon the legislator for education, fire and police services, health and sanitary protection, recreational opportunities, and the right to live in a civilized society.

Wisdom, courage, and integrity are the marks of an effective councilman, selectman, or other municipal elected official. Fortunate, indeed, is the community governed by men and women who possess these qualifications. And blessed is the manager who works with a legislative body comprised of respected citizens who voluntarily give their time and talent to the affairs of local government. Professional and business leaders are the ones best equipped to interpret the public welfare and to establish just and equitable laws. Many more such persons should be recruited for public legislative service if managers and their associates are to succeed in developing better communities. Wisdom is essential in choosing among alternative civic programs, courage is necessary in the assessing of adequate taxes, and integrity in the face of conflicting public desires and interests is vital to the legislative function.

My own brief experience as a public official has been revealing, challenging, and satisfying. Thus it is with enthusiasm that I describe some specific incidents and make some observations which are pertinent to the theme of this discussion. Interpreting the wishes and needs of the people is often a complex process. Education, for example, is a public activity which rightfully enjoys much popular interest and support. The city of Bangor has an excellent school system, but the construction of adequate new high school facilities has been seriously delayed by citizen disagreement on such matters as site location, choice of architect, and cost estimates.

One expression of the popular will indicated that the new facility should be established in the downtown business district, while another large segment of citizens favored a suburban site near the growing edge of the community. In the face of a divided popular will, the city councillors and the members of the school building committee sought diligently for a solution which would be in the public welfare. Because they acted with wisdom, courage, and integrity, their final proposal was accepted by the voters in referendum as in accord with the popular will, and the new high school will be opened in 1964. Similar procedures with respect to urban renewal, sewage disposal, parking facilities, and recreational activities have resulted in major community improvements which make Bangor the most desirable of the six cities and towns in

189

which I have lived.

The public welfare demands that the legislative function ideally should be in the hands of men and women with high principles who have been successful in their own vocation and who have demonstrated a genuine social concern. When such qualified people have been elected to office they are in fact the chosen representatives of the voters and they should fulfill their duties with self-confidence and initiative. In the democratic process it is neither desirable nor necessary for civic officials to seek advice on every issue which comes before the lawmaking body. They should consider each question on its merits, always in the context of the general public good, and then make the required decision. Of course, the wise legislator will be courteous and attentive to those citizens who express themselves on particular subjects, but must use his or her own best judgment in voting upon controversial matters. Otherwise, none of the constituents with opposing points of view will be pleased, and the net result will be in accord with neither the popular will nor the public welfare.

One of the most difficult problems facing the legislator involves the relationship between the popular desire for services and the unpopular need of paying for them through taxation. During the recent session of the 101st Maine legislature it was obvious from the time the governor presented his budget that a bill providing for major new revenues would have to be enacted; it was also widely known among informed lawmakers that a bill to increase the sales and use tax had the best chance of passage. Nevertheless, the legislature postponed the inevitable for more than five months because the majority did not have the wisdom and the courage to vote for an unpopular but essential tax increase.

Anyone who was willing to acknowledge the facts knew that additional tax dollars were needed for educational subsidies, health and welfare programs, maintenance and staffing of correctional institutions, expanding the state university and the teacher colleges, industrial and recreational promotion, and scores of other governmental functions vital to Maine's growth in the mid-twentieth century. Yet many members of the legislature were unduly influenced by pleas from constituents that there be no increase in taxes. They should have known that these same people back home would have cried out with greater agitation if any essential state services had been curtailed. One worried House member finally went home to ask his constituents to release him from an ill-conceived campaign promise not to vote for a sales tax increase. Eventually the legislature in its collective wisdom passed the necessary tax bill.

The matter of taxes illustrates very well the distinction I have suggested between the popular will and the public welfare. Since I believe it is a crucial issue surrounding the legislative function in community improvement, let me dwell on the subject for a moment longer. People will pay taxes with equanimity, if not with enthusiasm, when they understand the need and are asked to assume a fair share of support for state or local services. Whenever I have been criticized for favoring new taxes it has been my practice to explain in detail how the additional revenue was to be used; in most cases the opposition has abated, and often it has disappeared.

Here is an opportunity for interpretation in reverse. The informed and competent public servant will not only attempt to interpret the popular will in the performance of the legislative function; in addition a concerted effort will be made to explain to the citizenry why they should contribute tax dollars in support of the public welfare. Not only because I am a clergyman but because I am also a concerned citizen, do I suggest that tithes and taxes should be paid with an equal sense of responsibility, and with gratitude for blessings received.

Another issue which squarely confronts civic leaders interested in community improvement involves housing for minority groups. Discrimination against blacks, in particular, as they attempt to rent homes is prevalent in Maine cities, and I assume that the problem exists in other parts of New England. Racial tension poses a threat to our national well-being and it certainly warrants attention at the local level.

A bill to ban racial discrimination in rental housing bore my name as sponsor in this year's session of the Maine legislature. Evidence gathered at a public hearing before the Maine section of the United Civil Rights Commission clearly indicated the need for such legislation. Preliminary voting in both the state Senate and

House of Representatives favored passage of the bill as an instrument for protecting the public welfare. Then gradually and persistently opposition developed among citizens who feared for their property rights or for their economic gains. Strong public pressure led many legislators to change their votes and on final action the bill was defeated in the House of Representatives. Was this a victory for the popular will? Was it a valid interpretation of the public welfare? In any event the problem remains, and no manager or councilman in 1963 America can ignore its influence upon the local community.

Although I have placed considerable stress upon the prerogatives of the legislator once he or she has been chosen by the people, there is no intention on my part to suggest that the lines of communication between the elected and the electorate should not be kept open at all times. In fact, community improvement depends upon an orderly and effective use of this communication system. Thus the city of Bangor, for example, has provided in its charter and ordinances that committees shall be appointed by the City Council in such significant areas as planning and zoning, public health and hospital service, recreation, and industrial development. In addition, the Council also appoints the members of the Superintending School Committee and the Commissioners of the Urban Renewal Authority. Undoubtedly both the popular will and the public welfare are reflected in the deliberations, recommendations and actions of these various bodies, for they are composed of competent and dedicated citizens. They not only serve well the special responsibilities assigned to them, but their impact is felt in the legislative process through the guidance which they give to members of the City Council. Other towns and cities commonly use similar procedures, I am sure.

Two other techniques worthy of note have been developed recently within the legislative body of Bangor. At my suggestion the City Council has added to its own internal organization a standing committee on Public Relations, whose duties include the arranging of opportunities for semi-public exchanges of ideas related to the improvement of municipal government. The committee also arranges friendly and informal discussions between councillors and the several boards and agencies appointed by the Council. And it urges citizens to attend hearings and stated public meetings conducted by the legislative body. Another helpful procedure in the work of interpreting the wishes and needs of the people has been the appointment by the City Council of a special advisory group consisting of former Council chairmen. These experienced legislators are thus kept in public service and are called upon to assist the incumbent councillors when major issues of policy and planning are being considered.

It is no secret that I look upon the Council-Manager system as the most effective and desirable form of municipal government. I believe it produces superior results both in legislation and administration. I give this testimony in spite of the fact, or perhaps because of the fact, that half of my lifetime has been spent under the partisan system in which civic affairs are controlled by a mayor and aldermen.

Before concluding I want to make a brief statement about the role of the manager. Although primarily an executive officer, the manager rightfully exerts a crucial influence upon the legislative function in community improvement. Because of professional training, the manager knows the factors which enhance the life of a municipality and is aware of the laws and administrative procedures needed in the local situation. The manager should be encouraged and expected to present for consideration by the legislative body those ideas, plans, and suggestions which are believed to be proper interpretations of the popular will and the public welfare.

It has been a rare privilege for me to speak here today as one who is a proponent of the cooperation rather than the separation of Church and State. If my interest in political affairs seems strange for one in my profession, let me close by an historical reference which bears out my belief that the legislative function is a high order of endeavor which has its roots in the Creator's design for the life we know on this good earth.

More than seven hundred years ago the great Roman Catholic philosopher and theologian of the thirteenth century, Thomas Aquinas, set forth a theory of law which is still a classic. There is an eternal law in the mind of God, said Aquinas, a portion of *which is made manifest in the natural law known to man in his environment and in his personal experience. In response to this natural law man seeks to govern himself and his society through human laws of his own devising. But man is destined to fail in this enterprise without the guidance of the divine law which God has revealed through the teachings of the Jewish-Christian tradition, and which he continues to reveal through the holy spirit working upon the human conscience. As lawmakers of the twentieth century, and as we seek to interpret the popular will and the public welfare, we shall do well to remember that ours is a task of both divine and human significance. Thus we may discover that legislation dedicated to the public welfare is in truth a valid expression of the popular will.*

When the above address was delivered in the summer of 1963 I had already put into practice as a state senator many of my own political convictions concerning the public welfare. As an elected member of the 101st Maine Legislature I was given the oath of office in the Senate chamber at Augusta by Governor John H. Reed, a man whom I have been privileged to call "friend" in all the ensuing years. The date was January 2, 1963. Robert A. Marden, senator from Waterville in Kennebec County, was elected President of the Senate, a position which he filled with dignity and wisdom. I was greatly pleased by the opportunities he gave me through committee assignments. He asked me to serve as chairman of the State Government committee, as a member of the Education committee, and as a member of the committee on Health and Institutional Services.

These three assignments allowed me to promulgate my ideas and exert my influence in three areas of keen interest and need: equitable taxation through a state income levy; enhancement of educational programs in elementary, secondary, vocational, undergraduate, and graduate schools; and improvement of services offered by the state in its correctional and mental health institutions. The first six months of 1963 was the period when the 101st Maine Legislature did its work, and I was able to participate because it coincided with my sabbatical from the Seminary. During most of the weeks of the session I left home on Monday, stayed in an

Augusta motel for four nights, and returned to Bangor on Friday. Despite the time necessarily spent away from my family, this half-year was an exciting and fulfilling milestone in my career.

My maiden speech as a Maine State Senator was made on January 22, 1963, when I introduced an order calling for the appointment of a Joint Select Committee on Railroad Passenger Service for the purpose of negotiating with officials of the three Maine railroads with regard to ways and means of restoring railroad passenger service to and from points in Maine north and east of Portland. Here are some excerpts from my supporting testimony as recorded in the Legislative Record:

"I believe that the restoration of rail passenger trains north and east of Portland is necessary for the industrial, recreational, and cultural growth of the state. This opinion is supported by the Maine Public Utilities Commission ... The Commission ordered the Maine Central Railroad in 1960 to continue such trains for a period of not less than one year, but the railroad successfully petitioned the Maine Supreme Judicial Court to set aside this PUC order. Thus the state of Maine has been without through passenger service since September, 1960. In view of the Court decision, this situation will become permanent unless the railroads can be persuaded to restore service voluntarily, perhaps with the cooperation of the legislature."

The story of a theological school president serving as a state senator and introducing legislation concerning railroad passenger service was sufficiently unusual to get attention from the state's leading weekend newspaper, the *Portland Sunday Telegram.* On January 27, 1963, it published a commentary in its Legislative News column under the headline: "Clergyman-Senator Whittaker Makes His Mark Quickly." The article quotes my long-held conviction that "government affects the lives of people just as much as the church does, and it is important that those with real religious convictions should apply them in practical politics ... There is a good precedent for this in colonial times, when churchmen were the leaders of government ..."

The reporter of the Sunday Telegram noted that I made my presence felt in the fourth week of the legislative session by introducing the order calling for a study of railroad passenger service and empowering a special committee to confer with officers of the rail companies about the restoration of the trains which had been eliminated in 1961 and 1962. As indicated by the newspaper, the order was approved by both the Senate and House of Representatives. Subsequently a Joint Select Committee on Railroad Passenger Service was appointed, and negotiations were held with railroad officials.

Later in the legislative year the result of these negotiations was reported to the Senate and then to the House. The initial presentation is recorded in the Legislative Record of the Senate under date of June 13, 1963. The highlights of the report may be summarized as follows: Three separate meetings were held with representatives of the Boston and Maine, the Maine Central, and the Bangor and Aroostook Railroads. In the early stages there was consideration of the possible restoration of passenger train service through the use of self-propelled "Budd" cars on the lines of the Maine Central and Bangor and Aroostook Railroads; this type of equipment was then being used on the Boston and Maine Railroad between Boston and Portland. Later it was agreed that only service between Portland and Bangor on the Maine Central twice daily in each direction would be considered. The railroad indicated that this plan would be possible only if the State of Maine purchased the necessary equipment and paid the net operating cost, plus a nominal service charge.

After thorough investigation and due deliberation, the details of the proposal, as follows, were presented to the Senate by me in a minority report of one:

1. That the State of Maine enter into a contractual arrangement for a two-year trial period with the Maine Central Railroad whereby the Railroad will operate passenger train service in self-propelled "Budd" cars on a schedule involving two round-trips daily between Portland and Bangor.
2. That the State of Maine purchase the equipment necessary for this service, the estimated cost of which is $1,001,949.
3. That the State of Maine agree to pay the actual net annual operating cost for this service, estimated at $331,872, plus a fee to the Maine Central Railroad for services rendered not

to exceed six percent of the actual annual operating cost.

4. That State of Maine funds in an amount not to exceed $1,750,000 for the biennium 1963-65 be appropriated for the purposes stated in this report.

5. That legislation to implement the above recommendations be prepared and submitted to the 101st Legislature for consideration.

The majority of the Joint Select Committee, consisting of two Senators and two Representatives, presented their conclusion that the minority report should not be accepted by the Senate. They argued that there was no real need for the reestablishment of rail passenger service and that, in any event, state funds should not be used for this purpose in view of the multitude of financial problems confronting the legislature. There was extended discussion, during which I emphasized the opinion of the Maine Public Utilities Commission that there is a substantial public demand for and use of the passenger trains here involved.

Much to my surprise and delight, when the vote was taken the minority report was approved by the narrow margin of one vote. My elation was short-lived, however, for when the proposal was considered by the House of Representatives, it was soundly defeated. I have never been sure whether or not the the favorable vote in the Senate was genuine or was a personal favor to me by friends who knew that the House would not concur. Thus Maine has been without railroad passenger service for almost thirty years, except, ironically, for a daily Canadian train operated by its national government through the northern part of the state between Montreal and the Maritime Provinces with stops at such Maine rural stations as Greenville and Brownville. I still live in hope that one day American railroads will once again be recognized by state and federal governments as the national treasures which they truly are.

As chairman of the State Government Committee and a member of the Committee on Health and Institutional Services, I was instrumental in convincing the Senate to adopt a proposal to strengthen the Maine Department of Health and Corrections. For many years the Department had employed a Director of Mental

Health, but there was no comparable officer to supervise the state's five correctional institutions. These five — the School for Boys at South Portland, the Stevens Training Center at Hallowell, the two reformatories at South Windham and Skowhegan, and the Maine State Prison at Thomaston — had all been operating independently despite the fact that they had many problems in common, both in the training of personnel and in the need for an integrated underlying philosophy of treatment. The Commissioner of the Department of Mental Health and Corrections had requested the legislature to establish a Bureau of Corrections and to authorize the employment of a Director of Corrections. Under my leadership the State Government Committee successfully secured passage of a bill to achieve this important improvement.

Of all the issues facing the state of Maine in 1963, the most troublesome one involved the assessment of equitable taxes to pay for an expanding budget. On March 19, 1963, the Committee on Taxation presented to the Senate, with an "Ought Not To Pass" recommendation, "An Act Relating to a Net Income Tax Law for the State of Maine." That day I made the first of several speeches in favor of the state income tax as the most equitable of all levies since it is based on ability to pay; the only available other broad-based tax was the regressive sales tax then in effect at a five-percent rate. I began by quoting a recent report of the Legislative Research Committee: "Maine has more than an average number of problems to solve. No other state is in greater need of dealing with its taxation procedures with wisdom."

It was obvious to me that the Governor's budget for the next fiscal year was some $20 million less than requested by the several state departments. Left unmet would be critical needs in support of elementary and secondary education, expansion of teacher's colleges and vocational institutes, improvement of mental health and correctional facilities, and proper staffing of welfare programs such as aid to dependent children, rehabilitation and the care of retarded young people.

In support of my position I quoted from a report by Dr. John Sly of Princeton University, who in 1961 had made a careful study of the tax structure in Maine. He pointed out that Maine ranked

31st in 1960 among all the states in per capita taxes; in tax sacrifice, meaning, the rate of taxation as a percentage of income, it ranked 21st. Dr. Sly revealed that seven years earlier "Maine ranked 11th in tax sacrifice, which means that at the present time the people of the state of Maine are not making the same tax sacrifice they made in 1953." He concluded that "there is some leeway to increase taxes without increasing Maine's previous tax effort."

My argument continued by reference to some historical facts: In 1950 the Maine tax revision committee recommended a combination of sales tax and personal income tax. Fourteen times an income tax has been proposed to the Maine legislature, nine times by Republicans and five by Democrats; thus it is not a partisan issue. There was extended debate in the Senate, pro and con, before the vote was taken. A few converts were made, but once again a state income tax proposal was defeated, this time by a vote of twenty-seven to five. However, good seeds had been sown, and six years later the 104th Legislature adopted a graduated personal income tax which has remained in effect since 1969.

High on the list of satisfying experiences as a State Senator was the privilege of sponsoring for the National Association for the Advancement of Colored People a bill to prohibit discrimination in rental housing; this was to be an extension of the statute already in effect against discrimination in public accommodations, and it would have corrected an increasingly serious problem in Maine's larger cities where adequate rental housing was often denied to black families simply because of the color of their skin. The bill was passed in the Senate but failed of adoption by eight votes on final consideration in the House of Representatives. The way had been prepared, however, and two years later an identical bill was passed by the 102nd Legislature. In this same area, I was also the sponsor of a constitutional amendment, which was later approved by referendum, whereby discrimination against any person in the exercise of civil rights was prohibited in Maine.

As chairman of the State Government committee I presided over public hearings on approximately eighty pieces of legislation. Among major bills favored by the committee and eventually passed were those granting moderate salary increases to various state officers. A significant action was the adoption of a formula which I proposed for a new scale of compensation for future legislators whereby for the first time the state would pay expenses for meals and overnight accommodations; this should attract to public service capable persons who could not otherwise afford to seek state office.

Membership on the Education committee was probably my most important assignment. Here I was instrumental in securing passage of such measures as an increase in minimum wages for teachers, augmented appropriations for the University of Maine and the state teachers' colleges, and permissive legislation for the establishment of additional school administrative districts under the so-called Sinclair Act. My Senate colleagues and I were successful in defeating efforts by conservative legislators to abolish from the school laws certain incentives for the formation of districts, as well as attempts to lower standards for school accreditation and the certification of teachers. I was also appointed to an interim committee charged with responsibility for studying the public school subsidy provisions and recommending corrective measures to the next legislature.

As a member of the committee on Health and Institutional Services I was appointed by the Governor to serve as the Senate representative on the Maine Committee for the Mentally Retarded, in which capacity I sponsored and secured passage of legislation designed to support and expand State activity in a field of major need and concern. I was closely associated with the plan adopted by the legislature to retain the Boys Training Center at its location in South Portland and to appropriate substantial funds for its renovation and expansion; the Center is Maine's only institution for the rehabilitation of juvenile male offenders. I also used my influence for the improvement of the State's services through its other correctional institutions and its mental hospitals.

One other effort which gave me satisfaction as a Christian in politics was my witness in the matter of liquor control. One of the most powerful lobbies at the capitol in Augusta has sought continually to liberalize the Maine liquor laws. In 1963 the steady movement in this direction was stopped for the first time in many years. The principal effort of the liquor interests was to remove the restriction on the Sunday sale of alcoholic beverages. Legislation to do so was defeated after debate in which I had a major part.

When I completed my term as a State Senator I submitted a report of my sabbatical activities to the Seminary Board of Trustees in which I described the major legislative issues which received my attention. The report also set forth my gratitude for the privilege of engaging in the political life of the State, the philosophical basic for such participation, and an estimate of the import of my witness upon the reputation of the Seminary. Here are a few excerpts:

"As a Christian minister concerned with relating his faith to the real problems of society, and as a professor of history seeking to broaden his knowledge of history in the making, this has been a most rewarding experience ... The desire to serve in the state legislature was the natural result of a firmly-held and longstanding conviction that the so-called 'separation' of Church and State in the United States is a myth which should be dispelled both in theory and in practice ... For the past five years I have been demonstrating this theory in local and state government by action in the dual role of churchman and politician. By so doing I have increased my effectiveness as a professor, as a citizen, and as a Seminary president engaged in public relations."

Although I have not held elective public office since 1964, when my state Senate term ended, my interest in political affairs has remained intense, as later chapters in this life story will illustrate.

Photographs

TWO GOLFERS MEET AFTER OFFICE HOURS: PRESIDENT J. J. PELLEY of the New Haven Railroad Congratulates His Conqueror, Fred Whittaker, a Stenographer in the Road's Traffic Department, Following the Play-Off for the Golf Championship of the Company on the New Haven Municipal Course. (Sneiderman.)

New York Herald-Tribune, 1933

The Bride and Groom,
Shirley and Fred Whittaker,
September 14, 1940.

Bangor Seminary Faculty and the Class of 1943

Front row, left to right: Dr. Alex Dodd, Dr. Andrew Banning, Dr. Charles Gordon Cumming, President Harry Trust, Dr. Alfred Perry, Dr. Marion Bradshaw, Dr. Mervin Deems. Second row, left to right: William Bissett, Vincent Fischer, Maldwyn Parry, Edward Manning, John Lamprey, Frederick Whittaker, Willis McLaughlin, Theodore Webb, Charles Haas.

The Whittaker Brothers at the Huntington Congregational Church, Shelton, Connecticut, 1945. Left to right: Edward, Stanley, Fred.

President Whittaker delivers Inaugural Address, 1953.
Seated, left to right: President Emeritus Harry Trust, Trustees Chairman Willard S. Bass, Dr. Vaughan Dabney, Dean of Andover Newton Theological School.

Bangor Seminary Board of Trustees, 1957

First row, left to right: James Lenhart, Fred Thompson, Fred Hayes, President Fred Whittaker, Trustees Chairman Clarence Fuller, Charles Bragg, James Crockett, L. Felix Ranlett, Arthur Eaton. Second row, left to right: John Lowell, Alfred Hempstead, James Gannett, Fred Alden, Athern Daggett, Rodney Roundy, Judge Donald Webber, Arthur Macdougall, Judge Robert Williamson, Edgar Thompson, Ellison Beckwith, William Linnell.

National Hole-in-One Champion.

Penobscot Valley Country Club Professional Charles Emergy presents Fred Whittaker with national P.G.A. trophy for longest hole-in-one (196 yards) in Labor Day tournament, 1957.

The Whittakers at home in the Hannibal Hamlin House, 1960.
Left to right: Shirley, Mark, Fred, Barbara Anne.

Bangor City Council, 1960.
Left to right: Charles Higgins, Edward Keith, John Barry, Dr. Carl Blaisdell, Chairman Clifford Bailey, Edward Gross, Carl Delano, Fred Whittaker, Earle Brown.

Seminary President Fred Whittaker receives honorary Doctor of Divinity degree from President James Stacy Coles of Bowdoin College. Observing at right is Maine Governor John Reed. (1964)

Sesquicentennial Convocation Reception in the Moulton Library,
Bangor Seminary, 1964.
Receiving line, left to right: President Whittaker, Shirley Whittaker, Union
Theological Seminary President Henry P. Van Dusen, United Church of
Christ Vice President Truman Douglass, Trustees Chairman Clarence Fuller.

*Fred and Shirley Whittaker at Retirement Testimonial Dinner in Bangor, May,
1978, with Toastmaster Burton Throckmorton (right), senior faculty member
at Bangor Seminary.*

HEAR THAT LONESOME WHISTLE — *1978 Congressional campaign. Cartoon by Vic Runtz of Bangor Daily News.*

Son Mark and wife Pamela Livesay on their wedding day, June 21, 1969.

Daughter Barbara and husband Frank Toppa on their wedding day, May 11, 1985.

River-rafting on the Kennebec River Gorge in Maine. July, 1987.
Fred and Shirley Whittaker in right foreground.

Looking across "The Wall" from West Germany through "No Man's Land" to East Germany — September, 1988.

Family photo, Christmas, 1990

Front row: Fred and Shirley Whittaker with Isaac Anthony Toppa, adopted son of Frank and Barbara. Second row: left to right: Frank Anthony Toppa, Barbara Anne Whittaker-Johns, Pamela Livesay Whittaker, F. Mark Whittaker, Emily Dole Whittaker, Andrew Boyd Whittaker.

11.
Citizen and Churchman

Throughout my long term as a seminary president I maintained concurrently a keen and lively interest in community affairs and in the Christian church. In fact, I consider my witness as a community leader and as a layman to be of equal significance with my professional work as a theological teacher and administrator. In addition to my service as a city councillor and state senator, my activity as a citizen took many other forms. The local church and the state conference received a considerable portion of my time and effort.

For forty-five years I have been an active member of the service club known as Kiwanis International. In 1953, which was my first full year as president of Bangor Seminary, I was also president of the Bangor Kiwanis Club. On more than one occasion through the decades I have been chairman of the Kiwanis Committee on Support of Churches. Weekly contact with leading businessmen of the community has been both a public relations activity on behalf of the Seminary and a means whereby I have had vital contact with the secular life of the city. Many time I have been given the privilege of speaking on topics of the day at meetings of Kiwanis and its sister organizations: the Lions Club and Rotary International.

My feeling about service clubs is well expressed in an address to the Bangor-Brewer Lions Club in 1953, when I said: "Although religion is commonly associated with the church or synagogue, it becomes most significant when its teachings are applied in areas where men live and work together. Service clubs such as Lions, Rotary, and Kiwanis are religious organizations insofar as they promote social welfare, and their members perform religious duties whenever they minister to the needs of their fellowmen."

In seeking to fulfill my duties as a responsible citizen I also made my talents available to other civic and educational institutions. For example, I served on the board of directors of the Bangor Y.M.C.A., the local United Fund, and the area Chamber of Commerce. In 1964 I accepted appointment by Governor John Reed to membership on the board of trustees of the Maine Maritime Academy at Castine for a three-year term. This gave me an opportunity to take a leadership role in the affairs of a premier school for the training of officers for the merchant marine industry.

Following the completion in 1964 of my term as a Maine state senator I was asked to accept the position of chairman of the Educational Conference Board of Maine during its formative period; I served for the first two years of the Board's existence. Membership of the Board consisted of representatives from each of eight state-wide organizations concerned with educational matters, namely: American Association of University Women, State School Boards Association, Maine Congress of Parent-Teachers Association, Governor's Advisory Committee on Education, University of Maine, Maine State Board of Education, and Maine Teachers Association.

The Articles of Agreement of the Educational Conference Board set forth the following five objectives: to study proposed legislation; to advise the constituent membership of such proposed legislation; to develop and promote same most effectively; to keep fully informed the constituent membership as to the status of public education in the State of Maine; to make original recommendations concerning public education to the constituent membership.

During my tenure as its chairman, the Educational Conference Board adopted and supported publicly, after careful study, position papers on several important issues related to education in Maine. It endorsed a graduated personal income tax as the best way to raise money to improve the quality of schools and to reduce unequal property tax burdens. The Board supported a general purpose subsidy for education instead of many separate subsidies for special programs. It suggested that the federal government should return a part of income tax receipts to Maine and other states for the improvement of education under state administration, and that this funding should favor general purpose aid rather than categorical assistance.

Other recommendations made by the Education Conference Board had to do with curriculum and professional growth. The Board suggested that schools should augment staff and resources so as to provide a variety of courses that will relate education to individual student aptitudes and to the future life work of the student, thus providing a motivating incentive toward learning. Further, the Board encouraged developments designed to invigorate intercultural understanding, including more teacher and student exchange between Maine and foreign countries.

With regard to professional growth, the Board proposed experimentation for the improvement of teaching and learning, specifically by the greater utilization of teacher aides and cooperation among Maine schools in providing internship experience. It also supported the practice of payment by the state of professional incentives to teachers and superintendents. My work with this statewide Board was a source of personal satisfaction in that it provided an extension of my influence as a state senator and member of the legislative Education Committee. It also gave me the pleasure of becoming personally acquainted with many of the distinguished educators in Maine such as Dr. Lloyd Elliott, president of the University of Maine.

My avocational role as a Christian citizen found expression in several ways. In 1964 I was a delegate from Maine to the Republican National Convention in San Francisco. I was elected on the basis of my support for then Governor Nelson Rockefeller of New York state as a nominee for the office of President of the United States. At the convention Rockefeller was overwhelmed by the carefully orchestrated forces of Senator Barry Goldwater. This was the convention at which Senator Margaret Chase Smith of Maine became the first woman ever to be nominated for President. In the decisive vote Goldwater easily defeated Rockefeller, but the entire Maine delegation refused to support him as it cast all of its votes for Senator Smith. The Goldwater nomination marked the beginning of the conservative ascendancy within the Republican party nationally, which culminated in the Ronald Reagan presidency. For me it signalled the beginning of my own declining interest in a political party where liberal voices were destined to lose their influence.

Shortly after the convention I was surprised and pleased by an invitation from Republican leaders in Maine to support my nomination for the office of representative to Congress from the second district. It was a prospect which I had not envisioned despite a heightened interest in a political career following my term in the Maine State Senate. The offer came, I suspect, because two prestigious Maine institutions had recently recognized my contribution to the state as a political figure. In June of 1964 Bowdoin College awarded me the honorary degree of Doctor of Divinity upon the recommendation of Donald W. Webber, a Seminary trustee and associate justice of the Maine Supreme Judicial Court. Later in the same year the B'nai B'rith State of Maine Council presented to me the "Man of the Year Award" as "an outstanding humanitarian." The Bowdoin citation by President James S. Coles read as follows:

> FREDERICK WILLIAM WHITTAKER, of the Class of 1944, magna cum laude, President of the Bangor Theological Seminary. Ten years of practical experience in railroad operation preceded your studies at Bangor and at Bowdoin, your election to Phi Beta Kappa, and your doctorate from Yale University, in whose shadow you were born. Effective in three pastorates, you have been equally effective as Professor of Ecclesiastical History and President of the Bangor Theological Seminary, where your leadership has brought it to new glory. As a "fisher of men" you have caught for the church many able clergymen, sorely needed, for whom you

personify the ideal of the "mature ministry." You have now brought to all facets of community life and to the State of Maine — in education and civic affairs and public service — your many abilities, first as member and Chairman of the Bangor City Council, and most recently as Senator in the Maine State Legislature, where your cool head and balanced judgment have proved a wise and liberating influence.

Although I had some misgivings about the possibility of winning a Congressional seat as a Republican with Senator Barry Goldwater heading the national ticket, I decided to ask the Seminary Board of Trustees for permission to have my name entered in the primary election. I did so with mixed emotions, knowing that the Seminary was about to begin a three-year celebration and fund-raising campaign on the occasion of its 150th Anniversary. I rationalized that I had served as president of the school for twelve good years, that the political opportunity offered to me would probably never come my way again, and that service as a Congressman would bring some honor to the Seminary while fulfilling my strong avocational interest in the world of politics.

The Board of Trustees declined to grant my request; no doubt they had good and sufficient reasons. I was faced with the choice of entering my name in the primary election and resigning my position at the Seminary, or continuing my theological career. Responsibility to my family was the key factor in my decision to remain at Bangor. It was probably a wise move since very few Republican candidates survived the landslide Democratic presidential victory in 1964 of Lyndon B. Johnson over Barry Goldwater. Nevertheless, I have often wondered in the ensuing years what would have happened to my career if I had chosen the political alternative.

The Trustees did grant me permission to seek another term on the Bangor City Council, but I was defeated at the polls in the fall election, somewhat to my surprise and that of local political commentators. It was surmised that the Bangor electorate reacted negatively to my liberalism as a state senator in supporting a personal income tax for Maine and sponsoring legislation to prohibit racial discrimination in rental housing.

Two years later I tried again to resume my activity as a City Councillor. 1966 was a year of sharp difference of opinion among Americans with regard to participation of the United States in the Viet Nam war. From the beginning of our nation's unilateral involvement in this Far Eastern conflict, I had been an outspoken opponent of this policy. My positive argument was that only the United Nations had a legal and moral right to intervene. I urged the voters of Bangor to "send a message to Washington" by voting for me as a City Councillor. My ultimate defeat at the polls indicated that my fellow citizens did not agree with me about the Viet Nam war, or that they believed the issue was not germane to a local election.

My chagrin at losing another election was deepened by the fact that my wife Shirley also failed in her first and only attempt in the political arena. At a time when women were something of a rarity in the state legislature, she agreed to accept an invitation from the Republican party to be a candidate for election to the state House of Representatives. She was well qualified by virtue of her college education, her six years of teaching in the Bangor public schools, and her leadership in church and community activities. We presented ourselves to the voters as a "ticket," which was probably a mistake in view of my own defeat on election day. It was to be another eight years before I again became a candidate for public office. That is a story to be told later.

Now there is a narrative to be written about my life as a churchman. For thirty years my wife and I were active members of the Hammond Street Congregational Church (UCC) in Bangor. Together we have filled most of the offices held by lay people in the congregation. Since leaving the pastorate in 1948 I have always considered myself to be a layman despite my official status as an ordained minister. Shirley and I have been blessed by our association with four ministers at Hammond Street, most notably by the Reverend Harland G. Lewis and the Reverend Edward G. Ernst, together with their wives Anne and Helen. Many times I have preached from the pulpit of the church. For twenty-six years I presided in that pulpit over the annual Convocation Week program of the Seminary. I was even a member of the Hammond Street men's championship dart-ball team. Our two children, Barbara and Mark, were educated in the Church School. Barbara was married in the sanctuary in 1964. She still speaks reverently of Ed Ernst as a minister who had a very positive influence upon her life. Hammond Street Church has left an indelible mark upon the Whittaker family.

Beyond the local church my activities as a churchman began with leadership roles in the Penobscot Association of Congregational Christian Churches such as moderator and chairman of the Ministerial Standing Committee, the latter being the agency which authorizes prospective clergy to receive licenses to preach and eventually to be ordained. I was a regular attendant at Association meetings during my thirty years at Bangor Seminary. I have addressed the Association on many occasions, and my ministerial standing is still today in the Penobscot Association.

Under congregational polity the Maine Conference of the Congregational Churches has historically been the agency responsible for planning and effecting the cooperative work of local denominational churches within the state. It is headed by a Conference Minister or Superintendent, three of whom have been my close friends and associates over the years. It was Dr. Rodney W. Roundy who assigned me to my first student parish. Dr. Cornelius Clark and Dr. William Thompson, together with Dr. Roundy, were trustees of the Seminary during my tenure as president and were immensely helpful in supporting my work as chief executive.

My witness as a churchman was given major expression through the Maine Conference. As early as 1950 I was invited to address a seminar sponsored by the Conference. The assigned topic was "On Training a Christian Ministry Today." In my prepared remarks I set forth the following dual thesis which has been a hallmark of my lifelong philosophy or theology: "The modern minister should be prepared not only to lead and instruct the congregation in those aspects of life commonly known as 'religious' or 'spiritual,' although that is his major task, but he should be trained also to live sympathetically and helpfully with his brethren in those realms of life called the 'political,' the 'economic,' and the 'social,' that is, the 'total' life of man." I went on to say " that if this be true, then it follows that the education of a minister today is not the responsibility of the seminary alone, but is a project which must be shared by the home, the elementary and secondary schools, the church and the community-at-large.

In this same address I also espoused a suggestion which has been incorporated in my prophetic pronouncements for forty years: "If religious experience is as vital a part of the total life of man as historical records indicate, then the story of this experience should be an integral part of the curricula of our schools from the higher elementary grades through college or university. We assume that our youth should know about human achievements in the realms of science, political history, economics, sociology, and the like, but we exclude religion from our schools as a subject too 'controversial' for discussion. As a result, many young men and women turn to some other field of endeavor when, if their early education had been complete, they might well have chosen service in the religious sphere." Thirteen years later the U.S. Supreme Court, in its landmark decision banning prayer and Bible-reading as devotional exercises in the public schools, agreed that teaching "about" religion in the classrooms was constitutionally valid.

In 1957 the Maine Conference conferred upon me the honor of naming me its President. This office became a gateway for me to enter the wider sphere of denominational work nationally. One of the objects of the state Conference set forth in its by-laws was "cooperation with our national benevolent societies, with the General Council, and with other ecclesiastical bodies 'in the extension of the Kingdom of Christ on earth'." The principal means of achieving this object was financial support of a statewide contribution of the churches to the national program of the denomination known then as "Our Christian World Mission." During the year of my presidency the Maine Conference adopted the largest OCWM goal in its history, thus fulfilling a basic emphasis of my ministry — increasing support by local churches and state conferences of the missionary outreach of the denomination. Another important achievement of my administration was the implementation of a plan to locate a branch office of the Conference in Bangor for the purpose of better serving the needs of local churches and ministries in the northern and eastern sections of Maine.

A large segment of my time and effort as a churchman was spent in denominational work at the national level. As president of the Seminary I was given the privilege automatically every two years of attending, as an associate delegate, the biennial meeting of the General Council (the General Synod after the United Church of Christ was formed in 1957) of the Congregational Christian Churches, one of the national agencies of the denomination. For many years I was a member of this body's Commission on Christian Unity and Ecumenical Service; this is a story which will be told in a later chapter. Other major instrumentalities of the national church were the Board for World Ministries and the Board for Homeland Ministries; within the latter agency there was a Council for Higher Education, and it was with this group that I exerted my best effort as a churchman on behalf of education within the denomination.

The Council for Higher Education of the United Church of Christ has the following stated purposes: to serve as a means of communication between the Church and its educational institutions; to be a forum for the exchange of ideas and practices among the members; to sponsor the expression of the Christian faith within the academic community; and to provide the best possible training for the Christian ministry. Members of the Council include officers of the Church's Board for Homeland Ministries and the executives of thirty-one colleges, two academies, and fourteen theological schools related to the United Church. Within the Council there are two divisions, one for the colleges and academies, and one for the seminaries.

My national association began in 1955 when I started a term of several years as secretary of the Congregational Christian Council of Theological Schools. After the formation of the United Church of Christ I served as secretary and then chairman of the Council for Higher Education. Twice I was chairman, and once secretary, of the Seminary Section of the Council. Within the Council there was a further division of the constituent member schools, seven of which were designated as "closely related" to the United Church. One of the principal efforts of the seven — Andover Newton, Bangor, Chicago Theological Seminary, Eden, Lancaster, Pacific School of Religion, and United (Twin Cities) — was directed toward greater recognition and financial support of these schools by the national denomination. This effort was, at best, marginally successful. For reasons which are difficult for me to comprehend, the United Church of Christ has never given high priority to the sustenance of the schools which train its ministers.

In evaluating my twin role as citizen and churchman through the decades, I discovered that in many instances one function was indistinguishable from the other. When I spoke to citizen groups such as service clubs I was very much the churchman expounding religious viewpoints which were pertinent to a secular issue. When I preached as a churchman I consistently tried to apply the tenets of my faith to the practicalities of personal or community living. One good example is the Maundy Thursday sermon I preached in 1968 at the Hammond Street Church shortly after the assassination of Dr. Martin Luther King, Jr. In a front-page story in its edition of April 12, 1968, the *Bangor Daily News* ran a five-column headline, "Bangor Seminary President Urges City To Bury 'White Isolationism'." The following are some of the quotations and ideas taken from my communion meditation the previous evening:

"If Christians would keep alive the spirit of Jesus Christ and help redeem the martyred life of Dr. Martin Luther King, Jr., they must work for the Christian ideals of brotherhood, peace, and social justice." Declaring that Bangor should bury its "white isolationism," Dr. Whittaker suggested that members of local churches, business leaders, government officials and professional people "let it be widely known that Negroes will be cordially welcomed if they come to Bangor to live and work." He stated his opinion that "such a program will be a significant model for the nation in its time of racial crisis and it would, by bringing to the city a more substantial number of Negro residents, make available here the cultural advantages of a truly integrated community."

The Seminary president described his ideas as "not a crusade," but a constructive step to combat racism. He announced plans to contact alumni of the Seminary throughout the United States, urging

212

them to recommend qualified Negroes to the school. Advertisements will be placed in Negro periodicals in an effort to attract more non-white students. Traditionally the Seminary has enrolled a student body in which about five percent have been non-white, and the school would like to increase this ratio to fifteen percent. He pointed out that several Negro students had made significant contributions to local community life.

Asserting that he was not recommending the establishment in Bangor of a ghetto for Negroes, Dr. Whittaker stated his conviction that "the white community in Bangor, or in any city with few non-white residents, is culturally deprived when it does not have the opportunity of living with a minority group." Pointing out that "it is easy for us in Bangor to live in white isolationism while racial tensions disrupt the rest of the country," the Seminary president urged his fellow citizens to take positive action in combatting the growing racial crisis in the nation.

It was in the momentous decade of the 1960's that I was most active as a citizen and churchman. I include in this chapter of my life excerpts from some of the major public speeches made on behalf of current issues involving moral overtones. One of these was racism, as already shown above. Another was international relations and the cold war. On August 10, 1961, the *Bangor Daily News* reported on my address to the Bangor Kiwanis Club the previous day. The headline read: "Bangor Seminary Head Advocates Red China Be Admitted Into United Nations." I had pointed out to my fellow service club members that "large numbers of competent observers believe that the government of the People's Republic of China should be granted membership in the United Nations organization so that its policies and actions may come under the scrutiny of this world body."

Reminding my audience that the U.N. cannot function effectively while it denies membership to a nation of more than 400 million people with a civilization almost 4,000 years old, I lamented that "each year the United States is losing support for its position that Communist China should not be admitted to the United Nations ... Ominously, it is losing the respect of the colored races — yellow and black — which comprise two-thirds of all human beings."

213

In this speech, entitled "A Kiwanian Looks at War and Peace," I advocated that the United States should take the initiative in the struggle for world peace by offering to surrender its veto power in the U.N. Security Council, if others will do the same, by expressing its willingness to abide by decisions of the United Nations, and by support of a U.N. police force to carry out such decisions. Such leadership, I suggested, would be in accord with a Kiwanis objective "to advance peace through the rule of law in world affairs" and would bring far greater security to our nation and the world of nations than can possibly be achieved by continuation of a "cold war" which each day threatens to explode into a holocaust.

Drawing upon my experience as a professional historian, I told the service club members that "my study of history convinces me that some of our national policies can lead only to war and inevitable chaos; other national plans and aspirations have within them the possibility of peace and ultimate security for our nation and the world. On the negative side, "we are now engaged in an arms race which requires for its financial support 47 billion dollars annually. Enough nuclear weapons now exist in American stockpiles to exterminate every man, woman and child on the earth. The Soviet Union may have almost as many. Both nations are increasing their number of weapons and their ability to deliver them. This is a policy of war, which can only lead to international conflict, as all of history will testify."

On the positive side, I pointed out that one of the brightest lights on the horizon is the Peace Corps now being recruited and trained by the United States government. The tremendous and enthusiastic response of American young people to the idea and challenge of the Peace Corps is a great and encouraging demonstration of the desire of the people of this nation to strive for peace rather than prepare for war. "From my point of view," I concluded, "every dollar spent in support of the Peace Corps is worth a hundred dollars — and perhaps a thousand dollars — spent for the building of armaments."

Four years later, in 1965, at the height of the war in Viet Nam, I again espoused a viewpoint in support of the United Nations as a peace-keeping agency. Here are excerpts from a letter written to the editor of the *Bangor Daily News*:

"In 1945, just twenty years ago, the United Nations was born out of the turmoil of World War II. Under its charter an international police force has succeeded in peace-keeping missions in such war-torn lands as the Congo, the island of Cyprus, and India-Pakistan. Meanwhile in Viet Nam an undeclared war escalates daily as the unilateral action of the United States in responding to the pleas of South Viet Nam for military assistance is met with increasing military activity on the part of North Viet Nam ... It is my Christian conviction that the United States has no moral responsibility to send a police force to protect 'freedom' in Asia or other parts of the world. This is the responsibility of the UNITED NATIONS, with the United States providing its share of men and machines. I believe that my nation has no moral right to plead 'self-defense' as a justification for sending its military forces halfway around the world when, for example, a nearby neighbor to the Viet Nam conflict, Japan, feels no need for such self-defense ... the United States should request the Secretary General of the United Nations to seek urgently a cease-fire in Viet Nam and make arrangements for the conflict there to be placed under the jurisdiction of a U.N. police force...."

In November of 1963 an event occurred which shocked all Americans and left them searching for answers to eternal questions. President John Fitzgerald Kennedy was assassinated, cutting short a most promising political career. A grieving country participated in memorial services throughout the nation. One was held at Bangor Theological Seminary on November 26th, at which I spoke as a churchman and citizen under the theme, "A Time For Prayer." The BTS Alumni Bulletin of January, 1964, published my address:

This is a time for prayer — prayer of thanksgiving for the life and work of President John Fitzgerald Kennedy; prayer of intercession for his eternal well-being and for the sustaining of his loved ones; prayer of penitence for the guilt which all Americans share in the assassination of our President; and prayer of petition for divine guidance of the nation and its new chief executive. Prayer is our only sanctuary after a weekend of violence, shock, disbelief, grief, and sorrow which no one of us will ever forget. On the eve of this nation's traditional day of gratitude it will not be easy for us whose lives have suddenly been saturated with sadness to revive our faith and to sing praises to our God. But we shall turn from the darkness to the light because we know that under divine Providence gloom cannot for long overshadow hope.

John Fitzgerald Kennedy, in the moment of his cruel and untimely death, may have set in motion moral and spiritual forces which will guide the peoples of the world to a new era of mutual understanding and peace. His assassination by one of his own countrymen may have so dismayed the citizens of our beloved land that we shall seek and find new ways of living together in brotherhood from shore to shore.

Chief Justice Earl Warren has called President Kennedy "a great and good man." His goodness was shown in a lifelong series of "profiles of courage," in his dealings with other nations through a rare combination of strength and compassion, and in his fearless support of the rights of minority groups within the United States. His goodness was readily recognized through his love for his family, his concern for the senior citizens of our country, and his willingness to mingle with the people as friend to friend even at the risk of his life. Very few men in so short a period of time have captured the minds and hearts of such a worldwide multitude. Testimony to this fact was given by the representatives of fifty-three foreign states and the millions of Americans who have wept for him and brought him tribute. Our first prayer, then, should be of thanksgiving for the life and work of our departed leader.

As Christians we believe that death does not end our individual existence, but that by faith we inherit the everlasting life promised by God through Jesus Christ. Thus with confidence we may utter our prayer of intercession for President Kennedy and for the sustaining of his loved ones. There is no doubt he was a man of religious conviction and one who was strengthened in his private and public acts by the teachings of his Church. Our petitions for his eternal well-being will be echoed around the earth and with the assured hope that they will be answered.

When news of the President's death was finally accepted as true by a stunned and disbelieving world, the early reactions of many took the form of anguished sympathy for the widow and for the fatherless children. That Mrs. Kennedy was aware of this universal concern has been abundantly clear to all who have seen the majestic beauty and dignity of her composure in time of deepest grief. The spiritual stature of the first lady has been a source of inspiration and courage to innumerable men and women of lesser faith. God has indeed spoken through her abiding love for her husband and the obvious survival of that love beyond the grave. Yet we shall want to pray for Mrs. Kennedy, for her young ones, and for the members of the President's family in their present bereavement; and ask that the Holy Comforter may be with them steadfastly in the long days and years which are to come.

There is another prayer we must utter before the Creator and Judge. It is one of penitence and supplication, of begging forgiveness of the guilt which all Americans share in the assassination of our President. One man in a city far away fired the fatal shot. But my conscience has been burning within me ever since that fateful Friday. Do I not speak for you, too, and for countless others when I say that we and our fellow countrymen are implicated in this murderous crime because we have left undone those things which we ought to have done and we have done those things which we ought not to have done?

Have we not been responsible for the development in our land of a climate of hatred, intolerance, lust, suspicion, dishonesty, intemperance, violence, and a host of other evils, which served as a breeding place for the angry or misguided killing of our chief executive? Have we not condoned the glorification of sex, of lawlessness, and of greed for material possessions, in our literature, our legitimate stage productions, our moving pictures, and our television fare? Have we not waited almost a hundred years since the assassination of another great American President before beginning to redeem his death by granting at last a measure of real freedom and equality to our Negro citizens? Have we not established an unnecessary and an unhealthy enmity among political parties in our nation by seeking first to be partisan Republicans or Democrats rather than first to be loyal Americans, and by irrationally hurling at one another the epithets Communist, Fascist, left-wing and right-

217

wing, liberal and conservative? Have we not in our religious communities sought to dwell in splendid isolation as Protestants, Roman Catholics, and Jews instead of acknowledging our common heritage and joining hands to take our best spiritual insights into the world for the uplifting of our bewildered society? And do not our affirmative answers to these questions have relevance to the terrible tragedy which engulfs us? We are, indeed, standing in the need of a prayer of penitence!

As those who seek forgiveness from above we shall be most worthy of God's blessing if we now and for the future re-dedicate ourselves as a nation in a commonwealth of nations to those ideas and high purposes for which our fallen President gave his life and met his death. To this end our final prayer must be a petition for divine guidance of the people of the United States and of our new leader. President Lyndon B. Johnson has been unexpectedly charged with a responsibility of great magnitude, but there is welcome evidence that he is prepared for the task. One of his most challenging legacies is the dual problem of racial justice and peace. That he intends to follow in the footsteps of his predecessor on this issue was made manifest by the then Vice President at Gettysburg on last Memorial Day, when he declared at the close of an address marking the centennial of Lincoln's Emancipation Proclamation: "Until justice is blind to color, until education is unaware of race, until opportunity is unconcerned with the color of men's skin, emancipation will be a proclamation but not a fact. To the extent that the proclamation of emancipation is not fulfilled in fact, to that extent we shall have fallen short of assuring freedom to the free."

Our new President will surely need the help of the Almighty in the solution of this and a host of other vexing problems. He will also need the assistance of a people under God united in labor for holy and righteous causes. And so this day, in honor and memory of "a great and good man," we offer our prayers of thanksgiving, of intercession, of penitence, and of petition for divine guidance. Yet may we know that after our prayers are answered, and the divine guidance has been given, we cannot escape the awesome fact set forth by President John Fitzgerald Kennedy in his inaugural *address: "Here on earth God's work must truly be our own."*

I conclude this chapter on my activities as a citizen and churchman during the decade of the 1960's by quoting excerpts from an address inspired by President Kennedy's clarion call for human endeavor on behalf of God. Using the topic "The New-Time Religion," I have spoken often in the church and in the community. This is what I said in part to the Bangor Rotary Club at a luncheon meeting on September 30, 1969:

"Man cannot expect God to do for him what God has given man the power to do for himself ... God will not intervene by some new supernatural act to eliminate the many social evils which plague human society ... Man is on his own in dealing with war, racism, and poverty, to name but three of the major programs of contemporary life ... The 'old-time religion,' with its over-emphasis on the sinfulness of man and the sovereignty of God, needs to be replaced because it has not inspired man to realize his potential as a human being under divine guidance. It has been too much concerned with life after death in another world and too much motivated by a fear of God's judgment....

"The 'new-time' religion emphasizes the ability given to man by the Creator to choose between good and evil; it proclaims a God of love who expects his human creatures to cooperate with him in maintaining peace and justice and prosperity upon the earth; it believes that the deity who gives man life in this world will care for him after death, and that man should gratefully spend his days and years here as a partner with God ... God has revealed his purposes to man from the beginning of religious history down to this very moment of time ... In every age, including our own, God has spoken anew to every individual who would listen. Thus, contemporary man, using all the power and inspiration of past and present divine guidance, must solve his own moral and social problems — or suffer the consequences.

"The paralyzing hold which 'old-time' religion has on American Protestantism, in particular, is illustrated by statistics recently released by the National Council of Churches indicating that six out of every ten citizens believe that the church should not be involved in social and political issues such as war, racism, and poverty ... As a proponent of the 'new-time' religion I contend that these are the very issues to which a vital modern church should give the highest priority ... God has given man all the guidance he needs through past and present revelation ... Man is now on his own."

12.
President: The Middle Years

The decade of the sixties was perhaps the most volatile ten-year period in America during the twentieth century. It was the era of the Viet Nam war; it marked the assassination of three national heroes — John Fitzgerald Kennedy, Martin Luther King, Jr., and Robert Kennedy; students demanded more control over educational processes; and the women's rights movement had its beginnings. My own participation in politics as an avocation was an indication of the mood of the times. For the Seminary itself the 1960's was a period of both change and advancement.

During the middle years of my presidency, there were a number of changes in personnel, including the appointment of the first women to serve on the faculty. Women, students, and faculty members were appointed to the Board of Trustees for the first time. The school celebrated its 150th anniversary by building a new chapel and renovating its classroom and dormitory facilities. The number of students enrolled reached an all-time high as the percentage of female matriculants began to rise. A Roman Catholic priest became a member of the adjunct faculty. The financial condition of the Seminary improved by virtue of several substantial bequests, including the largest capital gift ever received. At the end of the decade national accreditation was finally granted

221

after a long struggle.

The decade began, soberly, with the death of President Emeritus Harry Trust on May 3, 1960, in Pittsfield, Massachusetts, at the age of 77. A memorial service was held in the Church on the Hill in Lenox, Massachusetts, where Dr. Trust had served as minister after his retirement from the Seminary. The address was given by Dr. Frederick M. Meek, a long-time friend and former pastor to Dr. Trust. Another service was held at All Souls Congregational Church in Bangor, where Dr. Trust had long been a member. Dr. Charles Gordon Cumming, senior faculty member at the Seminary, officiated and the prayer was given by Dr. Mervin M. Deems of the Seminary. Chairman of the Board of Trustees Clarence W. Fuller read a minute adopted by the Board, which stated in part:

"No resolution can comprehend the significance of his presidency. Inheriting from his distinguished predecessors a school of academic excellence which had been narrowly saved from financial collapse, he received it in one of the worst economic periods in the country's history. None excelled him in faith in its purposes, in work for its preservation and improvement, in devotion to those who became associated with it. Devotion, displayed not only in dedication but also in warmth of personality and friendly understanding, is perhaps the quality most associated with him by students, alumni, and colleagues. Giving of himself with wonderful fidelity to the school, he also honored it with far-flung service in church, fraternal organization and youth agencies, believing that such service, while worthy in itself, would reflect in glory to the school, a belief which has been justified in practical ways. Retiring from the presidency after nineteen years and returning to the parish ministry, where he was distinguished as a 'beloved pastor,' he continued to make known his love for the Seminary. The Trustees cannot fully measure his worth to the school, but for his devotion to its purposes, for maintaining it through a difficult time and preparing it for the future, for the credit he brought to it in many ways, they are eternally grateful to this consecrated servant of Jesus Christ who was their former colleague, chairman and friend."

It was my honorable privilege to give the memorial address at the Bangor ceremony. I include excerpts here for the historical record:

Two portraits hang upon the wall in my Seminary campus study. One is of Jesus Christ, the other of Harry Trust. Today we have met in the name of one to remember and honor the other. It is altogether right and good that these two names should be upon our lips and in our hearts this day, for we praise Harry Trust first of all as a follower and disciple of Jesus Christ. Many times in recent years the impact of these two portraits has been felt across my desk. The spiritual influence of the President Emeritus has often guided Seminary affairs, although he himself was many miles away. No less shall this be true in years to come; in fact, his power shall increase for he dwells now in the nearer presence of his own Lord and Savior....

Harry Trust had faith in the God revealed by Jesus Christ. He clearly heard and gladly received the gospel proclaimed by St. John: "For God so loved the world that He gave his only Son that whoever believes in him should not perish but have everlasting life." He preached this good news throughout a lifetime of devotion to the Christian "cause" — a word he often used. Inspired by this cause he led a generation of men and women by precept and example to a more abundant earthly life and to a firm expectation of greater glory yet to come....

Harry Trust had faith in the church of Jesus Christ. It impelled him to leave his native England in search of a theological and liberal arts education. Although we of the Seminary family esteem him most highly as an alumnus who became its president, it may well be that his testimony and work as a parish minister was of equal significance in his distinguished career. Multitudes of church people, old and young, have been blessed by his preaching and his pastoral care in many parts of Maine, in Ohio, and in Massachusetts during his retiring years....

Harry Trust had faith in Bangor Theological Seminary. This is the school which opened for him — as it has for countless others — the doorway to the Christian ministry. No man has been more devoted than he to the "school of the prophets," as he so fondly called his alma mater. No man could have toiled more diligently to

223

perfect its educational program, to sustain its physical plant, and to broaden its impact as an instrument of Christianity. He designed and established the Seminary's worshipful sanctuary, he brought to fruition the "Bangor plan," now uniquely famous for its preparation of mature men and women for the ministry; and he laid the financial, academic, and spiritual foundations upon which the present development plans of the school are being built. There are no words I can say which will so well express his love for the Seminary as these he spoke to me one memorable day: "I charge you to remember always that your first loyalty, after that due to God and to Jesus Christ our Lord, is to the Seminary as long as you shall continue to serve it."...

Harry Trust had faith in his fellowmen. Acknowledgement of this fact may be our greatest tribute to him. His doctrine of man was a positive one. He believed in the power of Christian man, under the guidance of God, to overcome personal sin and corporate evil. He told the faculty and students at the Seminary that "men go to church...to receive counsel from a man of God concerning the problems of the moral life and their obligations to their neighbors and the world at large." This was his "conclusion and faith," he said, at the end of forty-eight years of preaching the gospel of Jesus Christ: he counted himself among those whom he described as "definitely dedicated to advancing the Kingdom of God on earth." ...And so 'the cause' for which Harry Trust lived and died goes on!...

A most significant change in faculty personnel took place in 1961 when Dr. David W. Jewell resigned as professor of Christian Education to take a similar position in the Graduate School of Theology at Oberlin College. That same year the first woman ever called to the faculty at Bangor began her service on September 1st as Associate Professor. The Reverend Clarice M. Bowman was an ordained minister of the Methodist Church and was widely known as a denominational leader in Christian Education work, as a teacher and an author. Since 1952 she had been Assistant Professor of Religious Education at High Point College, a Methodist school in North Carolina. Previously she had been for sixteen years a member of the national staff of the General Board of Education of the

Methodist Church, working out of Chicago and Nashville, Tennessee. Her early experience included four years as director of Christian education at Plymouth Congregational Church in New Haven, Connecticut, where as a young layman in my home church I was well acquainted with her leadership qualities.

Born in Mount Airy, North Carolina, Professor Bowman studied at Duke University and received the A.B. and A.M. degrees with a major in Christian education. She completed further graduate study at Boston University School of Theology, Vanderbilt School of Theology, University of Southern California School of Theology, and the University of Chicago Divinity School. She had traveled throughout the United States as a lecturer and worship leader at many schools and among several denominations. Her special competence was in the fields of youth work, camping, leadership training, and worship. Among Miss Bowman's many publications are several books and more than 700 articles. She authored *Resources for Worship, Guiding Intermediates, Restoring Worship, Ways Youth Learn,* and *Spiritual Values in Camping.*

Because of our earlier association at Plymouth Church in New Haven, I was particularly pleased that Claire Bowman agreed to leave a successful teaching career in her native state and become a member of the Bangor faculty. We were both pleased to renew our friendship. She brought her mother to live with her in a campus apartment, where both were charming hosts to many students for several years. Claire also played a significant role in solidifying the growing relationship of the Methodist Church with the Seminary. She came to Bangor at a propitious time, for the Seminary was about to inaugurate a new degree program in Christian education.

Effective with the academic year 1961-62, the Seminary began to offer a program of studies leading to the degree of Bachelor of Religious Education. This was a four-year course and was offered only to women students. The first two years of study were in the liberal arts, and the curriculum was similar to that offered in the school's pre-theological department. The third and fourth years included study in basic theological disciplines and specialized work in Christian education courses. The stated purpose of the B.R.E. program was to prepare women for work in Christian education as staff members of local churches. It was also a means of increasing enrollments at the Seminary. Although the B.R.E. program was abandoned later in the decade in favor of specialization of Christian education within the theological degree program, the experiment lasted for a number of years and served to strengthen Christian education in its continuing struggle to achieve equity with other theological disciplines. It also marked the beginning of the recognition by B.T.S. of women as professional leaders of the Christian enterprise. It is worthy of note that today women at Bangor, and at many other theological schools, are equal in number to male students.

1961 also saw the beginning of a new program in mental health at the Seminary in cooperation with the Bangor State Hospital (later the Bangor State Mental Health Institute). This program was made possible by a three-year grant totaling $27,000 awarded to the Seminary by the National Institute of Mental Health through the United States Department of Health, Education and Welfare. To direct this new endeavor, the Seminary called to its resident faculty, effective September 1st, the Reverend Myron F. Klinkman, Th.D., and gave him academic status as Associate Professor of Psychology and Pastoral Counselling.

Dr. Klinkman was born in Lancaster, New York, in 1922. After serving in the U.S. Army during World War II, he enrolled in Capital University at Columbus, Ohio, earned its B.A. degree and then the B.D. degree of its School of Theology. In 1955 he was awarded the Th.D. degree of Boston University School of Theology. He then became chaplain of the Harrisburg State Hospital in Pennsylvania, where he conducted courses in clinical training for area ministers and theological students. He took his own clinical training at Massachusetts General Hospital and Boston Psychopathic Hospital and was accredited as a Chaplain Supervisor by the Institute of Pastoral Care.

During the middle years of my presidency, there was major emphasis upon the sesquicentennial anniversary of the Seminary. In 1964 the school was 150 years old with respect to the granting of its charter in 1814. A special convocation was held to mark the actual date on February 25th. The celebration continued for two years through 1966, when the school noted the 150th anniversary of its opening in 1816. Throughout the two-year period a financial campaign was conducted; it successfully raised $150,000 in capital gifts as a tribute to its sesquicentennial. Much of this money had been spent early in the decade as a part of a long-range development program adopted by the Board of Trustees. As soon as the school's book collection had been moved to the new Moulton Library, plans were made to renovate the Chapel Building. In 1960 and 1961 the entire second floor of the structure, which had previously housed a large lecture hall and a sanctuary, was converted into five modernized classrooms. The old and worn double staircase, which climbed the full distance between the first and second floors, was changed to a single set of stairs with an intermediate landing. Two classrooms at the first-floor front of the building were renovated, and the remainder of the first-floor space, which had previously housed the library, was transformed into a beautiful chapel.

The new sanctuary, which bears the name of Bangor's second president, David Nelson Beach, was dedicated at the Baccalaureate Service on June 4, 1961. The Beach Chapel was a worship center of unusual beauty. The prominence of the cross was accentuated by a series of wooden louvers and by special lighting effects. A new Allen electronic organ was installed. The movable pulpit, lectern, and community table made it possible either to use a divided chancel or to place the pulpit in the center with the community table before it at floor level. For the presentation of religious drama, the chancel furniture could be removed. These flexible arrangements allowed for a variety of worship and teaching experiences. Draperies at the windows and controlled recessed lighting added to the charm of the worship center.

At the dedication service the participants were Priscilla Hall Mague, who gave an organ recital; Dr. Cornelius E. Clark, secretary of the Seminary's Board of Trustees; Dean Mervin M. Deems; Dr. Walter L. Cook of the faculty, who preached the baccalaureate sermon; and the President, who gave the address of dedication under the title, "Hearts and Minds, and Hands and Voices." Here is what I said at one of the high moments of my presidency:

The mood and message of this holy moment is beautifully

expressed in a verse from one of my favorite hymns, "Angel Voices, Ever Singing." It was exactly one hundred years ago, in 1861, that Francis Pott wrote these lyrics of dedication: "Here, great God, today we offer of thine own to thee. And for thine acceptance proffer, all unworthily, hearts and minds, and hands and voices, in our choicest melody." For more than a century this Chapel building has been a sacred place of "Learning and Piety, Study and Devotion" — to quote the description used in the original dedicatory address. Tonight as we reconsecrate the sanctuary and classrooms to the same high purposes, may we remember the hands and voices, the minds and hearts — both past and present — which constitute the continuing mission of Bangor Theological Seminary.

The hands are symbolic of all the physical labor and material wealth involved in establishing and maintaining this building. The workmen of 1859 performed their task with such skill that the structure is still sturdy and sound; with the interior renovations now completed it is ready to serve for another hundred years. Interestingly, the original cost of $12,000 was used several times over to pay for the reconstruction. Dr. Calvin Clark, in his history of the Seminary, gives full credit to the ladies of the mid-nineteenth century "who had it in their hearts to build a Seminary Chapel." Quoting the 1859 report of the State Conference Visitors, he writes: "God bless the ladies of Bangor, who started this enterprise; and the ladies throughout the State and elsewhere who have been helping to move it on. They are entitled to all the credit of this noble undertaking." In the twentieth century many ladies have been joined by many men to make available through generous gifts the necessary funds for the restoration of this Chapel. They, too, shall be held in grateful remembrance. The trained hands of the architects, contractors, and artisans should not be forgotten in this hour. To one who watched the process with admiration, there is in the change from the old library to the new and lovely sanctuary something close to miraculous transformation by the hands of men.

We are blessed tonight by talented hands at the organ console. Our appreciation is shown by the reverent awe with which we receive this ministry of music. For years to come the organ, one of man's ingenious instruments of praise, will be a voice guiding and inspiring the devotional life of this school. Through it we shall hear the faith of Mendelssohn and Bach, and with its help we shall sing the hymns and anthems of Isaac Watts, Charles Wesley, and a host of Christian witnesses who speak to us in song. Other voices will be heard in this place. From the lectern we shall read and hear the voice of God as it has been recorded in the Scriptures by men to whom He has revealed Himself. While the world outside is filled with angry noises and bewildered cries we shall listen here to words of wisdom from the ancient prophets and apostles of the Jewish-Christian tradition. We shall come to know Jesus as the Christ, the son of God, the saviour of men. Thus shall we be prepared to minister in his name to the world outside.

Within these walls God will continue the revelation which began before the time of human history, and through the voice of the Holy Spirit modern Christians will feel the impact of Pentecost and the Damascus Road, of Gethsemane and Calvary. We shall be encompassed by a host of witnesses; but we shall ourselves be redeemed, converted, called, instructed so that we may be instruments of the divine will in our day of life upon the good earth. The voices of men also will be heard in this sanctuary. And, I should add, the voices of women. Faculty members and students, alumni and invited guests, will stand in this pulpit to proclaim the truth which is in them. With fear and trembling, yet with the confidence born of religious conviction, these will join the long line of faithful ones who for decade upon decade have uttered in this building the "good news" of Christianity. From this hearing of many voices in the house of the Lord surely there will come a spiritual blessing upon members of the Bangor Seminary family now and in the years ahead.

This is a school of theology, and in other parts of this building students and faculty members will gather to seek fulfillment of Jesus' commandment, "Thou shalt love the Lord thy God with all thy mind." Thus we also dedicate the classrooms where the voices of God and of man will be examined and discussed with full academic freedom and with all the intellectual power which the Creator has bestowed upon his children. Theology has been called "the queen of the sciences," and one of our great military heroes has declared that the problems facing contemporary society are "basically theological." If this be true — and I believe it is — the hours spent in classroom dialogue here in this Seminary are of tremendous import to God's providential plans. All of the discoveries of the physical, biological, and social sciences, all of the values of the fine and liberal arts, find their fruition and their ultimate meaning only in the context of theology.

We do well, then, to invoke divine favor upon the workings of our minds as we search for a unity of faith and reason. In the long history of academic life at Bangor Seminary the tradition of free inquiry after truth has grown up and flourished. Many disciplines have been involved in this search: the Greek and Hebrew languages, Old Testament and New Testament study, church history, systematic theology, philosophy and psychology of religion, Christian ethics, homiletics, and Christian education. A vast library of books, great stores of professional knowledge, and generations of student inquisitiveness have been the components of this holy enterprise. No one of these disciplines, no one of these components, has been sufficient unto itself; no one has been more significant than another; but each has had its distinctive part in enabling students and professors alike to love God "with all thy mind." This is a heritage worth noting and preserving.

Jesus also said, "Thou shalt love the Lord thy God with all thy heart." Hands, voices, and minds are interwoven in the "choicest melody" which we offer to God in this dedication service. In the final analysis, however, religion is an affair of the heart. It is in the experience of worship that man finds a covenant relationship with God which is truly called "holy communion." So we return to this chapel in search of the divine love without which we cannot live and dare not die. Essentially we come here not so much to hear the voices of men, but to seek the presence of God. He has created us so that we are comforted and redeemed not by the work of our hands or the conclusions of our minds, but by the transformation of our hearts. We turn, then, instinctively toward the cross and the table of our Lord. Here is the power and the grace by which we become the sons and daughters of God. Here on the cross we see the sacrifice of our Saviour whereby our sins are forgiven and we are made righteous again in the sight of his Heavenly Father and ours. Here we sit at the sacramental table and we are strengthened by the faith that the living Spirit of Christ abides in us as servants of the divine Kingdom. Here we know in our hearts that "God so loved the world that he gave his only begotten son, that whosoever believeth in him should not perish, but have everlasting life." And we are made ready to engage in the sacred act of dedicatory prayer.

In the administration of Seminary affairs, the President is very much dependent upon good public relations. I was particularly fortunate during my long tenure to have the assistance of several competent staff members who bore the title of assistant to the President, Business Manager, or Vice President. When Daniel Fenner resigned as Vice President in 1958, my new assistant was a prominent layman from Bucksport, Maine, Donald S. McCobb. For three years he had been president of the Maine Congregational Laymen's Fellowship. He served well for four years in the combined task of soliciting funds and recruiting students. In the latter capacity he was so successful in promoting the "Bangor plan" of theological education that in 1962 he resigned his staff position in order to become a student at the Seminary. Concurrently he served as part-time pastor of the United Church in Sangerville, Maine. McCobb was followed by another layman, Harold E. Hansen of Bangor, who had the title of Business Manager. Hansen was a veteran with nine years of service in the U.S. armed forces and held the B.S. degree in Business Administration from Husson College in Bangor.

As plans for the 150th Anniversary (1964-1966) Development Program continued, the Board of Trustees acted favorably in 1962 upon a suggestion which was based upon my early experience as a junior executive with a railroad company. All railroads find it profitable to have field representatives located in areas of the country where there are potential sources of business. I convinced the Board that this system would be beneficial to the Seminary. Thus on September 1, 1962, the Reverend John R. deSousa became Assistant to the President. He continued to make his home in Hartford, Connecticut, where he represented the President in such activities as the recruiting of students, solicitation of financial support for the school, visitation among the alumni, speaking engagements in churches and colleges, and general public relations. This appointment resulted from a recognition by the Trustees that the school should have a staff member in southern New England and the New York area, a region in which many Bangor alumni were serving and from which a large number of students come to the Seminary.

Mr. deSousa was admirably qualified for his work, since the majority of students enrolled at Bangor are mature Christian lay people who have begun their theological studies after careers in the business world. Since 1957 Mr. deSousa had served the Connecticut Conference of Congregational Churches as Minister for Men and Missions, in which capacity he worked closely with laymen in many churches. He had previously held pastorates in New London, Connecticut, and in Hawaii. Born in New York City in 1914, Mr. deSousa was a graduate of Franklin College and of Andover Newton Theological School. During his tenure on the Bangor staff the Seminary reached a high point in the number of students enrolled. His intimate association with graduates of the school over a period of years resulted in a strengthening of the Alumni Association which is still evident today.

On January 1, 1966, during the sesquicentennial celebration, the Seminary established an Office of Development, and called Dr. Daniel W. Fenner to rejoin the Seminary staff as Vice President. He had previously served in this capacity from 1953 to 1957 and for the ensuing eight years had been minister of the Grace Congregational Church (United Church of Christ) in Framingham, Massachusetts. His appointment coincided with the conclusion of John deSousa's tenure as Assistant to the President. The Board of Trustees had decided to close the Hartford office, despite my own recommendation to the contrary, and to concentrate public relations activities in the new Office of Development at Bangor. The Board appreciated the accomplishments of John deSousa in the areas of student recruitment and alumni relations, but felt that Dr. Fenner would be more effective in fund-raising. Fenner did help to bring to a successful conclusion the three-year sesquicentennial program but then, unfortunately for the Seminary, he resigned his second term as Vice President after only one year and returned to the pastorate, his preferred vocation, as minister of the First Church in Belfast, Maine.

The Development Office was now in need of new leadership, but it was well into the year 1969 before the right person was found to fill this important post. On August 15th the Reverend Larry E. Kalp of Mountain Lakes, New Jersey, began his work as Assistant to the President. Kalp was born in Tarrs, Pennsylvania, and received his undergraduate education at the State Teachers College of Indiana, Pennsylvania. He was a graduate of Drew University Theological School (B.D.) and of New York University School of Education (M.A.). For two years he had been an administrative assistant in public relations at Drew University, and for six years he was Minister of Christian Education at the Community Church in Mountain Lakes. As a specialist in Christian education and the use of the communications media, Larry Kalp produced filmstrips, directed workshops for teacher training, and taught courses on the use of educational media in the church. His graduate study was in the communications arts and involved television production and direction. Over a period of nine years, and until the end of the Whittaker administration, Kalp used his many talents in a distinguished career of service to the Seminary. The story of Vice President Larry Kalp during the 1970's will be told in a later chapter.

During "The Middle Years" of my presidency the Moulton Library became firmly established as a center of Seminary academic life. On September 18, 1962, the Reverend Ans J. van der Bent was installed with tenure as Librarian and faculty member. He first came to the school as Librarian on July 1, 1959, after serving the three previous years as a member of the library staff at Harvard University. He received most of his education in the Netherlands and in Germany. He held two degrees from the Municipal University of Amsterdam, and since coming to the United States in 1956 he had earned the degree of Master of Science in Library Science from Simmons College in Boston. The Seminary was indeed fortunate to have Ans van der Bent as its librarian during the formative years of the new facility. One of his noteworthy accomplishments was the establishment of an archive in the Rare Book Room which contained a collection of books published by

Seminary personnel as well as manuscripts, papers, pictures, memorabilia, and other documents related to the school's history. Van der Bent resigned in October of 1963 after accepting an offer to become Director of the Ecumenical Library of the World Council of Churches in Geneva, Switzerland. The faculty lamented his departure, but was proud of his new and significant appointment.

With Ans van der Bent on his way to Geneva, the Seminary was again in need of a competent librarian. Diligent search for a replacement discovered the availability of Leslie Ziegler of Corvalis, Oregon. She was born in Modesto, California, and received a B.S. degree in chemistry from the University of California at Berkeley. She spent thirteen years in industry, working in the pharmaceutical field as a research chemist, then in pilot plant development, and finally in the area of administration. Then, like many "Bangor plan" students, she sought a second career in a Christian professional field. She returned to academic studies and earned both the Bachelor of Divinity and Doctor of Theology degrees at Pacific School of Religion in Berkeley. Later she also received the Master of Library Science degree from the University of California.

Dr. Ziegler appeared ideally suited to fill the vacancy on the Bangor staff. For four years she had been on the faculty of Oregon State University, where she taught philosophy, religion and related subjects to undergraduates and was also engaged in library work. She had been active in church adult education courses and in campus ministry activities at Corvalis and other centers in Oregon. While at Pacific School of Religion Miss Ziegler held a Fellowship in Religious Studies and was an instructor in New Testament. She accepted an invitation from Bangor to begin a career on November 1, 1963, as Librarian and faculty member. Soon thereafter she was ordained in All Souls Congregational Church, Bangor, as a minister of the United Church of Christ. Leslie Ziegler thus became the second woman appointed to the Bangor faculty in the long history of the school. As events unfolded during her twenty-year tenure she also proved to be one of the most versatile scholars the Seminary has ever known. This will become evident as these memoirs continue.

An opportunity for Leslie Ziegler to demonstrate her many

talents occurred in 1965 when Dr. Arnold W. Hearn, Lowry Professor of Philosophy of Religion and Christian Ethics, resigned the faculty position he had held since 1958 in order to become Associate Professor of Christian Ethics at the Episcopal Theological Seminary of the Southwest at Austin, Texas. He had come to Bangor as a Methodist minister, but changed his denominational affiliation while at the Seminary. During his years at Bangor he was very active as a preacher and lecturer. He was closely associated with the work of the Bangor-Brewer Council of Churches, the Bangor Area Branch of the N.A.A.C.P., and the Eastern Maine Branch of the Academy of Religion and Mental Health.

It did not take the Seminary long to fill the vacancy left by Dr. Hearn. Although happy and effective as Librarian, Leslie Ziegler let it be known that her primary desire was to be a teaching member of the faculty. Since she was qualified by previous training and experience, her appointment as Associate Professor of Philosophy and Christian Ethics effective September 1, 1965, was natural and salutary. She agreed also to continue her work as Librarian, with the understanding that an assistant librarian would be added to the Seminary staff. This was another step in the career of Leslie Ziegler which led eventually to her appointment to the prestigious position of Buck Professor of Christian Theology after the retirement of Dr. Andrew Banning.

Meanwhile a second alumnus joined the President as a member of the Seminary staff. On September 1, 1965, the Reverend Clifton G. Davis of Concord, New Hampshire, became the school's Assistant Librarian. Since 1961 Davis had been serving as pastor of the Congregational Churches of East Concord and Loudon, New Hampshire. He was a graduate of the Seminary with the B.D. degree in 1961 and of the University of Denver with the B.S. degree. During his student days at Bangor he had been a library assistant. During his first two years on the Seminary staff Davis was encouraged by the faculty to pursue graduate study at the University of Maine; in August of 1967 he was awarded the University's degree of Master of Library Science. This degree, plus the tutelage of Dr. Ziegler and his own experience as Assistant Librarian, qualified him to become Librarian of the Seminary, with faculty status, on September 1, 1968, at which time Dr. Ziegler began to devote full time to her teaching responsibilities. Davis has remained in his post as Librarian until the present time and is now senior member of the faculty.

One more rearrangement of faculty personnel took place in 1966 when Dr. Myron F. Klinkman resigned in order to establish a private counselling practice. During his five years at Bangor, Dr. Klinkman had effectively developed clinical pastoral training as a vital part of the Seminary curriculum. For three years he was director of a mental health project involving cooperation between the Seminary and the Bangor State Hospital under a federal grant from the National Institute of Mental Health. He helped to begin and served as chairman of the Eastern Maine Branch of the Academy of Religion and Mental Health.

To succeed Dr. Klinkman the Seminary appointed the Reverend Dwight Wesley Cumbee, effective September 1, 1966, as Associate Professor of Psychology and Pastoral Counselling at the Seminary. Cumbee was born in Scranton, Pennsylvania, and was a graduate of the University of Richmond in Virginia. He also held the graduate degrees of B.D. and Th.M. from Southeastern Baptist Theological Seminary, Wake Forest, Virginia. He had completed two years of study for the Ph.D. degree, which he later received, at St. Andrews University in Scotland. He was married to the former Janet Stallings and the Cumbees had a family of four children. Dr. Cumbee was a specialist in pastoral care. He had served as staff chaplain of the Baptist Memorial Hospital in Jacksonville, Florida, and had studied at the C.C. Jung Institute in Zurich, Switzerland.

Other major changes were made in faculty assignments on September 1, 1968. This date marked the retirement of Dr. Mervin M. Deems as Dean and Professor; the trustees named him "Emeritus" in both positions. Dr. Andrew Banning, Buck Professor of Christian Theology and Registrar, became the new Dean. Dr. Stephen Szikszai succeeded Dr. Banning as Registrar. Two other tasks performed by Dr. Deems were reassigned: Dr. Burton H. Throckmorton, Jr., became Editor of The Alumni Bulletin, and the office of Chaplain was assumed by Professor Clarice M. Bowman. A new position, Director of Continuing Education, was established and filled by Dr. Leslie Ziegler.

Mervin Deems and I were colleagues in administration and teaching at Bangor Seminary for fourteen happy and productive years. As President and Dean we collaborated in many and diverse ways for the advancement of the school's mission. We shared the professorial leadership of the Church History Department. He was the one during my student days at Bangor, in his first term on the faculty, who inspired me to become eventually a teacher of Church History and a strong supporter of Christian missionary activity. At a special assembly of faculty and students to honor him I spoke these words: "Dr. Mervin Deems was my mentor twenty-five years ago when I was a student at Bangor Seminary. From him I learned the love of Christian History which inspired my own teaching career. My admiration and gratitude have grown continually through the years. I have known Dr. Deems as scholar, churchman, colleague and personal friend. His influence upon a generation of students, professors, and other fellow Christians has left an indelible mark for all the time to come."

The Alumni Bulletin of July, 1968, contains several pages of the tributes paid to Dr. Deems at the time of his retirement. A faculty minute stated: "We recall with gratitude the qualities which have made him a leader of stature among us: his untiring zeal for the ongoing life of the church, and his willingness to serve it unstintingly. Not sparing himself in fulfilling his responsibilities as preacher, teacher and scholar, he has given to the office of Dean of the Seminary loyalty, humility, and untiring devotion. His firmness of judgment has often been coupled with a disarming sense of humor which more than once relaxed a tense situation ... He has guided students with genuine understanding of their difficulties, giving unmistakable evidence of having taken counsel with himself before advising others ... Remembering with gratitude his influence and consistent witness, we are united in wishing for him and for his devoted wife, Cleta, many more years of fruitful service."

A bound volume of letters was presented to Dr. Deems as he retired. Scores of alumni praised him for his many talents and services. There was unanimous acclaim for his teaching of Church History and for his compassionate ministry as Dean. Here is an excerpt of one typical tribute: "You made Church History live ... I am very grateful that I have been one of the fortunate ones who profited from your scholarship and your friendship. Bangor Seminary will not be the same without you. But as you retire, may you do so with the knowledge that you have given of yourself unselfishly to a great many students ... My work in the ministry has been the richer and deeper because of having you as teacher and friend...." Another alumnus wrote: "My memory holds a tender gratitude for Dr. and Mrs. Deems' vital interest in the general welfare and happiness of all students and their families. They were confidants, warm-hearted neighbors and benevolent friends."

The Board of Trustees adopted and published a resolution which read in part as follows: "It is no small task for the Board of Trustees to record its appreciation of the Reverend Dr. Mervin M. Deems as he leaves his varied responsibilities as teacher of Church History and of Sacred Rhetoric, and as the Seminary's first Dean ... The student is the best evidence of his teacher. And Professor Deems' students rise up and bless him for encouraging a hunger for knowledge and love of scholarship and its rewards and disciplines. As an administrator Dean Deems played a crucial role in the developments which have marked the Whittaker administration ... He carried major responsibilities for the Chapel, for which faculty and students are in his debt ... Dr. Deems gave endless hours to the work of the churches. His honors as head of the Bangor Council of Churches and the Maine Council, his work for the Penobscot Association and as president of the Congregational Christian Historical Society, are instances of the labors for which he is held in gratitude among the churches ... In all his labors the Dean and the Seminary owe much to his wife, Cleta N. Deems. In honoring him we honor her."

The resignation of Dr. Deems necessitated one more change in faculty personnel during the 1960's. The Board of Trustees had decided in 1968 that the President should devote more of his time and effort to fund-raising and should relinquish most of his teaching responsibilities. Thus for the last ten years of my administration I taught no more than one course per semester and sometimes only one course per academic year. In retrospect, this was the beginning of a decline of interest on my part in the office of President. When I first sought the office, fund-raising was not a significant part of the portfolio. Teaching was my preferred vocation, and when this was restricted by the trustees in 1968 I was ready ten years later to retire when I reached the age of sixty-five, although I could have continued as President for at least another five years. In any event, it was now necessary to call a new professor of Church History to carry most of the teaching load in that department. After a somewhat lengthy search, an appointment was made.

On September 1, 1968, Dr. Roland H. Wessels joined the faculty as Associate Professor of Christian History. He was born in Los Angeles, California, in 1927, and he came to Bangor with his wife, Gisa, and three children. Dr. Wessels was an ordained minister of the United Church of Christ and had been serving a pastorate in Elk Grove, California, since 1966. He held the B.A. degree of the University of California and the B.D. and Th.D. degrees of the Pacific School of Religion. He had studied for a year in Germany on a World Council of Churches scholarship, and had spent another year in Germany as pastor of a church in Bremen.

The decade of the sixties was a time of innovation in the Seminary. In addition to those events and developments already noted, the school inaugurated during this period a successful Lay School of Theology and an ecumenical program of Continuing Education. The latter project featured the participation of Roman Catholic scholars, one of whom was the Reverend James E. Connor, J.C.D., a faculty member at St. Joseph's College in Standish, Maine, and a visiting lecturer at Bangor Seminary. Father Connor was appointed to the adjunct faculty in 1968 and taught a two-hour elective course on "Contemporary Roman Catholic Theology and Practice." Although the Seminary had previously presented Roman Catholic scholars as Convocation Week lecturers, this appointment to the visiting faculty was a new dimension in ecumenical relationships between the Roman Catholic Church and the Seminary. It would be another twenty years before the school called a Roman Catholic to its resident faculty.

Another ecumenical development of importance took place in 1966 when the Methodist Church formally recognized the Bangor

Bachelor of Divinity degree as meeting fully the requirements of the Methodist Ministerial Course of Study. This made official an arrangement under which Methodist students had long been a significant segment of matriculants at Bangor, second only in denominational affiliation to the Congregational Christian Churches (now United Church of Christ). For many years Bangor had offered elective courses in Methodist polity, history, and doctrine. The Methodist Church was consistently represented on the Board of Trustees by Bangor alumni, and often by Methodist bishops. Methodist scholars have served continuously on the Seminary faculty since Clarice Bowman was appointed in 1961. Noted Methodists have appeared regularly as Convocation Week leaders.

The alumni of Bangor Seminary are probably its most precious asset. The middle years of my administration were marked by a recognition of this fact. John deSousa's most significant work, as noted earlier, was his representation of his own and the President's concern for the welfare of Bangor graduates in the parishes where they worked. Each spring the alumni in New England and some adjoining states gathered at the Congregational Conference Center in Framingham, Massachusetts, for a meeting which featured two lectures by Bangor faculty members and a report by the Seminary president. 1964 marked the beginning of a continuous annual "Alumnus of the Year Award" to a nominee selected by the Seminary Alumni Association; an engraved citation has been presented to the awardee each year at the annual meeting of the Seminary Alumni Association during Convocation. The first award was given to the Reverend Gordon H. Washburn of the class of 1938, minister of the Congregational Church in West Medford, Massachusetts, and long-time member of the Seminary Board of Trustees. Recognition of the alumni took another form in the 1960's: Although graduates of the Seminary had previously served regular unspecified terms as trustees by invitation of the Board, now for the first time the Alumni Association was allowed to nominate graduates for a three-year term as Board member; concurrently the faculty was given the same privilege of representation on the school's governing body.

While recognizing the value to Bangor Seminary of trustees,

faculty, and alumni, not to be overlooked is the vital contribution to the school of the support staff: maintenance crew, dining room stewards, and office personnel. I cannot name them all, but in the period of which I am now writing one person deserves special mention: She is Helen A. Godsoe, my faithful and competent secretary throughout the decade. In 1964 she prepared and edited the Seminary's Historical Catalogue, thus bringing up to date biographical data on alumni and other personnel. To show my gratitude, I asked the Trustees in 1966 to give Mrs. Godsoe the title of Administrative Assistant, a task which she fulfilled with distinction for the remainder of my tenure and beyond. She continued to serve until the early 1970's as Secretary to the President and as assistant to the editor of The Alumni Bulletin. Her new responsibility was the keeping of academic records as deputy to the Registrar, Dr. Andrew Banning; in 1971 she was given the additional title of "Registrar." As Administrative Assistant Mrs. Godsoe supervised all business office operations and kept the minutes of faculty and trustees meetings. She was a support staff member without equal. Her death in 1990 saddened me deeply.

The "middle years" witnessed a substantial increase in the endowment of the Seminary and new recognition by benevolent foundations. Two of the major capital gifts were received in 1962 and 1969. The first was a bequest of more than $100,000 from the estate of William Edgar Lowry of Newton, Massachusetts. Mr. Lowry, who served as Deacon and Treasurer of the North Congregational Church in Newton for more than fifty years, had learned of Bangor Seminary's unique mission through his brother Franklin, a medical doctor. In gratitude for this generous gift the Seminary trustees attached the name of Lowry to the Professorship of Philosophy of Religion and Christian Ethics. The decade ended with the receipt of the largest amount of money ever given to the Seminary. The donor was Mrs. Genevieve E. Stratton of Rye, New Hampshire, and the amount was $375,000. Mrs. Stratton had once lived in Bangor near the Seminary and had been a regular contributor to the school. I recall that she once wrote to me as President, asking if I would accept for the library a small, red-covered Bible which was a family heirloom. I accepted with a letter of gratitude, but never did know whether this in any way prompted the unexpected later benevolence. The Stratton bequest was a stabilizing financial blessing for the Seminary through all the ensuing years.

The Walter Teagle Foundation of New York City has been a benefactor of the Seminary since the years of the Harry Trust administration. Each year the Foundation makes available to Bangor students a number of scholarship grants. The original amount in the 1940's was $1,500, but this award has increased during the Whittaker administration to its present level in the 1960's of $25,000 annually. When I retired in 1978 the Teagle Scholarships were still being maintained; over the decades a large number of Bangor students have benefited from these gifts.

In 1962 the Lilly Endowment, Inc., of Indianapolis, Indiana, began to recognize the validity of the Bangor Seminary educational mission by making grants to its faculty members. Dr. Burton H. Throckmorton, Jr., was the first Bangor professor to receive a Lilly Fellowship. The award was for study in England and Germany and was among the earliest offered by Lilly for post-doctoral fellowships for teachers of religion in "Associate" member seminaries of the American Association of Theological Schools. The next year, 1963, a similar award was made to Bangor scholar Dr. Stephen Szikszai for study in Germany during his sabbatical year. Others have followed in later years. This recognition of an "Associate" member of the ATS was a precursor to full accreditation of Bangor in the early 1970's, an action which was applauded by Lilly officials. The Lilly Foundation has in more recent times given even more substantial support to Bangor during the Glick and Warford presidencies.

If there is one issue upon which I was persistent as Bangor President, it was the effort to secure full academic accreditation for the Seminary. At three consecutive five-year intervals — 1957, 1962, and 1967 — Bangor submitted the required "schedules" and self-study to the Commission on Accrediting of the American Association of Theological Schools. After being turned down by the Commission with monotonous repetition, in each instance an appeal was made to an AATS Board of Review; in identical monotonous fashion the Board upheld the negative decision of the

242

Commission. In every decision both the Commission and the Board adjudged Bangor ineligible for accreditation because it admitted too large a proportion of students to theological study without the standard prerequisite of an undergraduate degree, even though the Seminary awarded its graduate degree to these students only when they had completed their undergraduate education — under the "Bangor plan" — through post-theological study for the A.B. degree or its equivalent. Never did the Commission or the Board take into consideration the widely-acknowledged fact that Bangor graduates were adequately trained — despite a non-traditional educational process — for an effective ministry.

The best illustration of the intransigence of the accreditation agency is the following quotation from the 1967 report of the Board of Review: "We reviewed all the improvements that have been brought out during the last few years, and believe that with the present facilities of the library, classrooms and other improvements, together with personnel advances both in the library and the faculty, and also the significant advance in the financial situation at the seminary, these indicate that they now have a first-class school for the Bangor Plan — but, the plan itself makes it inadvisable for the accreditation of the A.A.T.S."

It was in 1968, just a year later, that two events occurred which would eventually influence the A.A.T.S. to grant Bangor the accreditation it had so long desired. One was my election as Secretary of the American Association of Theological Schools, thus giving me a place on the Executive Committee. The other was accreditation by the New England Association of Colleges and Secondary Schools. After its third failure to secure recognition by the A.A.T.S. Commission on Accrediting, the Seminary trustees approved my recommendation that the school seek regional accreditation from the agency which grants academic standing to Yale, Harvard, Dartmouth, Bowdoin, Brown, and all other eligible colleges in New England. Bangor submitted the required self-study schedules, was visited by an inspection team, and on December 6, 1968, was granted membership in the New England Association as a specialized institution. The Seminary was gratified to be the first theological school to be so recognized by the Association and thus to achieve the national accreditation it had so long been denied. It has continued to be a member of the New England Association through the ensuing years.

Even as the decade of the 1960's began with the death of President Emeritus Harry Trust, so it ended on September 23, 1969, with the death of Professor Emeritus Marion John Bradshaw at the age of 82. Thus there passed from the earthly scene another of the men who so greatly influenced my own career. My admiration of Dr. Bradshaw has already been amply expressed in these pages, but I add here just one paragraph from my memorial address at the time of his death: "He was indeed a philosopher-theologian who brought reality to the things of the spirit by the full use of his God-given power of reason. In all the thirty years of my relationship with him I count as the greatest contribution to my life his proclamation of a reasonable faith."

I close this story of the middle years of my presidency with reference to the one single event which marked for me the pinnacle of Bangor Theological Seminary's development and promise. It was the Sesquicentennial Convocation commemorating the 150th Anniversary of the granting of the school's charter in 1814. The Sesquicentennial Lecture was given at a birthday celebration on February 25, 1964, by Dr. Henry P. Van Dusen, President Emeritus of Union Theological Seminary in New York City and one of the great theologians and ecumenists of the twentieth century. Dr. Van Dusen had long been an advocate of the Seminary in its struggle for accreditation, and on one memorable occasion at a biennial meeting of the American Association of Theological Schools had threatened to withdraw his prestigious Union Theological Seminary from membership if the Commission on Accrediting did not grant full recognition to Bangor.

In his address entitled, "Theological Education in the Ecumenical Era," Dr. Van Dusen began with a "sincere felicitation to Bangor Seminary on the occasion of this sesquicentennial celebration." He went on to make this unforgettable declaration: "Bangor is a national institution; in a fashion which is literally unique, it serves the entire nation — the only seminary of highest standards and quality which accepts and trains qualified candidates lacking a college degree. It deserves to enlist support from the whole country. Indeed, if the whole truth be told, all other seminaries should contribute to its maintenance. For it is doing for them an essential task which they cannot or will not do for themselves. It has been often, and rightly, said: 'If Bangor did not exist, a Bangor would have to be created to do its job.' As a study team of the A.A.T.S. declared: 'We know of no other theological school, standing on the educational level of Bangor, which so conceives of its special vocation in these terms.' I am proud to be here tonight to declare that fact, and to pay grateful tribute on behalf of all who revere Bangor for its invaluable service."

13.
The "Always Right" Reverend

The story of my professional career pauses now so that I may bring up to date the memoirs of my personal life as husband and father. The chapter title discloses the moniker bestowed upon me by my daughter and son, Barbara and Mark, during their teenage years. As they explained it to me, the designation "always right" did not reflect their opinion of me, but rather my opinion of myself. It was a value judgment spoken both in frustration and in love. I did not think of myself as a strict disciplinarian, but from their point of view apparently I was. In any event, most of the time they grudgingly admitted that my only motivation was fatherly love.

I have no reason to believe that my children were not proud of my activities as a "reverend." But I know it was not easy for them to grow up in a minister's home where moral values were held in high esteem and public behavior was expected to be exemplary. While I was serving in the state legislature, my automobile displayed a "State Senator" license plate; one evening Mark was apprehended for speeding on a Bangor city street and was escorted to the Whittaker home by the arresting officer. My son was deeply chagrined, but had the presence of mind during our discussion of the incident to remind me that three years earlier I had experienced a similar embarrassment while serving on the city council.

Barbara has been an attractive and delightful daughter. During her growing years she developed a strong bond of love with her brother which remains to this day. When Mark was just a toddler he crawled through the backyard fence one day, crossed two major highways, was picked up by a friendly neighbor half a mile away, and returned safely to our home. Barbara was disturbed by this escapade just as much as her parents were. Some time later, when Shirley had reason to discipline Mark, ten-year-old Barbara staged a protest on behalf of her brother by packing a suitcase and leaving home. Shirley found her down at the local bus station and persuaded her to return to the family.

Because a state highway passed in front of our home, Barbara was not allowed to ride a bicycle until long after she felt ready to mount the wheels. However, when Mark won a bike at a local sportsman's show, the restriction against Barbara had to be removed. She still remembers this "injustice." Shortly thereafter Mark disobeyed parental instructions and took his vehicle across the highway to a friend's house. Enroute the bike malfunctioned and Mark found himself on the ground with multiple, if not fatal, injuries. Both children had some second thoughts about the "always right" reverend.

Barbara will always remember her tenth birthday. She was surprised by a delivery from the florist in the form of a corsage which I had ordered as a sign of my love for her. Shirley and I wondered if it would be appreciated by a young lady of such tender years, but her delight indicated that nothing could have pleased her more. This was one of the "right" things I did as a father. I have reason to believe that Barbara remembers with gratitude that when the time came for her to have a car, I taught her how to drive. With Mark, however, I decided for no perceived reason that he would do better to take the high school "driver education" course.

Both of the children were educated in the Bangor public school system, and both were well prepared for productive careers. Barbara found the academic experience to be a happy and successful one. Like her father before her, she skipped a grade in elementary school and was graduated from Bangor High at the age of sixteen. Mark was an "average" student academically but excelled in such activities as amateur dramatics and public speaking. His mother worried more than I did about Mark's report cards, but he knew that I never really doubted his ability to meet the requirements for graduation. In this respect I was, in truth, the "always right" reverend. Eventually, in his senior year of college Mark was on the dean's list.

During high school days Barbara received recognition on more than one occasion for her natural beauty and pleasing personality. She was "Queen" of the ROTC Military Ball on one occasion, and another year was named the March of Dimes "Queen." She was Vice President of the Junior Class and a featured speaker at her graduation ceremonies in 1960. Barbara has had a life-long interest in music and is a talented violinist and pianist. While in high school she played the violin in the Bangor Symphony Orchestra. Her teacher was Gwendolyn Spaulding, the mother of our lifelong friend Judith MacNeil Merrill.

Mark was also involved in extra-curricular activities. He excelled in amateur dramatics while in high school. After Bangor High won local, state, and regional contests, Mark reached the climax of this early career by being named "All-New England Actor." In 1964, as he prepared to graduate, Mark received his greatest honor as a high school student. He was named President of the National Association of Student Councils when the Association met in Bangor that year. I was privileged to give the invocation when Mark presided at the annual conference of the Association held at the University of Maine in Orono. Earlier that year Mark had represented the youth of the state when he spoke at the Tenth Annual Conference of the Maine Highway Safety Committee in Augusta.

During their adolescent years Barbara and Mark were nurtured in a family setting where mutual love was a dominating factor. They experienced none of the trauma which has become so prevalent in broken marital relations during recent years. Shirley and I both were active participants in the life of Hammond Street Congregational Church, and the two children received basic training in Christian living by attending the Church school, the morning worship, and the youth groups. Barbara has often spoken in later years of the significant lessons she learned from our long-time minister and friend, the Reverend Edward G. Ernst. In the home Shirley and I made an earnest effort, by precept and example, to bring up our children in the "right" way. Shirley has always protected the physical health of our family members by providing nutritious and appetizing meals.

The Whittakers were blessed during the formative years of the children by attractive and unusual housing facilities. Beginning in 1954 we lived in the historic "Hannibal Hamlin House," adjacent to the Seminary campus at the corner of Fifth and Hammond Streets. The Bangor home of Abraham Lincoln's first Vice President was given to the school early in the twentieth century by the Hamlin heirs. Its spacious interior contained a double formal parlor, a living room, dining room, and kitchen on the first floor. On the second floor were four large bedrooms and two baths, which meant that each of the children had their own rooms, judiciously separated by a guest suite. On the third floor, unused, were three more bedrooms, a bath, and a large storage area replete with metal hooks which once held stored meats. Our children and their guests were also fascinated by the ghost-like appearance of the abandoned third floor. On occasion a stray bat would wander from this area into the living quarters below, much to the discomfort of the Whittaker family, especially me.

In 1957 Shirley and I decided to rent a camp for a month of vacation at Phillips Lake in Dedham, Maine, just fifteen miles and thirty minutes by car from our Bangor home. Earlier we had belonged to the "Beach Club" at the northern end of the same lake, which gave the children an opportunity to enjoy swimming with their mother. I was a "landlubber" until I was more than seventy years old. We fell in love with camp living, and indicated to the owner that we would like to buy the facility if they ever decided to sell it. The offer was made at the right moment, and that fall we became property owners for the first time. With the financial help of Shirley's mother, Blanche Johns, we bought a summer home and 150 feet of prime lakefront property for the amazingly low price of $5,500. It was one of the best investments we have ever made. "Whittaker's Whereabouts" has been our summer residence for more than thirty years, and will remain in the family for at least another generation. Today the property is worth fifteen or twenty times its cost.

The next year Shirley's mother added to the camp facilities by purchasing a prefabricated building containing a living room, two bedrooms, and a bathroom. She spent every summer with us until her death in 1981, and delighted to have her granddaughter Barbara sleep in her adjoining bedroom. The new addition came to be known as "Maga's Mansion," to distinguish it from the original building called "Shirley's Shack." "Maga" is the name given to her grandmother by Barbara when she first began to talk. One of the beautiful relationships of the Whittaker family has been the love affair between our daughter and her maternal grandmother.

It was at Lucerne that Mark began his lively interest in boats. It began with a rowboat equipped with a three-horse motor, in which he explored every remote cove of the lake and visited his many young friends along the shoreline. It was here that he and his sister, along with their mother, learned to waterski behind a powerboat owned and operated by our next-door neighbors, the Brountas family, many of whom have been our personal friends for three decades. The "girls," Helen and Georgia, have been swimming companions with Shirley for many years. When Mark later lived in Virginia he had his own powerboat and, more recently, owned a houseboat in Florida.

Both of our children have fond memories of life in the Hamlin House and at "Whittaker's Whereabouts." Both of them have had romantic episodes in each setting. During high school days Barbara entertained many friends in our Bangor home. Some of them were serious boyfriends, and in most instances Shirley and I approved of our daughter's emotional involvements. As I recall, we intervened on only two occasions; once when we felt that she was too young for a "going steady" commitment; and again when we advised against becoming serious about a Roman Catholic suitor whose parents were unhappy about their son's interest in a Protestant girl. I have no doubt that these two incidents evoked in Barbara her judgment about the "always right" reverend. Mark had his many romantic moments, too. He introduced us to many beautiful and lovely young ladies at Lucerne, the last of whom was Pamela

Livesay, now his wife for more than twenty years. I well remember the day he first brought her to the lake, for I knew immediately that marriage between them would be the ultimate reality. "Always right," as he would say.

Barbara's time within the Whittaker household was all too short. She was born while I was a student-minister at Bowdoin College and a Yarmouth church. Until she was five I was similarly involved at Yale University and the Huntington Church in Shelton. For her next ten years I was busy as a professor and president at Bangor Seminary. Then at age sixteen she was off to college in Boston. I have always regretted that I did not make time to be with my daughter on a more intense one-to-one basis during the years of her childhood and youth. The situation was somewhat improved with Mark, partly because he was at home for a longer period and partly because we developed a common interest in the recreational game of golf. I taught him the rudiments of the sport when he was quite young, and he was gainfully employed as a golf course worker at Lucerne, in Bangor, and on Cape Cod. We still play together whenever the opportunity arises, and we can both score under eighty on occasion. When I am "right," I win. When I am not, he wins. All of it in good fun.

When she was a very young girl, Barbara wanted to be a nurse. This interest led her to enroll in the nursing program at Simmons College in Boston after graduation from high school in 1960. However, after two years of successful study, which had advanced her to duty in an operating-room setting, she decided that nursing was too "impersonal." She transferred to the social studies program at Simmons and graduated in 1964, earning a Bachelor of Science degree. Her senior year was marked by two traumatic experiences. During the spring "break" she and a group of several other students from Boston area schools participated in the early "civil rights" movement by going to North Carolina. She lived for several days during the lenten season with a black family in a "prayer vigil" on behalf of equal treatment for minorities in the United States. It was a testimony of which I was very proud, even though the time and effort spent was at least partially responsible for a failing grade at Simmons in a required course. As a result she had to redeem the failure — the first and only of her academic career — in summer study before she could graduate.

Since I was paying for her college education, Barbara and I had an understanding that she would not marry until she had received her degree. During her senior year she became deeply involved romantically with Donald Bakker, a young doctoral student at the Massachusetts Institute of Technology. They planned to marry early in September in spite of parental suggestions that they should wait a bit longer since Barbara was not yet twenty-one years old. However, the young lovers decided that the "always right" reverend was wrong again, and a church wedding was scheduled for late summer. Meanwhile, Shirley and I had planned early in the year to take the family on a cross-country automobile trip in June so that I could attend, as a delegate from Maine, the national Republican convention in San Francisco. Mark was eager to go, but Barbara only reluctantly agreed to leave Donald for four weeks so that the Whittakers could enjoy what was to be the last family excursion for the four of us.

Thus for thirty days we shared the beauty and the splendor of the United States, and for thirty nights we occupied double beds in a motel, Barbara sleeping with her mother, and Mark with me. Each night three of us tried not to listen while Barbara talked on the telephone with her beloved back in New England. Each night Mark unloaded, and the next morning re-loaded, the golf clubs we had brought with us for the purpose of playing just one round at the famous Pebble Beach course. It all seemed worthwhile when I scored a "birdie" two on the spectacular par-three 17th hole which all television watchers know is surrounded by water on three sides. At the convention itself Mark had an experience which he has never forgotten. His gregarious personality emboldened him to approach Harry Reasoner, the well-known television commentator. His conversation with this famous man left an indelible impression upon my teenage son, and made the whole trip worthwhile.

Barbara's wedding that fall to Donald Bakker in the Hammond Street Congregational Church was a social event of some significance. It was a high point of my career to officiate at the marriage ceremony for my daughter. Guests and relatives came from various parts of New England. A reception was held inside and outside the Hannibal Hamlin House, the Whittaker home. The happy bride and groom left for a honeymoon on Cape Cod, which later was to be the locale of the Bakker home. At the end of eight years, however, the union ended in divorce.

Meanwhile, Barbara and Don lived for a few years in New Jersey, first in Hackensack and then in Ridgewood. Don had become disenchanted with his doctoral studies at M.I.T. and had transferred to another program of graduate work at Columbia University in New York City. Barbara enrolled for a short period at Union Theological Seminary, indicating her latent interest in a career similar to her father's. When Don was not supportive of this endeavor, Barbara withdrew from the Seminary and engaged for a brief period in volunteer social service work among minorities sponsored by a church in Hackensack. She then matriculated at Yeshiva University in New York City and earned a master's degree in special education, which qualified her to teach emotionally disturbed children; she worked in this field both in New Jersey and Cape Cod.

Don's graduate study at Columbia had progressed to the point where he had only a dissertation to complete. However, again he failed to earn the doctoral degree because of a major disagreement with his faculty advisers. He withdrew from Columbia and established a home with Barbara at Brewster on Cape Cod, where he began a career as a high school teacher which still continues. It was obvious to Shirley and me during our frequent visits with our daughter that she and her husband were no longer living compatibly. Shirley was distressed, and I was concerned, on the occasion of our last visit with them when we left Barbara in a tearful mood. We were deeply saddened, but not surprised, when the marriage ended in 1972. No children were born during the eight years of the union, due to Don's reluctance to become a father, we have been told; this may have been one reason, but certainly not the only reason for the divorce.

The next few years of Barbara's life was a time of transition for her. She worked for a while as an executive of the Cape Cod Family and Child Service. She established relationships with a number of men, but none of them ended in a serious commitment. She had a positive influence upon young people from broken homes whom she befriended from time to time. Occasionally she augmented her income by doing some commercial clamming. I well remember her reaction to a serious suggestion I once made out of concern for her well-being. She often went to the clam flats alone early in the morning. "Are you not afraid of being raped?" I asked. Her hilarious negative response indicated clearly that once again I was not the "always right" reverend. By the time I retired in 1978 Barbara had begun to show interest in the program of the Unitarian Church in Brewster. This was the beginning of a new era of professional fulfillment and personal happiness for her, a story which will be told in a later chapter of these memoirs.

1964 marked the end of family living for the Whittakers as a unit of four. At the same time that Barbara began her married life, Mark went off to Florida as the first male student enrolled in the charter class of New College in Sarasota. This honor came to him partly because of the prestige he had gained at Bangor High School as the president of the National Association of Student Councils. Another factor was the encouragement given by long-time family friend, the Reverend Doctor John Whitney MacNeil, who was at the time minister of the First Congregational United Church of Christ in Sarasota and one of the founders of New College. The school itself was patterned after New College at Oxford University in England and featured self-directed study under the guidance of professors. The unstructured curriculum proved to be unsuited to Mark's academic abilities and he withdrew after three semesters. The time spent in Florida was for Mark an excellent introduction to college life. For Shirley and me it was an opportunity to visit the state which later became our permanent home.

Mark came back to Bangor in mid-1965 and enrolled at the University of Maine, from which he later graduated. He lived at home during the first year and then went to Orono as a fraternity house resident. During his senior year he was on the Dean's list. This was after he met Pamela Dole Livesay, also a University graduate, who has greatly influenced his life ever since. Pam and he were married in 1969 at Brunswick, Maine, at the First Parish

Church in a ceremony at which I officiated. The union has blessed them and us with two delightful grandchildren: Emily Dole, who is a student at Stetson University in Deland, Florida, and Andrew Boyd, who is a teenager in high school.

After graduating from the University, Mark was employed for a year in the Alumni Office in the field of public relations. This followed a semester of study at Bangor Theological Seminary, during which Mark decided that he did not want to be a minister. With the encouragement of the University President in 1970 Mark applied for and received appointment to the development staff at Sweet Briar College, an all-girls school in Virginia. He remained there for fifteen years, with the exception of one year spent in public relations at the University of Massachusetts in Boston. When he left Sweet Briar he held the title of Vice President. By this time he had achieved a wide reputation as an expert fund-raiser and held a leadership role in the activities of the Washington-based Council for the Advancement and Support of Education (CASE). The story of Mark's career and his family life will continue later.

One more illustration of the significance of this chapter's title, "The 'Always Right' Reverend," needs to be recounted here. Mark and I have had a delightful father-son relationship, with one or two possible exceptions. We both remember the day when we were driving separate cars in opposite directions on the camp road leading to our summer home. We met on a curve and narrowly escaped a serious collision. In the ensuing discussion there was no agreement as to whether he was driving too fast or I was too near the middle of the road.

Even more memorable — and traumatic — was the evening when Shirley and I decided to take my mother for a twilight drive to our summer place at Lucerne. At the time Mark was a student living at the University. He had free access to the camp, but Shirley and I were not prepared for the scene we discovered that evening. As we entered the driveway, Mark's car was parked ahead of us. We found Mark and a pretty young lady whom we knew preparing a party for some of their friends. Very much in evidence were some bottles of liquid refreshment — perhaps beer, perhaps something stronger. I did not wait to identify the contents. Indignant at my son, and embarrassed by the presence of my mother, I grabbed the offending containers, rushed down to the dock, and threw them as far as I could into the lake. That was the end of the party. For all the ensuing years I have had the guilty feeling that on that particular occasion I was not the "always right" reverend. I am sure that Mark would agree.

When Barbara went off to college in 1960, Shirley offered to supplement the family income by returning to the teaching profession she had left twenty years earlier. For six years she taught general science in the Bangor public school system, thus providing a service to young people in the community while taking a major role in subsidizing the cost of higher education for our own two children. She stopped teaching in 1966, partly because our financial situation was stable and partly because she was taking increasing responsibility for the care of her aging mother. "Maga," the name given to her maternal grandmother by our daughter when she was a baby, spent three months with us during the winter and another similar period in summertime. Shirley's loving care of her mother through the years has been a beautiful thing to see. She was also most kind and thoughtful in her relationship with my mother, who visited with us from time to time.

Shirley was always willing to share her talents in community activity. She was at one time president of the Athene Club, a women's literary club. For several years she was a director of the Phillips-Strickland House, a Bangor retirement home for aging men and women. In the church she was president of the Women's Fellowship and for many years superintendent of the Hammond Street Church School. She was an active environmentalist both at Lucerne-in-Maine and in the League of Women Voters; she served as president of the Bangor League and was a state director and environmental chairman for the Maine League.

My wife will be remembered by many as one who set the highest of standards for the position of "first lady" of the Seminary. She was beloved and respected by members of the faculty and their wives. Students were pleased to be entertained in our home. Convocation guests came back year after year to meet the lecturers and be nourished by refreshments served graciously in the Hamlin

House dining room. Visitors were always welcome to inspect our historic home. On one memorable occasion Shirley invited members of her public school class to an "open house" scheduled especially for them. It was the first time many of them had been to "tea," and they reveled in examining every nook and cranny of what had been the home of Lincoln's first vice president.

One of our favorite forms of indoor recreation during the Bangor years was playing pinochle with members of the faculty. Eight of us met regularly for an evening of fun. For many years, winter and summer, the octet consisted of Walter and Merle Cook, Dwight and Janet Cumbee, Larry and Carol Kalp, and ourselves. When the Cumbees left the Seminary they were replaced by church friends Clayton and Kay Lothrop. This circle of light-hearted enjoyment was broken only by the death of Clayton and then of Walter and Merle, but the good memories linger on.

I have marveled through the years that Shirley has been so efficient and so uncomplaining about providing nutritious meals for the Whittaker family, day after day after day. That all of us have remained in good health is certainly attributable to her expertise and her patience. Throughout our long marriage I have prepared my own simple breakfast, but Shirley has carefully provided the other two meals. My major contribution to the household affairs has been the management of budgets and finances, an activity appreciated by my wife. Amazingly, my only other chore in the home after the children left has been vacuuming. I know this is an unequal partnership not to be countenanced by the modern generation. My children agree that I have been, indeed, fortunate and "right" in choosing Shirley as my bride.

During the past twenty-five years Shirley and I have traveled throughout the United States and in several foreign lands. This experience has given us a healthy perspective on world community and has added zest to our personal lives. We have crossed this country three times by automobile and have visited every state on the mainland. In 1970 we spent part of my second sabbatical in Hawaii, and since retirement we have had a memorable trip by plane and ship to Alaska. All of our overseas travel has occurred since I left the Seminary and will be recounted in a later chapter entitled, "President Emeritus."

My professional career required me to attend meetings of theological school personnel in various American cities and in Canada on a biennial basis. In the intervening years I was a delegate from the Seminary to national conferences of the Congregational Christian Churches and, after the merger, the United Church of Christ. On many occasions Shirley was my companion; this has been a feature of our married life and a source of increasing devotion to one another. Shirley has been the "tour guide" on all of our trips. Barbara, Mark, and I well remember that on the last family tour to California in 1964 Shirley gave us daily lessons in geology, one of her favorite subjects, as we rode through the spectacular terrain of the western states.

The good health which Shirley and I have enjoyed has been due in part, we both believe, to the sporting activities we have engaged in since early youth: her swimming and my golf. Only occasionally have I been in the water with her, and only infrequently has she walked the fairways with me. Yet I am as proud of her swimming ability as she is of my prowess on the links. Even my children will agree that most of the time I have been the "right" reverend on the golf course. For twenty years I was a member of the Penobscot Valley Country Club in Orono. It was here that I spent most of my Saturday mornings and holidays during the season. It was here that I achieved two of the "firsts" which every golfer dreams about. On Labor Day in 1957 the United States Professional Golf Association sponsored the first in an annual series of hole-in-one tournaments for amateurs. One that day I stood on the tee of the 196-yard par three 16th hole at Penobscot Valley and hit a three-woodshot on two bounces directly into the cup on the distant green. That shot won the national contest for the longest hole-in-one of the day, and I still proudly display the two-foot tall trophy presented to me by the U.S. PGA.

Not many months later the second achievement was a sub-par round of seventy strokes at the same Penobscot Valley golf course, two shots less than the par of seventy-two. Only once since then have I had an under-par round, a seventy-one on the par seventy-two Bangor Municipal Golf Course. There was just one more goal for a golfer to seek: to score a round equal to or below his age. This quest is a story to be told in a later chapter during the time of my retirement years. Meanwhile there are more serious and professional matters to be discussed in these memoirs.

14.
Ecumenical Executive

The word "ecumenical" first became meaningful to me as a young layman in the 1930's when the Christian church of which I was a member held annual joint services with a Jewish congregation. Ecumenicity took on an added dimension for me as a graduate student in the 1940's when as a candidate for a degree in church history I learned of the dependency of Protestantism upon its Roman Catholic base. In all my later teaching I have stressed the crucial importance of the ecumenical movement within the Jewish-Christian tradition.

In 1950, when I was a young professor of church history at Bangor Theological Seminary, an invitation was given to me to participate in the negotiations which eventually led to the formation of the United Church of Christ through the merger of the Congregational Christian Churches with the Evangelical and Reformed Church in 1957. I was one of twenty-one members appointed to a "Committee on Free Church Polity and Unity" whose purpose was to discover the ways in which congregational polity makes possible the relating of "free autonomous churches to the ecumenical movement." When I was appointed secretary of the Committee it marked the beginning of that phase of my professional career which I have designated "Ecumenical Executive."

260

That career was to culminate in the biennial 1974-1976 when I served as president of the Association of Theological Schools in the United States and Canada.

The Committee on Free Church Polity and Unity was chaired by Dr. L. Wendell Fifield and became known popularly as The Fifield Committee. It was judiciously chosen to represent all points of view with regard to the proposed formation of the United Church of Christ. Strong proponents of the merger included Roland Bainton, Ross Cannon, and William Halfaker. Ardent opponents were Malcolm Burton, Edwin Williams, and Norman Whitehouse. Active "mediators" were Fred Meek, Fred Whittaker, and Henry David Gray; this is the title given us by Dr. Gray in his 600-page book, "The Mediators," which is a detailed account of the process leading to the formation of the United Church of Christ.

The Fifield Committee met on numerous occasions during the biennium prior to the meeting of the General Council of the Congregational Christian Churches in Claremont, California, in June of 1952. The Committee made a report of progress to the General Council, at which I was a delegate for the first time in my role then as president-elect of Bangor Seminary. Ninety-five percent of the delegates voted in favor of "The Claremont Resolution," whose major provisions were as follows: The General Council continues to look forward to a united fellowship; the Executive Committee will seek meetings with the General Council of the Evangelical and Reformed Church for the purpose of agreeing to prepare a draft constitution for the proposed merger; the Executive Committee will establish a consulting relationship with the Committee on Free Church Polity and Unity (the Fifield Committee); and in the preparation of the draft constitution every effort will be made "to preserve all the spiritual and temporal freedoms now possessed by the individuals, churches, associations, conferences, and boards of this communion."

During the next two years the Fifield Committee worked diligently on its various assignments. There was a collection of documents from every level of denominational activity for the purpose of determining the nature of Congregational polity. A correlated study was made of the documents versus actual practice, and a consensus was reached that there was very little variance between the two. After prolonged discussion at many meetings a unanimous report was submitted to the General Council meeting in New Haven on June 24, 1954, with the recommendation that a copy be sent to each church for information and study only. In accordance with a previous arrangement, the report was discussed at three two-hour seminars during the Council meeting. One of many points of friction was caused by a legal opinion circulated by Loren Wood, attorney for the General Council, that the Committee report was inaccurate. Before it adjourned the 1954 General Council voted to reaffirm the Claremont Resolution of 1952, thus moving forward the negotiations for merger and the preparation of a draft constitution for the United Church of Christ. It also voted to appoint a commission to study any constitutional problems. Henry David Gray, one of the "mediators," was named to this commission.

The final decision to establish the United Church of Christ was made at the General Council meeting in Omaha during the June meeting of 1956. Meanwhile, there was discussion throughout the denomination, both pro and con, of the proposed merger. As one of the mediators I addressed the Massachusetts Convention of Congregational Ministers in Boston on May 2, 1955, on the subject "Crisis and Choice for Congregationalism." My comments included the following basic premise: "As a Congregationalist I am concerned that our churches shall participate with all possible effectiveness in the modern ecumenical movement. Thus I am in favor of the merger if it can be accomplished without denominational schism."

That schism was inevitable became apparent in November of 1955 when the National Association of Congregational Christian Churches was formed by a coalition of merger opponents known respectively as the Committee for the Continuation of the Congregational Christian Churches and the League to Uphold Congregational Principles. When the United Church of Christ actually became a reality in 1957 large numbers of Congregational Christian churches remained independent, and to this day have not become affiliated with the United Church.

Meanwhile the "mediators" continued to strive for a union without schism. A letter missive was sent to the delegates who would meet in Omaha, Nebraska, at the General Council meeting of 1956. It contained three recommendations: vote not to ratify the vote of the General Council Executive Committee calling for consummation of the union in June of 1957; vote to make a fresh approach to the Evangelical and Reformed Church; and vote to re-submit to the Congregational Christian churches the question of whether or not to consummate the union.

The Omaha General Council voted overwhelmingly to proceed with the formation of the United Church of Christ, and a uniting synod was scheduled for June, 1957, in Cleveland. I was a delegate at the creation ceremony, and it was a memorable occasion. But I must confess that more than thirty years later my enthusiasm for this historical ecumenical event has dwindled. The new denomination is much more united at the national and state level than it is locally. The United Church of Christ is still a parenthesis or a secondary allegiance in the three churches where I have been a member during the past forty years: the Hammond Street Congregational Church (UCC) in Bangor, Maine; the Huntington Congregational Church (UCC) in Shelton, Connecticut; and the First Congregational United Church of Christ in Sarasota, Florida. The United Church has not yet fulfilled its promise to be a "Uniting Church of Christ," although this was one of its original purposes.

After the formation of the United Church of Christ I continued my interest in ecclesiastical union by serving for ten years or more on the national UCC Commission on Christian Unity and Ecumenical Service. My most vivid memory of this decade was the laborious, but ultimately fruitless, pursuit of a merger between the United Church and the Disciples of Christ denomination; this would have been a significant step toward the realization of a "Uniting Church of Christ." I participated on two different occasions with representatives of the two church bodies in "conversations" designed to foster an eventual merger. However, leading officials of the United Church became more and more enamored of the larger community of major denominations envisioned by the Consultation on Church Union (COCU), with the result that interest in the possible merger with the Disciples became a secondary concern, and finally all but disappeared. Ironically, the dream of a united Protestantism under COCU has not been realized and in recent years there has been a revival of interest in a United Church-Disciples union.

One of my important contributions to the UCC dialogue with the Disciples of Christ was a paper entitled "One Ministry" which I presented in November, 1964, to a joint meeting of the Commissions on Christian Unity of the two denominations in Chicago. The paper was a commentary on a statement issued by the Consultation on Church Union. I include excerpts below as an illustration of my ecumenical thinking:

The Consultation on Church Union has rightly concentrated its current negotiations upon a consideration of the doctrine of the ministry, for this doctrine is the chief obstacle to the further advance of ecumenicity in our time ... The Consultation has based its statement on the ministry very largely upon sources of authority and theological concepts which over the centuries have been divisive in the ordering of church life, and not sufficiently satisfying as articles of faith to effect a transformation of the individual or of society. For example, churches participating in the Consultation are urged to re-examine their understanding of the ministry "in the light of the Tradition expressed in the Scripture, whose unique authority is affirmed...."

Two premises set forth here do not establish a sound foundation upon which to build the structure of today's Christian unity. Certainly there is a tradition expressed in the Scripture, but to designate it as "the" Tradition by use of a capital letter is to give the faith and order of the first Christian century an unwarranted priority over developing beliefs and practices which properly constitute the traditions of later centuries. The Church of today and tomorrow will become increasingly irrelevant if it is patterned exclusively after "the New Testament Church." Secondly, the assignment of "unique" authority to the Scripture in determining a modern understanding of the ministry does not lend itself to the openness of intellectual and spiritual sensitivity whereby the living God can speak to men now as authoritatively as He did at the time of Pentecost.

We cannot dismiss the historical fact that reliance upon the

Scripture for guidance has been a major factor leading to the divisiveness which has characterized the Christian movement, especially in matters of theology and polity. "One Ministry" for the contemporary Church will not be achieved unless we can somehow reach a consensus based upon consideration of at least three authorities: the authority of Scripture, the authority of nineteen centuries of post-scriptural Christian experience, and the authority of the Holy Spirit speaking with fresh insight in the year of our Lord nineteen hundred and sixty-four." ...

The "one ministry" I have in mind involves a de-emphasizing of the Pauline concept of sin and reconciliation, and a proclamation of the good news which can be found in parts of the synoptic Gospels and in some of the Johannine literature; it is good news which has been embodied in Jesus Christ and in many of his followers throughout successive generations. A portion of this gospel is most succinctly stated in John 3:16: "For God so loved the world that he gave his only Son, that whoever believes in him should not perish but have eternal life." Here is a clear doctrine which requires only simple belief in God's revelation through Christ to assure every human being of everlasting care by his Creator.

Yet for more than nineteen hundred years, confessing Christians have built and established a complicated scheme of so-called salvation based upon the legend or myth of an "original" sin and the ensuing necessity of "redemption" through a sacramental system and a hierarchical priesthood or ministry. This "orthodox" way to salvation has nourished the fear of death rather than the hope of eternal life; it has taught man to expect redemption through the priestly intercession of the Son of God and his vicars instead of inspiring man to fulfill his spiritual potential by patterning his own life after that of the historic Jesus; and it has diverted the manpower of the Church from its principal task of building the Kingdom of God on earth. Let the Church accept by faith the good news of John 3:16 with respect to life beyond this planet and begin to concentrate the attention of all its members, both ordained and unordained, upon the primary duty of ministering to the world....

In ministering to the world the Church needs to rediscover the neglected portion of the gospel which is contained in John 3:17:

265

"For God sent the Son into the world not to condemn the world, but that the world might be saved through him." The Consultation rightly directs attention to the importance of a ministry to the world, but it emphasizes redemption of the world by God through "Christ's reconciling power." I speak for another emphasis. It is obvious to observers of the contemporary human scene that the world has not been saved by God through his Son, as proclaimed in John's gospel. Still, the potential for such Christian redemption remains if we, like God, do not condemn the world but work to save it in the name of the Christ whose living Spirit is constantly at hand to guide us. This is a major purpose of our ministry. It involves words and deeds by Christians who are assured of their eternal salvation and who, in gratitude for this divine gift of faith and in self-confidence of their ability to lead a Christ-like life, are anxious and willing to dedicate themselves to the task of transforming the world around them....

As we consider the future of the Church and its "one ministry," a most salutary reform would be the removal of the barrier between clergy and laity as laborers in the harvest of the Lord ... The Reformation doctrine of the "holy calling" which presumably qualifies a clergyman to be an ordained Christian minister is no different from the holy calling which qualifies a lawyer, a merchant, a doctor, a farmer, a teacher, or a politician, for example, to be an unordained Christian minister ... The Consultation has listed as "the particular responsibility of ordained ministers" several functions of the Church, and has declared that "only by the effective exercise of their ministry does the Church realize its intended health, growth, and mission." The functions listed include praying, teaching, witnessing, care and nurture, all of which laypeople can and should perform in a vital church; and while the Consultation acknowledges that other members of the Church have a share in these functions, the role of the laity as unordained ministers deserves greater emphasis....

The Consultation does recognize that "ministry belongs to the whole people of God," but it gives special divine sanction to the ordained ministry as one which "God calls forth" and which should be "set apart." This is not conducive to the concept of "one ministry" ... *Ordination should be considered as a recognition of the functional role of professional leadership for which the ordinand has been educated and trained; this rite marks the beginning of a vocation within the Church which is different from the vocations of Christian laypeople primarily because it involves the performance of professional ecclesiastical functions in addition to the personal witness which is required of all members of the Church. This interpretation of ordination avoids the separation of clergy and laity as Christian ministers and imposes upon laypeople the same responsibilities for witness by faith and works which lie upon clergymen, thus making possible a community of effort which is difficult to achieve when ordained ministers are "set apart" from the unordained.*

My major role as an "ecumenical executive" was as an officer of the Association of Theological Schools in the United States and Canada. By 1968 I had become well-known, perhaps infamous, within the ATS by virtue of continuing and persistent appeals to its Commission on Accrediting on behalf of full recognition for Bangor Theological Seminary. I had attended regularly the biennial meetings of the two hundred or more theological schools in North America, and in 1968 I was invited to become Secretary of the organization and a member of its Executive Committee for a two-year term. Then after a hiatus in 1970 and 1971, I was elected Vice President in 1972 and President in 1974. After my presidential term ended in 1976, I remained on the Executive Committee, as was the custom, for another two years and thus completed eight years of service on that Committee.

The time of service with the Association of Theological Schools (ATS) was in a very real sense the culmination of my professional career, both at Bangor Seminary and in the larger Christian community. One evidence of this fact was the full accreditation given to Bangor for the first time while I was an ATS officer. There are two events which will suffice to illustrate my witness and work as an "ecumenical executive": One was a two-month study of ATS-governmental relationships conducted in Washington, D.C., and the other was my ATS presidential address, "Freedom's Holy Light," delivered at the biennial meeting in Boston in 1976.

Excerpts from both the study and the address will constitute most of the remainder of this chapter.

For context, the following is a brief description of the ATS itself: During my tenure the Association maintained a headquarters and staff in Vandalia (Dayton), Ohio. Dr. Jesse Ziegler was the executive director and his principal associates were Dr. David Schuller, Dr. Marvin Taylor, and Charlotte Thompson, all of whom I remember with gratitude and affection because of their many kindnesses to me over a period of eight years. The ATS has approximately 200 member schools in the United States and Canada, including Protestant, Roman Catholic, Orthodox, and Jewish institutions. It serves as an accrediting agency, publishes a quarterly scholarly journal, and issues an annual "Fact Book on Theological Education." Under a foundation grant it has completed a three-year study and maintained an ongoing program entitled "Readiness for Ministry." The ATS receives each year substantial grants from foundations which it distributes among its members as subsidies for sabbatical activities by administrators, faculty members, and librarians. It also conducts programs for the encouragement of theological education for blacks, Hispanic Americans, and women, as well as for the general improvement of theological education.

Early in 1976 theological leaders throughout the United States and Canada met to discuss long-range planning for the ATS; a key document prepared for use in a series of meetings described two significant "purposes" of the Association: to function in an advocacy role on behalf of the seminaries to agencies of government, and to provide these agencies with adequate information regarding the theological education enterprise. In accordance with these stated purposes I was commissioned as the ATS president to conduct a two-month study in Washington, D.C., among key governmental and educational personnel, and to submit a report with recommendations to the ATS; I spent March and April of 1976 on this task while on a leave of absence from the Seminary.

My instructions were to develop in depth an earlier study made by vice president Bill Barnes of Christian Theological Seminary in Indianapolis. The Barnes report indicated that the communication of information about theological education and the federal government is a two-way process in which the data often require expert interpretation in both directions, and that a knowledgeable representative of the ATS in Washington is needed for this purpose. To test this latter thesis, I had personal interviews with seventy-five individuals. Thirty-two were Congressional personnel, including eleven Senators and eleven Congressmen; six were Senate staff members and four were staff members related to the House of Representatives. In each branch of the Congress most of those consulted were serving primarily on educational committees, although some also had responsibility on such committees as Judiciary, Ways and Means, Budget, and Government Operations. I am particularly indebted to my own Senator from Maine, William D. Hathaway, for arranging many of the appointments with his colleagues. Most memorable were half-hours spent with such national luminaries as Senators Edward Kennedy, Walter Mondale, and Edmund Muskie.

Among those interviewed were six representatives of the executive branch of the federal government, including members of the Department of Health, Education and Welfare, the National Endowment for the Humanities, the National Institute of Mental Health, and the White House staff. I had discussions with ten leaders of church organizations which maintain offices in Washington; among them were the United States Catholic Conference, the National Council of Churches, the Lutheran Council in the U.S.A., the Baptist Joint Committee on Public Affairs, and the United Methodist Church. Six officers of member institutions in the Washington Theological Consortium were also consulted. There are at least 250 national educational associations with offices in the nation's capital. Interviews were held with officers of twenty such organizations, including the Association of American Colleges, the National Catholic Educational Association, the Association of American Law Schools, the Association of American Medical Colleges, the Council of Graduate Schools in the United States, and the American Council on Education.

Consultants were told of the tentative proposal to establish in Washington a representative, and perhaps a branch office, of the Association of Theological Schools with a three-fold purpose in mind, as follows:

1. *Communication.* To gather pertinent information, for distribution among its member institutions, concerning federal government activities such as legislation, administrative policy-making, and distribution of funds; to provide information about theological education to various federal agencies; to make available a two-way process of communication.

2. *Advocacy.* To provide a spokesman for ATS points of view when legislation is being drafted and policy is being made on such matters, for example, as moral and social issues, charitable contributions, tax exemptions, lobbying laws, recognition of accrediting agencies, confidentiality of school records, and allocation of funds for education.

3. *Grantsmanship.* To protect the interests of theological schools and theological students in the distribution of federal funds for education.

In my report to the Executive Committee of the ATS I summarized the testimony of the Washington personnel interviewed by stating, "There is no doubt that a substantial majority believe that the ATS should establish an office in Washington if it wishes to fulfill effectively the purpose of relating the theological education enterprise to agencies of government in the nation's capital." A further commentary on this conclusion will be made in my 1976 presidential address to the ATS which will complete this chapter. I include here the major recommendations made to the Executive Committee:

Recommendations: That the ATS establish a Commission on Government Relations; that the Commission develop and implement a program of governmental relations which will include the purposes of "Communication, Advocacy, and Grantsmanship"; that the ATS establish a branch office in Washington; and that the ATS seek a foundation grant sufficient to cover the expenses of the first two years of operation of the proposed program of governmental relations.

The Whittaker report was considered by the ATS Executive Committee in June, 1976, following my presidential address to the

ATS biennial meeting, in which I urged its adoption. Dr. Jesse Ziegler, Executive Director of the ATS, reports the action taken on the recommendations in his book entitled *ATS Through Two Decades*: "The Executive Committee essentially rejected the thrust of the recommendations but did establish a Committee on Government Relations ... by December, 1977, the committee was dissolved and the work of government relations was picked up by the Executive Committee itself. Other actions by the Executive Committee in the late 1970's made completely clear that neither the schools nor the Executive Committee were prepared to turn over to a paid staff person representation of ATS interests with the federal government." Dr. Ziegler went on to explain that "the whole issue of church and state" made many members of the ATS "very uncomfortable."

And so until this very day the ATS has no branch office in Washington. Meanwhile, the Whittaker report lies dormant in some ATS filing cabinet. It is my hope that someday it will be rediscovered, and its recommendations implemented, so that the theological schools may exercise their dormant power to revitalize the religious, educational, ethical, and cultural life of the nation. The conservatism of the ATS is a subject upon which I shall comment in a later chapter of the section of these memoirs on "The Years of Reflection." Now this chapter ends with major excerpts from my presidential address in 1976 to the biennial meeting on the subject "Freedom's Holy Light": (I consider it to be among the most important speeches of my lifetime.)

In this bicentennial year it was the hope of the program committee of ATS that a national political figure might give the keynote address at this biennial meeting in Boston. With this goal unfulfilled, it has become my privilege and responsibility to serve as a substitute. My credentials are modest: a quarter of a century of teaching in the field of American Church History, with emphasis upon the relationship of religion and politics; five of the twenty-four years of my incumbency as a seminary president spent, uniquely perhaps, on the city council of Bangor and in the Maine state senate; and two months of conversations this spring in Washington with some seventy-five of the nation's policy-makers while on special

271

assignment for the Association. If the ATS president's address of 1976 should be adjudged inadequate, ill-founded, or offensive, I can do no better than to present for my defense the 200-year-old words of Thomas Jefferson in his Virginia Statute for Religious Freedom: "...all men shall be free to profess, and by argument to maintain, their opinions in matters of religion...."

The theme for this 30th biennial meeting is "Readiness for Ministry in a Pluralistic Setting." It reflects the desire of the executive committee and the staff that the varied programs of the ATS shall be of maximum value to its member institutions as they seek to prepare men and women for effective religious leadership in the real world of the late twentieth century. This kind of leadership requires, in my opinion, a new philosophy and program of cooperation *between the agencies of the church and the state; the time-honored tradition in the United States of the separation of these two instrumentalities will not suffice for the third century of our national history now beginning. To speak in philosophical or theological terms, I am proposing a new instrumental trinity for our time in which religion and the church are not the only agencies appointed for the sacred purposes of God. The kingdom on earth also needs for its fulfillment the witness and ministry of politics and the state, of education and the school. The ATS should be vitally involved in this three-fold process, and it is especially well-structured to do so.*

It is obvious that our Association is intimately related to the mission of the church; most of our member schools conduct a major program for the training of local leadership in the parish and for religious outreach. We are also concerned through our several institutions with the preparation of teachers for church-related colleges, universities, and seminaries. I suggest here for elaboration later that in our contemporary pluralistic setting this concern should be expanded to include the training of personnel capable of teaching about *religion in the public schools, as permitted by the United States Supreme Court. However, the principal thrust of this address is a defense of the thesis that "readiness for ministry" in the post-bicentennial era demands an imaginative new cooperation between church-related agencies and national, state, and provincial government bodies; it is my hope that the ATS will be at the forefront of this project....*

Before turning to some specific issues, this address needs a topic of its own and a rationale for its central message. As a historian looking at 1776 and 1976, I call upon two witnesses from the last quarter of the 19th century: one is Samuel Smith and the other is Samuel Harris. During morning worship at two of Washington's churches not long ago I noted the effective use of the fourth verse of Smith's prayer-hymn written to the tune "America," so well known in both the United States and Canada: "Our father's God, to thee, author of liberty, to thee we sing; long may our land be bright with freedom's holy light; protect us by thy might, great God, our King." For a hundred years, more or less, we have been singing in our churches and our schools about "Freedom's Holy Light"; it becomes our topic today because at no time in our national history has our cherished secular freedom more desperately needed the holy light of religion.

In 1876 Samuel Harris was the Dwight Professor of Systematic Theology at Yale University, where he served for twenty-five years until his retirement; earlier he had occupied a similar position at Bangor Theological Seminary during the Civil War period. Still to be appreciated by many modern scholars, Harris wrote three major volumes of theology and many shorter works; I quote for our purposes these 100-year-old prophetic words from his essay on "Religion and Politics": "We have separated the Church and the State, but we have not separated, and we cannot with impunity separate, religion and politics. The separation of the Church and the State does but render it the more necessary to healthy political action that, throughout the entire population, the true principles of religion and their proper application to all human affairs should be clearly explained and diligently inculcated. This is essential to preserve to politics their true dignity and to make the political agitations, incident to a democracy, purifying and ennobling rather than corrupting and belittling ... In our country all men are politicians and a large portion of daily conversation and action is political; therefore, to exempt the preaching of the gospel in its application to politics is to exempt it from one of the large and significant areas of human life."

Fortunately, the ATS is not unaware of its responsibility to be concerned about the national character and to make its influence felt among the agencies of government. Among the sixty-four core clusters of the Readiness for Ministry study are the following: "Initiative in Development of Community Services," "Relating Faith to the Modern World," "Active Concern for the Oppressed," and "Aggressive Political Leadership." The long-range planning report submitted by a task force to this biennial meeting identifies one of the major objectives of the ATS as service in an advocate role for theological schools to various agencies of government. And the Executive Committee is giving consideration to a report on "The ATS and Government Relations" which I submitted after an investigation in Washington during March and April authorized by the committee. I share with you now some of the principal findings of that report, together with a few supplementary opinions.

My study disclosed, first of all, a consensus among a representative sampling of Washington personnel — in Congress, the federal executive branch, national church and educational association offices, and local seminary administrators — that the ATS should establish a major program of governmental relations. This consensus is based upon the belief that theological education, as represented in the ATS, is broadly ecumenical, is distinctive in character as graduate professional education, and would add through this program new and beneficial dimensions to the academic, social, and ethical life of the United States. Typical of the comments made to me are these: "The United States urgently needs ethical and moral guidance at this time," said a member of the Senate. And a highly-placed executive branch officer added: "An ATS presence in Washington would serve as a reminder of the spiritual life and would help to arouse the national conscience." ...

A major conclusion of my investigation is that the proposed ATS program of governmental relations should involve the establishment of a branch office in Washington; this was the opinion of eighty percent of those whom I consulted. One of the more effective government liaison officers serving a church organization made a statement which is typical of many others: "To be influential with the federal government there is no substitute for a Washington presence." The vice president of the prestigious American Council on Education reports in a recently-published book that there are at least 250 educational organizations at work in Washington and then predicts that "as far ahead as anyone can see, the federal government will exercise a crucial leverage ... on the future of the entire educational enterprise"; he concludes that "the national need for effective spokesmen for education was never greater." Among the professions, the absence of an ATS office in Washington is made more conspicuous by the presence there of such organizations as the Association of American Medical Colleges and the Association of American Law Schools.

In the remaining time allotted to me, I presume to share with you some personal opinions, based upon a career-long interest in the subject, about what I have called the cooperation of church and state, especially as it concerns the ATS. My recent experience in Washington only confirms my belief that the religious, educational, and political leaders of this nation — the instrumental trinity of which I spoke earlier — have a God-given responsibility to join forces in a concerted effort to restore what Samuel Smith called "Freedom's Holy Light." A night of darkness has descended upon our land in these post-Viet Nam, post-Watergate years, but there is an earnest desire among people in all walks of life to rediscover the moral illumination — the "holy light," if you will — which inspired the early struggle for freedom 200 years ago. Some of the results of the primary elections this spring are a clear indication of this desire. Although it is very popular right now to denigrate Washington and all that it represents, I am here to testify that there are large numbers of our fellow citizens in the Congress and in the other branches of the federal government who are dedicated to the protection of the national welfare and who will welcome any guidance or assistance offered by an organization like the ATS.

It was in the Congress that special appreciation was expressed for inquiries made on behalf of the ATS. A good many members commented that never before had a request for interview been made by a representative of the theological schools. There was a general tendency to equate the programs of seminaries with sectarian religion; gratitude was expressed for a new understanding of theological education as essentially graduate professional in character and of the public-service dimensions of such seminary-related activities as clinical pastoral education, the training of military and other chaplains, and the preparation of teachers of religion for private and public institutions of higher education. Members of the Senate and House asked to be kept advised of developments in theological education; several indicated an interest in dialogue with seminary professors and administrators, and stated a hope that they might be invited to speak on the campus of ATS member schools. As one senator, a member of the committee on education, told me: "Political and religious people need to get together." It is also instructive to hear this opinion of a Washington-based national church agency leader: "Congress depends upon special interest groups to educate its members; the desire of Congress is to meet real needs."

Our Association is a special interest group. We are primarily concerned with theological education, which means that we have an orientation both religious and academic, related to both the church and the school. If then we can combine this special interest with that of the state in an area of real need, we can achieve the instrumental trinity which I have designated as a desirable goal, and at the same time implement our biennial theme, "Readiness for Ministry in a Pluralistic Setting." Let me suggest, briefly, just one program for the ATS with this dual aim in mind: If and when we move more adventurously into the field of governmental relations, let our member schools and the Association itself make plans to provide the trained leadership required to establish on a broad national basis in our local public schools the instruction about religion permitted by a 1963 decision of the U.S. Supreme Court. I can conceive of no more effective long-range project for the rekindling in this land of what Samuel Smith poetically described as "Freedom's Holy Light."

In its decision entitled, "Abington School District v. Schempp," this nation's highest court recognized in two important ways the religiously pluralistic setting which is twentieth century America today. On the one hand, it prohibited in the public schools such religious exercises as prayer or reading from the Bible if they are required by the state or its agents. On the other hand, the court declared constitutional "the teaching about religion, as distinguished from the teaching of religion, in the public schools." During the past thirteen years this decision has made possible in more than one thousand U.S. high schools a curriculum in which the Bible is used as a resource in English and American literature courses, units on the development and influence of the various religions of the world have been included in social studies, and the understanding of history has been enhanced by the use as primary sources of some of the great religious documents. This program of teaching about religion in the public schools has tremendous potential as a ministry to pluralistic America in the re-forming of its political, social, and moral life. Yet there is today a reported shortage of teachers trained to teach about religion, and of curriculum materials for teachers interested in such a career. Here, I suggest, is an ideal opportunity for the ATS, as a church-related, ecumenical, and pluralistic organization, to cooperate with the state.

This cooperation, however, should be a two-way arrangement in which agencies of government, without violating constitutional principles, participate in the funding of the theological education enterprise. An important step in this direction has already been taken through the eligibility of theological students for federal loans and work-study grants. In Maine, students at Bangor Theological Seminary who have low family incomes may legally receive state tuition equalization funds. In a related educational sphere, the U.S. Supreme Court has ruled by majority vote that four Roman Catholic colleges and universities in Connecticut are eligible to receive federal funds totalling almost two million dollars under Title I of the Higher Education Facilities Act; this decision was made in 1971 in Tilton v. Richardson.

Under the doctrine of the separation of church and state, seminaries are still not permitted to receive state or federal funds for institutional purposes; this may be the last vestige of discrimination by a government which specifically forbids all inequities based upon sex, race, ethnic or national origin. I ask the rhetorical question: Since the church comprises both laity and clergy, can the state which subsidizes education for laity in church-related colleges and universities justify its refusal to subsidize education for clergy in church-related theological schools? The question may require no answer, since every indication out of Washington suggests that future federal aid to education will be in the form of assistance to students, including seminarians, rather than grants to institutions.

This address must end. I add one further thought, then close this biennial/bicentennial message with a final word from the one quoted at the beginning. When this nation was born, political freedom and religious freedom jointly provided the power which shed a kind of "holy light" over a liberated people. Separation of church and state ended the bondage imposed upon many of the colonies by sectarian "establishments of religion." Two hundred years later we live in a different era. As exemplified by the ATS, ecumenism is a guarantee against any possible sectarian control of our society. Through our Association we seek a "Readiness for Ministry in a Pluralistic Setting." That readiness, I believe, requires a new relationship of cooperation between the political and religious institutions of our country, and in this endeavor I cherish a place of leadership for the ATS.

Last April my wife and I spent an inspiring hour at the Thomas Jefferson Memorial in Washington. One of the inscriptions engraved in bronze I chose then for this address and quote to you now; it is from a letter which Jefferson wrote to a friend: "I am not an advocate for frequent changes in laws and constitutions, but laws and institutions must go hand in hand with the progress of the human mind. As that becomes more developed, more enlightened, as new discoveries are made, new truths discovered and manners and opinions change, with the change of circumstances, institutions must advance also to keep pace with the times."

15.
President: The Later Years

The final eight years of my presidency at Bangor Seminary began quietly enough with a sabbatical spent by my wife and me in visiting alumni throughout the southern and western states, including a month in Hawaii. The period ended on a more dynamic note in 1978 when I retired at age 65 after a confrontation with the Board of Trustees over the process they adopted in choosing my successor. Significant events of the intervening years included the accreditation of the Seminary by the Association of Theological Schools, my presidency of the ATS, my recovery from a serious illness, and my renewed involvement in politics as an independent candidate for Governor of Maine and, later, for election to the Congress of the United States. As the story unfolds it will take on characteristics both peaceful and frenetic.

Prior to 1970 my only sabbatical in twenty-two years on the Seminary staff had been the six months spent in 1963 as a State Senator in the Maine legislature. Following the 1970 Convocation late in January, Shirley and I began what I have called a "working sabbatical" by spending three months in Florida. There I met with several of our alumni, preached in a number of churches, and participated in the academic life of New College at Sarasota, where I had study privileges. A major purpose of the sabbatical was to establish contact with as many Bangor graduates as possible. Thus in May we started on a cross-country tour through the southern states to California and on to Hawaii.

My wife and I have fond memories of time spent in New Orleans with former classmates Ralph Kimball and Kingsley Hawthorne. Ralph was the rector of St. Andrews Episcopal Church and Kingsley was director of development for the Tulane University Medical School. In San Antonio, Texas, we had a pleasant reunion with another former classmate, Lt. Col. Bradley Morse, who was a career chaplain with twenty-seven years of service and then chief of chaplains at Randolph Air Force Base. We also enjoyed a visit with a former student of mine, Major William Cleary, Jr., who was involved with the pastoral care of cancer and surgical patients in the 1000-bed hospital at Lackland Air Force Base.

In Louisiana and Texas I functioned in my capacity as secretary of the Association of Theological Schools and secretary of the Council for Higher Education of the United Church of Christ by conferring with the presidents and deans of the following institutions: New Orleans Baptist Seminary, Dillard University, Brite Divinity School of Texas Christian University, Southwestern Baptist Seminary, and Perkins School of Theology at Southern Methodist University. In Austin we had a pleasant social evening with Dr. Arnold Hearn and his family; Dr. Hearn had become Professor of Christian Ethics at the Episcopal Seminary of the Southwest in 1965 after serving on the Bangor Seminary faculty.

Our month-long stay in Hawaii was a memorable one. I was guest preacher at Honolulu Central Union Church, the largest in Hawaii, and at the Kailua Christian Church (UCC) where Bangor alumnus Charles Schuetz was the pastor. We shall always be grateful to "Chuck" and Arlene Schuetz for the many hours they spent as our unofficial hosts in the islands; I especially appreciated the golf games Chuck arranged for me. He also scheduled me to speak on "Contemporary Theological Education" at a meeting of the Windham Coalition of Hawaiian Ministers. On another occasion I spoke to the Ala Moana Kiwanis Club in Honolulu on one of my favorite subjects, "Religion and Politics." We were also privileged to have a guided tour of the campus of the University of Hawaii, where we were introduced to faculty members and honored at a luncheon.

Before returning to California in early June to attend the biennial meeting of the Association of Theological Schools in Claremont, Shirley and I spent some time on the beautiful island of Maui, where we had many unforgettable hours with Bangor alumnus Takashi Yamashita and his family. Takashi was the minister of the Pookela Church, and is one of the long line of men trained in Maine's only theological school for Christian service in far-flung corners of the world. One of the earliest Bangor-educated missionaries to Hawaii was Daniel Dole of the class of 1839; we relived history by visiting the site of his ancient parish on the island of Kauai.

On the trip to Hawaii two members of our touring party were Harry and Sue Ota, American citizens of Japanese ancestry. I include them in these memoirs because of the indelible impression they made upon the Whittakers. They were most gracious to us during the trip and they met us at the airport after our extended stay in Hawaii so that they could be our companions and guides in Los Angeles. Harry was the maintenance supervisor for the Los Angeles Parks and Recreation Department. We had an extraordinary visit to Disneyland because of Harry's knowledge and expertise as a public relations representative; due to his familiarity with the foreign language he was often called upon by the city to entertain visitors from Japan. Our friendship deepened the following year when Harry and Sue came to Maine for a visit in our summer home. Unfortunately, this episode ended suddenly shortly thereafter when Harry died unexpectedly.

I tell the Ota story for another reason. During our all-too-brief friendship, we discovered that Harry and Sue had been interned, despite the fact that they were American citizens, in one of the many camps established by the U.S. government during the hysteria which followed the Japanese attack on Pearl Harbor; the Otas were relocated in a camp for several months, during which time Sue was delivered of the first of her two sons. Despite the shabby and unjust treatment they received as U.S. citizens, the Otas never lost their patriotism and love of country. When World War II was over, and the family had returned to their California home, Harry was among the first to volunteer to serve his nation as an interpreter when the United States began rehabilitation work in Japan after the atomic bomb attacks. I am pleased to testify that the Otas were, in truth, loyal Americans.

The Whittaker sabbatical came to a close in July after the return trip to Bangor by automobile through Oregon, Washington, British Columbia, and other parts of Canada. I came back to the campus secure in the knowledge that alumni of the Seminary were serving effectively as Christian ambassadors throughout the United States. I also learned first-hand, a truth I had long suspected, that the school would easily survive the extended absence of its chief executive officer. The task immediately awaiting my personal attention was still another appeal for full academic accreditation of Bangor by the Association of Theological Schools.

Applications had been submitted to the ATS Commission on Accrediting in 1957, 1962, and 1967, all to no avail. Then early in the 1970's there were developments within the ATS which led to changes in the standards for accreditation and, eventually, to full recognition of Bangor Theological Seminary. These developments coincided with my membership on the ATS Executive Committee as an officer of the Association. As early as 1970 there was an omen of things to come when the ATS permitted Bangor and other member schools to change the nomenclature of the first professional degree from Bachelor of Divinity (B.D.) to Master of Divinity (M.Div.). A related factor favorable to Bangor's status was the action of the New England Association of Colleges and Secondary Schools in 1971 reaffirming for ten years the accreditation of Bangor voted in 1968 for a three-year period.

It was in 1972 that the ATS was finally persuaded to modify its standards. The biennial meeting accepted a report from a special committee which had studied the matter of accreditation for several months and had held hearings in which I participated. The Association reaffirmed its longstanding position that "admission to theological study shall normally be based upon graduation with a bachelor's degree" from an accredited college. It then adopted this exception: "Schools which are principally concerned with the specialized mission of training men of mature years and experience for ordination may follow admissions policies which significantly deviate from this standard." The exception was tailor-made for Bangor and marked the end of a twenty-year struggle for national recognition of the "Bangor plan."

Once again Bangor Seminary submitted the required information to the ATS Commission on Accrediting. Under date of January 23, 1974, I received a communication from Dr. Marvin Taylor of the ATS staff which read in part as follows: "I write to confirm our telephone conversation regarding the action taken by the ATS Commission on Accrediting last Friday. That decision was to recommend to the accredited members of ATS that Bangor be awarded preliminary accreditation for the Master of Divinity degree until January, 1976 ... All of us here are delighted that this very significant step, both for Bangor and ATS, has at long last been taken." A copy of the letter, significantly, was sent to the New England Association of Colleges and Secondary Schools.

The ATS Commission requested the Seminary to make an in-depth study during the two-year period of "preliminary accreditation," with particular reference to such matters as the definition of "the mature person," data to demonstrate that the level of academic work at Bangor is comparable to that given in other accredited schools, an augmented faculty, and an increase in the library budget. Such a "Self-Study" was prepared by a joint committee consisting of trustees, faculty, alumni, and students; the committee gathered information from many sources over a period of several months before submitting its report to the Commission on November 10, 1975. (The Joint Committee report is on file at the Seminary and is a valuable resource for those interested in the status of the school in the mid-1970's.) For these memoirs it is sufficient to report that in 1976 the ATS granted full accreditation to Bangor Seminary for the normal ten-year period. Since that time it has never again been necessary to explain to foundations, prospective faculty members and students, and potential benefactors why this unique theological school was not fully accredited nationally.

In 1971 Dr. Walter Cook of the Seminary faculty was the author of a book entitled *Bangor Theological Seminary — A Sesquicentennial History,* in which he commented on the long struggle of the school for national accreditation: "There is no hint that full recognition by the Association of Theological Schools is near. President Whittaker, nevertheless, has worked zealously and continuously to advance the standards of the school, and his endeavors have been acclaimed by his associates in theological education. A less persevering administrator would have ceased his exertions long ago...." Five years later the perseverance, happily, was finally rewarded.

I am deeply gratified that my dear friend and colleague, Walter Cook, responded favorably to my appeal that he become a historian of the Seminary in succession to Dr. Calvin M. Clark. Walter not only updated the Bangor story, but in a scholarly and refreshing way gave vitality to the events and the persons involved in the unfolding drama of Maine's only theological school. For these memoirs I am proud to include this brief "profile" concerning me which Walter recorded about my election to the presidency: "...a most complicated personality exhibiting many qualities that are seemingly contradictory ... conservative in certain things yet astonishingly innovative; reserved yet capable of real warmth and friendliness; usually contained and composed yet at times unexpectedly impulsive; rather austere and straitlaced but capable of a relaxed appreciation of the ridiculous; fastidious and correct in dress and manner but often in summer casually attired, swinging a most effective golf club."

1971 is a year to be remembered because it marked the retirement of Dr. Andrew Banning after thirty-six years as a member of the Bangor faculty. He was the last of the "Harry Trust faculty," and the last of the professors of my student years, to complete his service to the Seminary. The trustees named him Buck Professor of Christian Theology emeritus, and established the Andrew Banning Student Loan Fund in his honor. During his tenure he also served for thirty-three years as Registrar and three years as Dean. As I said publicly at the time, "Dr. Banning is completing one of the longest and most distinguished careers in the 156-year history of the school. His Christian ministry to a generation of students and colleagues will remain a blessing for all the years to come." Nell Banning was Andrew's wife for most of his time at Bangor and will be remembered with affection by decades of students and faculty families. For ten years she was a teacher in the Bangor public schools. She and Andrew still live in retirement in Grand Rapids, Michigan.

In appreciation, and for the historical record, it should be noted that Andrew Banning was a leader in church and community affairs for more than three decades. During his Seminary career he also served for seven years as minister of the Forest Avenue Church in Bangor, and in other interim pastorates. He was three times president of the Bangor-Brewer Council of Churches, twice moderator of the Penobscot Association of Congregational Churches and Ministers, and deacon and clerk of All Souls Congregational Church. He was a member of the Bangor Kiwanis Club. He served the United Church of Christ nationally as a member of its Commission to Study Basic Doctrine. Dr. Banning was an accredited visitor to the first Assembly of the World Council of Churches. He was an officer of the American Theological Society and one of the founders of the Maine Philosophical Institute.

Two other members of the Seminary staff also retired early in the 1970's. One was Elwood G. Cookson, who for twenty-five years was Superintendent of Buildings and Grounds for the school. Representatives of the trustees, faculty and students attended a testimonial for Elwood and his wife Mildred, at which I read the following statement on behalf of the trustees: "Throughout a quarter of a century the Seminary has benefited from the many technical and personal talents of Elwood Cookson. At a modest cash salary he has been heating engineer, electrician, plumber, carpenter, road builder, truck driver, purchasing agent, and general handyman ... Equally important ... he has been a friend to a generation of students, faculty, and staff members."

A second staff member retired at the end of the academic year in 1972. She was Mrs. Elvira M. Hilyard, who for fourteen years had been stewardess of the Seminary's dining room. One of the distinguishing features of the Bangor program through the years has been the offering of food services in a home-like atmosphere to

285

a host of grateful students. Thus I told Mrs. Hilyard that she had "effectively taken her place in the long tradition of those who have cared for generations of students in this place where food and fellowship abound. Your ministry here has been not only to the human physical need for nutriment but, even more important, to the spiritual need for understanding and friendship." Throughout the remainder of my tenure, and beyond to this day, the providing of food services by a caring stewardess has been directed by another gracious lady, Carolyn Trundy.

No institution of higher learning can fulfill its mission without the day-by-day devoted witness of its support staff. And so I record here, inadequately to be sure by the listing of their names, my deep appreciation of some of those not previously mentioned who have left their mark on the Seminary during the Whittaker years: Margaret Bradbury, my competent and faithful secretary; Charles Knowles, buildings and grounds superintendent; Virginia Miles, assistant to the librarian; Inez Toothaker, development assistant; Margaret Smith, bursar; Irene D'Angelo, secretary; Sally Kaubris-Kowalzyk, assistant librarian; and Linda Cray, who rose from the ranks of the business office to become today's treasurer of the Seminary.

One of the features of life at Bangor Theological Seminary throughout the twentieth century has been the annual Convocation Week program, inaugurated in 1905 by President David Nelson Beach. Now eighty-six years old, this program has continuously attracted to Bangor during the twentieth century most of the nation's outstanding religious leaders. During my administration this included, in addition to those named earlier, such luminaries as: Roland Bainton, George Buttrick, James Forbes, William Sloan Coffin, Harvey Cox, H. Richard Niebuhr, Erwin Canham, David Trueblood, Amos Wilder, Bishop G. Bromley Oxnam, John Bennett, Krister Stendahl, Charles Shelby Rooks, and Robert Calhoun. The 1971 Convocation is one I remember with special fondness because it brought to Bangor one of the two or three friends who have been most influential upon my life. Leader of the Beach Quiet Hour that year was Dr. Dwight S. Large, minister of the Central United Methodist Church in Detroit, Michigan.

As indicated in a previous chapter, Dwight Large was a Yale

Divinity School student who served on the staff of my church, Plymouth Congregational, while I was still a layman living in New Haven. He was responsible for my early avocation in amateur dramatics and was a major factor in my decision to study for the ministry. Our reunion at the 1971 Bangor Convocation was an exciting and nostalgic occasion. Dwight made such a favorable impression as a lecturer and worship leader that the faculty invited him two years later to spend a semester on the Seminary campus as pastor-in-residence. While at Bangor, Dwight taught a course on pastoral theology and pastoral care; in addition, he was available for group and individual conferences with students, alumni, and area ministers. The pastor-in-residence program emphasized the importance of preaching and pastoral relations in the Bangor curriculum during my administration. I shall always be grateful to Dwight Large for his role in my life and in the life of the Seminary.

In 1970, concurrent with the adoption of the M.Div. degree nomenclature, the faculty established a revised curriculum which was a source of strength in Bangor's impending successful appeal for accreditation. Student representatives were deeply involved in preparing an academic program designed to provide maximum flexibility both in the choice of courses and the sequence in which they may be taken. A required core of study, distributed over four areas, constituted slightly less than half of the thirty-three courses needed for graduation. The student was introduced to several disciplines involved in theological education, but was otherwise free to proceed according to interests and inclinations. Each student was assigned to a faculty advisor. Five courses were to be taken during each of the two semesters over a three-year period, plus one course of independent study during January each year. The "January session," so-called, was a popular feature of the curriculum which enabled the student to engage in concentrated study of a favored subject. An alternative four-year plan was designed for students who had major field work responsibilities or who had difficulty in maintaining an average academic grade of "C."

There were four designated areas of studies, namely: Biblical, Historical, Theological, and Pastoral. The resident faculty members in the early 1970's were Burton Throckmorton (New Testament),

Stephen Szikszai (Old Testament), Roland Wessels (Church History), Fred Whittaker (American Church History), Andrew Banning (Systematic Theology), Leslie Ziegler (Christian Ethics), Walter Cook (Homiletics and Field Education), Clarice Bowman (Christian Education), and Dwight Cumbee (Pastoral Care and Counseling). One other required course (Non-Christian Religions) was taught by an adjunct professor from the University of Maine. Various electives were offered in each of the four major areas. Each M.Div. degree candidate was also required to write a thesis on a chosen topic.

There is no doubt in my mind that the fine quality of the faculty was a principal reason for the favorable action of the Association of Theological Schools in accrediting the Seminary during the later years of my presidency. There was a time during the mid-1970's when the Board of Trustees became apprehensive about reported tensions and disagreements within the faculty; at one point it was suggested by the board that an outside counselor be employed to deal with alleged personality conflicts among the teaching staff. This suggestion was never implemented because the president, with the strong support of the then senior member of the faculty, Burton Throckmorton, convinced the chairman of the board that such action was unnecessary and would be counter-productive.

To be sure, Bangor professors have usually been competent scholars with unique individual personalities and strong academic convictions. Inevitably there were some who believed they were better teachers than others and that their chosen field of expertise was somehow more significant than another. There was at Bangor, as in many theological schools, a rivalry between biblical and theological studies, on the one hand, and such "practical" disciplines as pastoral care and Christian education, on the other hand. From my point of view this was a natural and a healthy situation — a source of strength for the Seminary — despite the uneasiness it caused among some students and alumni. In any event, the Commission on Accrediting of the ATS placed its strong stamp of approval on the Bangor faculty it examined in the 1970's.

There were three more changes in resident faculty personnel before I retired in 1978. The first occurred in 1972 after Dr. Andrew

Banning retired. To succeed him the trustees accepted the recommendation I presented on behalf of the faculty that Dr. Leslie Ziegler be named Buck Professor of Christian Theology. Dr. Ziegler came to the Seminary in 1963 as Librarian. In 1967 she was installed as Professor of Philosophy of Religion and Christian Ethics. She was also Director of Continuing Education, in which position she supervised the Bond Lecture series, Lay Schools of Theology, and theological education programs for clergy and educators. In 1969-1970 she studied in Europe on a sabbatical under a Lilly Foundation Fellowship. The appointment of Dr. Ziegler was a recognition of her versatility as a faculty member; she became one of very few women who in 1972 were serving as professors of theology in American seminaries.

A second change in the resident faculty took place in 1975 following the resignation of Dr. Dwight W. Cumbee as Lowry Professor of Pastoral Psychology and Counseling. He accepted appointment to the faculty of the North Carolina Baptist Hospital School of Pastoral Care, with adjunct teaching responsibilities at the Southeastern Baptist Theological Seminary, of which he is an alumnus. Dr. Cumbee was a member of the Bangor faculty for nine years, during which time he served for a short period as Dean of Students, as well as a faculty representative on the Board of Trustees. During a sabbatical leave in 1972-1973, he did research at the Georgia Mental Health Institute under a faculty fellowship awarded by the Association of Theological Schools; subsequently, he was certified as a supervisor by the Association of Clinical Pastoral Education. Dr. Cumbee will be remembered at Bangor Seminary as the genial and competent supervisor of clinical pastoral education programs carried out in cooperation with the Bangor Counseling Center, Eastern Maine Medical Center, St. Joseph Hospital, and Bangor Mental Health Institute. As an ordained minister of the American Baptist Churches he added a welcome ecumenical spirit to the Bangor community. He and his wife Janet were well-loved members of a faculty pinochle club.

On September 1, 1975, Dr. Cumbee was succeeded by Dr. Alexander B. Cairns, who had been an adjunct professor at the Seminary for five years. During that period he had been employed as Coordinator of Pastoral Services and Director of Clinical Education at the Bangor Counseling Center. Dr. Cairns was born in Edinburgh, Scotland, in 1935. Educated at the University of St. Andrews, he had served as associate minister of the Glasgow Cathedral. Earlier he was pastor of a rural church after working for ten years in the real estate business. He came to the United States in 1967 to study for the Master of Theology degree at Crozer Theological Seminary, and in 1975 earned the Doctor of Ministry degree at Andover Newton Theological School. Dr. Cairns also held the diploma in psychiatry from the Hahnemann Medical School in Philadelphia, was a social worker with the State of Maine Board of Social Workers, and was accredited as a chaplain supervisor by the American Association of Clinical Pastoral Education. For the balance of my administration and beyond, Dr. Cairns continued and expanded the fine tradition in his chosen field earlier established by his predecessors, Myron Klinkman and Dwight Cumbee.

The third and final change in the resident faculty during the later Whittaker years took place after the resignation in 1976 of the Reverend Clarice M. Bowman as Jonathan Fisher Professor of Christian Education. She had been a faculty member for sixteen years and, as indicated earlier, was the first woman ever appointed as a resident professor at Bangor seminary. The Board of Trustees fittingly named her professor emeritus. During her tenure Miss Bowman firmly established the discipline of Christian Education in the school's curriculum, which was a significant factor in the Seminary's successful bid for full accreditation. Her work as chaplain, in the book store, and as supervisor for the Audiovisual center was also outstanding.

To succeed Miss Bowman, Dr. Andrew P. Grannell was called to become Associate Professor of Christian Education effective September 1, 1977. He was born in Waterville, Maine, in 1943 and received his early Christian nurture in the Methodist Church. He had been Ministry and Education Secretary of the New England Yearly Meeting of Friends since 1973, having previously served for four years as pastor of a Friends Meeting in Massachusetts. Dr. Grannell was well qualified for the Bangor appointment by virtue of four earned degrees: the B.A. of Earlham College, the M.R.E. of

Princeton University, the B.D. of Earlham School of Religion, and the Ph.D. in Christian Education of Boston University.

1973 is most remembered as the year in which their earthly pilgrimage ended for a most admired faculty colleague and a deeply cherished mother. Dr. Charles Gordon Cumming died at the age of eighty-eight after fifty-four years as a member of the Bangor faculty, thirty-six of them as George A. Gordon Professor of Old Testament and eighteen as professor emeritus. His biography is outlined in an earlier chapter, together with an account of accolades given him at the time of his retirement in 1955. I include here some of the words spoken by Dean Mervin M. Deems and by me at a memorial service of faith and thanksgiving in the David Nelson Beach Chapel on November 27, 1973.

I spoke this "Word of Faith": On rare occasions there appears upon the good earth a human being who gives credibility to the proclamation of the Psalmist concerning man: "Thou hast made him little less than God, and dost crown him with glory and honor." (Psalm 8:5) ... Charles Gordon Cumming's mortal life ended in Syracuse, New York, on Sunday, November 18, 1973, but it is my faith that one like him will never die ... It has been my blessing to have known Dr. Cumming as a revered teacher during student days at Bangor, as a faculty colleague who inspired me and guided me in the early years of my presidency, and as a gracious neighbor to my family while he resided in an apartment attached to our home. He will be remembered as one who evoked faith in God and man. Mervin Deems uttered this "Word of Thanksgiving": If an institution is the lengthened shadow of a man, or men and women, then much that is worthy in Bangor Seminary today reflects the rugged honesty, the keen intellect, the stalwart character of Charles Gordon Cumming. And I am thankful to have called him friend.

Earlier in 1973, at springtime, the earthly life of Annie May Penney Whittaker, my beloved mother, came to a conclusion at age eighty-five after several years of lingering debilitation. Death came, I remember, while Shirley and I were on our annual vacation in Florida. We rushed by automobile to the memorial service in New Haven. Mother had lived for several years in the home of my younger brother, Stanley, and his wife Dorothy in Thomaston,

291

Connecticut. I shall always be grateful to Dorothy and my brother for the loving care they gave, beyond the call of duty, to mother in her declining years. A good measure of thankfulness belongs also to grand-daughters Cheryl and June.

In the first chapter of these memoirs I paid tribute to my parents, especially my mother, for setting a moral and spiritual tone in my childhood home which has been a source of strength throughout my life. Later years have brought many fond memories of the one who gave me birth. We were together every Christmas, and she often spent extended visits with Shirley and me in our home. As long as she had the physical capacity, mother was at work. For several years she lived as a companion to elderly women in Massachusetts. She was intensely proud of her four children, and regularly presented them with gifts of love, according to her means, on birthdays and at Christmas. I shall always remember my mother with deep thanksgiving for the many ways in which she enabled me to achieve the goals of my own life. Each year I visit her gravesite in the Evergreen Cemetery at New Haven, where she rests in peace alongside her husband, her mother, and her brother.

1974 was a twelve-month period simply unforgettable. In January I delivered a series of five lectures in Florida on one of my favorite themes, "Church and State Re-examined." In May and June I was for a brief period an independent candidate for the office of Governor of Maine. In mid-June I was elected president of the Association of Theological Schools in the United States and Canada. In July I was hospitalized and operated upon for cancer of the cecum. The month of September was spent in the hospital recovering from an attack of serum hepatitis. That same fall the Seminary was accredited by the Association of Theological Schools.

The Florida Conference of the United Church of Christ invited me to give the 1974 "Chautauqua" lectures at the Conference center in Avon Park. This experience was one of the highlights of my career. UCC ministers and lay leaders from many states gathered for the occasion. My assignment was to give a fifty-minute lecture each morning for five days, to be followed by a discussion period. The afternoon was left free, and each day I could be found on the golf course. Shirley was with me, and each evening was spent in fellowship with the conference participants.

The titles of my five lectures were: "Man's Kingdom of God," "Religion and Politics," "Religion and Education," "Religion and Morality," and "The Church in Context." Each lecture was an exposition of the central theme that a new instrumental trinity is required for the last quarter of the twentieth century: "Religion and the church should no longer be defended as the primary agencies divinely appointed for the purposes of God. The holy Kingdom on earth also needs for its fulfillment the witness and ministry of politics and the state, of education and the school." I shall not present here even an abridged version of this lecture series since a major part of the content is revealed in other pages of these memoirs. I do remember with satisfaction, however, this opportunity in 1974 to present in some detail, before a knowledgeable and receptive audience, a compendium of my basic religious philosophy.

It was during the week of the Florida "Chautauqua" that I was conscious of the first warnings of an impending serious physical problem. A certain feeling of tiredness came over me in the middle of each day following the morning lecture. The fatigue increased during the afternoon golf game, to the point where I eschewed my usual walking pattern in favor of riding in a golf cart. The feeling of weariness persisted, but did not increase, during the next few months; thus I was not deterred from a decision I had made in late 1973 to again enter the political arena.

With the permission of the Seminary Board of Trustees, a permission they had denied me ten years earlier when I wanted to run for a seat in the U.S. Congress, I had announced my intention to compete as an independent candidate for the office of Governor of Maine. During the early part of 1974, with the help of many friends, I gathered a sufficient number of signatures (3,254 was the minimum requirement) of registered Maine voters to qualify for the November, 1974, statewide election. On June 5th I filed with the Secretary of State petitions containing 3,443 valid signatures, and thus became the first independent candidate to qualify for the fall election.

My first public announcement of a possible bid for the office of Governor was made in September, 1973. It was contingent upon my ability to secure the required number of voter signatures. Formal candidacy was not declared until early June in 1974. Meanwhile I organized a campaign committee, all of them volunteers, and distributed a letter among five hundred friends in which I asked for both moral and financial support. Many of these friends circulated petitions in search of the required voter signatures. The campaign theme was "Win with Whittaker," and one of the campaign rules was a limitation of contributions to no more than one hundred dollars per voter.

Over a period of several months I made a number of campaign appearances before service clubs, school organizations, and church-related groups in which I described many items in my political platform. Among them were the following: tax reform, with emphasis upon the state income tax; opposition to a proposed state lottery; restoration of railroad passenger service; and expansion of state services in such areas as health care, education, housing, economic growth, and recreational facilities.

In answer to questions about my motivation I replied that a principal reason for my candidacy was a desire to use my lifelong experience and training for the advantage of Maine and its people. Serving as Governor, I explained, is a natural development of many years of interest in promoting the cooperation of church and state. When challenged about the propriety of a clergyman running for political office, I pointed out that there are many more lay persons in the church than there are clergymen; thus I contended that if ministers should be excluded from political participation so should lay people since they are as much a part of the church as the clergy.

Many of my friends questioned the practicality of an independent candidacy for the office of Governor. For me it was the only practical way I could run. My duties at the Seminary and my lack of money precluded participation in a primary election. Further, as a "Rockefeller Republican" my views were too liberal for me to expect nomination by Maine Republicans. Although I publicly supported such Democrats as Senator Muskie and Congressman Hathaway, I could not hope to win primary election as a Democrat. Most importantly, I believed that an independent Governor would have the advantage of freedom from party pressure and influence in making decisions on legislation presented and in the appointment of various state officials. Although my candidacy was withdrawn shortly after it was officially announced, for reasons which will be revealed, it is satisfying to note that in the 1974 November election an independent candidate, James Longley, was in fact elected Governor of Maine.

On June 12, 1974, I made my first and only public address as a candidate for Governor. I record as an historic moment in my life part of what I said to the weekly luncheon meeting of the Rotary Club in Belfast, Maine: "Maine has the human and natural resources, together with adequate financial wealth, to set an example for the rest of the nation under enlightened executive and legislative leadership ... Sound economic principles and procedures, as suggested by the Maine Management and Cost Survey Commission, should be adopted by state officials, but the goal of meeting human needs should have priority as it does in other service agencies such as Rotary and Kiwanis ... If Maine is to prosper in the years ahead it must have expanded leadership from the state capitol. The next governor should challenge the affluent and talented people of Maine to share more of their material wealth and more of their skills through participation in the government process itself...."

The campaign speech at Belfast was presented while Shirley and I were enroute to the biennial meeting of the Association of Theological Schools in Atlanta, Georgia. As a result of events at that meeting my life was about to experience a dramatic change, both professionally and personally. I had been vice president of the ATS for two years and had been asked informally if I would accept election as president for the next biennium. I was faced with a difficult decision. Did I want to be Governor of Maine or President of the ATS? I could not do both. Once the Atlanta meeting elected me as chief executive officer I immediately chose to accept this honor and to forego the unlikely possibility of state political leadership. Within a few days I withdrew from the contest for Governor of Maine. To be President of the two hundred and more theological schools in the United States and Canada was an opportunity which comes less than once in a lifetime and especially to a seminary as small as Bangor. There was to be another reason why the decision was a wise one

After the excitement of Atlanta my physical problem, which had been noticed as early as January but had been dormant for some time during my preoccupation with the political campaign, suddenly accelerated during the trip home to Bangor in late June. I was tired beyond reason. A quick visit with the doctor disclosed that I was anemic and losing blood from an undisclosed source. I was hospitalized immediately and, after four days of testing, a small malignant tumor was discovered in the cecum, where the small intestines join the colon. Today I look back in amazement at how calm I apparently was when the doctor told me I was suffering from cancer. An operation was performed a few days later. The cancer was completely removed, together with my appendix, without incident or complications. I began my recuperation at home ten days later, and was back playing golf in six weeks. I remain deeply grateful to my long-time personal physician, Dr. Lawrence Cutler, and to my surgeon, Dr. Lloyd Brown, for saving my life.

It is not certain that the cancer surgery would have prevented me from carrying on a political campaign, if I had decided to do so, but the unexpected aftermath two months later would have ended any such endeavor. On Labor Day in 1974, just as I was preparing to leave for the golf course, I experienced a physical attack which sent me to the hospital that same day. Prior to the cancer surgery in early July I was transfused with just two pints of blood. As a result I spent most of the month of September in the Eastern Maine Medical Center, the victim of serum hepatitis. The disease lingered without abatement for three weeks, at which time a liver probe disclosed some damage to the organ. The so-called "miracle drug," prednisone, was then administered and I was out of the hospital within a week. Fortunately, there have been no recurrences during the ensuing years.

After my recovery from the hepatitis attack I was told that those afflicted by the disease in the 1970's had a mortality rate of five percent. This fact inspired me to ask the hospital administrators why tainted blood had been given to me in the transfusion process. They reported that the two pints given to me had tested negative for the hepatitis virus, but that the test itself was then only fifty percent accurate. I learned that 17,000 persons each year in the United States shared an experience similar to mine. I understand, thankfully, that the situation has improved greatly since 1974. This most serious illness of my life occurred when I was sixty-one years old. It did have one important beneficial effect. Shirley and I agreed that when I reached age sixty-five, my resignation as Seminary president would be offered. It was a decision we have never regretted.

In January, 1975, at its annual banquet during Convocation week, the Alumni Association of the Seminary presented to me its annual "Distinguished Alumnus Award." The citation given to me by Ernest B. Johnson, alumni president, made specific reference to my efforts, now finally successful, to secure accreditation for Bangor from the Association of Theological Schools. This recognition is one which I cherish because it is a testimony by my peers, the graduates of Bangor Seminary. The remembrances of the 1970's would not be complete without an expression of the gratitude I feel toward the alumni I have known over a period of fifty years. Many have been mentioned in these memoirs, but I wish to write of a few others, without intending any slight of the hundreds who remain unnamed, as illustrations of the distinguished service rendered by those trained at Bangor.

Of all those chosen through the decades as "Alumnus of the Year," one who lingers in my memory, although he has since departed this world, is Dr. Peter Gordon Gowing of the class of 1953. He was one of my students during early teaching days at Bangor, and I remember that he took seriously the challenge presented to him in my course on Christian Missions. The citation presented to him as the alumnus honored in 1973 summarizes his unique service: "As a Pastor to churches in Maine and men in the U.S. Navy; as a Missionary to churches of Southeast Asia; as a Teacher at the Divinity School of Silliman University in the Philippines and the South East Asia Graduate School of Theology in Singapore; as an Author of two important works about Religion in the Philippines, and as a Student whose scholarship has earned him among other degrees a Th.D. and Ph.D." Peter Gowing's two books are *Mosque and Moro: A Study of Muslims in the Philippines* and *Islands Under the Cross: The Story of the Church in the Philippines*. He earned doctoral degrees at both Boston University and Syracuse University.

As an alumnus of Bangor Seminary myself, I have had a career-long appreciation of the significant role played by its graduates in the history of the school. It was in the 1960's, while John deSousa was assistant to the president, that the General Alumni Association came to greater and greater prominence. This development was accelerated in the 1970's when Vice President Larry Kalp was also Alumni Secretary. Bangor graduates have perennially been enthusiastic attendants at the annual Convocation, which has featured a banquet at which a succession of "Distinguished Alumni" awards have been made. Through the years a goodly number have attended a spring meeting in Framingham, Massachusetts, to hear lectures by Seminary faculty members.

All of the officers of the General Alumni Association have been supportive of the Whittaker administration. Four of its many fine presidents during the 1970's were: Ernest B. Johnson, William E. Flynn, Ronald Beinema, and Ian Stewart. For longevity and loyal service the honors must go to Raymond J. Cosseboom, who took office in 1961 as Secretary-Treasurer of the Association and was still alumni Treasurer when I retired. Among the Seminary trustees I have previously acclaimed Clarence W. Fuller, long-time chairman, and Gordon Washburn. Other alumni, representative of all who have served on the governing board, were: Cornelius Clark, David Beach, Robert Fiske, John Lacey, Eric Bascom, Robert W. Mayhew, and John Webster.

The later Whittaker years were marked increasingly by the need to have the president spend more and more of his time in fund-raising activities. For most of my tenure as chief executive officer I was able to continue my teaching career, at least to the extent of offering one course each semester. During the 1970's my participation in classroom leadership was reduced to a one-semester course each year and eventually I was forced to give up teaching altogether in favor of administrative responsibilities. This only confirmed my decision, made following my illness in 1974, to resign in 1978 when I reached the age of sixty-five.

For the last five years of my administration, Vice President Larry Kalp and I engaged in strenuous efforts to improve the financial condition of the Seminary. Such an effort was made mandatory by a decision of the General Synod of the United Church of Christ in 1973 that within two years the financial support of related seminaries like Bangor should be provided on a regional basis by state conferences and local churches. The impact upon Bangor was substantial. The $32,000 received in 1974 from the U.C.C. national budget was reduced in 1975 to $15,000, and in 1976 this revenue income disappeared completely. As chairman of the Seminary Section of the United Church I had made an appeal, without success, to a national meeting of denominational officials in May, 1975, through a position paper urging the UCC to continue "National Responsibility for Support of Theological Education." One of the major failures of the United Church of Christ has been its unwillingness to give financial aid to the seminaries which train its professional leadership.

Administrative efforts by seminary officers, trustees, and alumni managed to offset in large measure the loss of national denominational support. Helpful in this endeavor was a filmstrip produced by Larry Kalp. The Maine Conference assisted by increasing its annual gift to Bangor. A modest increase in student charges was made possible by the beginning of federal support for theological students. In 1976 Bangor received $92,192 in National Student Loans, Work-Study Grants, and Basic Educational Opportunity Grants.

Most significant in undergirding the financial stability of the Seminary during the Whittaker administration was the support given by The Lilly Endowment, Inc., of Indianapolis, Indiana. On several occasions this philanthropic organization made grants to Bangor faculty and staff members for sabbaticals and study leaves of absence. Then in 1976 it made a gift of $5,000 to the school itself for the dual purpose of (1) employing a qualified consultant to examine the whole development program and make recommendations for improvements and/or expansion; and (2) with the help of this consultant, preparing and submitting a proposal in the Lilly competitive grants program under a category called "Creation of Strategies for Development of Lay Support."

The consultant employed under the Lilly grant was Herbert L. Jones, Director of Development at Garrett-Evangelical Theological Seminary in Evanston, Illinois. Under his guidance a proposal was devised which may be summarized as follows: "Bangor Theological Seminary will implement a development program designed to broaden its base of financial support by identifying and systematically soliciting, for both annual and estate gifts, a lay donor constituency within the principal geographical area served by the school. The program requires the intensive involvement of alumni and trustees; it includes a plan for reorganizing the governing board. Staff support will be provided by the Seminary president and vice president."

In November, 1976, the Lilly Endowment notified the Seminary that it had been awarded a two-year grant of $32,025. In a congratulatory letter the Seminary consultant, Herbert L. Jones, wrote: "It is a wonderful vote of confidence that something distinctive and important can happen at Bangor in the area of fund raising." One result of the Lilly grant was a revision of the Seminary by-laws and a reorganization of the Board of Trustees to provide for additional lay representation. To accomplish the latter purpose, voting membership on the board for faculty and student representatives, which had been initiated during the 1960's, was eliminated. This was my own recommendation as well as that of the outside consultants who helped the Seminary implement the program suggested by the Lilly Endowment.

A unique feature of the Lilly grant was the provision of funds for "continuing education seminars for trustees." The first such seminar was held in April, 1977, and this program has been expanded throughout the two succeeding administrations until the present day. I include in these memoirs my deep appreciation to the Lilly Endowment and to its Senior Vice President, Dr. Robert W. Lynn. Dr. Lynn was a firm supporter of Bangor Seminary during the crucial 1974 appeal for accreditation by the Association of Theological Schools, he negotiated with me the first Lilly Award to the Seminary in 1976, and he is today a Bangor "Scholar-in-

Residence" and Distinguished Professor of Religion and Education.

When I retired in 1978 the Seminary was in a far stronger financial position than it was twenty-six years earlier when I became its president. The school was free of all debt, as it had been throughout my administration. The operating budget had been balanced every year by judicious use of reserve funds under the direction of the Board of Trustees. The amount of these unrestricted funds "functioning as endowment" in 1978 was $189,109, almost twice as much as in 1952. Endowment Funds, Trust Funds, and Plant Funds had more than doubled to respective amounts of $2,178,852, $1,044,581, and $1,385,336. The annual operating budget had grown from $79,843 to $611,811. Annual gifts had increased from $12,232 to a record high of $130,033. Student aid funds in 1978 totaled $82,911, compared with a mere $4,200 in 1952. One other significant statistic is the nearly 100% increase in student enrollment during the quarter-century, from 70 to 134. Other major advances at Bangor, in academic program and physical facilities, during the tenure of the fifth president have been delineated in earlier pages of this book.

Early in 1977 I announced to the trustees my intention to resign as president at the end of the academic year in 1978, thus giving them more than a year to find my successor. A Search Committee headed by Dr. Nathanael M. Guptill began its work later in the year and advertised for applicants and nominations in the media. One of those who applied was Dr. Larry E. Kalp, the incumbent Vice President of the Seminary. Just a day after receiving this application the Search Committee met and reached a decision that "no one presently employed by the Seminary will be nominated by this committee." This action effectively eliminated from consideration not only Larry Kalp but at least one other faculty member who was qualified to be my successor. Both Larry Kalp and I were surprised and disturbed by the action of the Search Committee. He soon resigned his position in order to accept an offer which had been pending for some time to join the staff of the United Church Board for Homeland Ministries in New York City. At my request he agreed to postpone the move to New York until the end of my tenure at Bangor. Meanwhile my last year as Seminary president was beclouded by a lengthy confrontation with the Search Committee and the Board of Trustees, only a part of which I record here.

The heart of my protest is contained in a letter I wrote to Chairman Guptill of the Search Committee under date of August 16, 1977. I quote below some of its content:

"The decision is discriminatory. It establishes the principle that no one employed by the Seminary can aspire to higher office. If applied in earlier years it would have prevented Enoch Pond, Warren Moulton, and Fred Whittaker from serving as president ... My whole administration has been marked by the encouragement of personnel to excel in their work so that they might be eligible for advancement ... The committee decision is a repudiation of this policy of motivation....

"The decision is ill-advised because of the divisive and deleterious effect it will have among the various constituencies which support the Seminary. Because of his personal attractiveness, his professional abilities, and his widespread activities as Seminary vice president, Larry Kalp is well known and highly respected among the alumni, the local churches, the business community, the Higher Educational Council of Maine, the Maine Conference, the UCC Council for Higher Education, and the Association of Theological Schools. There are many friends of Bangor who consider Larry Kalp to be a likely candidate to succeed me as president. When it becomes evident that he has been summarily dismissed as a candidate without consideration of his qualifications, there will undoubtedly be strong negative reaction....

"...Let me be crystal clear on one point. I am not trying to select my successor as president ... It is true that I believe Larry Kalp to be exceptionally well qualified to be the next president of Bangor ... I only ask that Larry Kalp be given the same careful consideration which will be accorded other applicants. If the committee then nominates someone they judge to be better qualified than Larry, I shall be completely satisfied — and so will Larry...."

As I predicted, there was strong negative reaction to the Search Committee's decision regarding Vice President Kalp. It came from many directions: from four members of the faculty, from the president of the Alumni Association, from the student newspaper, from leaders of the Bangor business community including a former trustee, and from such long-term trustees as L. Felix Ranlett and James U. Crockett. Mr. Crockett's letter of October 26, 1977, to the Search Committee chairman is illustrative: "...In these days of intense public and legal pressure to show no prejudice and to observe absolute equality of treatment to all applicants, this move seems to put the Board in an untenable position, certainly morally and, very possibly, legally. At the very least, the action must have already created a sense of disillusionment among the faculty and staff and was, I believe, unnecessary and prejudgmental...."

It is true that Larry Kalp and I were disillusioned by the Search Committee's decision. However, with the help of the trustee Committee on Personnel and Academic Program, chaired by Eric W. Bascom, we were able to deflect most of the negativism caused by that decision. The Bascom committee met on November 15, 1977, at my request, for the primary purpose of discussing ways and means of implementing the new development program made possible by the recent two-year grant from the Lilly Foundation. Retaining Larry Kalp as Vice President for the second year of the program was critically essential. He had just spent a sabbatical at Andover Newton Theological School under a Lilly grant and had earned the Doctor of Ministry degree. Both the Lilly Endowment and the Seminary were counting on him to continue as a central figure in the development program. Larry agreed to remain on the Seminary staff until the time of my retirement in mid-1978, an unselfish action which protected the best interests of the Seminary.

At the December, 1977, meeting of the Board of Trustees I presented one final appeal for a reversal of the exclusive policy adopted by the Search Committee. However, a majority of the Board supported the chairman of the Search Committee, Dr. Nathanael M. Guptill. Subsequently, the Committee nominated Dr. G. Wayne Glick to become the sixth president of Bangor Theological Seminary effective August 1, 1978. For three years Dr. Glick had been Director of the Moton Center of Independent Studies in Philadelphia. Earlier he had been President of Keuka College in New York State for eight years and for fifteen years a member of the faculty and staff of Franklin and Marshall College in Lancaster, Pennsylvania; he was Dean of the College for five years and also held the positions of Vice President and Acting President. Dr. Glick was born in Bridgewater, Virginia, and graduated from Bridgewater College in his native state; his alma mater awarded him the honorary degree of L.L.D. in 1969. He also received earned degrees from Bethany Theological Seminary in Chicago (B.D.) and the University of Chicago (M.A. and Ph.D.) His doctoral thesis on "Adolph Harnach as Historian and Theologian" was published in 1967 by Harper and Row under the title *The Reality of Christianity*.

My appreciation of Dr. Glick will be recorded in a later reflective chapter entitled "President Emeritus." I state here only the fact that I applauded the appointment of my successor and was his strong supporter during the eight years of his Bangor presidency. My only regret is that he was not chosen from a field of candidates which included Dr. Larry Kalp. This process would have avoided much unpleasantness and would have made my final year at Bangor a happier and more productive one. It should be added that my strong disagreement with Dr. Guptill on this issue has not weakened the bond of respect and friendship we have enjoyed for forty-five years and more. Today we belong to the same local church and frequently play golf together.

Before Larry Kalp left the Seminary in the summer of 1978 he and his wife Carol were honored at a luncheon meeting sponsored by the Development and Public Relations Committee of the Seminary's Board of Trustees. Committee Chairman Robert W. Mayhew presented Larry with a scroll expressing the Board's "heartfelt appreciation of his most valuable contributions to the Seminary over the past nine years." These contributions included expertise in public relations, service to students and alumni as Dean of Students and Alumni Secretary, teaching a course in Art, leadership in the audio-visual library and closed-circuit television studio, membership on the faculty, and fund raising. Larry is the author of "A Feasibility Study for a Program of Continuing Education for Clergy Persons at Bangor Theological Seminary, with Models and Strategies for Development."

Off campus Larry was active in local, state, and national church work, and in the Association of Theological Schools. He was a member of the Bangor Lion's Club and of the executive committee of the United Way. With his wife Carol and children Karen and Robert, Larry was deeply involved in the life of the Hammond Street Congregational Church in Bangor. Carol was a teacher in the Vine Street elementary school.

My own gratitude to my colleague was expressed by the public comment that "the many talents which Larry Kalp used as a staff member in advancing the welfare of the school will leave a lasting impression upon the institution; he will not easily be replaced as a faculty member and administrator." The record shows that during his years at Bangor annual gifts increased by 47% despite the loss of $32,000 per year from the United Church of Christ, and that trust and endowment funds received totaled $847,706. Further, Vice President Kalp was the coordinator of activities under the Lilly Endowment two-year development grant which he helped to secure. During the first year of the grant the faculty and trustees participated one hundred percent in making gifts to the Seminary, and contributions from alumni increased by twelve percent. A most significant recognition of their debt to Larry Kalp was made by the Board of Trustees at the 1978 commencement when he was awarded an honorary Master of Divinity degree, thus making him a Bangor Seminary alumnus. He then went to his new position as a major staff member of the United Church Board for Homeland Ministries in New York City. In 1991, he was Secretary for Publication in the Division of Education and Publication, and Editor of The Pilgrim Press when he resigned to become minister of the Community Church, UCC, in Mountain Lakes, New Jersey.

As my long tenure as Seminary President began to approach its conclusion, various forms of recognition took place. As early as 1976, when I started my twenty-fifth year as Bangor's chief executive officer, the *Bangor Daily News* published a feature article entitled, "Whittaker Seen as Phenomenon," written by its educational staff member Wayne Reilly. I quote some of my favorite words from the editorial: "Frederick W. Whittaker, educator, social critic, former politician, former cleric, is something of a phenomenon ... In an age when social reformers cry for reform in politics and society, Whittaker has backed his ideals by successfully hopping into the political arena ... As a politician and social critic Whittaker has shown himself to be well-insulated against the proverbial heat in the kitchen. Both in and out of office he has proven himself unafraid of the barbs of conservative critics in his liberal stands on a host of controversial issues...."

In July of 1977 two honors were bestowed upon me in Washington, D.C., at the biennial meeting of the General Synod of the United Church of Christ. The first was a citation presented at a dinner meeting of the UCC Council for Higher Education by its chairman, Dr. Robert T. Fauth. The "Resolution of Recognition" read in part as follows:

"Frederick William Whittaker this year is completing a quarter of a century as President of Bangor Theological Seminary ... The occasion for our recognizing him is his length of service to his institution. The reason we recognize him is the distinguished service he has given to Bangor Seminary, which, because of its unique approach to theological education, required his long and persistent efforts to achieve recognition through accreditation by the Association of Theological Schools; the leadership he has given to the Association of Theological Schools in the United States and Canada as its President from 1974 to 1976; and his active participation in political processes as a member of the Bangor City Council and of the Maine Senate.

"We recognize him further as a faithful colleague in the Council for Higher Education of the United Church of Christ, and particularly in the Seminary Section of that Council.

"We offer our congratulations upon his anniversary, and we wish him and his devoted wife, Shirley Louise, well, and ask God's blessing upon them as they move together into the years yet to come."

At the General Synod itself Shirley and I were called before the assembly for the presentation of a "Special Tribute" in the form of a plaque given "In recognition and thanksgiving for twenty-five years of distinguished service as President of Bangor Theological Seminary." The plaque was signed and presented by Joseph H. Evans, President of the United Church of Christ. It now hangs proudly on the wall of my study.

The General Alumni Association devoted part of its annual meeting on January 30, 1978, to a testimonial honoring Shirley and me as we faced our time of retirement. Alumni President Ian Stewart presented me with a beautifully engraved citation which read in part: "We pay tribute to you for twenty-six years of memorable service as President of the Seminary ... We present this citation in recognition of your courageous leadership and your legacy of credibility ... We honor you, and establish this day The Whittaker Fund for the Bangor Theological Seminary Library." A substantial check was given to the Seminary to begin the Fund, with the promise of additional gifts. Only the interest from the Fund is to be used annually for the purchase of books. I was particularly pleased by the establishment of the book fund since the building and maintaining of the Moulton Library was a major interest of my administration. I was also grateful to the alumni for presenting a corsage to my wife Shirley "for her unique contributions to the Seminary," not the least of which was her gracious service as the First Lady of the Hannibal Hamlin House at Convocation receptions and many other occasions.

The major social event of my retirement year was a testimonial dinner on Sunday evening, June 4th, in the Red Lion Restaurant of Bangor, with two hundred guests in attendance from various points in New England and beyond. Included were my wife Shirley, our children Barbara and Mark, and other members of our families. Toastmaster for the evening was Dr. Burton H. Throckmorton, Jr., senior member of the faculty and chairman of the arrangements committee.

Other speakers were Clarence W. Fuller, Trustee Chairman; Dr. Kenneth Brookes, Executive Director of the Higher Educational Council of Maine; Dr. Harvey Guthrie of the Episcopal Theological School in Cambridge, Massachusetts, member of the executive committee of the Association of Theological Schools in the United States and Canada; Dr. Otto E. Sommer, Minister of the Maine Conference of the United Church of Christ; former trustee Charles F. Bragg, II, who represented the Bangor community; Thomas Meehan, President of the Bangor Kiwanis Club; Ernest B. Johnson,

Past President of the Alumni Association; the Reverend Ansley C. Throckmorton, Associate Minister of the Hammond Street Congregational Church; and Timothy Hanley, President of the Student Christian Association at the Seminary.

Highlight of the testimonial dinner was an announcement by Chairman Clarence Fuller of the Board of Trustees that historic Maine Hall, the student dormitory where I had once resided and in which my office as President was first located, had been renamed Whittaker Hall in my honor. Maine Hall was built in 1834 and is a landmark listed with other Seminary buildings on the National Historic Register. Before the festivities concluded I was presented with gifts which included a check for $1,000 from trustees and other donors, $100 from Seminary students, and a new set of golf clubs for my retirement years.

On Monday, June 5, 1978, I presided at my final graduation ceremony. I shall be forever grateful to the Senior Class for granting me the privilege and honor of delivering the Commencement Address. It was entitled, "Little Less Than God — A Humanology for Tomorrow," and its content will be disclosed in a later chapter of these memoirs. I was now ready to retire. Or was I? Ready to retire from theological education, yes! But not quite ready to retire from politics! For I had announced on my sixty-fifth birthday in January that I would be an independent candidate in the fall election for the office of Representative from Maine's second Congressional district. This is the exciting story of the next chapter of my life.

16.
Candidate for Congress

I shall always remember my sixty-fifth birthday, not because I first became eligible for Medicare, but because it was the occasion for announcing publicly that I would be an independent candidate for election to the U.S. Congress from the second Congressional district of Maine in the November, 1978, election. This was a carefully conceived plan which was part of my strategy when I told the Seminary Board of Trustees in mid-1977 that I would retire at the end of the academic year in 1978. It seemed to me possible that I could win election as an independent since James Longley was then a popular Governor of Maine, an office which he had won as an independent candidate in the 1974 election. There were some practical considerations involved also: I could not begin serious campaigning until mid-1978 when my duties at the Seminary would end; and I did not have sufficient financial resources to participate in the pre-election primary contest as a Republican or a Democrat.

Thus on January 26, 1978, I scheduled a press conference in the parlor of the historic Hannibal Hamlin House which had been my home for twenty-five years. My wife Shirley was at my side as I announced my plans to a group of invited friends and several media representatives. A news release issued the same day explained the rationale for my candidacy: "Serving in the United

States Congress would be a natural application of my long interest in relating religious principles to social problems." I indicated that my platform would stress "conservation of natural, human, and economic resources." Specific issues would include: a secure Social Security system, expansion of education subsidies to students, restoration of railroad passenger service in Maine to save energy and create jobs, greater use of hydroelectric power, and careful scrutiny of military expenditures as a major means of reducing federal taxes.

At the initial news conference I also explained that my campaign would be short-term and low-budget, with activity concentrated between Labor Day and the November election. Financial resources would include a limited amount of my own savings plus whatever funds were made available by friends and supporters. During the four-month period of February through May, I concentrated on forming my campaign committee and securing the required 1,000 signatures of registered voters in order for my name to be placed on the ballot for the November election. Petitions were circulated throughout the second Congressional district by more than fifty friends, including several alumni of the Seminary, and on June 1st I filed with the Secretary of State a total of 1,427 authenticated signatures; I was now officially in the political contest.

The "Whittaker for Congress" committee was chaired by my long-time friend and former colleague on the public relations staff of the Seminary, Donald S. McCobb, who was then serving as principal of the Bucksport High School. The Treasurer was Clayton R. Lothrop of Brewer, churchman, businessman, and fellow-member of the Kiwanis Club. Irene D'Angelo of Argyle, member of the secretarial staff of the Seminary, was Secretary of the Committee. Campaign Manager was my gregarious and talented wife Shirley. She was ideally qualified for the task by educational background and record of service in the church and community. During the next few months we were to have one of the most challenging and exciting times of our lives as we traveled throughout the vast second Congressional district of Maine.

Maine has only two representatives to Congress by virtue of its total population of about one million. Roughly half of these citizens live in the nine counties which comprise the second district. Geographically it is the largest Congressional district east of the Mississippi River; it extends from the New Hampshire border in the west, to the Canadian border in the north and east, and to the Atlantic Ocean in the south. During September and October Shirley and I traveled by car in all of the nine counties, a total distance of several thousand miles. I spoke in churches and high schools, in meetings of teachers, at service clubs, and on radio and television programs. I wrote letters to the editors of area newspapers, and issued weekly news releases stating my position on major campaign issues.

The principal components of my campaign paraphernalia were a letterhead, a one-page, two-sided pamphlet, and a medium-sized button. The letterhead contained the following statement at the top: "You have a choice — WHITTAKER for Congress." At the bottom was a major campaign theme: "Integrity and Accountability in Government." The button featured the campaign symbol in black on a yellow background. The symbol was a railroad crossing sign with the words "Whittaker" and "Congress" on the crossbars, thus emphasizing one of my platform planks: restoration of rail passenger service in Maine. The symbol was in the form of the letter "X" and served also to indicate the mark to be placed by the voter on the election ballot.

The pamphlet, also in yellow and black, had my photo on the front; on the back was a resume of my platform and a list of my credentials. About a third of the space was taken up by the following: "A VOTE FOR ME X IS A VOTE FOR MATURITY AND EXPERIENCE — Kept Bangor Theological Seminary financially stable during 26-year presidency — First-hand knowledge of the Washington scene as officer of U.S. theological schools — Ten years of business experience with a railroad company — Led fight to keep railroad passenger trains in Maine — As State Senator initiated law ending discrimination in Maine rental housing — Long-time proponent of taxes based on ability to pay — Three years a Christian minister in Washington County — A generation of service to the local and national church as a layman — Inaugurated Kenduskeag Stream restoration project as Bangor City Council chairman — A principal founder of the Bangor Municipal Golf Course — Member of building committee for new Bangor High School — Three years a trustee of the Maine Maritime Academy — Early (1966) public opponent of Viet Nam War — Specialist on church-state relations through thirty years of history teaching.

After the June primary I knew that my party-nominated opponents would be Republican Olympia Snowe, a popular State Senator, and Democrat Mark Gartley, the incumbent Secretary of State. These two would be difficult indeed to defeat at the polls, but my situation was made more precarious by the entrance into the race of four other independent candidates. Political commentators agreed that had it been a three-way contest my chances for election would have been enhanced. As it was, the media concentrated on the relative merits of the two party candidates and failed, for understandable practical reasons, to give comparable attention to five independents.

Another disadvantage for me was the relatively meager amount of funds available for my campaign. Before election day I spent a total of less than $14,000, about two-thirds of which was my own money. Meanwhile, Olympia Snowe, the eventual winner, expended a treasure chest of more than $200,000. My ability to pay for necessary television coverage was severely limited, although in the final few weeks of the campaign I did run some effective spots, especially one featuring an endorsement by Jim Crockett, my personal friend and long-time member of the Seminary Board of Trustees; Jim was then nationally known for his popular weekly television program, "Crockett's Victory Garden," which appeared on the public station in Boston.

In the campaign I emphasized the importance of my experience in public office and my maturity. At age sixty-five I was old enough to be the father of both party candidates. I compared my own record as mayor of Bangor and Maine State Senator with Democrat Mark Gartley's complete lack of legislative experience. I also challenged Republican Olympia Snowe to take a more definite stand on some of the major issues facing the nation. I pointed to my own publicly-stated position favoring tax reform rather than a constitutional restriction of government spending, and my proposal to fight inflation by transferring some of the waste in the military and welfare budgets to such productive uses as health protection, aid to education, and restoration of railroads.

Speaking to the weekly meeting of the South Paris-Norway Kiwanis Club, I stated that "party candidates need the challenge of independents ... The taxpayer revolt now developing is the result of too much party loyalty and party competition, too little concern for the welfare of the people who need government services and who pay the bills." Expanding on the theme of the independent challenge, I suggested that because of my broad experience and record of service, I would be more influential in Washington than a young party candidate. I proclaimed that "I would be bound by no party loyalty or party platform, and would be better able to resist the lobbyists and special interest groups."

The viability of the Social Security system was an issue in the 1978 election. Speaking at a local meeting of the American Association of Retired Persons (A.A.R.P.), I proposed that members of Congress and Congressional employees should be required to participate in the national Social Security system, thus eliminating an inequity which gives preferential treatment to a special interest group in the nation's capitol. I asked my fellow retirees: "Why should those who impose Social Security taxes on most other American employers and employees be exempt from the same provisions of the laws which they establish?" I explained that members of Congress have their own private pension plan to which they contribute eight percent of their salaries; American taxpayers contribute a matching amount through the federal income tax. Those with long service are eligible at age sixty for a maximum pension of $46,000 annually, which is eighty percent of the current $57,000 congressional salary. In contrast, the maximum amount now available under Social Security is $5,871 annually for a person reaching sixty-five in 1978. "As a member of Congress I would work to eliminate all inequities in the Social Security system so that those who are now retired and those who will retire in the future will be protected by a national pension program which is financially sound."

The imposition of equitable taxes was a political issue of the first magnitude in the 1978 election, just as it is today. Since my days in the Maine legislature, more than twenty-five years ago, I have been a strong and outspoken proponent of the personal income tax as the fairest of all government levies. I have been an equally ardent opponent of constitutional amendments which mandate a balanced budget. Many times over the years I have written letters to the editors of newspapers in Maine and Florida under the general theme, "Fair Taxes, Wisely Spent." In a statewide television debate during the 1978 campaign, I criticized the position taken by my opponents Gartley and Snowe in favor of a constitutional amendment to limit federal taxes and expenditures.

Such a constitutional amendment, I declared, is directly contradictory to the 200-year-old tradition of representative government under which our nation has prospered. It would stifle the initiative of members of Congress and prevent them from performing their normal duties of proposing legislation to meet genuine human needs and assessing equitable taxes to support federal social programs. "What we need in Congress," I asserted, "are experienced, competent, and courageous men and women who are self-confident enough to make the hard decisions required in a democratic society. Those who want to hide under the protection of an arbitrary limit on taxes and spending should not seek to serve in the national government."

It was at a political forum at the University of Maine at Presque Isle that I presented one of the major planks in my platform: reduced military spending. I spoke in favor of a balanced federal budget, a reduction in the national debt, and a stabilization of federal taxes. These goals cannot be achieved, I pointed out, without a substantial reduction in the largest item in the national budget: $135 billion for military expenses, which is twenty-seven percent of the total federal expenditures.

Concentrating on the elimination of "waste" in the military appropriation, I suggested that "many billions of dollars in federal funds can be saved, or transferred to more productive purposes such as health protection or education, by (1) eliminating the 'overkill' in our nuclear arsenal; (2) modifying the military retirement policy so that full pension benefits are not available until at least age fifty-five; (3) requiring other nations to share the cost of a continuing military presence in South Korea, which is a United Nations project;

314

and (4) making military duty in Europe a 'hardship' tour, thus reducing transportation and family living costs." To those who feared the economic consequences of a reduction in military programs and personnel, I outlined a possible partial remedy.

I believed in 1978, as I do today, that the restoration of railroad passenger train service in the United States, together with a modernization of the whole railroad infrastructure, "will help to solve many of the problems facing the nation: inflation, unemployment, energy conservation, national and civil defense. These are all related to a sound transportation network." This is what I told the members of the Bangor Kiwanis Club, of which I am a past president, in one of my early campaign speeches: The dollars saved from a reduction in military spending could be invested in rebuilding the railroads; personnel removed from military forces could be retrained to work on this transportation project.

Here is a paragraph from a campaign speech made to several audiences throughout the second Congressional district: "Maine deserves its fair share of the Amtrak operation now being carried on in all but one or two of the other states. However, to be attractive the trains would have to make the trip between Boston and Bangor, for example, in no more than three and one-half hours. Such a schedule would require the improvement of road beds, rails, signal systems and grade crossings. It would mean the expenditure of millions of dollars, but it would create hundreds of new jobs and provide an alternative form of mass transportation which will be urgently needed if the predicted energy crisis develops within the next few years."

I defended the proposed subsidy for the railroads by maintaining that they should have tax support comparable to that given for many years to automobiles and trucks through the building of an interstate highway system, and to airlines through the construction of airports. The rail subsidy would also be justified, I argued, by the resultant decrease in allocations of federal dollars for welfare and unemployment compensation as new jobs became available on the railroads. I also contended that a strong network of railroads is vital to national defense. The series of derailments over a period of years has not only illustrated a serious national neglect of a transportation system which would be a vital asset in time of war, but has endangered the lives of citizens in peacetime when they happen to reside near the scene of derailments which cause the release of noxious materials from ruptured tank cars.

There is no way to determine how many voters cast ballots for me in the November election because of my stands on reducing military expenditures and renovating the railroads. On two occasions, however, I caught the attention of Vic Runtz, the popular cartoonist of the *Bangor Daily News*. He once depicted me as a guide leading legislators in search of funds for meeting the social needs of the nation; I pointed them in the direction of a large field marked "Military Expenses" which they had decided to pass by. In the other cartoon, the original of which he presented to me for framing, he showed me in the role of a railroad man with a conductor's cap reading "Congressional Independent." This portrait sat on a desk near an open window. On the desk was a placard showing the platform plank "Restoration of Passenger Train Service in Maine." Through the window came the sound of a passing train. The cartoon caption read, poignantly, "Hear That Lonesome Whistle."

Among the more important opportunities granted to me as an independent candidate were invitations to present my views to the labor organization AFL-CIO, the National Association for the Advancement of Colored People (NAACP), and the Maine Teachers Association. At the annual conference of the Maine AFL-CIO I was given five minutes to seek their endorsement. I sought their immediate attention by opening my remarks with words designed to establish rapport with my hearers: "I appear before you as the son of a laboring man and as one who has been earning his own living for fifty-five years since beginning as a paper boy at the age of ten. This week I ended twenty-six years as president of Bangor Theological Seminary, and I am temporarily out of work. With your help on November 7th I hope to have a new job in Washington next January as your Congressman."

For the next few minutes I described briefly my working experience as a caddy, a drugstore clerk, and railroad employee, which enabled me to augment the salary of my father as he labored in an oven-manufacturing plant and a dairy. "It is important for a political candidate to know the value of a dollar," I said. "I learned this lesson very early when it became necessary for me to help my father support his wife and four children, of which I was the oldest." Referring next to my professional career as a clergyman, professor of history, and seminary president, I added this comment: "Fiscal responsibility has long been important in the pattern of my life. My business training prepared me for the successful management of a small professional school of theology for more than a quarter-century. This is one of my most significant credentials at a time in our nation's history when taxes and government expenditures are headline issues. My financial accountability is reflected in my campaign budget. While other major candidates will each spend well over $100,000, or at least twice as much as the annual salary of a member of Congress, my campaign costs will probably not exceed $15,000. In the Congress I shall be as careful with your money as I am with my own."

I concluded by assuring my listeners that I would seek funding for national programs which meet genuine human need. Such areas of need are well known to me, I claimed, because of my experience as a pastoral minister, a city councilor and mayor, a state senator, and service club member. In Washington I would promote careful budgeting, equitable taxation, a secure Social Security system, national health protection, aid to education, energy conservation, and jobs rather than welfare. Of particular interest to labor, I suggested, was my proposal to renovate the railroads in Maine with federal help, thus creating hundreds of new jobs while saving energy and providing an alternative form of fast transportation for passengers and freight.

The Maine Chapter of NAACP invited me and other candidates to submit written answers to several questions. My responses to two pertinent inquiries were as follows: With regard to the situation in South Africa, I wrote: "The pressure of world opinion and the economic power of American corporations in South Africa should continually be brought to bear upon the racial problem in that country. The example of Rhodesia, if indeed it does adopt majority rule by blacks, should eventually bring about a similar transformation in South Africa." When asked how my election

317

might benefit blacks and other minorities, I replied: "My record of activity on behalf of blacks, other minorities, and women is clear. As a state senator, I sponsored a law which eliminated discrimination in rental housing. The school of which I am president encourages the enrollment of blacks, hispanic Americans, and women. Women are employed in key administrative positions and on the faculty. As a national officer I have worked on behalf of blacks and other minorities through the Association of Theological Schools in the United States and Canada ... Indians deserve to be first-class citizens of Maine ... Non-Indians can benefit from the influence of Indian traditions and customs — folklore, religion, language, arts and crafts ... Indian land claims in Maine should be settled by the federal courts."

The Maine AFL-CIO did not offer me their endorsement, but followed their traditional practice of favoring the Democratic candidate. The NAACP does not state a preference for individual candidates. It was the Maine Teachers Association which gave new hope to my campaign. Early in September I was invited to appear with Olympia Snowe and Mark Gartley at a meeting of the Political Action Conference of Educators (PACE) in Lewiston. After my opening remarks, specific questions were directed to me, and I was later given an opportunity to submit a prepared statement of my political platform. After two weeks of deliberation PACE then announced its preference for the candidates. I was chosen over both Republican Snowe and Democrat Gartley and was the only independent so honored. The MTA president announced that the decision was made on the basis of positions taken on education-related issues.

In my opening remarks I stated that my position on education was similar to that of Senator Edward Kennedy's view on national health care: "Education is a national right ... It is everyone's birthright to receive the kind of education consummate with one's ability. Achieving this goal is a matter or reordering national priorities." On a specific question about the desirability of creating a federal Department of Education, I responded affirmatively by saying: "I am clearly in favor of a separation of the three-headed Department of Health, Education, and Welfare ... We need an educational expert as Secretary of Education." On another question I commented on the propriety of teachers being permitted to strike: "As a teacher myself I do not believe that educators should use the striking process, but should make every possible effort to settle disputes through negotiation, using arbitration when all else fails." During the last month of the campaign I sought votes by advertisements asking: "DO YOU TRUST YOUR TEACHERS?"

As the date of the election drew near, I continued my itinerary in the nine-county district with my wife at my side. Some appearances were more meaningful than others. Some themes were more significant than others. I remember well a political rally in the Grange Hall at Robbinston, the small town in Washington County on the St. Croix River where I had been the student minister thirty-five years earlier; it was a nostalgic experience to ask for the votes of many old friends. Some of the most satisfying events were informal talks with high school students in their classrooms; they were not old enough to vote for me, but many promised to speak to their parents on my behalf. I felt most at home when speaking to service club members or preaching in the churches. My favorite sermon, preached somewhere every Sunday a pulpit was available, was entitled "Freedom's Holy Light." The sermon had political implications, but it was in no way a partisan presentation. I quote below some of its major points:

"American politics needs an infusion of religion ... The traditional separation of church and state does not require the separation of religion and politics. On the contrary, the person who has religious convictions about social issues should be expected to express that faith as a responsible citizen ... Church members should take a more charitable attitude toward government and government service. Government is not the enemy; it is essentially the servant of the people; its effectiveness and its character will reflect the effectiveness and the character of those who are elected or appointed to public office." Quoting from a sermon by Henry Ward Beecher, a famous 19th century preacher, I affirmed that "when the politics of a nation are made contemptible in the eyes of the people ... then the nation is far advanced in degeneracy, and every political agitation hastens its decay."

Even as the endorsement of my candidacy by the Maine Teachers Association was a highlight of my campaign, there was also a major disappointment. Just a few weeks before election day, the Maine Conference of the United Church of Christ was scheduled to meet in annual session in Presque Isle, a location in Aroostook County within the second Congressional district. In August I wrote a letter to the Reverend Otto E. Sommer, minister of the Conference, asking for permission to address the annual meeting, with the hope that the Conference would then endorse my candidacy.

Part of the rationale for my request is found in the following early paragraph of my letter: "The Christian churches and their agencies make voluminous studies of the relationship between Christianity and the social problems of the world. They pass vast number of resolutions designed to influence public opinion on a wide variety of moral and ethical issues. Rarely, however, do church agencies have an opportunity to make these studies and resolutions effective through the leadership of a churchman who is elected to national political office. The Maine Conference has such an opportunity now. As a thirty-year member of the Conference, I ask it, through you, to consider what action it should take."

I then outlined the various ways in which I had exercised my ministry during three decades of Conference membership: as President of the Conference and one of its directors; as a teacher of Church History with special emphasis on Christian social teachings and the relationship of Church and State; as President of Bangor Theological Seminary; as moderator, trustee and deacon of a local church; as an officer of the national UCC Commission on Christian Unity and Council for Higher Education; and as President of the Association of Theological Schools.

Before concluding the letter I presented two further reasons why I was asking for endorsement by the Conference. First, "I have put my Christian faith into action throughout the secular community. I have been a councilman and mayor of the city of Bangor and a state senator in the Maine legislature. My influence has been felt through leadership given to the Kiwanis Club, the Y.M.C.A., the United Way, the Chamber of Commerce, and other community agencies. No other candidate for the office I seek can match my record of experience and service." Secondly, "I shall probably not win the election because I have chosen to campaign as an independent, thus forgoing both party influence and party financing. If I am to have the opportunity to serve in the Congress I must have the support of educators, business and professional leaders, senior citizens, and especially church people. Thus I ask what the Maine Conference will do for one of its own."

The answer to my request came in about three weeks in a brief letter from the President of the Maine Conference. The Board of Directors wished me well in the forthcoming election, but was not willing to grant me permission to address the Conference or to seek its endorsement. Knowing the basic conservatism of the Conference leadership, I was not surprised by the negative decision. Still, I was deeply disappointed. My church colleagues of Maine were unwilling to give me the same consideration granted freely by the teachers of Maine. A sad commentary, indeed, on the state of religion.

Shirley and I now made preparations for the time following the election on November 7th. We had moved out of the Hannibal Hamlin House, our Bangor home, in August and had put our furniture in storage near our son Mark's home in Virginia. When we were not on the campaign trail, we had been living in our summer cottage at Lucerne-in-Maine, which fortunately was equipped with electric heat. On election day we voted and awaited the decision of the people, not really expecting to be sent to Washington. The official tally showed Republican Olympia Snowe to be the winner with 87,939 votes. Democrat Mark Gartley was second with 70,691 votes. I was a distant third with 8,035 votes, 3,062 of which were cast in my home county of Penobscot. Although I led all of the independent candidates with fifty-five percent of the votes cast for independents, my 4.7% of all votes was less than I had expected. There was some consolation in the editorial comment of the *Bangor Daily News* that I had conducted my campaign with effectiveness, dignity, and integrity.

Olympia Snowe and I developed a respect for one another which continues through the years. I hear from her every Christmas season and on other occasions when she responds to letters I feel free to write her on political issues of the day. For thirteen years now she has been an able representative of Maine in the Congress. Here is the statement I released to the press following the election: "My hearty congratulations go to Olympia Snowe. I send her every good wish for the important task she faces in Washington. I am deeply thankful to all who voted for me and to the host of friends who worked so diligently for my election. To my beloved wife and campaign manager, Shirley, I am especially grateful. My debt extends to the Maine Teachers Association, whose endorsement of my candidacy was a principal factor in helping me to achieve credibility among the voters. It has been an unforgettable experience to meet and to talk with many hundreds of Maine citizens. Shirley and I have many fond memories for the years ahead."

The years ahead began on the day after the election when my wife and I left for our retirement condominium home in sunny Florida. In the next chapter of these memoirs, I begin the final part of my life's story: "Years of Reflection." The Bangor years are now history, a history which ended — perhaps fittingly — with a political campaign reflecting one of the goals of my life: to apply the Christian faith as a solution to the human problems of our society. I note here only that I accepted the results of the election philosophically. When my new friends in Sarasota asked me why I had retired to Florida, this was my response: "The voters of Maine sent me!"

PART III

Years of Reflection

17.
President Emeritus

In this thirteenth year of my retirement, I bring this book to a close with a segment entitled, "Years of Reflection." There is only one way to begin this story of retrospection and nostalgia: It is to record my heartfelt appreciation of Shirley Louise Johns Whittaker, my beloved wife for half a century.

It was more than fifty years ago during the Christmas season that Shirley and I spent eighteen consecutive wonderful days together in New Haven while I was on holiday vacation from my first-year studies for the Christian ministry at Bangor Theological Seminary in Maine. We had been separated for three months, and we soon acknowledged the mutual feeling that this was too long a period for us to be apart ever again. We discovered a bond between us — emotional, intellectual, cultural, and sensual — which demanded an early marriage.

So it was that in September of 1940 we returned to Bangor as husband and wife to begin a long love affair which is even more exciting and fulfilling now than it was then. I shall never forget that she left a promising high school teaching career in a metropolitan city to join me in a rural parish in eastern Maine where I earned a paltry twenty-five dollars per week as student-minister of two struggling Downeast churches. It was an act of faith and devotion on her part.

Life has been good to us through the years. More accurately, Shirley has been good to me. During three winter seasons she was my companion and co-worker in the Washington County parishes to which we commuted three hundred miles every weekend of the Seminary school year. Especially memorable are the many nights we spent in an unheated bedroom provided by one of the church members. The torture of being cold was offset by the pleasure of cuddling under many layers of blankets.

Among the greatest gifts given by Shirley to me are the two children we adore: Barbara Anne and Frederick Mark. They in turn have enriched our lives by marrying Frank Toppa and Pamela Livesay. From these unions have come further delights: Mark and Pam's Emily and Andrew, now talented teenagers, and Frank and Barbara's recently adopted infant son, Isaac, who has made his grandparents feel young again. Shirley and I rejoice, too, that Barbara and Mark have chosen careers similar to our own: she in ministry and he in education.

Whatever success I have achieved professionally is due in large measure to Shirley's constant and unwavering support in all my endeavors: educational, ecclesiastical, political, and recreational. She encouraged me to go to graduate school and thus prepare for a teaching career, although it meant that she carried extra responsibilities in caring for our children. She has been enthusiastic about my involvement in church activities, in teaching, and in seminary administration. My avocation in practical politics would not have been possible without her concurrence and help. Shirley has been an expert swimmer since her youth, but she did not expect me to follow her example; golf is my game, and very fortunate I am that she has always told me to play as often as my heart desires. We do sit together at the bridge table at least once a week; since she taught me the game I usually lose any arguments we have about technique, but my love for her remains.

That Shirley and I have lived together in relative good health for fifty years is due in no small measure to her culinary expertise. When we married she was a novice in the kitchen, but soon learned to be proficient in preparing meals by the judicious use of recipes gleaned from the files of her mother and grandmother. During my years as seminary president we often entertained at lunch or dinner. Many church leaders and other dignitaries still remember, after a lapse of years, the extraordinary lobster stew and blueberry pie prepared for them in our home. Our children rave about the mocha torte Shirley always puts on the table when they are with us. I feel as young and as fit as I do because my nutrition-conscious wife gives me the best meals available.

Our long marriage has blossomed and remained beautiful because, as I told Shirley not long ago, she has been great fun to live with. This was true in the parish ministry, at the seminary, on our several trips exploring the United States, and in our recent world travels to many foreign lands. It was true when she induced me at age seventy and more to go river-rafting on the Kennebec gorge, and when she drove with me hundreds of miles in seven counties of eastern Maine as campaign manager during my 1978 candidacy for election to the Congress of the United States. Her unique sense of humor, which has enhanced both our public life and our most intimate private moments, is well illustrated by a comment she made during our joint appearance in the Congressional campaign before the Bangor Lions Club, many of whose members were our personal friends. This is a good example of the "Shirley-isms," as I call them, which pop up unexpectedly from time to time. When she was asked why she agreed to serve as campaign manager, my wife replied blithely: "Oh, I'm doing it for sexual favors." She was one of my best vote-getters!

I could write a book just about Shirley, but one more commentary must suffice for the purposes of these memoirs. Her multitude of friends have joined me in admiring Shirley for her compassion, especially in relationships with older people. This virtue was abundantly shown in a lifelong love of her mother and a selfless caring for an aging parent in declining years. It was manifested in service on the board of directors of a home for the elderly infirm in Bangor, as current ministry on a church visitation committee, and long-time volunteer work among the old and the lonely at the Pines of Sarasota. A recent conversation with a lady resident of the Pines provides a poignant backdrop for my final testimony about my marriage to Shirley. Near the close of a pastoral visit the lady gave my wife an affectionate pat on the head and said, "My, I'll bet your husband is crazy about you!" "I don't know," Shirley replied, "but I'll ask him." For fifty years I have told my beloved on a daily basis how much I adore her, but for the time ahead I shall be certain to exclaim, "Honey, I'm crazy about you!"

The paragraphs with which this chapter have begun were written and read by me at a special party on December 27, 1989, sponsored by our children Barbara and Mark in the social room of Harbor Towers, our condominium home in Sarasota, Florida. It was an early celebration of Shirley's 75th birthday on January 8, 1990, and our 50th wedding anniversary on September 14, 1990. The date was determined by the time when both of our children and their families could be with us in Florida during this anniversary year. More than fifty of our southern friends gathered with us for a sit-down dinner celebration. A similar event was held in the Wellman Commons of Bangor Theological Seminary on July 22, 1990, at which time our friends in Maine were dinner guests of our two children. On the actual date of our 50th anniversary, Shirley and I were at the Chateau Frontenac in Quebec for the beginning of a "second honeymoon" tour of eastern Canada.

I have now been "President Emeritus" of Bangor Seminary for thirteen years. Before writing of my relationship to the school as a retired chief executive officer, I record first some of the principal events and developments of this period involving my personal, family, and community life. The chronicle includes my activities in church, condominium, service club, and political affairs. It involves my exploits as a senior golfer, tennis player, and bridge enthusiast. I have been a writer of two books, including this one. Twice I have encountered relatively minor physical problems. Shirley and I have thoroughly enjoyed several travel adventures to many fascinating places overseas. Our two children have firmly established professional careers. Grandchildren have evoked in us deep pride and great happiness. On several occasions I have officiated at weddings and memorial services. And I have engaged in a limited amount of preaching, lecturing and social commentary.

Soon after establishing our new residence in Florida I realized a long-held ambition by learning to play the piano. It proved to be helpful transitional therapy for one who was entering upon retirement. For three years I was diligent in taking lessons and achieved a proficiency on the instrument which was satisfying to me, if to no one else. Then other interests became more important to me, and I gradually abandoned piano-playing. I have not performed on the keyboard during several recent years, but have promised myself and Shirley that I shall return once again to this challenging hobby when the time comes that I must give up some of my other interests. Meanwhile Shirley and I maintain our inherent affection for music by attending each season the series of concerts presented in Sarasota by the Florida West Coast Symphony Orchestra.

My interest in the piano began to wane when I became deeply involved in preparing for publication my Yale doctoral thesis on "Samuel Harris, American Theologian." The manuscript had gathered dust on my library shelf for thirty years during my teaching and administrative career at the Seminary. When I could not find a commercial publisher I subsidized the production of several hundred copies in 1981. While only a modest number of the volume has been sold, it was widely distributed among American theological schools, church-related colleges, Maine libraries, and alumni of Bangor Seminary. The story of Samuel Harris constitutes a major part of an earlier chapter of this book entitled "Doctor of Philosophy." I had the privilege of speaking about the book at the annual Seminary Convocation luncheon in 1982. I was gratified by the favorable review which appeared in the *Bangor Daily News* on February 27, 1982, under the by-line of James B. Vickery, president of the Bangor Historical Society; he wrote in part: "Whittaker's biography strives to restore the forgotten reputation of Harris and provide due recognition of this important, but neglected, 19th century theologian ... The biography is amply documented ... and has an impressive bibliography. It is chiefly directed to the student of theology who may find an example from this peerless shepherd of the flock."

During the Bangor years my wife and I were active layleaders in the Hammond Street Congregational Church (UCC). In Sarasota we have been similarly engaged as members of the First Congregational United Church of Christ. I have served three-year terms on the Board of Outreach, the Board of Trustees, and the Stewardship Board; in these capacities I have been instrumental in expanding the budgets for both home expenditures and support of the Church's wider mission. I have also preached the Sunday morning sermon on several occasions, both in my home church and in other area congregations. Shirley has been a member of the Board of Education and of the Board of Deacons; on the latter body she was the first woman chairperson.

Work in First Church has given us the privilege of counting among our many friends the senior minister, Dr. John Syster. John is the son of the Reverend Paul Syster, a classmate of mine at Bangor Seminary during the early 1940's, and Barbara Colby Syster. Barbara is the daughter of the late Reverend Rensel Colby, an earlier graduate of Bangor. Thus, by unusual coincidence, the one who is our pastor is bound by family ties through his father and grandfather to the Seminary which has been such a vital part of our lives. Further, other members of First Church are Nathanael and Helen Guptill. "Nat" participated in my 1944 ordination at Yarmouth, Maine, when he was minister of the South Portland Congregational Church; he was a trustee of Bangor Seminary during my administration, and later served as chairman of the Board.

Another blessing of our relationship with First Church was a renewal of the friendship Shirley and I had established long ago with John and Judith MacNeil when John and I were students at Bowdoin College and pastors of churches in Cumberland County. When we moved to Florida in 1978 John had retired, for reasons of health, after serving nine years as minister of First Church. During his active pastorate he had been the founder of Plymouth Harbor, a premier retirement and health center, and the leader of a community effort which established New College of Sarasota. Both of these institutions were later to be significant factors in the life of Whittaker family members. Unfortunately, our reunion was short-lived, for in the spring of 1979 John died of a long-standing heart ailment. It was my sad but honorable privilege to participate in his memorial service. This was another in a succession of significant events which have marked the continuing long and strong friendship of Judith MacNeil and the Whittakers. In the fall of 1980 I officiated at Judith's marriage to Robert Merrill, a widower whom she had met at her summer home. Judy and Bob, Shirley and I, spend meaningful time with one another at regular intervals in both Florida and Maine.

John MacNeil had a considerable influence upon our son Mark. When Mark was a senior at Bangor High School, John persuaded him to apply for admission to the charter class of New College. Mark was the first male student to be accepted. He stayed for three semesters, but found that the innovative and loosely structured academic procedures were not compatible with his study experiences. Although invited to continue at New College, Mark decided to transfer to the University of Maine at Orono, from which school he graduated in 1969. As has been indicated in an earlier chapter, Mark spent a year working in the alumni office of the University before beginning his long tenure as a development officer at Sweet Briar College in Virginia. When he left there in 1986 he held the title of Vice President. Since then he has had an expanding career in development work and public relations as Vice President for University Relations at Stetson University in Deland, Florida.

The life of our daughter Barbara took a new turn in the late 1970's when she became interested and involved in the work of the Unitarian-Universalist Church in Brewster, Massachusetts. Eventually, at the age of 38 in 1981, she enrolled as a student at the Harvard Divinity School with the new vocation of the pastoral ministry as a goal. After graduation with the Master of Divinity degree she was ordained as a Unitarian-Universalist minister in the Brewster Church, where she had served an intern year during her Harvard studies. June 9, 1984, was a proud day for me as I delivered an ordination meditation challenging my daughter to incorporate in her ministry these three major components: the pastoral, the philosophical, and the prophetic. This she has done very well during the past six years as minister of the Unitarian-Universalist Society in Amherst, Massachusetts. She has also extended her influence by assuming a leadership role in the national organization known as

331

IRAS (Institute of Religion in an Age of Science). It was my privilege in the fall of 1987 to preach a sermon in the Amherst Church on one of my favorite subjects, "Religion in the Public Schools." On September 1, 1991, Barbara assumed the pastorate of the Unitarian-Universalist Church in Arlington, Massachusetts.

Barbara's personal life, as well as that of her parents, has been blessed by her marriage on May 11, 1985, to Frank Anthony Toppa. My wife Shirley thinks he is an ideal son-in-law, and I agree. Like Barbara, Frank has many musical talents. He served the Amherst Church as organist and choir director, taught music in the local public schools, gave private piano lessons, repaired and rebuilt pianos and organs, and occasionally directed community musical productions such as "Man of La Mancha." Frank also engaged in graduate study leading to a Master's degree in organ teaching.

A dramatic change occurred in the lives of Barbara and Frank, Shirley and Fred, on April 9, 1989. Our newest grandchild was born that day in Newport, Rhode Island, the son of one of Frank's nieces. For two years our daughter and son-in-law had been trying unsuccessfully to adopt an infant through an international agency. Then Frank learned that his niece was about to give birth to her fourth child in Newport, Rhode Island. Because of a "broken family" situation, and because the mother was a cocaine addict, the newborn was to be turned over to a state agency for adoption. Barbara and Frank offered to be the adoptive parents, despite apprehension about the baby's physical condition, and the mother readily agreed. The baby was born prematurely and weighed just a little over three pounds. Fortunately, however, all hospital tests done at birth for basic bodily functions indicated that the baby was normal and healthy; he is in the same condition more than two years later.

What should the new member of the family be named? After her divorce from her first husband, Barbara had reclaimed her maiden name, but added to it her maternal grandmother's name of Johns. Known henceforth as Barbara Anne Whittaker-Johns, she has retained the hyphenated surname during her second marriage. The new parents readily concurred that their adopted son should be named Isaac Anthony Toppa. Isaac means "she laughs," according to the Old Testament biblical story of Sarah, mother of Isaac, who laughed when she discovered she was pregnant in her old age. Isaac Toppa is, indeed, a handsome and happy child, who brings laughter and joy to his parents, grandparents, and other members of the family.

Shirley and I, as grandparents for the third time, never forget the blessings brought to our lives through the years of our retirement by Emily and Andrew, the offspring of our son Mark and his wife Pamela. Emily is now a beautiful young lady of nineteen, and has completed her second year of college at Stetson University. Andrew is a handsome high school teenager with considerable talent as a golfer and a tennis player. Many times he and I have had enjoyable foursomes on the course and on the court with his mother and father. Mark and Pam and the two young people have enriched our senior citizen years by regular visits to our homes in Florida and Maine. Not long ago our sturdy dock on Phillips Lake at Lucerne was designed and built by Mark and his family. Shirley and I plan that our summer home in Maine will eventually belong to our children and grandchildren.

Having written about the current careers of Barbara and Frank, I conclude the story about our immediate family with an appreciation of the professional work of Pam and Mark. Pam has been a public school teacher during most of her married life — in Maine, Virginia, and Florida. While Mark was at Sweet Briar College, Pam also served the school for several years in the dual capacity of director of institutional research and assistant to the registrar. Since moving to Florida she has been employed at the Deland Middle School in Project SMILE, one of the Volusia County School District's dropout prevention programs. It is Pam's responsibility to work with "at risk" students on academic skills and self-concept, and to lead them in group discussions on such topics as decision-making. In 1991 she earned the graduate degree of Specialist in Education from Stetson University. Meanwhile, Mark is busily engaged as Vice President in a cooperative effort with the President to raise the millions of dollars and to maintain the public relations program which have helped to make Stetson University a premier institution of higher education. He also continues his contribution, begun while he was at Sweet Briar, to the regional work of Washington-based

CASE, the Council for the Advancement and Support of Education.

The retirement years for Shirley and me have been enhanced by our involvement in several community activities. Shirley's Christian witness as a member of the Board of Deacons at First Church included participation on a visiting committee which called on members of the parish who were ill or infirm. Although no longer on the Board, she continues to visit with selected church friends. In addition she has spent a day each week as a volunteer at the Pines of Sarasota, a resident home for the elderly who need special care. I am in my forty-fifth year as a service club member and am involved in the social work program of the South Sarasota Kiwanis Club. For several years I also served on the Sarasota County Democratic Executive Committee, including a term as chairman of its finance committee. For three years I was a board member of the Siesta Key Association, a group dedicated to local civic improvement.

When we moved to Florida Shirley and I had our first experience with condominium living. In 1977 we bought a two-bedroom unit overlooking the swimming pool on the second floor of Harbor Towers, a 210-unit seven-story condominium located on the barrier island of Siesta Key just south of the city of Sarasota and between the Gulf of Mexico and the Florida Intracoastal Waterway. We were just half a mile from four-mile long Crescent Beach, a county facility which is rated among the world's finest. Fortunately or wisely, we made the purchase just in time to avoid a meteoric rise in condominium prices, with the result that our unit became worth twice as much as we paid for it. In early 1991 we moved to a waterfront apartment in Sarasota at "Plymouth Harbor," a lifetime care retirement community.

It was not long before both Shirley and I became involved in condominium activities. She was chairman of the social committee and I began as chairman of the budget committee. Soon I was a member of the Board of Directors, then Vice President, and finally President for three years of the Harbor Towers Owners' Association. Through this volunteer work we established some close friendships with talented and congenial people, thus adding to the enjoyment of retirement years. The following list is not all-inclusive but names

334

those to whom we are most grateful for becoming an important part of our lives: Helen and Harold Bahm, Peggy and Holmes Dyer, Lee and Oscar Hartman, Mae and Elwood McCracken, Ruth and Herbert Rosenberg, Natalie and Eugene Schram, Helen and Aaron Elfenbein.

My wife and I have reason to be thankful for good health. Through competent medical care, regular exercise, and reasonable eating habits, both of us have reached the seventy-five year mark and beyond. Our most serious physical encounters in recent years have resulted in the removal of Shirley's benign ovarian cyst and my operation for a benign prostate problem. Mildly troublesome and worrisome for Shirley has been some arthritis, and a gradual deafness which requires her use of two hearing aids. As for me, I have learned to live with chronic hypertension and diabetes, each controlled by one pill a day.

Exercise has been a part of our daily routine. Regular swimming, beach walking, and work around the house, have kept Shirley in good physical condition. I play golf twice a week or more, walking most of the time. Occasionally I may be found on the tennis court, playing doubles or singles. I use an electric treadmill as supplemental exercise. I even learned to swim after I was seventy years old when my doctor suggested that I take some lessons at the Y.M.C.A.; however, I spend more time walking the beach than in the water. After an experience with river-rafting during a trip to Alaska, when I was seventy-four Shirley and I had the most thrilling ride of our lives on a raft in Maine's Kennebec River gorge; my children still do not believe I was so adventurous.

The climax of my long career as a golfer came to pass after I was seventy-five years old. When I was seventy I scored my second hole-in-one after a lapse of twenty-seven years since the first one in 1957; it was on the 165-yard 17th hole at the Rolling Green course in Sarasota on January 14, 1984. The following year, on August 22, 1985, the third "ace" was recorded on the 165-yard 16th hole at the Bangor Municipal course. Two holes-in-one after the age of seventy was spectacular enough, but the best was yet to come. There was one more goal yet to reach — to shoot my age on a par-72 golf course. When I was seventy-two I had scored a 73 at

Rolling Green in Florida. Then on December 6, 1989, at the age of seventy-six, unexpectedly I achieved the ultimate goal. At six over par with two holes to play I had just about given up hope of shooting my age that day. A "birdie" two on the par-3 17th hole gave me another chance. On the par-5 18th, I was on the green in three shots with a 15-foot putt for another birdie. When the ball went straight into the hole I had my four-over-par 76, and my long-cherished ambition was fulfilled.

Now that my golfing career has achieved all of its major goals, I include a paragraph in these memoirs to record my gratitude to the many good friends who have spent countless happy hours with me chasing a golf ball from tee to green; I list the names of some among many who have shared and enriched my recreational hours: son Mark, his wife Pamela, and my grandson Andrew; my friend for sixty years, John Robinson; Henry and Craig McKown, Andy Wright, Roy Malmberg, Bob O'Neill, Bernie Jarvis, Elwood McCracken, Oscar Hartman, Nat Guptill, Jack Smith, Jim Robinson, Bob Woodward, Bob Reynolds, Page Belding; and my brother-in-law, Elmer Schlegel.

But life is more than a game of golf! It may also be a game of bridge — or of pinochle — or of "Scrabble" — or of crossword puzzles. These have been my principal sedentary activities during the "senior citizen" years. Doing the daily newspaper crossword puzzle is good exercise for the mind. Shirley and I find that a hotly contested game of Scrabble is fine recreation during evening hours when we are alone. Bridge is our favorite indoor sport. We play at least once a week during the months we are in Sarasota, most often with those who are among our closest friends. Making an occasional "grand slam" bid of seven no-trump helps to keep us young at heart. We have not played much pinochle lately, but weekly games with faculty colleagues and friends in Maine are fond memories, broken only by the deaths of Clayton Lothrop, and Merle and Walter Cook.

On a more serious note of reflection, I turn now from the games I have played to the impact upon my life of family members and friends whose earthly days have ended in recent years. A deep feeling of personal loss came to me in the spring of 1988 when my youngest brother, Stanley, died unexpectedly at the age of sixty-five. He and his wife Dorothy had renewed an earlier close relationship with Shirley and me when they made annual vacation visits to Florida with my cousin Shirley and her husband Neil Gabrielson from Rhode Island. We are grateful to Stan and his wife for reuniting us with the Gabrielsons after many a long year. We remain most thankful to Stan and Dorothy for the loving home care they gave to my mother during her declining years.

Heading the list of all who are constantly remembered with love is Blanche Louise Johns, Shirley's mother, who died in the fall of 1981 after ninety-three years of a full and vibrant life. The following are a few of the words I had the privilege of speaking at her memorial service: "For three decades and more she was the matriarch of the family ... Two sons-in-law shared with daughters Shirley and Barbara the joy which flowed from her generous spirit and gracious personality. Following the early death of her husband, the bond of affection between Blanche and her two daughters was one of the strengths of her life. It was a mutual love and reached its culmination in the tender and constant care given by Barbara and Shirley in the declining years of their mother's earthly existence. Compassion and concern were hallmarks of the life of Blanche Johns. This truth was shown most completely in the relationship she had with four grandchildren and seven great-grandchildren. To them, and to many others, she was 'Maga', a term of endearment first given to her by infant granddaughter Barbara. Let Barbara's words, written in poetic form on Maga's ninety-first birthday, be our final tribute to her:

'Dear God:
      We know you are it —
    Dancing a life in each one of us
    When you came to be as Maga
        menacing was no more than
        the Red Caped Cavalier hung
        over the mantle and
        Hasselbach's-made
        strawberry ice cream sodas.

Backyard flowered brick walks
    a garden swing
    big-bosomed laughter perfumed
    under a broad sunny hat
    tales of muslim linens —
    of tough times.
Happy Birthday, Dear Maga,
    you are the gift —
Each thought of you dawns
    another stubbornly joyous day.'"

My heartfelt appreciation of Clarence Fuller is made clear in earlier pages of this book. My administration as President of Bangor Seminary was blessed through twenty-two of its twenty-six years by his leadership as chairman of the Board of Trustees. After we both retired, our friendship continued through visits in our respective summer homes in Maine and by good times in Florida, where "Chuck" and Anora spent the winter months in their nearby Sarasota residence. His death in the spring of 1987 was a personal loss felt more deeply only by Anora and the three Fuller children. I made this clear in a eulogy at a memorial service in Melrose, Massachusetts, where for thirty years "Chuck" had been minister of the First Congregational Church. The Whittaker bond of affection with Anora remains.

Nostalgia sweeps over me as I write in my summer home overlooking beautiful Phillips Lake at Lucerne-in-Maine. The distant hills remind me of departed loved ones, Walter and Merle Cook, for whom the mountains and waters of Maine were a life-sustaining force. Walter's contribution to the churches of Maine and to Bangor Seminary has been memorialized in an earlier chapter. I recall here the joy which he and Merle brought to Shirley and me in our retirement years during our annual visits to Maine. A year after his death in 1987 it was my privilege to speak in praise of Walter in a memorial service in the First Baptist Church of Bangor, where he had previously spent many years as pastor; the occasion was the rededication of an organ in his honor. I have recently finished writing an introduction to a book of prayers by Walter which was published posthumously. Merle survived Walter by only a year. It is difficult to believe that they have departed the good earth. They live on, in hallowed memory.

Life as a retired Christian minister has its moments of happiness, too. Officiating at the marriage of Judith MacNeil and Robert Merrill is one example already given. Another was the pleasure of joining in wedlock good friends Natalie Hatfield and Gene Schram on April 4, 1987. The occasion is remembered with some mirth by all concerned because of a slip of the tongue by me during the ceremony; without realizing it at the time, but reminded later, I inadvertently asked Eugene: "Will you have Natalie to be your husband...?" Fortunately, he repeated the proper vow, "I, Eugene, take you, Natalie, to be my wedded wife..." I wondered then whether or not I was getting too old to officiate at weddings, but recently I thoroughly enjoyed offering the prayer at the reception following the marriage of Karen Kalp, daughter of my dear friends Larry and Carol.

Since coming to Sarasota in 1978 I have continued my long-established practice of writing occasional letters to the editors of local newspapers, and have also accepted a few invitations to speak at local forums on major issues of the day. The substance of some of these articles and lectures will appear in the following two chapters concerning my role as "Theological Analyst" and "Social Critic." Among the topics discussed are: "Religion and the Public Schools"; "Tithes and Taxes"; "Church and State"; "Abortion"; "The Biblical and Theological Perspective of Peacemaking"; "Freedom's Holy Light"; and "Education for Ministry." On two occasions I have returned to Bowdoin College, my alma mater, to serve as chaplain at commencement exercises.

One more activity during the past thirteen years is worthy of description before I turn, finally, to my relationship with Bangor Theological Seminary as its President Emeritus. As senior citizens Shirley and I have become world travelers, which is a new experience for us. During my active years at the Seminary we traveled extensively throughout the United States, but never went overseas except for a visit to Hawaii in 1970. When we went to Alaska a few years ago we achieved the goal of setting foot in all fifty states of the U.S.A.

Our first adventure to Europe took place in the fall of 1980. We flew to Vienna and traveled by bus through Austria, Switzerland, and West Germany. Since then we have explored England, Scotland, Wales, and Ireland; Greece and Italy; France, Denmark, Norway, and Sweden; Russia and adjacent areas of the Soviet Union, Poland, and East Germany, including East and West Berlin. Other trips have been to Alaska and the islands of the eastern Caribbean.

To record all of the sights and sounds which have come to me in reflection following our extensive travels would constitute a book in itself. For the purpose of these memoirs I write a few pages to illustrate the major impacts upon Shirley and me made by the natural wonders and the human achievements we have witnessed in foreign lands. First, we stand more and more in awe and reverence before the Creator God since we have seen the majesty of the Swiss Alps, the fjords of Norway, and Alaska's Mount McKinley. The physical beauty of the planet earth has led us to re-examine our own humanity in relationship to a Higher Being.

A second significant retrospective experience has stemmed from our first-hand contact with the inhumanity we mortal beings have inflicted upon ourselves through the scourge of international warfare. The beaches of Normandy and the nearby cemetery with 10,000 graves; the war memorials in Russia, Poland, East and West Germany, honoring the hundreds of thousands who died in conflict; the Berlin Wall dividing the peoples of a great European city; the devastation of property by aerial bombing; all of this demonstrates for us the stupidity and the degradation of mortal beings.

On the other hand, an unforgettable visit to the English city of Coventry was a third highpoint of travel which convinced me of the human potential for good. On November 14, 1940, the Coventry Cathedral was a magnificent center of worship, one of many such church edifices throughout Europe built by the skill and artistry of devout Christians. That night the Cathedral was destroyed by German firebombs, leaving intact only the outer walls, the tower and spire. A few days after the bombing, two irregular pieces of the charred oak roof beams were tied together by wire and set up at the eastern end of the ruins behind a stone altar. To complete this now-famous worship center two words were carved in the still-standing cathedral wall — "Father Forgive."

A decision to rebuild the cathedral was made on the day following the bombing destruction, although it was to be sixteen years before the new foundation stone was laid. The spectacular beauty of the new church, which is connected by an archway to the old ruins, is impossible to depict in words; it must be seen in all its glory. As one enters the cathedral, which was completed in 1962, one is immediately transfixed by the majestic figure of Christ woven into the largest tapestry in the world. At the base of the worship center is a human figure, signifying the central theme of reconciliation between God and every man and woman. A sermon was born that day in Coventry Cathedral. It is a sermon about forgiveness, but it is also a sermon about repentance. More than that, it is a sermon about reconciliation. Titled "Father Forgive," it will be a feature of the next chapter of these memoirs called "Theological Analyst."

The wide scope of human ingenuity is another truth impressed upon my wife and me as we have journeyed abroad during the past decade. The incomparable beauty of Greek architecture and Italian art we found to be awe-inspiring. Days spent at the Vatican and in churches of the Protestant Reformation reinforced our conviction that spiritual rather than material values still hold the only hope for human salvation in this world — and the next. Saint Francis rather than Adolph Hitler or Joseph Stalin is our role model for the future; this became our faith during a unique evening in Assisis as we participated in an anniversary celebration for Italy's patron saint. The Eiffel Tower in Paris, and Pisa's Leaning Tower, pointed upward as symbols of the direction we are moving.

The story of the Whittaker travels would not be complete without reference to the personal pleasures, and one unpleasant episode, which we have known. Our travels abroad have been in groups of twenty-five to thirty-five persons, most of whom during our week or ten days together have changed from strangers to congenial companions. We have on two or three occasions established lasting friendships, the most recent of which has been with May and Bob Brown of Gasport, New York. We met them on the Alaska trip, and we have since exchanged visits in our respective homes. We introduced them to river-rafting in Maine and they gave us some memorable hours at Niagara Falls near their home. A recent adventure was a whale-watching excursion off the New England coast.

Perhaps the most memorable of our overseas trips is our visit in the fall of 1988 to Moscow, Minsk, Berlin, and other cities then under Communist domination. Certainly we have been amazed, and deeply heartened, by the changes made in eastern Europe in less than two years under the policy of "perestroika" initiated by Mikhail Gorbachev. We remember being favorably impressed by the friendliness of the Russian people, including our official tour guide. We believe this was a portent of things to come. We recall the warm welcome we received inside an active Russian Orthodox Church when our group arrived just before a worship service was to begin. Shirley enjoys telling about her cordial recognition outside our Moscow hotel by one of the Russian working women, which involved a series of bowing to one another and of shaking of hands, thus overcoming the language barrier.

A story worth telling and re-telling had as its setting a theatre in Minsk where we witnessed a most beautiful ballet performance. During the first intermission we noticed that a woman and two young girls were sitting in the row behind us. In a gesture of friendship, my wife asked if any of the group spoke English. When the youngest girl nodded, Shirley engaged her in a brief conversation, but soon discovered that the young lady had only a rudimentary knowledge of English. She then presented each of the girls with a ballpoint pen, a token which our guide had told us would be warmly received. The broad smiles which we got in return were reward enough. However, during the second intermission my wife felt a tap on her shoulder and then was given a note signed by both girls which said in English: "Thank you very much." It was for us a symbol of the greatly improved relationship between the Soviet Union and the United States which has now become a reality. The note has a cherished place in our scrapbook.

It was in East Berlin that we had a somewhat disturbing experience, although in retrospect it seems quite amusing. After dinner one evening we were returning to our room on the third floor when the elevator moved swiftly to the top of the building without stopping. We pushed all available buttons, but there was no response. We banged on the door, but no one heard us. Feeling very much alone, we wondered if we were destined to stay in confinement all night. Although it seemed like an eternity, after about ten minutes the elevator descended to the third floor, the door opened, and we rushed out. From our room I telephoned the hotel front desk and described the incident to the attendant. She listened to my story and then made her first reply in an unforgettable single word: "Impossible!" When I indicated my annoyance at her flippant remark, she then made this comment: "Well, you are out now, are you not?" It was as if I was talking to the Berlin Wall!

I conclude this travelogue with a reflective thought about the infamous wall. The few hours Shirley and I spent in East and West Berlin were unique indeed, for never again can they be repeated, by us or by anyone else. We viewed the wall from both sides. On the East Berlin side it was bleak and white. In West Berlin it was covered by animated graffiti, perhaps an indication of the freedom of expression not permitted on the other side of the wall. The difference in economic and political conditions, and in lifestyle, in the divided city was immediately evident when one moved from East to West through the tightly-guarded "Check-point Charlie." And now, unbelievably, the wall is down and the check-point building has been removed to a museum. East and West Germany, and Berlin, are reunited. To me this is the greatest example in my lifetime of a reconciliation among peoples achieved through the innate human power to choose the good over the evil. I am blessed to have lived long enough to see it as a sign of the better world community now in the making.

The historical account of my early years and my professional career needs only one more segment for completion. So I turn to the story of my relationship to Bangor Theological Seminary as President Emeritus during the past thirteen years. It is not my plan to record in detail the progress of the Seminary through the Glick and Warford administrations which followed mine. This account is for someone else to write. From time to time I shall refer to developments at Bangor which have been of special interest to me in the reflective period of my life. Some of these I shall applaud; about others I shall offer constructive criticism for what it may be worth. Overall, I have a genuine and deep feeling of appreciation for all the courtesies extended to me as one of their predecessors by Presidents G. Wayne Glick and Malcolm L. Warford.

On August 1, 1978, Dr. G. Wayne Glick became the sixth President of Bangor Theological Seminary. Biographical data about him is given in an earlier chapter of this book. It was my privilege to speak at the inauguration luncheon for Dr. Glick on May 5, 1979, at which time I said, in part:

"The coming of Wayne and Barbara Glick to Bangor has pleased me particularly in two respects: I applaud the election of another church historian as the chief executive officer of the Seminary, thus assuring the continuation of the liberal academic tradition which has been a hallmark of the school from its earliest years. Secondly, Shirley and I are delighted that Barbara has come, with her grace and charm, to be the first lady of the Hannibal Hamlin House ... My concluding word to you, Wayne, is this: You and I are the only two people on earth who know what it really means to be President of Bangor Theological Seminary. May you be as happy and as fulfilled as I have been before you. And be assured that I am just as near as your telephone if ever you need me for any reason at all."

Wayne and Barbara Glick have become our good friends over the years. They visited with Shirley and me in our Florida home while Wayne and I did some public relations work on behalf of the Seminary early in his administration. In the fall of 1989 the Whittakers spent three exciting days with the Glicks in their retirement home in Lancaster. We explored the countryside and had a meeting of one of the most exclusive organizations in the world, The Presidents Emeriti Club of Bangor Theological Seminary, of which Wayne and I are the only members. In retrospect we were happy with the progress of the Seminary during our respective administrations.

Among many notable developments at Bangor during the eight years Wayne Glick was its president there were two which I found most impressive. Under his guidance, and with the help of Vice

President John Zehring, the school greatly strengthened its financial base both in terms of capital improvement and support by foundations, churches, trustees, alumni, and friends. Because of this first accomplishment, a second was made possible: the building of the new Ruth Rich Hutchins Center connecting the historic Chapel building with the Wellman Commons, which had been the gymnasium since 1895 and is now an attractive dining room and lounge area.

The Hutchins Center was built in honor and memory of the wife of Curtis Hutchins, prominent Bangor business leader and trustee benefactor of the Seminary during the Glick administration. The Center is a multi-purpose complex containing seminar and classrooms, a modern kitchen, an attractive lounge, and other facilities. The adjoining Wellman Commons is named for a Bangor family well-known for its contributions to the community, one of whose members, Alice Wellman, was a trustee of the Seminary for several years. It is a well-appointed auditorium, large enough to serve the school and the public for social functions such as the annual Convocation luncheon, and musical presentations of various kinds.

It has been my practice as President Emeritus to be available to my successors for assistance in fund-raising if they desired my help, to be as generous as possible in making family financial contributions to the school, to attend graduation and opening ceremonies of the Seminary when I was in Maine, and to speak upon request at special occasions such as recognition parties marking the retirement of former faculty colleagues like Dr. Burton H. Throckmorton, Jr. Otherwise, with one exception, I have been meticulous in avoiding any semblance of intervention in Seminary affairs. I did communicate with the President and with the Trustees chairman at the time preliminary plans for construction of the Hutchins Center proposed major changes in the David Nelson Beach Chapel so as to provide a passageway to the new building. Fortunately, they agreed with me that as a memorial to Bangor's second President, the Chapel should not be disturbed.

I do remember one other occasion when I was able to be of assistance to the Seminary on a matter very close to my heart. In

1986 the accreditation of Bangor by the Association of Theological Schools was scheduled for renewal after a period of ten years. When the Association decided to add a notation against the Seminary because it admitted to graduate study a higher-than-permissible percentage of non-college graduates, which was a long-standing unique feature of the "Bangor plan," President Glick asked for my counsel and assistance. I assured him that the Association was in error and, with my help, he was able to have the offending notation removed. The Association's Commission on Accrediting of 1986 had overlooked the fact that its counterpart in 1976 had given Bangor a special accredited status which exempted it from the notation concerning enrollment of non-college graduates. Having worked for twenty years to achieve this special status, I am gratified that it remains.

When Wayne Glick retired in 1986, the Seminary called its seventh President in the person of Dr. Malcolm L. Warford, who had for several years held the same position at Eden Theological Seminary in St. Louis, Missouri, another of the seven theological schools closely related to the United Church of Christ. Educated at Transylvania College (B.A.), Andover Newton Theological School (B.D.), and Columbia University (Ed.D.), Dr. Warford is also Dean and Professor of Pastoral Theology at Bangor. His wife Pamela has been on the faculty of the University of Maine and, in 1990, assumed a senior staff position at Husson College in Bangor.

Dr. Warford has been widely acclaimed by the alumni and other constituencies of Bangor Seminary as an excellent choice for leadership of the school in the final years of the twentieth century. He has consolidated the financial gains of the Glick administration and has widened the support given to the Seminary by national foundations such as the Lilly Endowment, Inc. He has strengthened a first-rate faculty by the addition in 1988 of an Old Testament scholar who is a woman and the first Roman Catholic on the full-time teaching staff. He has inaugurated a Doctor of Ministry program in Bangor and in Hanover, New Hampshire, as well as a Master of Theology program in Portland, Maine. Under Dr. Warford's leadership, the Seminary Board of Trustees has been restructured into a more effective governing body. I have been pleased to introduce my predecessor, once-removed, as a speaker in the Sarasota church where I am a member and where there is strong support of the Seminary.

The progress of the theological school at Bangor since I have retired has been due in considerable measure to the work of John Zehring as Vice President for Development during the administrations of my two predecessors. It is with John that I have often cooperated in seeking additional financial support for the school. One instance in which we have both taken considerable pleasure involved the changing of the Whittaker will in 1987. Shirley and I had planned to add a modest sum to the Whittaker Library Fund after our deaths, but John convinced us that it would be advantageous to all concerned if we made the contribution during our lifetime in the form of a Charitable Gift Annuity. He asked for and received our permission to use this change in an advertisement challenging others to follow our example. When the announcement was made public, the headline of the advertisement read: "Former President Fred Whittaker Just Removed Bangor Seminary From His Will — With Our Blessing!" John has told me that this promotional piece has been the most successful of all he has produced.

When I return to the Bangor campus now I find only five active staff members who were part of my administration. With the recent retirement and subsequent death of Dr. Stephen Szikszai after more than thirty years of distinctive service as George A. Gordon Professor of Old Testament, there are only two remaining faculty members who were my colleagues: One is Librarian Clifton G. Davis, who is now senior faculty member, and the other is Church History Professor Roland Wessels. Linda Cray has fulfilled all the promise I saw in her by rising to the position of Treasurer and Business Manager. Her husband, William, continues to give excellent care to the buildings and grounds as Director of Physical Plant. Carolyn Trundy is still the congenial and competent Director of Food Services. The presence of these five at the Seminary gives me a real sense of being there too.

As President Emeritus I have one perennial concern which is worthy of mention. Throughout my long tenure there was a continual struggle to increase enrollments. Significantly, this is a national trend. The United Church of Christ, in its summer 1990 newsletter "Keeping You Posted," reported that the number of Master of Divinity students within the denomination is at its lowest level since 1979. Several reasons are given for this situation, but I shall reserve reference to them until the next chapter of this book when I shall discuss some theological and sociological factors which I believe are involved. Here I want to include a recommendation made by me twice, without success, to the faculty and trustees of Bangor many years ago, which still has the potential of enlarging enrollment in the unique "Bangor plan."

The pre-theological program at Bangor offers non-college graduates a two-year course in the liberal arts and sciences, many of the subjects being taught by visiting faculty from the University of Maine. Most of these students then continue theological work for the Master of Divinity degree. However, no degree is granted at the end of the pre-theological study. Herein lies an opportunity to increase enrollments at Bangor. If the Seminary awarded an Associate in Arts degree for the two-year program, it could attract a much larger number of students for the A.A. degree and at the same time provide an expanded pool of potential registrants for the Master of Divinity degree.

There are two other elements missing from the Bangor scene today, the revival of which would enhance the service of the Seminary to its constituencies. One is "The Alumni Bulletin," a scholarly journal issued quarterly during the Moulton, Trust, and Whittaker administrations. In my time this publication was edited by Dr. Mervin Deems and Dr. Burton Throckmorton, and was widely appreciated by alumni and other readers. It provided full coverage of school events such as Convocation lectures as well as important addresses given by prominent speakers at Commencement, Baccalaureate, and fall opening services. My second comment has to do with the Convocation luncheon. For many years it was the social event of the winter season. Tickets were sold out shortly after announcements were mailed. Many prominent Bangor area citizens came to hear the famous lecturers tell their favorite stories in after-dinner fashion. All this is changed. When I attended the luncheon a few years ago, there was just the meal and an announcement of the speakers for next year. Most of those in attendance were alumni and other ministers. The lecturers were nowhere to be seen. Only glorious memories of an historic Seminary highlight experience remained.

One more event occurred just as I was about to finish this account of my retirement years. The "New Commons" building, where Shirley and I once lived in a student apartment and where our first child was conceived, is now known as "The Whittaker House." Today it serves as a dormitory for both single and married students. "Maine Hall," which was the dormitory in 1978 when I retired, was redesignated then in my honor as "Whittaker Hall." It is now the building which houses the Seminary offices and it has been given its original name of "Maine Hall." President Warford requested that I permit this change of nomenclature to be made, and I readily concurred. There is an amusing aspect to this story of "musical offices": In 1979 Dr. Glick moved the office of the President, along with other offices, from the Moulton Library to the former residence at 310 Union Street; later these offices were moved into the "New Commons." When the dormitory, then "Whittaker Hall," was more recently declared a fire hazard if used for student housing, it was renovated to become the Seminary office building. The President's office has now come full circle; it is back in the same building where it was located in 1952 when I began my administration

This final chapter of my relationship to Bangor Seminary must end. I close with an item which has brought me some sadness, but also some satisfaction. In its April 1989 issue, *Down East* magazine published an article entitled "Expanding the Vision," written by freelance writer Cynthia Bourgeault. The subheading reads: "Restored vigor and innovative teaching at the Bangor Theological Seminary prepare a new breed of student for small-town pastoring." Ninety percent of the article I have applauded enthusiastically, but there is one paragraph of misrepresentation which brought forth from me a response which the magazine published in its next edition.

"Expanding the Vision" properly extols the unique "Bangor plan" of theological education. The reader must be favorably impressed by the current status of the school which includes a "Small Church Leadership Program" sponsored by the Lilly Endowment, and a new Master of Theology course offered in Portland, Maine, to lay people not pursuing the traditional goal of ordination. But then there is the following statement, apparently based upon the opinion of recent students, which has no basis in fact: "A reputation for being practical, unassuming, and not too fussy about entrance requirements, will produce a continuing flow of warm bodies to the ministry, but it can also be a ticket to mediocrity. And for considerable periods in Bangor Seminary's long history — including the not-too-distant past — mediocrity has in fact been the status quo. Students from as recently as a decade ago remember the 'passive atmosphere' and 'Sunday-school level of teaching.'"

The reaction to this statement by alumni and former faculty members was not long in reaching me at my Florida home. I talked with the editor of the magazine by telephone and he readily agreed to give me space for a rebuttal. The June 1989 edition of *Down East* contains my two-column letter to the editor with the headline "Seminary Defender." Here are some excerpts, with particular reference to the alleged "mediocrity" during the "not-too-distant past":

This not-too-distant past surely includes the fifty-year span (1939-1989) during which I have been intimately involved in Seminary affairs as student, student-minister, alumnus, faculty member, and president. Let me assure you and your readers that there was no mediocrity at the Bangor Theological Seminary this particular half-century. The era in question includes the perfection of the famous "Bangor plan" for non-college graduates by my predecessor, Dr. Harry Trust. It is the period when many great religious leaders spoke at Bangor's annual Convocation week, as your article noted; mediocrity would not have attracted them to the Seminary. This was the time when the school so perfected its academic program that it achieved national accreditation. It was not mediocrity which brought to Bangor in the 1960's the largest number of students ever enrolled, and which saw the addition of two new faculty positions.

350

Speaking of faculty, let me add this testimony: The faculty at Bangor which taught me in the early 1940's was so competent that my later graduate studies at Yale University seemed easy in comparison. There is empirical evidence (national accreditation, for example) that Bangor faculties in the ensuing decades have been equally effective teachers. The description by the author of academic offerings at Bangor in the past as "Sunday-school level of teaching" is a caricature.

"Expanding the Vision" emphasizes the "reawakening" of Bangor Seminary. From observation over the the past fifty years, the school has been wide awake throughout this period. In addition to the many accomplishments already noted, it has built a new library and a new chapel, renovated its classroom building and its dormitory facilities, and paid its faculty and staff an ever-expanding living wage. Throughout this period it has never been in debt and has substantially improved its modest endowment. Much of this has been due to the wise and dedicated leadership of its board of trustees, especially its chairmen for more than thirty years, Willard S. Bass and Clarence W. Fuller, of blessed memory.

This letter should not be interpreted as in any way a criticism of my successors in the office of President of Bangor Theological Seminary. I greatly admire what they have done in "Expanding the Vision" they have inherited from their predecessors, dating back to the 19th century and Enoch Pond, the first President of the Seminary. I have intended only to correct a few of the misrepresentations about the Bangor Theological Seminary set forth in the April issue of your magazine.

Thus it is with satisfaction that I conclude this historic account of my long love affair with Bangor Theological Seminary by defending its mission and extolling its virtues. In the remaining two chapters I shall enter the realms of theology and sociology and set forth some of the beliefs and practices which I hold dear after more than three-quarters of a century of Christian living.

18.
Theological Analyst

Throughout the chapters of these memoirs I have disclosed many of the theological tenets which have guided my life, as well as the application of my faith to most of the social issues which have been prominent during my years in the twentieth century. Now in these reflective pages I shall assume the role, first, of theological analyst and then of social critic as I reveal in some depth the guiding factors and the practical applications thereof which have been hallmarks of my seventy-five years and more. The words I write are inspired by my experiences as Christian layman and clergyman, theological school professor and president, politician and community leader, husband and father.

Before I retired in 1978, it was my privilege to give the Commencement address to the graduating class. It was entitled "Little Less Than God — A Humanology for Tomorrow." I quote here the first two paragraphs of the address:

"When a president of Bangor Theological Seminary has a final opportunity to deliver the commencement address there is a momentous decision to be made: What should be the single most important message to proclaim on this significant occasion? Very little reflection was required to determine that, if I am to be true to my own lifelong faith and conviction, a good word must be spoken

352

tonight about the human moral potential. From 1939 to 1943, when the world was at war, I learned as a student in this school a theology which will now be shared with this year's new alumni and with this congregation. My teachers were 'the Harry Trust faculty,' of which I am the last remaining active member.

"During my graduate student days at Yale, thirty years ago and more, a theological professor once wrote on a term paper, 'You are an unrepentant and unreconstructed liberal.' I have tried to live up to this reputation ever since, for it is my opinion that a liberalism which retains its Christian character has the only Gospel which can lead modern men and women from the death of despair to the life of hope. Lest you accuse me of espousing humanism, I hasten to explain that the God who speaks through the Jewish-Christian scriptures, and who is supremely revealed in Jesus of Nazareth, is essential to my theology. Only in this context do I dare to suggest a 'humanology' for tomorrow. You will not find this word in the dictionary; it is coined specifically to describe the moral potential of creatures of God like you and me."

Many times during retirement years I have preached an amended version of the 1978 Commencement address in Maine and Florida churches; I paraphrase it now. *My humanology, "Little Less Than God," has a biblical base in both the Old and New Testaments. I have selected two passages because they represent for me a major biblical emphasis which I consider superior to other estimates of the human condition that I readily admit may also be found in the book of faith. However, in constructing a philosophy, a theology, or a humanology, one must make a choice if there are viable alternatives. I have chosen for my guidance the pronouncements of Psalm 8 and of Jesus in the Sermon on the Mount. Read them again (and do not be put off by the sexist language of these ancient spokesmen):*

"When I look at thy heavens, the work of thy fingers, the moon and the stars which thou hast established, what is man that thou are mindful of him? ... Yet thou hast made him little less than God, and dost crown him with glory and honor..." "You are the light of the world ... Let your light so shine before men that they may see your good works and give glory to your Father who is in heaven."

353

*These optimistic estimates of the human role in the divine econ-
omy have inspired much of my preaching and teaching during
thirty years at Bangor Seminary. The best summary elaboration of
their effect upon my thinking is found in the following excerpt from
an address entitled, "Man's Kingdom of God," which was one of a
series presented in 1974 to the mid-winter convocation sponsored
by the Florida Conference of the United Church of Christ:*

*"I believe in both the transcendence and immanence of God,
who is the Creator and Sustainer of the universe. I believe that
God partially reveals Himself in this world through the natural
order of physical being ('the moon and the stars which thou has
established'); through the spiritual and moral factors which
distinguish man from other creatures ('thou hast made him little
less than God'); and especially through the life and teachings of
Jesus Christ ('you are the light of the world'). For the full revelation
of God we humans must await the eternal life yet to come for all
who accept the gospel proclaimed by Christ. (The biblical text
here, of course, is John 3:16: 'For God so loved the world that he
gave his only Son, that whoever believes in him should not perish,
but have eternal life.')*

*"I believe, further, that Jesus Christ is the Son of God; but I
believe also that men and women are sons and daughters of God,
and that they differ from Christ in degree but not in kind. I believe
that the evident sinfulness of human beings is a relative
phenomenon; that as creatures of a good God we are essentially
good rather than evil; that we have the power through the free will
granted by the Creator to diminish progressively the control of sin
over our lives as we respond more and more to the gracious
influence of God's continuing and manifold revelations. I believe
also that the 'Christian way of life,' so-called, offers the most
satisfying and complete 'salvation,' to use a theological term, for
both the individual and the community; both must experience this
salvation before the 'kingdom of God on earth,' as envisioned by
Jesus himself, can become a reality. (The biblical text at this point
is what I call 'the other side of the gospel,' John 3:17: 'For God
sent the Son into the world not to condemn the world, but that the
world might be saved through him.')"*

In one of my most significant Chapel talks at the Seminary, given at the opening of the school year in September, 1972, I elaborated on this relationship between God and the world; here is a pertinent excerpt: "God has given men and women an assignment to fulfill — to establish the divine dominion or kingdom on earth — and the task will not be completed until human beings accept and achieve this responsibility. God will not intervene directly on our behalf; neither will he send Jesus Christ again to accomplish the divine purpose. This does not mean that God is a passive factor in the drama of human redemption. God has acted in the past: through the physical creation, including the creation of men and women with moral and spiritual sensibilities; through the revelation of His will and way in the Hebrew prophets; and through the example of human potential in Jesus of Nazareth. God also acts today: through the continuing creative process and the renewing of human powers by the Holy Spirit."

At first glance, my "humanology" may seem hopelessly naive or, at best, a fanciful delusion; perhaps, even sacrilegious. Here are some questions I have asked myself: Is it not true that the world is on the brink of its greatest disaster through international nuclear warfare? (An affirmative response seemed more likely in 1972 when I first raised the query than it does as I reflect upon it in 1991.) Are not the lofty professions of medicine, the law, and education sinking to an unprecedented low point in public esteem? Are not elected officials and appointed government leaders being widely denigrated as "politicians" and "bureaucrats"? Is not the religious ideal of the family unit being destroyed by easy divorce and widespread acceptance of pre-marital and extra-marital relationships, even among those who purport to be leaders of the church? Has not the "work ethic" been largely replaced by the concept that "the world owes me a living"? Does not the increasing abuse of alcohol and other drugs signify the low estate of the contemporary human condition? And is there any hope of providing the spiritual and material resources required by a kingdom of God on earth when church members withhold their tithes, and citizens decline to pay equitable taxes?

Against all these negatives, however, there is a positive —

especially for those who profess to be inheritors of the Jewish-Christian tradition. For every sin there is a virtue. Our Creator has given us a choice. We can live up to our God-given potential, or we can deny our birthright. Jesus announced to his followers, "You are the light of the world!" Yet this challenge issued to the first disciples is largely ignored by Christians today. As a student of the history of Christianity I have been continually and increasingly dismayed by the emphasis placed upon human sinfulness rather than upon the human potential for righteousness. Ecclesiastical empires have been built, and multitudes have been held in religious slavery over many centuries, by the proclamation of a theology which portrays men and women as helpless sinners instead of "the light of the world," instead of creatures "little less than God."

In my considered judgment, God is degraded by the notion that man is essentially or basically a sinner. To be sure, sin is an historical fact of human life, but men and women have the God-given power, the potential, to overcome sin — yes, even to be morally "perfect," as Jesus told his early followers on the mountainside. The conclusive word on human sinfulness is contained in John's gospel when Jesus speaks to the woman accused of adultery: "Neither do I condemn you; go, and do not sin again!" (John 8:11) Yet in many contemporary churches, including my own United Church of Christ, the worshippers are led each Sunday through the ritual of a prayer of confession, followed by an assurance from the minister in the name of Jesus Christ that their sins are forgiven. This suggests to me that as Christians we are free to continue our daily sinning so long as we make a confession each Sunday and receive a weekly absolution. This is not the message Jesus gave to the adulterous woman!

In the final chapter of my book I shall become a social critic and indicate in various ways how this doctrine of Jesus, "do not sin again," may be applied to major contemporary ethical problems. At this point I continue the theological analysis by answering the question, how did the insistence upon intrinsic human sinfulness become orthodox doctrine? *The classical historical statement of the so-called human "plight" is set forth in the seventh chapter of Paul's letter to the Romans when he cries out: "I can will what is right, but I cannot do it. For I do not do the good I want, but the evil I do not want is what I do." (Romans 7:18,19) The Pauline idea that the taint of Adam's sin had been transmitted to all of his descendents, and had resulted in an impairment of man's will so that he could not choose the good over the evil, was later elaborated in the fifth century by the orthodox Bishop of Hippo, Augustine. It was restated by churchmen Anselm of Canterbury and Bernard of Clairvaux during the scholasticism of the Middle Ages, and was transmitted to Protestantism by the reformer John Calvin of Geneva in the sixteenth century.*

This pessimistic teaching concerning human moral capabilities has not gone unchallenged in any age. Alternative points of view stretch through the centuries from Jesus to Pelagius to Abelard to Erasmus. It was a contemporary of Augustine and a member of a British monastic order, Pelagius by name, who questioned the validity of the Pauline-Augustinian theory of original sin. The Pelagians argued that Adam's sin injured only him and not the human race; that every child is born as free as Adam was before the fall, and can choose to do what is morally right; and that a human being can fully keep God's commandments. God's grace is involved, to be sure, but for the Pelagians it is made manifest in the free will given at the time of human creation, in the proclamation of God's law as a guide for human behavior, and in the sending of Jesus Christ as a teacher and example to men and women in choosing the good life. A favored principle of the Pelagian "heresy" was that God does not ask his creatures to do what they are unable to do.

In the twelfth century another unorthodox one, Abelard of Brittany, took up the cause of liberal Christianity against the more prosaic teachings of his colleagues Anselm and Bernard. Abelard is popularly remembered for his famous love affair with Eloise, but he deserves applause as the great scholastic leader who attracted thousands of students from all over Europe to hear his lectures in Paris. Like Pelagius, Abelard also rejected Augustine's view of original sin. He believed that human beings have weaknesses which incline them toward wrong-doing, but that they are also endowed by God with tendencies toward good. By the divine gift of reason, men and women are empowered to discover what is good, and they can then employ their wills to follow the good.

Abelard held that Anselm was in error on the doctrine of the atonement when he declared that the death of Christ on the cross was a necessary satisfaction to God so that He could forgive the sins of humanity. Forgiveness is an act of grace, and it is freely given without demand for compensation. God forgave sins before the time of Jesus' birth. So Abelard believed. The reconciliation between God and His creatures is effected in the Christian era by the response which is evoked in the human heart when men and women see the divine love personified in Jesus Christ. For in Christ we behold what we ourselves should be — "little less than God"; "the light of the world" — and by this contrast we are brought to a realization of our sinful ways; this self-knowledge releases within the human being a new love for God and a desire to obey the divine commandments. Thus Abelard gives to the bewildered Christian today a basis for revitalized faith in God, a sense of human dignity in relationship to the Creator, and an incentive for good works done for the glory of God.

When the Pauline-Augustinian-Anselmic line of thought concerning human sinfulness was carried over into Protestantism by the reformer John Calvin, there was again an opposing point of view ready to meet it. Erasmus of Rotterdam is described by historian Kenneth Scott Latourette as the "prince of Christian humanists." Erasmus sincerely desired the reformation of the church and wished to see it purged of superstition through the use of intelligence and a return to the ethical teachings of Jesus. His approach to religious belief was of a practical nature and he cherished the conviction that through the use of human reason both church and society could be vastly improved.

Before concluding this historical journey toward a "Humanology for Tomorrow," there is one other stop along the way which I have found spiritually and intellectually refreshing for my own life. Come with me for a moment to the city of Hartford in Connecticut of a hundred years ago and more. There lived Horace Bushnell, theologian-pastor of a local church for a quarter of a century. During his long ministry Bushnell became the liberator of the New

England theology, with its strong Augustinian flavor, which he saw was out of tune with the temper of the age and with the actual experience of those who came under his influence. While he is remembered best for his book entitled Christian Nurture, *which is a classic in the field of religious education, there is among his several other works a volume called* The Vicarious Sacrifice, *which has left me indebted to him for an idea central to my own belief and practice.*

Following the theme which stretches to him from Pelagius and Abelard, Bushnell refutes the teaching that Christ takes all the sins of the world upon himself and by his death redeems the world. It is obvious that the sins are still with us and that the world has not been redeemed. Instead, Bushnell proclaims that there is a universal obligation upon all Christians to enter into the life of Christ, there to suffer with Christ, and thus to become one with him and God. His incisive and prophetic conclusion is that — to quote him directly — "Christ does nothing for a man beyond what the man himself is required to do for other men; it is exactly at this point that the world is redeemed."

As I said to the graduating class at Bangor Seminary in my final commencement address in 1978, and as I have told many churchgoers since who have listened to my sermon "Little Less Than God," the decision to accept my optimistic view of the human moral condition is an option which is available to every human being. Here are my exact words:

As you face the manifold individual and social problems of the late twentieth century you may decide that the orthodox way — dependence upon God to establish His own kingdom on earth — is the only salvation for hopelessly sinful human beings. You may agree with the black father of five children whose pitiful story was told on a national television newscast during the latter years of the war in Southeast Asia. His home had just been burned to the ground during a racial riot. He had lost his job because of a strike in the automobile industry. His younger children were out of school because the teachers were involved in a labor dispute. And he had just received word that his oldest son had been killed in Viet Nam. When he was asked by a reporter how he felt about all the troubles

359

which had come to him, his response was: "I'll just have to depend upon 'the Man upstairs'."

Or you may choose, if you will, the more difficult way suggested by unorthodox religious leaders in many different centuries. You may decide that your mission is to uphold by precept and example the humanology that establishing the earthly kingdom depends upon the cooperation of the One upstairs and all those who live downstairs. This is the way proclaimed by a great national martyred president, John F. Kennedy, in his unforgettable inaugural address: "Here on earth, God's work must truly be our own." This is the way of the Psalmist who described us mortals as "little less than God." This is the way of Jesus who called his disciples "the light of the world." This is my way. May it be your way!

When I assume the role of social critic in the next chapter I shall apply the theology stated above to ways and means of solving some of the major personal problems of the day, such as drug addiction, abortion, marriage infidelity, and sexual relationships.

Even as the theology set forth in "Little Less Than God" is a basis for personal ethics, so does a reflective sermon of mine created during retirement years illustrate a theological premise pertinent to the most significant corporate moral problem of our world society: international warfare. Entitled "Father Forgive," it was preached in my home church, First Congregational United Church of Christ in Sarasota, Florida, on January 22, 1984. Its origin dates back to the fall of 1983, as indicated in a previous chapter of this book, when my wife and I visited in Coventry, England, and were inspired by the new cathedral built next to the ruins of the old church which was destroyed by German firebombs in 1940.

"Father Forgive" are the two words carved in the still-standing old cathedral wall. Before the wall is an altar featuring a "Cross of Nails" fashioned from the hand-forged nails which fell to the floor of the church when the roof beams burned and disintegrated during the bombing. From this distinctive altar has come a program sponsored by the restored Coventry Cathedral which has sought to establish links of fellowship with worship centers in many lands to study means of Christian reconciliation in a divided world. Crosses of Nails have been presented to such centers in Oslo, Hamburg,

Kiel, Munster, Berlin, Dresden, Volvograd, as well as to similar centers in Africa, Asia, the United States, Canada, and Australia.

This multi-national effort at peace-making has been guided by the scriptural words on the old cathedral wall: "Father Forgive." However, reconciliation in a divided world could never have been achieved by the doctrine of "Father, forgive them, for they know not what they do," which at first glance would be the obvious interpretation of the inscription. Rather, Coventry Cathedral adopted another of the famous teachings of Jesus: "Father ... forgive us ... as we also have forgiven ... for if you forgive people their trespasses, your heavenly Father also will forgive you...."

As I said in my sermon, "The true meaning of repentance and the best hope of reconciliation lies not in the prayer, 'Father, forgive THEM.' These high Christian ideals, repentance and reconciliation, can be achieved only through the prayer, 'Father, forgive US!'" It is instructive to examine how this God-inspired principle governed the rebuilding of Coventry Cathedral. Christians in Coventry were challenged to say and do something dramatic about the situation of division and hatred which followed the destruction of the city and its cathedral.

As a beginning experiment, a small International Centre was established in 1960 within the walls of the still unfinished new cathedral. The Centre was furnished by an anonymous German citizen who had lost his entire family in an air-raid on Berlin. The facility was extended by the work of a team of sixteen young Germans who gave up paid employment for six months, came to Coventry with large sums of money contributed by individual Christians throughout Germany, and built for the International Centre a reception room, a lounge, a canteen, a library, and an oratory.

This act of repentance by a group of German youth was one of the most significant enterprises of reconciliation ever conducted in Great Britain. It was a prime expression of the sermon theme: "Father Forgive" — not them, but US. More than that, it was the first of many examples of international repentance without which the new Coventry Cathedral could not have been built. During the construction of the great church, gifts arrived from near and far as shares in this process of reconciliation. To name but a few, there was a black ebony crucifix from Tanganyika, from China a carved piece of the font of a church destroyed by Japanese bombers, from Germany money to pay for the Cathedral library and several stained glass windows, from Hong Kong a gift of communion vestments, from Sweden the marble mosaic floor for one of the chapels, and from Canada ten thousand pounds toward the cost of an organ.

Another aspect of reconciliation — the first being international — to which the Coventry Cathedral dedicated itself was ecclesiastical. In 1944 a plan for Christian unity was launched. Out of the suffering of the war the idea was born that a place in the new cathedral could provide the center around which Christians of different denominations would grow together by mutual understanding, common prayer, and join service in the community. The idea eventually took form in a Chapel of Unity and its adjacent Christian Service Centre, out of which emanated a broad program of activities led by the cathedral staff in such areas as industry and commerce, education, and social services, music and the arts, ministry to youth, liturgy, and international affairs.

The Declaration of the Joint Council administering the Chapel and the Centre was signed on the fifth anniversary of the destruction of the cathedral — November 14, 1945. It is instructive to hear the opening words of the Declaration: "We who belonging to different Christian communions now set apart this place as a Chapel of Unity for the worship of God, acknowledge our Lord Jesus Christ as God and Saviour of the whole world ... We believe that He has guided us to establish for His people a Christian Service Centre. We also believe that our undertaking will be in vain unless we seek His guidance, and it is for this purpose that we hallow this Chapel of Unity...."

Two lessons can be learned from the narrative of Coventry just unfolded. One is the theological truth that as Christians our primary concern must be God's "whole world" — not just a self-centered interest in a local church, the city or state in which we live, or in the United States of America. The second truth is that our divided world is desperately in need of reconciliation, a reconciliation which demands the kind of repentance represented by the prayer "Father Forgive" — forgive US, not them.

Consider first the "whole world" concept epitomized by the Declaration of Coventry. Not long ago I heard the world-famous evangelist Billy Graham answer the question posed by a television interviewer, "How has your mind changed in the past twenty years?" While he is not my favorite theologian, Graham responded with a Christian truth which I trust he is repeating in all of his crusades: "I have come to realize that the United States of America is not the kingdom of God. The kingdom encompasses all of humanity."

It is difficult for Americans to concede that the United States is not the most favored nation in the sight of God. Political patriotism demands that we believe America to be a "superpower" and "No. 1" among nations. But Christian faith requires that we accept the truth we are one among many in the sight of the God of the "whole world." Patriotism, because it is an emotional loyalty shared by the citizens of every sovereign nation on earth, has led the world to the brink of annihilation during our lifetime. While the tension has eased somewhat at the beginning of the 1990's, our best hope of achieving a true international peace lies in universal acceptance of the Coventry theology that our God is the God of all human beings throughout the world.

The "whole world" theology of Coventry gave birth to the cathedral's "Ministry of International Reconciliation." Through this ministry many of the people of Germany and England forgave one another for the horrors of World War II, and in repentance, helped to rebuild the bombed-out church. During the same period there evolved a plan among the war-weary nations of the world which led to the formation in 1945 of the United Nations, an organization to promote peace and international security.

But there was a fatal flaw in the United National Charter because of the veto power granted to five of the major sovereign nations in the Security Council, including the United States and the Soviet Union. We are still reaping the harvest of that tragic mistake. Instead of a UN police force to sustain international reconciliation under the "whole world" concept of Coventry, there have been a series of futile and enormously costly attempts to achieve universal peace through unilateral and multilateral military confrontations in such places as western Europe, the Middle East, the Far East, and Central America.

After a lifetime as a minister of the Gospel, a professor of religious history, and an activist in the political arena, I still search in my reflective years with some optimism for ways and means of collectively reconciling our world-wide society. I explore here a bit further the second truth I discovered in my Coventry experience: that redemption and reconciliation demand the kind of repentance found in the prayer "Father forgive, forgive US — not forgive them."

As American citizens of Christian persuasion, of what should we repent and ask God's forgiveness? We can ask divine forgiveness as a nation for ignoring the role of the United Nations as a peace-keeping force in such wartorn areas as Viet Nam and, more recently, in Lebanon and Central America. On its own initiative, the United States has engaged in acts of war against Nicaragua, Libya, and Panama without even the formality of a declaration of war by the Congress, as required by the Constitution. In August of 1990 President George Bush, acting as Commander-in-Chief, deployed the nation's military power in Saudi Arabia in anticipation of possible further territorial expansion by Iraq. While the Security Council of the United Nations, strengthened by the new cooperation of the Soviet Union, invoked political and economic sanctions against Iraq for its invasion of Kuwait, this international body did not authorize military action by a UN police force. It was the Soviet Union, rather than the United States, which gave support to the United Nations by declining to send military forces to Saudi Arabia until a UN police force was authorized by the Security Council. Father, forgive US!

While this chapter of my memoirs is designed primarily to present some of my major views as a theological analyst, in the interest of continuity I digress momentarily to write as a social critic. For forty-five years, since the United Nations organization was established in 1945, I have stated publicly my opinion that acts of war among the nations should no longer be tolerated, but that future disputes requiring military action should be settled by a United Nations police force. Until now, unfortunately, this was not possible because of the veto power given by the UN charter to the permanent members of the Security Council. With the end of the "cold war" between the United States and the Soviet Union, an ideal opportunity was at hand to eliminate this veto power by amending the UN charter. The offer of the Soviet Union to participate in a UN police force designed to settle the dispute between Iraq and Kuwait was an act of statesmanship which signified the possibility of a whole new relationship among the members of the United Nations. The United States should have welcomed this opportunity to establish a UN police force in Saudi Arabia. By so doing, it would have been true to the "whole world" theological concept of the Declaration of Coventry. Instead, a coalition of nations engaged in "Desert Storm" under American leadership rather than under the flag of the United Nations.

One other major theological proposition deserves enunciation before this chapter ends. Throughout my professional career I have given special attention to the relationship between church and state as two of the most significant instrumentalities affecting human life. In fact, I have devoted much of my time and talent to leadership roles in the areas of religion and politics, which are the principal concerns, respectively, of the church and the state. More than once, I confess, I have asked myself: Given an opportunity to begin again, would I have been primarily a churchman or a statesman? In my personal theology the two roles are of equal significance. This is made manifest in one of the five lectures, referred to earlier, which I presented at a Florida religious conference in 1974 under the theme, "Church and State Re-examined."

The final lecture of the series was entitled "The Church in Context." I paraphrase first one of its opening statements: My study of history has convinced me that the church is one among other voluntary associations created by human beings in response to their needs of a physical, social, and spiritual nature. Other associations similarly established may be described simply by the common terms, school and state. I do not suggest that God is not involved in the formation of these institutions. God creates men and women and He is, therefore, the primary cause of all human activity, but He creates them with the power to make voluntary decisions affecting human earthly destiny; thus, men and women are the secondary but vital causes of much that constitutes temporal history. The church is not an end in itself, but a means to an end. The end is the establishment of the kingdom of God on earth. But the church is not the only means to this end. Of equal importance are the school and the state. It is my thesis that the church is to be understood only in this perspective or in this context.

In my lecture I went on to point out that the Christian, in order to be spiritually prepared to deal with the problems of temporal living, must have a strong belief that when the individual's earthly time is over, God's care will continue eternally. While the ministrations and worship of the church should aid in the development of such a faith, the church has no God-given authority to guarantee the gift of immortality to its members in return for their obedience and devotion. In the Christian dispensation eternal life is a blessing bestowed directly by God upon those who believe in His abiding love as revealed in and through Jesus Christ. The chief business of the church in the world is to dramatize this revelation for all who will receive it, and then to organize grateful believers as effective workers in God's earthly kingdom. When the church so functions as a means to an end in cooperation with other agencies such as the school and the state, it is in truth the church in context.

When thinking about the church in theological terms it is important to emphasize the central significance of the laity. All too slowly have the ordained clergy and the theological professors who train them acknowledged that the lay members constitute the best hope for today and tomorrow that the institutional church will accept its divine commission as an agency of the kingdom of God on earth. The tendency is all too prevalent to think of the organized church in terms of its clerical leadership. Many times during my career I have been told that under the doctrine of the separation of Church and State, and because I am an ordained minister as well as a seminary president, I should not seek to serve in political office. My response has been: "As a clergyman I am not to be considered 'Church' any more than the Christian lay person; the laity and the clergy have an equal right and responsibility to serve the State."

As long ago as 1954, at its meeting in Evanston, Illinois, the

World Council of Churches issued the following pertinent challenge to the laity: "Our world is characterized by unprecedented technical, organizational and scientific achievements, and at the same time by disillusionments, cynicism and fear of final destruction. The church must not become an escape for those who do not dare to look such a world in the face. The time has come to make the ministry of the laity explicit, visible and active in the world. The real battles of the faith today are being fought in shops, factories, offices and farms; in political parties and government agencies; in countless homes and schools; in the press, radio and television; and in the relationships of nations. Very often it is said that the church should 'go into these spheres'; but the fact is that the church is already in these spheres in the persons of its laity."

This is an appropriate place to re-introduce an item reported in an earlier chapter concerning the decrease of enrollments in American theological schools to the lowest level since 1979. An article in the summer 1990 newsletter of the United Church of Christ, "Keeping You Posted," reported that among the reasons for this decline, according to an officer of the Association of Theological Schools, was the following: "The profession of ministry is not respected as it used to be. And the values associated with parish ministry are considered less important by today's society."

When I chose to leave a career with the railroad in favor of the vocation of Christian ministry more than fifty years ago, I was certain that the choice was a promising one. I still believe it was a wise decision. But today I am disappointed that the institutional church has declined in its influence and has not reached its potential as an instrument of God's earthly purposes. I am convinced that the reported diminution of respect and importance suffered by the parish ministry is due primarily to the failure of many professional leaders of the church to deal effectively with the major social problems which plague the latter part of the twentieth century. The church is still dominated by a concern for the eternal welfare of its members while leaving them without sufficient instruction and inspiration regarding the establishment of a good life in this world.

Faith without works is dead, the Bible tells us. Eternal life is a gift of God received by faith. Earthly life places a responsibility on believers to be achieved by good works. Too many parish ministers are timid about challenging the laity to apply Christian principles to social problems. In the United States the traditional "separation" of Church and State, which properly protects the Church from domination by the State, has been erroneously interpreted to mean that the Church has no right or responsibility to make its influence felt upon affairs of State. Much of the blame for this situation can rightly be placed upon the seminaries and the Association of Theological Schools. A pertinent illustration, reported in an earlier chapter of this book, is the decision of the Association not to establish a branch office in Washington for the purpose of communication and cooperation with government agencies. The rationale for this decision was that, in the eyes of some conservative members of the Association, it would be a violation of Church-State separation.

I close this chapter on my role as a theological analyst by elaborating upon a theme which has been the subject of many sermons and addresses during both my active and retirement years. "Religion and the Public Schools" has received a positive and appreciative response wherever it has been presented. This topic is an excellent expression of my theological doctrine, stated earlier in this chapter, that the church, the state, and the school are agencies developed by human beings under divine inspiration as instruments for the advancement of God's kingdom on earth.

Many of the people who have heard my address on "Religion and the Public Schools" have expressed surprise when they learned that there is a widespread program of teaching "about" religion in American high schools sponsored and promoted by the National Council on Religion and Public Education, with headquarters in Lawrence, Kansas. These listeners have usually been aware of the decision entitled "Abington School District vs. Schempp" by the United States Supreme Court in 1963, which prohibited prayer and Bible reading in the public schools. However, there is a positive aspect of this decision not so widely known and appreciated; it was set forth by Justices Goldberg and Clark in these words: "The Court would recognize the propriety ... of teaching *about* religion, as distinguished from the teaching *of* religion, in the public schools

... One's education is not complete without a study of comparative religion or the history of religion and its relationship to the advancement of civilization ... thus the Bible is worthy of study for its literary and history qualities. Nothing we have said here indicates that such a study of the Bible or of religion ... may not be effected consistently with the First Amendment of the Constitution...."

Many states have taken advantage of the Supreme Court decision by preparing curriculum material which includes religion as an item of study in connection with other related subjects. In Florida, for example, the state department of education has prepared three courses for high school students taking Social Studies which cover Old Testament Bible History, New Testament Bible History, and World Religions. The course in World Religions, to use one significant illustration, has this stated purpose: "To provide students the opportunity to acquire an understanding of the ways people in different cultures satisfy their spiritual needs ... the importance that has been attached to religion in people's lives ... and the relationship between religion and other social institutions."

Major content of the course includes a study of the principal living religious traditions and practices such as Hinduism, Buddhism, Confucianism, Taoism, Judaism, Islam, and Christianity. The Florida Department of Education's publication describing this course indicates that upon its completion the student will be able to identify the criteria upon which religious beliefs are based, analyze the relationships between religious and social institutions; trace the development of the world's major living religions and know the similarities and differences among them; synthesize information and ideas from conflicting religious beliefs; and interpret the development of a society as reflected by religious beliefs.

In a pluralistic American society — and in a world where events in the Near East, India, Japan, China, and other nations different from our own are as close as our television sets — enlightened citizens should vigorously support the teaching about religion in the public schools. Think of the long-range consequences: High school students who choose to study "World Religions" will have a working knowledge of the history and major teachings of Judaism, Islam, Christianity and other significant faiths. This process will eventually produce a large body of American citizens who are religiously literate, and thus well prepared to deal with the opportunities and problems of our complex world society. Gone will be much of the ignorance which now produces anti-Semitism, tension between Roman Catholics and Protestants, antagonisms among liberal and conservative Christians, and misunderstandings about the Moslem, Hindu, and Buddhist faiths.

Only those with an unbiased knowledge of the principal religions of the world will be able to act as mediators in Israeli-Arab and Arab-Arab conflicts, Latin American relations, problems in Northern Ireland, and racial tensions in South Africa. These words are written as a potentially explosive situation is developing in the Middle East as the result of intermingling sociological, economic, and religious factors. Thus there is no more meaningful way of my ending this chapter as a theological analyst than by emphasizing the need for increasing understanding of world religions.

19.
Social Critic

In this final chapter I shall present the highlights of my avocational witness as a social critic. Throughout the course of my active career and my retirement years I have considered it important to apply Christian faith to the multitude of personal and corporate problems which have stymied individuals in a quest for fulfillment of their moral potential, and have prevented the human community from growth toward the ideal of the kingdom of God. My views have been expressed in various forms such as sermons, public addresses, newspaper guest columns, and letters to editors.

I begin with one of the most controversial issues of the day: abortion. The following paragraphs contain a paraphrasing of an article published in the *Bangor Daily News* on July 18, 1989, after the U.S. Supreme Court decision permitting the several states to enact their own laws regarding abortion. The newspaper gave the article a headline reading, "Hardline positions endanger 'One nation, under God, indivisible.'"

The recent Supreme Court decision on abortion has destroyed the cherished concept of national unity set forth in the pledge of allegiance to the flag. On this vital and emotional issue the United States of American now has the legal potential of becoming fifty separate states, each with the sovereign right to establish by statute its own rules and regulations on abortion as determined by its elected representatives in the several state legislatures.

With the issue now politicized, a woman's choice to have an abortion under the court decision in Roe vs. Wade will soon depend upon action taken in state capitols from Maine to Hawaii, from Alaska to Florida. No longer will the U.S.A. be "one nation, under God, indivisible." Instead there will be a divided nation under state political mandates. I fear that our beloved country will be torn asunder unless a compromise position on abortion can be found. As one who has had experience as both a theologian and a politician, I am searching for such a compromise.

As a theological professor and ordained minister, my basic instincts and my acquired moral standards tell me that abortion should be the last alternative available to a pregnant woman. Thus I have considerable sympathy for the "pro-life" position. However, I do not believe that the life of the individual begins at conception, or that the fetus in the first three months of pregnancy has a right to live equal to the right of the mother to have an abortion for good and sufficient reasons. In this respect I agree with the Supreme Court decision in Roe vs. Wade. A compromise is needed at this point between "pro-life" and "pro-choice."

As a citizen and politician I applauded the 1973 court decision because I felt that it protected a valid right of the woman to choose abortion during the first trimester of pregnancy. It established a national policy on a divisive social issue. It eliminated the necessity of a woman having to travel from state to state in search of a legal abortion. It protected the right of a woman living in poverty to end an unwanted pregnancy with the assistance of public funds and medical facilities. It meant that women no longer needed to resort to illegal or unsanitary abortion procedures.

In my search for compromise I do not defend the "pro-choice" position without reservations. Ideally, the woman and the man involved should recognize that their first "choice," if they do not wish to conceive a child, is to abstain from sexual intercourse unless anti-pregnancy measures are employed. Realistically, when unwanted pregnancy becomes a fact, another kind of "choice" is the only alternative. If I were the spiritual counselor I would

372

certainly urge the mother to carry the child through birth and then offer it for adoption. Emphasis upon adoption rather than abortion is one of the key elements of a possible compromise. "Pro-choice" advocates should be very flexible at this point.

There is room for compromise in another way. My support of Roe vs. Wade was predicated in the early years after the decision by the rationale then prevalent that the choice of abortion in the first trimester of pregnancy would be made not by the woman alone but by consensus reached among four parties after careful consideration of all the alternatives. In addition to the mother, a key participant in the decision-making process would be the doctor, but also taking part would be the man involved, whether husband or not, and a spiritual adviser.

The choice of abortion should not be made in isolation by the mother, or by the mother and doctor in tandem, except in the case of rape, incest, or danger to the life of the mother. Abortion should never be an instrument of birth control. The "pro-choice" movement should accentuate the emphasis upon choice by consensus. The "pro-life" advocates should recognize the validity of rape, incest, and danger to the mother as reasons for the abortion procedure, and should relinquish their theologically questionable doctrine which proclaims that the life of a new human being begins at conception.

Unless both protagonists in the abortion struggle are willing to ameliorate their hardline positions, the United States of America cannot be "one nation, under God, indivisible." As one who has been involved in practical politics at the local, state, and national level, I shudder at the inherent danger to our nation if the abortion issue is left in the hands of state legislatures. Other major issues, which rightfully belong in the political domain, will be neglected as the struggle over abortion takes center stage. As a theologian, I am enough of an optimist and a liberal to believe in the ability of human beings to use the God-given powers of reason to resolve the social crisis caused by the abortion debate.

Another major social issue upon which I have expressed my opinion countless times during the past quarter-century is taxation. Since my days as a Maine state senator in 1963 I have been a vocal proponent of the personal income tax, at both the state and national level, as the fairest of all government levies. On November 12, 1987, it was my privilege to present an essay on this subject in Florida before the Sarasota Institute of Lifetime Learning as it celebrated the bicentennial of the Constitution of the United States. Entitled "Tithes and Taxes," I record below excerpts from this address as indicative of my long-held views on this important matter.

The Constitution of the United States, which we celebrate in this series of lectures, sets forth in the preamble a litany of goals for our nation which I call to remembrance as a prelude to my essay on "Tithes and Taxes." The stated Constitutional aims are: to form a more perfect Union; to establish Justice; to insure domestic Tranquillity; to provide for the Common Defence; to promote the General Welfare; and to secure the Blessings of Liberty to ourselves and our Posterity....

The concept of the "separation of Church and State" needs to be interpreted properly if it is to be a ruling principle of American society today. My own studies, and my own experiences in religious and political activities, have convinced me that the contemporary problems which beset the cultural fabric of our nation today can best be resolved by the cooperation rather than the separation of the spiritual and secular powers which we designate as "Church" and "State." Thus I use the terms "tithes" and "taxes" as symbolic of these two distinctive but related powers....

For fifty years my activities as a minister, educator, politician and administrator have involved fund-raising for the mission of the Church and for the social agenda of the State. My efforts have been both sacred and secular, both religious and political. As a teacher of ecclesiastical history I have been keenly aware of the Jewish-Christian tradition as a source of inspiration and guidance. The concept of tithing is set forth both in the Old Testament and the New Testament scriptures. In the book of Genesis the patriarch Jacob promises his God that "of all you givest me I will give the tenth to thee." (Genesis 28:20-22) The gospel of Luke records the generosity of the Pharisee: "I give tithes of all that I get." (Luke 18:12)....

The giving of tithes is first of all a religious act of thanksgiving through which men and women of faith return to their Creator a portion of the wealth with which they have been blessed. It is a voluntary act influenced by conscience or spirituality, not by the requirements of the civil law ... The giving of tithes is more than donating money to a religious organization. Very few of us give a tenth of our income to a church or synagogue. However, we do move closer to the ten percent goal if we include the dollars we contribute to other social service agencies, to organizations concerned with public health problems, and to the educational institutions from which we have graduated....

Tithing for religious and secular purposes is important in the quest for fulfillment of the ideals set forth in the preamble to the Constitution: a more perfect union, justice, domestic tranquility, common defence, the general welfare, and the blessings of liberty. But these ideals cannot be achieved by tithes alone. There must also be taxes! ... Taxes are the secular counterpart of religious tithes! I refer here to equitable taxes properly assessed and spent by duly authorized governing bodies. It is time for the American people to reassess an almost universal negativism about taxation!.....

Taxes, like tithes, are referred to in the Bible. Both Jesus of Nazareth and the apostle Paul speak of taxes in a way which should be a guideline for men and women today. In the gospel of Matthew Jesus is asked by the Pharisees: "Is it lawful to pay taxes to Caesar?" His reply was this: "Render to Caesar the things that are Caesar's and to God the things that are God's" (Matthew 22:17,21). Interpretations of this episode have varied through the years. Some scholars have made a sharp distinction between the sacred tithe and the secular tax. Others have held that citizens have obligations to both Caesar and God. The latter view is held by the apostle Paul in his letter to the Romans, wherein he writes: "Let every person be subject to the governing authorities. For there is no authority except from God ... the authorities are ministers of God ... pay all of them their dues, taxes to whom taxes are due, revenue to whom revenue is due ..." (Romans 13:1,6,7) It is the position of Paul which I have espoused for my own in the matter of taxes....

Early in my five-year period as an elected officer of local and state government in Maine, as I have indicated in an early chapter of these memoirs, it became obvious to me that the social needs of the community could be met adequately only through the assessment of equitable taxes. The state of Maine was desperately in need of additional revenue for the maintenance of its extended highway system, for the expansion of its university into outlying geographical areas, for the improvement of its mental health institutions, for the support of its public schools at the elementary and secondary levels, and for welfare assistance to its poor and homeless. The only broad-based state tax was a five percent sales assessment. To raise this levy would have been regressive and would have imposed an additional burden upon low-income families. As a state senator I became one of the leaders within the legislature to introduce a modest state income tax. After two years of effort it was passed by a narrow margin. It has proved to be a blessing for Maine both then and since, for it is the fairest of all taxes in that it is based upon ability to pay. Two years after the income tax was inaugurated an attempt was made by statewide referendum to rescind the levy. It was reaffirmed by a vote of more than two to one, and it has now been in effect for thirty-five years....

A discussion of "Tithes and Taxes" cannot end without a consideration of the national dilemma created by a huge federal deficit, an unfavorable trade balance, and the growing crisis in the fields of education, health protection, agricultural sustenance, and general welfare needs. The dilemma is best illustrated by the irrationality of executive and legislative programs which give priority to so-called national defense against foreign antagonists while failing to mount an all-out assault upon the enemies within such as the mushrooming drug abuse and AIDS epidemics. Meanwhile, a bipartisan committee of Congress is engaged in a tortuous, and so far unsuccessful attempt, to cooperate with the President in reducing the federal deficit. A solution to this problem demands an increase in the federal income tax!

Throughout half a century of fund-raising by "Tithes and Taxes" it has been a cardinal rule of mine that I have no right to ask others to make contributions to social causes until I have made my own donation. When I have been a member of the stewardship council of a local church I have announced my own pledge before asking others to support the budget. As president of a theological school I have always made my own gift before encouraging others to follow my example. When I was a state senator in Maine I proclaimed my own willingness to pay a state income tax when speaking in favor of such a levy. And now as I urge the readers of this book to assume an unselfish and enlightened attitude toward the payment of taxes as the secular equivalent of the offering of sacred tithes, I first declare my willingness as a citizen to support the national welfare, based upon my ability to pay, through increased contributions to the federal personal income tax. This is an act of patriotism and compassion for all who may participate.

I turn now as a social critic to some of the more individualist and personal issues which are among the basic causes of turmoil within the lives of countless men and women. I do so in the context of the theological principle set forth in the previous chapter, "Little Less Than God," which is the unfulfilled goal of the human moral potential. Among the issues are lust for money and power, abuse of alcohol and other drugs, and marital infidelity. I acknowledge that there are hereditary and environmental factors, especially in the undeveloped nations but also in our own, which may prevent universal realization of the ideals I espouse. Yet I am compelled to challenge the masses of my fellow citizens in this land and others to share the experience of my own fulfilled living during three-quarters of a century and more upon the good earth.

The reluctance to pay equitable taxes is one powerful manifestation of the lust for money and power. Those who have more than enough wealth to provide for the well-being of self and family are among those unwilling to diminish their fiscal resources by contributing the taxes, based on ability to pay, which are assessed by government agencies charged with the responsibility of maintaining the social services required by the common welfare. There is a widespread consensus in a nation like the United States that individual power and prestige are enhanced proportionately to the amount of wealth one can accumulate. Yet there is ample evidence that many of those with the greatest of material riches do not enjoy the experience of happy and productive living.

Perhaps it is because I have never been a wealthy man in terms of material things that it is difficult for me to understand or appreciate why exorbitant salaries are paid to star performers in the movie and television industry, to those who excel in various professional sports, and to chief executive officers of many industrial corporations. Their talents are certainly not more worthy than those of elected and appointed government officials, doctors and nurses, educational administrators and teachers, for example. The Internal Revenue Service has recently reported that 28.5 percent of America's personal wealth is in the hands of 3.3 million persons. In 1986, the latest year for which figures are available, the richest 1.6 percent of adults in the United States — those with holdings of $500,000 or more — had total assets of 4.3 trillion dollars, an amount exceeding the entire gross national product. These are the ones who should be setting an example for others less fortunate by willingly paying proportionate increases in personal income taxes, and generously contributing tithes to eleemosynary agencies.

It is commonly believed, and often expressed, that lust for money and power — which is really a form of greed — is simply a manifestation of "human nature," which is inevitable and cannot be changed. This is a fallacy which I have exposed in earlier chapters. Men and women do have the power, inherent in the free will granted by the Creator, to make choices between such opposite characteristics as generosity and greed. I have illustrated the truth of this belief by my own attitude, for example, toward tithes and taxes. Let me elaborate by disclosing my own experience with regard to money. If in so doing I appear to be self-righteous, I enter the disclaimer that I know my story can be matched by a multitude of other people.

Never in my life have I desired to be a millionaire. Frankly, I do not envy those who spend most of their waking hours accumulating wealth and trying vainly to find ways of spending it which are worthwhile and satisfying. As son of a laborer I spent my adult years until age twenty-six helping to support my mother, father, and three siblings. Married at age twenty-seven, I embarked upon a career in ministry, teaching, and educational administration with only five hundred dollars in the bank. When I retired in 1978 my total package of compensation had not reached beyond $30,000 annually. My salary was augmented for a period of only six years when my wife went back to public school teaching while our two children were in college. We paid for their college education, and they are firmly established in careers of their own. No member of our family has ever been deprived of the necessities or the amenities of gracious living. To be sure, we were blessed during our active years by a modest bequest from my wife's father, and more recently by one from her mother, in a total amount not exceeding five figures. Wisely invested, this money has enabled us to retire to a Florida apartment and to maintain a modest Maine summer home.

Another social plague upon the American way of life is the abuse of alcohol and other drugs. Fortunately the effect of nicotine in our land is on the wane through an educational policy which is convincing an increasing number of smokers that the use of tobacco is basically unhealthy, and even life-threatening. The excessive use of alcohol, however, remains as one of the principle causes of disruption in the lives of people of all ages and social levels. In fact, the process of self-deception has prevented it from being recognized as a drug in many circles; it certainly is not classified in the same danger zone as cocaine and heroin, for example. Hopefully, alcohol will one day soon be treated as a menace to health in the same fashion as tobacco. Meanwhile it continues to have a growing deleterious effect in the workplace, on the highways, and in family relations, to name but a few. The burgeoning menace of the cocaine traffic needs no elaboration from me. Tragic stories of its human degradation are told every day in the news media.

What is the antidote for the poison of drug abuse? Education is certainly an important part of the corrective process. Much progress has been made by the national campaign against drunk driving, and by instruction in our schools about the evils associated with drug abuse. There is some value to the massive drug interdiction programs carried on by federal and state governments. No one should be deceived, however, by thinking that this problem will disappear, or even be appreciably diminished, unless and until the drug demand ends. The drug abusers, and even the casual drug users, are the real culprits; for they have the ability, through innate God-given will power, to choose not to partake of non-prescription drugs, thus circumventing the power of the economic force called supply and demand. Here again, there comes into play the human potential to elect the good and to deny the evil.

Although to many it may seem simplistic, I am a strong supporter of Nancy Reagan and her public campaign known as "Just Say NO!" In the final analysis this is the most effective way to deal with such social problems as drug abuse and sexual abnormalities. I have chosen the subject of marriage infidelity as the third example of personal issues which are unraveling the social fabric of contemporary society. This specific problem is only one of many involving human sexuality or sensuality. The worldwide epidemic of AIDS, which seems to be growing rather than abating, is obviously one which demands the full attention of experts in the fields of medicine, counseling, education and government. Yet the passage of laws, instruction in the classroom, psychological treatment, and medical preventative measures, will not succeed in changing human sexual practices; ultimately, only free choice by morally sensitive individuals will eliminate the devastating effect of AIDS as it is related to sexual behavior.

The problems of abortion and AIDS have this much in common: they can be resolved in proportion to the willingness of human beings to abstain from sexual relationships, or to use contraceptive and antiseptic precautions. Similarly, marriage infidelity and divorce are twin curses upon contemporary society which can be ameliorated by individual human decisions motivated by moral principles. The broken family syndrome, with its devastating effect upon children, is an American tragedy without parallel in our time. The fabric of the nation disintegrates a bit further every time a divorce is granted, every time a husband or wife indulges in an extra-marital sexual relationship. When children are involved, the more devastating the consequences. Parenthood demands a marital fidelity which cannot be abrogated validly by the old excuse that "human nature" prevents a man or a woman from choosing the good over the evil.

One more autobiographical episode seems pertinent at this point. It is my belief that personal human relationships as the last decade of the twentieth century begins are not as volatile or as disoriented as they are portrayed in the various communications media. Sensationalism, with its concurrent objective of economic profit, is blatantly evident in contemporary literature, newspapers, movies, videos, television dramas, and stage presentations. While these all depict the realism of a segment of modern society, they should not be allowed to obscure the multitude of the beautifully ordered, emotionally satisfying lives which abound in every hamlet and metropolis of the nation. I have seen many of these lives among my circle of friends. Moreover, I have experienced such living in my own home.

Readers of this book will have discovered early in these pages how much my wife Shirley and I have been in love for half a century. There has been a sensual aspect of this relationship so mutually satisfying that neither of us has ever been remotely tempted to contemplate an extra-marital sexual experience. It is as vital today as it was fifty years ago. I illustrate by recounting one more so-called "Shirley-ism," which occurred on the occasion of our fortieth wedding anniversary. To commemorate the occasion I had purchased for my wife a small ruby set in gold and hung on a chain. I wrapped it appropriately in a small square box, and placed it in the waistband of my pajamas as I prepared for bed shortly after midnight. Since it was then the first hour of our anniversary date I invited myself into Shirley's bed. She readily welcomed me and, as we embraced, her hand soon came in contact with the package in the waistband. Her comment still brings a chuckle when the story is retold among family and friends: "Oh," said Shirley, "something square!" My later observation was: "I knew she would find it." She still wears the ruby constantly around her neck.

This book might have ended here except for the fact that the month of August in 1990, when I was finishing the story, brought forth an event which I could not ignore as a social critic. I have stated in the previous chapter my initial reaction to the conflict in the Middle East between Iraq and many of the other nations of the world led by the United States. My opposition to unilateral military action by my native land has been clearly expressed. My support of a United Nations police force, now made readily possible by the end of the "cold war" with the Soviet Union, as a substitute for international warfare has been consistent since the UN was founded in 1945. Throughout this volume I have clearly demonstrated by precept and example my conviction that the institutions of Church and State, with the latter to include the School, are instruments in the divine economy which should cooperate in the advancement of God's kingdom upon the earth. My final thrust in these pages is to elaborate and emphasize these basic principles.

As the world faces its greatest confrontation since World War II, it is not yet evident whether it will be resolved by peaceful means or by military action. At this moment in history I have become mindful again of the words written by President Dwight D. Eisenhower, one of the most distinguished military leaders: "Every gun that is made, every warship launched, every rocket fired, signifies in the final sense a theft from those who hunger and are not fed, those who are cold and are not clothed. This world in arms is not spending money alone. It is spending the sweat of society's laborers, the genius of its scientists, the hopes of its children...."

The truth of this proclamation by a beloved American president is manifested by the countless thousands of refugees now languishing without home or hope in the Middle East and elsewhere. It is abundantly clear to thoughtful citizens of the United States who see the time and effort of the President and the Congress diverted from the domestic crises of an unspeakable national debt, an uncontrolled AIDS epidemic, a drug abuse growing by leaps and bounds, homeless people sleeping in the streets, inadequate public health programs, weaknesses in educational systems, and deterioration of the nation's roads and bridges, to name but some of the issues which threaten the common welfare. In order to protect "the American way of life," he says, President George Bush mobilized far from home the largest military force since the Viet Nam conflict. In so doing he risked the self-destruction of the very domestic structure he seeks to protect.

In these days of disillusionment and frustration, I ask myself, "What can one religiously-oriented person do to support the goals of personal faith?" I can only repeat what I have suggested throughout my adult lifetime: Let the members of religious institutions become pressure groups — yes, lobbyists — with officeholders in the executive and legislative branches of government. Churches, synagogues, and mosques in the United States have members who are also citizens. As citizens these members have both individual and corporate power and responsibility, if they are true to their faith, to have vast influence upon the political decisions made by the nation.

Fortunately, there is already well established in Washington, D.C., an effective religious lobby called "Contact," which is a network of twenty-three national Protestant, Roman Catholic, and Jewish agencies. It publishes and distributes to its constituents position papers on various social and moral issues of the day. Here is a relevant quotation from "Prepare," a monthly bulletin dated December, 1981:

"We affirm our faith in one universal God, the Creator and Sustainer of a world in which all people are full members of the human family. No nation or group of people can be considered expendable or subordinate to any other nation or group ... We affirm that God is a loving God whose will it is that the human family become reconciled and live in peace without threats of violent destruction. Warfare is not the will of God; it is rather evidence of human failure to establish he kinds of relationships which God intends."

In support of the corporate religious influence of "Contact" in the nation's capitol, now is the time for individual Moslem, Jewish, and Christian citizens to say to the Congress and to the President:

With the end of the cold war, there are no more superpowers among the nations. The Soviet Union has publicly acknowledged this truth. The United States should do the same.

In a nuclear age, war can no longer be tolerated as an instrument of international relations. All disputes between sovereign stages should be resolved either through diplomatic negotiations or, if force becomes necessary, through the deployment of a multi-national police force as prescribed in the charter of the United Nations.

Since control of a major portion of the world's oil reserves is not a valid reason for engaging in a potentially catastrophic war in the Middle East, the United States should immediately plan to develop its own oil reserves while seeking other energy sources such as clean-burning coal; nuclear, hydro-electric, geo-thermal, and solar power; and natural gas.

Instead of wasting billions of dollars, and putting countless human lives at risk by diversionary military ventures, agencies of government should devote full time and talent to the domestic problems plaguing the United States, beginning with the federal deficit as a first priority.

And if it be argued that only God can establish his own worldly kingdom and that men and women with religious convictions should be principally concerned with life after death, my reply is to quote again the profound words of President John F. Kennedy in his inaugural address: "Here on earth God's work must truly be our own." And I would add an anecdote told about President Abraham Lincoln when he was a candidate for election to the Congress of the United States. In a public debate with Lincoln, his opponent sought to arouse the crowd by the rhetorical device of asking all who wanted to go to heaven to stand up. When few responded he then demanded that all who did not want to go to hell should stand. This time all arose except Lincoln. "Where do you expect to go?" asked the adversary. Lincoln stood to his full height and replied, "I expect to go to Congress!"

To conclude and to summarize: In these years of reflection my basic faith has been confirmed that heaven and hell are religious concepts whose validity will be disclosed in whatever may lie beyond life in this world. Here on the good earth we have a divinely-ordered mission "to go to Congress," to use the Lincoln metaphor; which is to say that we are called to be agents of the Creator's temporal kingdom. And, God be praised, we are fully equipped for this task. For as the Hebrew psalmist declared: We are "little less than God." And as Jesus, known as the Christ, assured us: We are "the light of the world!"